Praise for the first editions of the Great Family Vacations series

"Stapen is a respected travel writer who has done some awfully good books on family travel. They're well researched, very well done."

—*USA Today*

"The *Great Family Vacations* series is an inspiration to parents in search of worthy destinations. Stapen is an eminently practical parent and travel expert, down to fine details. Perhaps even more important, she understands that exploring new places is a thrill that brings families closer together."

—Alexandra Kennedy, *FamilyFun Magazine*

"Stapen provides a reassuring and enthusiastic voice for families on the go."

—Christine Loomis, *Family Life Magazine*

"We found enough useful information to give these guides an A. Each section offers at-a-glance info and a What to See and Do section that includes everything from hot-air balloon rides to zoos, sports, theaters and shopping."

—Barbara Hertenstein, *St. Louis Dispatch*

"Candyce is a recognized authority on the subjects of family travel and vacations. . . . [These books] are well laid out for efficient use. The exposition is clear and friendly and kids as well as parents can read and profit from these books. Covering places all over the U.S. and Canada, it's a good set for the family to have."

—Robert Scott Milne, *Travelwriter Marketletter*

EXPERIENCE THE WONDER OF FOXWOODS.

Nestled in the beautiful New England countryside, you'll find the world's favorite casino. Foxwoods Resort Casino, now even more breathtaking than ever. Inside our magnificent new Grand Pequot Tower, you'll find a world class hotel, with 800 luxurious rooms and suites. With gourmet restaurants, and more table games, slot machines and chances to win.

Our new hotel is the perfect complement to our 312-room AAA rated four diamond Great Cedar Hotel, and our quaint Two Trees Inn, with 280 charming rooms.

Foxwoods is fine dining with 24 fabulous restaurants. And room service is available 24 hours a day, for your convenience. Foxwoods is five different gaming environ-

ments, with over 5,750 Slot Machines, Blackjack, Craps, Roulette and Baccarat, including a Smoke-Free casino.

Foxwoods is High Stakes Bingo, Keno, a Poker Room and the Ultimate Race Book.

Foxwoods is entertainment. With stars like Aretha Franklin, Engelbert Humperdinck, Paul Anka and Bill Cosby. It's two challenging golf courses. It's Championship Boxing. It's Cinetropolis, with the 1,500-seat Fox Theater. It's a Turbo Ride, Cinedrome, and our Dance Club. With its Hotels, Restaurants, Gaming and Entertainment, it's no wonder that Foxwoods has become the hottest entertainment destination in the country.

EXPERIENCE THE WONDER OF THE CONNECTICUT WOODS.
Conveniently located in Mashantucket. Exit 92 off I-95 in southeastern CT.
Call 1-800-PLAY-BIG
Visit our website at www.foxwoods.com
Mashantucket Pequot Tribal Nation

Great Family Vacations

Northeast

Second Edition

Candyce H. Stapen

Guilford, Connecticut

Cover photo background: © PhotoDisc, Inc.

Cover design by Schwartzman Design

Photo credits: page 4 Michael Melford, courtesy Msytic Aquarium; page 25 courtesy
Washington D.C., Convention and Visitor's Association; page 54 courtesy Kennebunk-Kennebunkport Chamber of Commerce; page 69 by George Grall/courtesy
National Aquarium in Baltimore; page 82 courtesy Greater Boston Convention and
Visitors Bureau, Inc.; page 94 courtesy Cape Cod Chamber of Commerce; page 106
courtesy New Brunswick Department of Tourism; page 117 courtesy Mount Washington Valley Visitor Bureau; page 131 courtesy Cape May Department of Tourism
and Economic Development; pages142, 157, 181 ©1993 New York State Department
of Economic Development; page 188 courtesy Nova Scotia Department of Tourism
and Culture; page 196 courtesy Ottawa Tourism and Convention Bureau; page 211
by L. Albee, courtesy Longwood Gardens; page 220 courtesy Gettysburg Travel Council; page 227 courtesy Hersheypak; page 240 courtesy Philadelphia Convention and
Visitors Bureau; page 254 courtesy Greater Memorial Convention and Tourism
Bureau; page 265 courtesy Quebec Tourism; page 278 courtesy Rhode Island
Tourism Division; page 288 courtesy Metropolitan Toronto Convention and visitors
Association; page 302 courtesy Shelburne Museum.

Library of Congress Cataloging-in-Publication Data

Stapen, Candyce H.
    Great family vacations. Northeast / Candyce H. Stapen. — 2nd ed.
      p.   cm. — (Great family vacations series)
    Includes index.
    ISBN 0-7627-0386-5
    1. Northeastern States—Guidebooks. 2. Ontario—Guidebooks.
3. Québec (Province)—Guidebooks. 4. New Brunswick—Guidebooks.
5. Nova Scotia—Guidebooks.   I. Title.   II. Series: Stapen, Candyce
H. Great family vacations series.
F2.3.S73 1999
917.1—dc21   99-12614
                                                       CIP

Manufactured in the United States of America
Second Edition/First Printing

To my favorite traveling companions
Alissa, Matt, and David

Acknowledgments

I want to thank Luisa Frey Gaynor and Katy Saldarini
for their contributions, and my agent, Carol Mann, for her support.

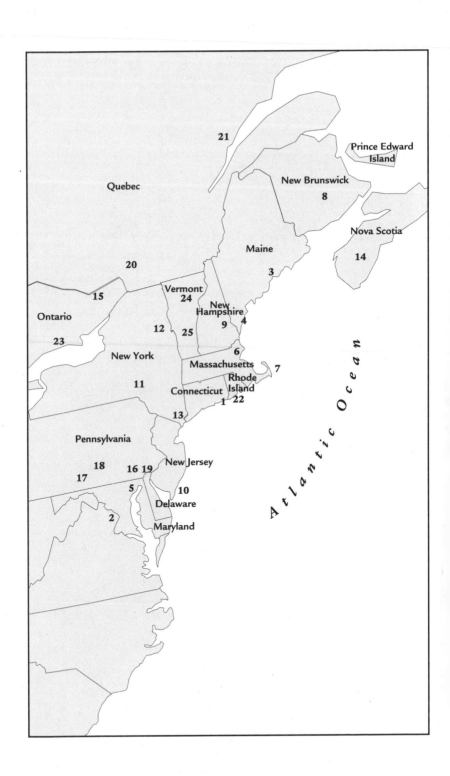

21

Quebec

Prince Edward
Island

New Brunswick
8

Nova Scotia
14

Maine

3

20

15

Vermont
24

New
Hampshire
9

4

Ontario

23

12

25

New York

6

Massachusetts

7

11

Rhode
Island

Connecticut

1   22

13

Atlantic Ocean

Pennsylvania

18

16 19

New Jersey

17

5

10

2

Delaware

Maryland

Contents

Help Us Keep This Guide Up to Date

Every effort has been made by the author and editors to make this guide as accurate and useful as possible. However, many things can change after a guide is published—establishments close, phone numbers change, facilities come under new management, housing costs fluctuate, and so on.

We would love to hear from you concerning your experiences with this guide and how you feel it could be made better and be kept up to date. While we may not be able to respond to all comments and suggestions, we'll take them to heart and we'll make certain to share them with the author. Please send your comments and suggestions to the following address:

The Globe Pequot Press
Reader Response/Editorial Department
P.O. Box 480
Guilford, CT 06437

Or you may e-mail us at:

editorial@globe-pequot.com

or email the author at:

stapenc@aol.com

Thanks for your input, and happy travels!

About the Author

Candyce H. Stapen is an expert on family travel. She appears on many television, cable, and radio shows, including *Good Morning America,* CBS *This Morning,* WUSA-TV, D.C., and National Public Radio. A member of the Society of American Travel Writers and the Travel Journalists Guild, she is a contributing editor/columnist for *National Geographic Traveler, FamilyFun,* the *Washington Times,* and *Vacations.*

Her articles about family travel appear in a variety of newspapers and magazines, including *Parents.com, Good Housekeeping, Ladies' Home Journal, Family Circle, USA Weekend, Better Homes and Gardens,* the *New York Post, Family Travel Newsletter,* and *Diversion.*

Other books by Stapen are *Great Family Vacations: South, Great Family Vacations: Midwest and Rocky Mountains,* and *Great Family Vacations: West* (Globe Pequot); *Family Adventure Guide: Virginia* (Globe Pequot); and *Cruise Vacations with Kids* and *Ski Vacations with Kids* (Prima).

Stapen lives in Washington, D.C., and travels whenever she can with her husband and two children.

Introduction

There is a Chinese proverb that says the wise parent gives a child roots and wings. By traveling with your children, you can bestow many gifts upon them: a strong sense of family bonds, memories that last a lifetime, and a joyful vision of the world.

Traveling with your children offers many bonuses for you and your family. These days no parent or child has an excessive amount of free time. Whether you work in the home or outside it, your days are filled with meetings, deadlines, household errands, and carpool commitments. Your child most likely keeps equally busy with scouts, soccer, music lessons, computer clinics, basketball, and/or ballet. When your family stays home, your time together is likely to be limited to sharing quick dinners and overseeing homework. If there's a teen in your house, an age known for endless hours spent with friends, your encounters often shrink to swapping phone messages and car keys.

But take your child on the road with you, and both of you have plenty of time to talk and be together. Traveling together gives your family the luxury of becoming as expansive as the scenery. Over doughnuts in an airport lounge or dinner in a new hotel, you suddenly hear about that special science project or how it really felt to come in third in the swim meet. By sharing a drive along a country road or a visit to a city museum, your children get the space to view you as a person and not just as a parent.

Additionally, both you and your kids gain new perspectives on life. Children who spend time in a different locale, whether it's a national forest or a city new to them, expand their awareness. For you as a parent, traveling with your kids brings the added bonus of enabling you to see again with a child's eye. When you show a six-year-old a reconstructed Colonial village or share the stars in a Tennessee mountain night sky with a thirteen-year-old, you feel the world twinkle with as much possibility as when you first encountered these sights long ago.

Part of this excitement is a result of the exuberance kids bring, and part is from the instant friendships kids establish. Street vendors save their best deals for preschoolers, and, even on a crowded rush hour bus, a child by your side turns a fellow commuter from a stranger into a friend. Before your stop comes you'll often be advised of the best toy shop in town and directed to a local cafe with a kid-pleasing menu at prices guaranteed to put a smile on your face.

New perspectives also come from the activities you participate in with your children. Most of these activities you would probably pass up when shuttling solo. Whether it's finding all the dogs in the paintings at an art museum, playing miniature golf at a resort, or trying horseback riding in a park, you always learn more when you take your kids.

Surprisingly, traveling with your kids can also be cost-effective and practical. By combining or by extending a work-related trip into a vacation, you save money since your company picks up a good part of your expenses. Because tag-along-tots on business trips are an increasing trend, several hotel chains have responded with a range of family-friendly amenities including children's programs, child-safe rooms, and milk and cookies at bedtime.

For all these reasons traveling with your children presents many wonderful opportunities. It is a great adventure to be a parent, and it is made more wondrous when you travel with your children. You will not only take pleasure in each other's company, but you will return home with memories to savor for a lifetime.

Family Travel Tips

Great family vacations require careful planning and the cooperation of all family members. Before you go you need to think about such essentials as how to keep sibling fights to a minimum and how to be prepared for medical emergencies. While en route you want to be sure to make road trips and plane rides fun, even with a toddler. You want to be certain that the room that is awaiting your family is safe and that your family makes the most of being together. When visiting relatives, you want to eliminate friction by following the house rules. These tips, gathered from a host of families, go a long way toward making your trips good ones.

General Rules

1. Meet the needs of the youngest family member. Your raft trip won't be fun if you're constantly worried about your three-year-old being bumped overboard by the white water the tour operator failed to mention or if your first-grader gets bored with the day's itinerary of art museums.

2. Underplan. Your city adventure will dissolve in tears—yours and your toddler's—if you've scheduled too many sites and not enough time for the serendipitous. If your child delights in playing with the robots at the science museum, linger there and skip the afternoon's proposed visit to the history center.

3. Go for the green spaces. Seek out an area's parks. Pack a picnic lunch and take time to throw a Frisbee, play catch, or simply enjoy relaxing in the sun and people watching.

4. Enlist the cooperation of your kids by including them in the decision making. While family vacation voting is not quite a democracy, consider your kids' needs. Is there a way to combine your teen's desire to be near

"the action" with your spouse's request for seclusion? Perhaps book a self-contained resort on a quiet beach that also features a nightspot.

5. Understand your rhythms of the road. Some families like traveling at night so that the kids sleep in the car or on the plane. Others avoid traveling during the evening cranky hours and prefer to leave early in the morning.

6. Plan to spend time alone with each of your children as well as with your spouse. Take a walk, write in a journal together, play ball, share ice cream in the snack shop, etc. Even the simplest things done together create valuable family memories.

7. Have a sense of humor. Attractions get crowded, cars break down, and kids spit up. Remember why you came on vacation in the first place—to have fun with your kids.

Don't Leave Home Without

1. *Emergency medical kit.* The first thing we always pack is the emergency medical kit, a bag I keep ready to go with all those things that suddenly become important at 3:00 A.M. This is no hour to be searching the streets for baby aspirin or Band-Aids. Make sure your kit includes items suitable for adults as well as children. Be sure to bring:
   - aspirin or an aspirin substitute
   - a thermometer
   - cough syrup
   - a decongestant
   - medication to relieve diarrhea
   - bandages and Band-Aids
   - gauze pads
   - antibiotic ointment and a physician-approved antibiotic, just in case
   - a motion-sickness remedy
   - sunscreen
   - insect repellent
   - ointments or spray to soothe sunburn, rashes, and poison ivy
   - something to soothe insect stings
   - any medications needed on a regular basis
   - tweezers and a sterile needle to remove splinters

   Keep this kit with you in your carry-on luggage or on the front seat of your car.

2. *Snack food.* As soon as we land somewhere or pull up to a museum for a visit, my daughter usually wants food. Instead of arguing or wasting time and money on snacks, I carry granola bars with me. She munches on these reasonably nutritious snacks while we continue on schedule.

3. *Inflatable pillow and travel products.* Whether on the road or in a plane, these inflatable wonders help me and the kids sleep. For travel pillows

plus an excellent variety of light yet durable travel products including hair dryers, luggage straps, alarms, adaptor plugs for electrical outlets, and clothing organizers, call Magellan's (800-962-4943). TravelSmith (800-950-1600) carries these items as well as clothing, mostly for teens and adults.

4. *Travel toys.* Kids don't have to be bored en route to your destination. Pack books, coloring games, and quiet toys. Some kids love story tapes on their personal cassette players. For innovative, custom-tailored travel kits full of magic pencil games, puzzles, and crafts for children three and a half or older, call Sealed With A Kiss (800-888-SWAK). The packages cost about $35. Surprise your kids with this once you are on the road. They'll be happy and so will you.

Flying with Tots

1. Book early for the seat you like. Whether you prefer the aisle, window, or bulkhead for extra legroom, reserve your seat well in advance of your departure date.

2. Call the airlines at least forty-eight hours ahead to order meals that you know your kids will eat: children's dinners, hamburger platters, salads, etc.

3. Bring food on board that you know your kids like even if you've ordered a special meal. If your kids won't eat what's served at mealtime, at least they won't be hungry if they munch on nutritious snacks.

4. Be sure to explain each step of the plane ride to little kids so that they will understand that the airplane's noises and shaking do not mean that a crash is imminent.

5. Stuff your carry-on with everything you might need (including medications, extra kids' clothes, diapers, baby food, formula, and bottles) to get you through a long flight and a delay of several hours . . . just in case.

6. Bring a child safety seat (a car seat) on board. Although presently the law allows children under two to fly free if they sit on a parent's lap, the Federal Aviation Administration and the Air Transport Association support legislation that would require all kids to be in child safety seats. In order to get a seat on board, the seat must have a visible label stating approval for air travel, and you must purchase a ticket for that seat. Without a ticket you are not guaranteed a place to put this child safety seat in case the plane is full.

7. With a toddler or young child, wrap little surprises to give as "presents" throughout the flight. These work wonderfully well to keep a wee one's interest.

8. Before boarding let your kids work off energy by walking around the airport lounge. Never let your child nap just before takeoff—save the

sleepy moments for the plane.

9. If you're traveling with a lot of luggage, check it curbside before parking your car. This eliminates the awkward trip from long-term parking loaded down with kids, luggage, car seats, and strollers.

Road Rules

1. Use this time together to talk with your children. Tell them anecdotes about your childhood or create stories for the road together.
2. Put toys for each child in his or her own mesh bag. This way the toys are easily located and visible instead of being strewn all over the car.
3. Avoid long rides. Break the trip up by stopping every two or three hours for a snack or to find a rest room. This lets kids stretch their legs.
4. When driving for several days, plan to arrive at your destination each day by 4:00 or 5:00 P.M. so that the kids can enjoy a swim at the hotel/motel. This turns long hauls into easily realized goals that are fun.

At the Destination

1. When traveling with young children, do a safety check of the hotel room and the premises as soon as you arrive. Put matches, glasses, ashtrays, and small items out of reach. Note if stair and balcony railings are widely spaced or easily climbed by eager tots and if windows lack screens or locks. Find out where the possible dangers are, and always keep track of your kids.
2. Schedule sight-seeing for the morning, but plan to be back at the resort or hotel by early afternoon so that your child can enjoy the pool, the beach, miniature golf, or other kid-friendly facilities.
3. Plan to spend some time alone with each of your children every day. With preteens and teens, keep active by playing tennis or basketball, jogging, or doing something else to burn energy.
4. Establish an amount of money that your child can spend on souvenirs. Stick to this limit, but let your child decide what he or she wants to buy.

With Relatives

1. Find out the rules of your relatives' house before you arrive, and inform your kids of them. Let them know, for example, that food is allowed only in the kitchen or dining room so that they won't bring sandwiches into the guest bedroom or den.
2. Tell your relatives about your kids' eating preferences. Let the person doing the cooking know that fried chicken is fine, but that your kids won't touch liver even if it is prepared with the famous family recipe.

3. To lessen the extra work and expense for relatives and to help eliminate friction, bring along or offer to shop and pay for those special items that only your kids eat—a favorite brand of cereal, juice, frozen pizza, or microwave kids' meal.
4. Discuss meal hours. If you know, for example, that grandma and grandpa always dine at 7:00 P.M. but that your preschooler and first-grader can't wait that long, feed your kids earlier at their usual time, and enjoy an adult dinner with your relatives later.
5. Find something suitable for each generation that your kids and relatives will enjoy doing together. Look over old family albums, have teens tape-record oral family histories, and have grade-schoolers take instant snapshots of the clan.
6. Find some way that your kids can help with the work of visiting. Even a nursery-school-age child feels good about helping to clear a table or sweep the kitchen floor.

A Few Words about Canadian Travel

Canada is foreign but familiar. Most Canadians speak English (although French predominates in the eastern province of Québec), and exciting cities, excellent ski resorts, and an expansive countryside of less-traveled areas make Canada a great travel destination for families.

Monetarily speaking, there's never been a better time to visit Canada. Although rates fluctuate, for the past year (and at press time) the U.S. dollar was worth between $1.35 and $1.50 Canadian. That means that a trip to Canada is great for budget-minded travelers, since you're getting between 35 and 50 percent more for your money. When we were skiing in Mount Tremblant, outside of Montréal, for example, the two-bedroom condo we were staying in cost $150 per night (compared to more than $220 for comparable units at northeastern U.S. resorts), lift tickets cost about $30 U.S. dollars (compared to the typical $55 charge at U.S. ski resorts), and, because of exchange rates, a meal that cost $20 Canadian cost about $12 U.S. For a family of four, the savings quickly add up!

The numerous rail, highway, and air connections from major U.S. cites make traveling to and around Canada easy. Several U.S. carriers service Canada. Canada's major transcontinental airlines are **Air Canada** (800-776-3000) and **Canadian Airlines** (800-426-7000). **VIA Rail** (800-561-3949) provides most of the passenger rail service within Canada, while **Amtrak** (800-USA-RAIL) has service into Canada.

Entry Rules. U.S. citizens and legal residents do not need passports or visas to enter Canada, although passports are a preferred means of identification. If you don't have a passport, native-born U.S. citizens can use a birth certificate or voter's registration card that shows citizenship, plus a photo identification card (a driver's license works well). Naturalized citizens need a naturalization certificate or other proof of citizenship. Permanent U.S. residents who are not citizens need alien registration receipts.

Note: To foil non-custodial parents in their attempt to kidnap their children and escape U.S. laws by fleeing to a foreign country, Canadian officials (along with officials from Mexico and several other countries) regularly check the passports and papers of children traveling with only one adult, regardless of whether that adult is the child's parent, grandparent, or custodial or non-custodial parent. Even if a divorce is not involved, an adult traveling with one or more child may be stopped and questioned, especially if the parent and child have different last names. This is the case with my daughter, and we are almost always questioned by officials when entering and leaving Canada.

What to do: Before leaving the U.S., obtain a notarized statement from your spouse or ex-spouse stating that you have his or her permission to take your child on a trip to Canada from a specific date to a specific date. This will reassure Canadian authorities and allow you to pass through immigration with little or no problem. Although a notarized statement is not a legal requirement, it's mighty helpful. Without it, you might experience unanticipated delays.

On one family trip to Montréal, I arrived on an earlier flight, passed through immigration, and waited at the airport for my husband and daughter to arrive. Despite having the same last name, my husband and daughter were questioned for more than twenty minutes by an immigration officer who wanted to know why "the mother" wasn't traveling with them. Of course this happened to be the one time we didn't obtain a notarized statement, since I was literally on the other side of the immigration area!

Family Travel Planners
These specialists can help you assess your family's needs and find the vacation that's best for you.

- *Family Travel Network.* (FTN) on AOL has lots of information and advice about family vacations and destinations as well as bulletin boards. Find out what other parents think of various places. Once on AOL, click "Keyword" and type in "Family Travel Network."
- *Family Travel Times.* This newsletter offers the latest information on hotels, resorts, city attractions, cruises, airlines, tours, and destinations. Contact Travel With Your Children, 40 Fifth Avenue, New York, NY 10011. For information call (212) 447–5524.

- **Family Travel Forum.** This newsletter has information about family trips. You can contact them at 891 Amsterdam Avenue, New York, NY 10025; (212) 665-6124; www.familytravelforum.com.
- **Rascals in Paradise.** Specializing in family and small-group tours to the Caribbean, Mexico, and the South Pacific, some Rascals' tours include nannies for each family and an escort to organize activities for the kids. Call (800) U-RASCAL for more information.
- **Grandtravel.** This company offers a variety of domestic and international trips for grandparents and grandchildren seven through seventeen. Call (800) 247-7651.
- **Grandvistas.** Grandparents can take their grandkids on a few trips, too. Destinations typically include South Dakota, Nevada, and Wyoming. Call (800) 647-0800.
- **Families Welcome!** This agency offers travel packages for families in European cities and New York. With rental of a hotel room or apartment, you receive a "Welcome Kit" of tips on sight-seeing, restaurants, and museums. Call (800) 326-0724.
- **Family Explorations.** Trip destinations include Ireland, Costa Rica, and Honduras, plus service-oriented trips overseas and stateside getaways such as Pennsylvania and Maine. Call (800) WE-GO-TOO.

The prices and rates listed in this guidebook were confirmed at press time. We recommend, however, that you call establishments before traveling to obtain current information.

MYSTIC COAST AND COUNTRY

This section covers Mystic and the surrounding towns of Stonington, North Stonington, Noank, Groton, New London, Ledyard, Niantic, and Essex.

For centuries, ever since Native American tribes migrated in hot weather to the seashore, Connecticut's seacoast has drawn summer visitors. Many of the attractions detail sea life, making the various facets of life on and in the water come alive in an interesting manner.

But summer isn't the only time to visit, although it is the prime time. The state's two top attractions, both of which are open year-round, are in Mystic. Mystic Seaport, a living history museum, re-creates life in a whaling village, and the Mystic Aquarium and Institute for Exploration displays schools of brightly colored fish as well as dolphins, whales, seals, sea lions, and penguins. The U.S. Coast Guard Academy, one of four military institutions, is located in New London, and when the training ship *Eagle* is in town, you can come aboard. The *Nautilus,* the first nuclear-powered submarine, is berthed in Groton. The region's seacoast towns, Niantic, Noank, Stonington, and Waterford, come with plenty of beaches and parks for play.

GETTING THERE

Major carriers fly into **Bradley International Airport,** Windsor Locks (860–627–3000), about a ninety-minutes' drive from Mystic. **T.F. Green Airport,** Warwick, Rhode Island (401–737–4000), about a one-hour drive from Groton's New London Airport, is served by commuter lines.

Greyhound bus lines arrive and depart from New London. Call (860) 447–3841. **Amtrak** (800–USA–RAIL) serves Mystic daily on a limited schedule and nearby New London on a more regular basis.

Several ferries serve the area. The **Block Island Ferry** goes to New London (seasonally); call (860) 442–7891. The **Cross Sound Ferry** serves

Mystic Coast and Country

AT A GLANCE

▶ Tour Mystic Seaport, the largest maritime museum in the United States

▶ Cruise on a coal-fired passenger steamer or a replica of a nineteenth-century schooner

▶ Discover 4,000 marine creatures at Mystic Aquarium, one of the top aquariums in the nation

▶ Mystic & More, (800) TO-ENJOY; www.mysticmore.com

New London–Orient Point, Long Island; (860) 443-7394. The **Montauk Passenger Ferry** provides New London–Montauk, Long Island, service, May through October; call (516) 668-5709 or (800) MONTAUK.

To reach Mystic by car, take Connecticut Route 27 approximately 1 mile south of I-95, exit 90.

GETTING AROUND

SEAT (Southeastern Area Transit, 860-886-2631) has buses that serve Mystic on a limited basis.

Yellow Cab Company, 64 Brainard Street, New London (860-536-8888), provides twenty-four-hour service within Mystic as well as to Mystic and to the airport. Mystic is 9 miles east of New London and 5 miles northwest of Stonington.

WHAT TO SEE AND DO

The Mystic area offers history that comes with docks of fun. In the nineteenth century Mystic served as a busy whaling port; many of the impressive homes of the prosperous sea captains still grace the town's streets. Mystic's top two attractions are **Mystic Seaport** and the **Mystic Aquarium and Institute for Exploration.**

Mystic Seaport

Set on seventeen acres on the Mystic River, **Mystic Seaport,** 75 Greenmanville Avenue (860-572-5315 or 888-9SEAPORT; www.mysticseaport.org), is the largest maritime museum in the United States. This living-history facility re-creates the nineteenth century, when Mystic bustled as a shipbuilding and whaling center. At the start of your visit, check *Today* for daily events and special demonstrations and note the "Kids' Today" section, which lists daily performances and events of special interest to children. *Note:* The north entrance is closer to the parking lots and is often less crowded.

With young children and grade-schoolers, consider taking a horse and buggy or wagon ride around the Seaport. The rides are a good way to get oriented while saving little feet. The twelve- to fifteen-minute carriage rides depart from the village green.

It's a long way from the deck to the crow's nest of the **Charles W. Morgan,** an 1841 whaling bark that is the pride of Mystic Seaport. But gaze up and it's easy to imagine the cry of "Thar she blows" when sailors of long ago spied a pod of whales breaching the waves. As part of the hands-on history, watch the hearty crew hang from the rigging to unfurl the massive sails of this majestic ship. Then watch as in tune to the rhythms of the shanty man and with a chorus of "Haul 'em away," the crew pull hard to raise or lower the dories (small boats). Children are charmed by the working songs that were belted out not for fun but to get the mates to pull in rhythm. Go below and see the crew's quarters. Children are often amazed to compare the average length of the ship's voyage (three and a half years) to the cramped space for each crew member.

The **L.A. Dunton,** a 1921 fishing schooner, is also docked at Mystic. The crew demonstrates raising the anchor and splitting and salting cod. Climb aboard the **Joseph Conrad,** built in 1882. Originally used to train Danish teens for the merchant marine, this ship is now employed as a live-aboard dormitory for teenagers enrolled in Mystic's seamanship program. Interpreters are glad to answer questions. Find out what a capstan is (it's used to haul in the anchor) or why some of the rigging is black (it has been tarred for preservation).

The **Sabino,** a 1908 steamboat that has one of the last remaining coal-fired steam engines, operates from a pier at the Seaport. From mid-May to mid-October the *Sabino* takes passengers for thirty-minute outings on the Mystic River (additional fee). Mystic Seaport is in the process of building a replica of the **Amistad,** a slave ship whose captive slaves mutineed, taking over the vessel for a short time when it was in port in New London. When completed in 2000, the ship will tour U.S. waterways.

Mystic Seaport's reconstructed village has such shore necessities as the barrel maker, the cordage company for rope manufacturing, the one-room schoolhouse, and the Tavern, a favorite gathering place for land-thirsty sailors. Some salty characters you might catch sight of in town include a master worker creating a figurehead at the ship carvers and a clockmaker at his shop readying a timepiece for the *L.A. Dunton.*

In summer try to be at the village green near Chubb's Wharf (opposite

At Mystic Aquarium you can get up close and personal with Atlantic bottlenose dolphins.

the Children's Museum) when costumed interpreters enact *A Tale of a Whaler.* With lots of help from child volunteers (and from some adults, too), these actors relate some real facts about whaling as well as some rollicking fiction. The best part for some child thespians: enacting "green" (new), woefully sick sailors by making lots of loud "throw up" sounds.

Save time for the **planetarium show** (additional admission), which describes how mariners employed the stars as guides. A display case has antique navigational instruments such as an astrolabe, used to measure angles, and the ceiling has an orrery, a model of the solar system. The **Stillman** and **Wendell** buildings, with their nautical exhibits, feature everything from scrimshaw and ship models to huge figureheads. Another reason to visit: These buildings are air-conditioned, and on a hot, muggy day a visit here is most welcome.

At the **Children's Museum,** best for young grade-schoolers, kids can move cargo, swab decks, and climb on the outdoor rigging.

For snacks, Mystic Seaport offers the self-serve **Galley.** For a more formal (but comfortable for children) restaurant with waiter service, there's the **Seamen's Inne** (see Where to Eat).

If your kids like Mystic Seaport, they may want to return some day for the six- and nine-day youth sailing courses for ages twelve to fifteen, and ages sixteen to nineteen. If you're staying in town for awhile, consider the Seaport's Summer Day Camp, which offers one-week sessions for ages seven and eight and two-week sessions for ages nine to eleven.

Great Family Beaches

- The **du Bois Beach,** Stonington Point, Stonington, is a small, relatively quiet beach. Pluses include a lifeguard on duty from 10:00 A.M. to 5:00 P.M., good breezes, fishing and crabbing from the jetty, and a parking lot. There's a nominal fee.
- **Esker Point Beach,** located at Connecticut Route 215 and Marsh Road, Noank, is small but nice for tots because the water tends to be shallow and gentle. The beach has a picnic grove and a nice view.
- For ocean swimming, **Watch Hill,** Rhode Island, about 13 miles east of Mystic, is popular.
- You can have a beach without crowds at **Rocky Neck State Park Beach,** Route 156, Niantic (860-739-5471). In addition to the 0.5-mile-long stretch of sand, the park offers hiking and fishing. This is a very good beach for young children, as the water is especially shal-low during low tide and always calm. Because the beach is located on the Long Island Sound, there are no waves. Lifeguards are on duty. The park has a boardwalk for strolling, bathhouses, picnic tables, and a concession stand.
- **Ocean Beach Park,** 1225 Ocean Avenue, New London (860-447-3031 or 800-510-SAND), draws crowds for its wide swath of fine sand and its facilities, including shower rooms. Located at the meeting point of the Long Island Sound and the Atlantic Ocean, the beach has gentle surf. For those who still prefer pools to waves, there is an Olympic-size outdoor pool.

  A broad boardwalk makes promenading (and pushing strollers) easy. Off-the-sand fun includes such classic boardwalk activities as miniature golf and skeeball.

Mystic Aquarium and Institute for Exploration

One of the top aquariums in the United States, **Mystic Aquarium and Institute for Exploration,** 55 Coogan Boulevard, exit 90 off I-95 (860-572-5955), has recently completed a $52 million renovation. With 4,000 marine creatures displayed in twenty-four new exhibits, there's plenty to see. Young kids especially like watching sand tiger and bonnet head sharks circling a 30,000-gallon coral reef exhibit, the centerpiece of the redesigned interior.

In **Where Rivers Meet the Sea,** a gallery presenting shoreline habitats from salt marsh to mangrove swamp and rocky shore, kids can get close to such marsh critters as seahorses, green crabs, silversides, and mudskippers.

The **Pribilof Islands** complex features two species of seal and sea lion, including the largest of all, the Steller's sea lion. Kids like watching the

Great Family Cruises

By signing on for a naturalist outing, your kids learn about whales and other deep-sea wonders, and by sailing on a replica of a nineteenth-century ship, they get a firsthand feel for old-fashioned sea life. (Because the sun can be fierce, be sure to wear hats and long-sleeved shirts and slather on lots of sunscreen.)

- **Whale Watch Sunbeam Fleet,** Captain John's Sport Fishing Center, 15 First Street, Waterford (860-443-7259). Spend a day watching for whales with a naturalist and research teams from **Mystic Aquarium and Institute for Exploration.** From late June through Labor Day, the tours head out toward the waters of Montauk Point.
- From February to early March, Sunday excursions look for bald eagles along the Connecticut River. From mid-March to May there are three-hour Sunday cruises to Fishers Island, south of Mystic, to visit harbor seals. Call ahead for schedules.
- **Project Oceanology,** Avery Point (860-445-9007). On this two-and-a-half-hour trip aboard a 55-foot research vessel marine scientists teach you how to measure lobsters,

identify fish, and test seawater. During the winter, cruise Fishers Island Sound to study harbor seals, and in warmer months cruise the Thames River to study lighthouses.

- **The Mystic Whaler,** 15 Holmes Street, Mystic (800-697-8420), an impressive ship, is a replica of a nineteenth-century schooner. There are day and evening outings plus extended two- to five-day trips. The minimum age for day and evening sails is five years. For overnight sails—except for special family excursions—the minimum age is ten.
- The *Argia,* operated by **Voyager Cruises,** Steamboat Wharf, Mystic (860-536-0416 or 800-243-0882), is a replica of a nineteenth-century gaff-rigged schooner, complete with varnished mahogany interiors and brass lamps. This 81-foot ship offers half-day and full-day excursions. All-day sails come with a buffet lunch and, if the weather is warm, a stop for swimming. Mostly couples board for the sunset sails from 6:00 to 8:00 P.M., although well-behaved children are welcome.

sea lions plunge in the water, transforming themselves into sleek, swift swimmers. And everybody loves the penguins: View African blackfooted penguins as they fly underwater and waddle on land.

At the **World of the Dolphin** theater, Atlantic bottlenose dolphins and beluga whales demonstrate various behaviors. The dolphins "tail" backwards, jump over poles, and select objects blindfolded, a feat performed through echolocation—identifying objects by sound. The whales wave their flukes, spin in the water to demonstrate agility, and splash to show what they can do to enemies. If you can, try to attend a show in the middle of your visit; that way everybody gets to sit down and rest.

The aquarium's newest attraction is the **Alaskan Coast,** a one-acre outdoor beluga whale exhibit, and the **Institute for Exploration's Challenge of the Deep,** headed by explorer Dr. Robert Ballard. Exhibits detail the technology used in deep-sea exploration and a dive theater provides visitors with the scenes and sounds of a simulated 3,000-foot-deep ocean dive.

In the summer parents and kids ages three to four enjoy guided beach walks, and families can sign up for seining and for marine educational day outings aboard the *Peter W. Anderson,* a U.S. Navy gunboat converted to a marine laboratory vessel. Kids ages five to six, seven to eight, nine to twelve, and teens have their own water workshops of one- to four-day programs of beach explorations and whale-watching.

Niantic

Preschoolers and young grade-schoolers will enjoy **The Children's Museum of Southeastern Connecticut,** 409 Main Street, Niantic (860–691–1255). In addition to rotating exhibits, some of the permanent features of the museum are KIDSville, the Science Discovery Room, and Science Park. KIDSville is a replica of a town scaled down to size for little ones, where children can try their hand at being a doctor, a firefighter, a DJ, or a teacher. In the Science Discovery Room, kids are encouraged to handle the assortment of artifacts, fossils, and bones. For those three and under, there is an enclosed infant-toddler area, with tunnels to crawl through and lots of stuff to look at. Outdoors is Science Park, which includes animal tracks, a waterfall, and a "smell garden."

Parks and Green Spaces

For some quiet time, walk the trails of the **Denison Pequotsepos Nature Center and Peace Sanctuary,** 109 Pequotsepos Street, Mystic (860–536–1216). Preschoolers and young grade-schoolers like this nature center, which offers a break from the crowds at the larger attractions. The museum itself is not much to see, consisting mainly of cases of bird eggs and mounted birds. Mr. Bill, a Great Horned Owl who is a resident, is a real kid-pleaser.

The delights here are really the 7 miles of self-guided trails. Be sure to bring a canteen of water (there are no water fountains along the way) and leave the stroller behind, as the paths are rocky, but do enjoy the walks. Because the 125 acres on Pequotsepos Road in Mystic incorporate fields and wooded swamps, as well as groves of oak and maple trees, more than 150 species of birds inhabit the area. This is a quiet place to regroup and gather energy for more sight-seeing.

An area oasis is the 425-acre **Connecticut College Arboretum,** Williams Street, Connecticut College, New London, (860-447-7706). At the Williams Street entrance pick up a self-guided map of the twenty-acres of nature trails that wind through these wooded groves past flowering shrubs, wildflowers, and a marsh pond. The 2-mile main trail loop takes moderate walkers about one hour, but don't do it all if that's too much for your children. Simply enjoy the woods and the birds.

Gillette Castle State Park, 67 River Road, East Haddam (860-526-2336), with its "castle," an odd structure built by an actor, will interest some children, but more likely the 184 acres of grounds overlooking the scenic Connecticut River will be the real draw. Arthur Conan Doyle, the author of the Sherlock Holmes tales, never slept here, but the man who did, William Gillette, owed much to the Holmes' tales. Gillette wrote a play based on the detective stories and gained fame for his portrayal of Holmes, a part that lasted from 1899 to 1932. In 1919 Gillette built this large stone-and-wood home, whose towers suggest a castle. The main hall, with its three-sided balcony and high ceilings, is impressive, and the second-floor re-creation of Holmes' sitting room at 221 B Baker Street will interest Holmes' fans. Much of the rest of the house is likely to bore children. However, the surrounding park offers a great space to enjoy the outdoors. Stroll along the nature trails, enjoy the river views, and bring a picnic.

Native American History and Casinos

The conflict-ridden history of New England settlers and native tribes takes a curious turn in Mashantucket, Connecticut. As a result of various lawsuits and resultant federal regulations, two Connecticut tribes, the Mashantucket Pequots and the Mohegans, gained rights to construct and operate gambling casinos on their tribal land. In February 1992 the Mashantucket Pequots opened **Foxwoods Resort Casino,** Route 2, Ledyard (860-752-9244). The Mohegans opened the **Mohegan Sun,** Mohegan Sun Boulevard, Uncasville (888-226-7711), in October 1996. These two tribal reservations are not far from one another. To travel from one casino to another, cross the Thames River on I-95 in New London/Groton or follow Route 2 between Norwich and Preston.

The Foxwoods Resort Casino has been a hit, drawing people by the busloads. The casino has been a source of millions of dollars in revenue for the Mashantucket Pequots and also a boon for the surrounding region. As a sovereign nation, the Mashantucket Pequots negotiated with the state of Connecticut to pay the state 25 percent of overall slot revenues each year, or a minimum of $100 million per year. Tourists drawn by the gambling stay to explore the Mystic region.

Many families bring their children to shop, eat in the restaurants, and enjoy the video and virtual reality games in what Foxwoods calls "the theater district." Foxwoods does not offer child care, but Mohegan Sun has Kids Quest, supervised child care for ages six weeks to twelve years. Kids Quest has Barbieland and Lego City play areas, a kids' theater, a stage, and nonviolent arcade games. Reservations are suggested.

Consider carefully, however, whether you really want to spend family time at these casinos. After all, gambling is the main attraction, and this is off-limits to anyone under age twenty-one.

What Foxwoods does have that is of interest to children is the **Mashantucket Pequot Museum and Research Center,** 110 Pequot Trail, Mashantucket (860-396-6800). The 308,000-square-foot facility interprets the culture and the complicated history of the Mashantuckets and other Native American tribes. Guests enter the Gathering Space, a vast meeting hall with views of the surrounding tribal land. To witness life before European contact, visitors "descend" via escalator through simulated glacial crevasses, complete with sounds of cracking ice and blasts of frigid air, to a 9,000-year-old prehistoric community created with dioramas. The depiction of the caribou hunt is especially impressive, as is the museum's centerpiece, a 22,000-square-foot re-creation of a Pequot village featuring life-size figures and a cedar swamp, the place where the few Pequots who survived a massacre in 1637 by Colonial forces sought refuge.

There are three hotels on the Mashantucket Pequot reservation: the Great Cedar Hotel, the Two Trees Inn, and the Grand Pequot Tower. For reservations, call (860) 885-4777 or (800) FOXWOOD.

Performing Arts

The 1876 **Goodspeed Opera House,** Route 82, East Haddam (860-873-8668), a jewel of a Victorian building, overlooks the Connecticut River. Saved from demolition and restored in 1963, this venue offers American theater, particularly classic

Norwich Navigators

Baseball fans might like attending a game of the **Norwich Navigators,** Yantic (860-887-7962 or 800-64-GATOR), a team affiliated with the New York Yankees. The 500-seat Senator Thomas J. Dodd Memorial Stadium not only is attractive but is also small enough to enable fans to feel involved with the game. As a result, this is a great place to take young children for whom the action at a big stadium may seem just too far away to follow or care about. The "sunken bowl" design, with a concourse around the edge and seats going down to the field, also contributes to the facility's friendliness. There is a designated family section in which alcohol and smoking are banned. Tater the 'gator, a green alligator in pinstripes, entertains the crowds. Tater's Playhouse is the video arcade.

and new musicals. Successes that have debuted here include *Man of La Mancha* and *Annie*. Theater productions run from April through December, Wednesday to Sunday. For theater tours, call (860) 873-8864, June to September.

Garde Arts Center, 325 State Street, New London (860-444-7373 or 800-ONGARDE), is a professional performing arts center that features family theater, Broadway shows, and comedies. **Summer Music at Harkness Park,** Route 213, Waterford (860-442-9199 or 800-969-3400), offers Saturday evening concerts ranging from jazz to classical. Summer children's theater is held on Friday or Saturday at the **Ivoryton Playhouse,** 103 Main Street, Ivoryton, near Essex (860-767-8348).

Shopping

Olde Mistick Village, Route 27 at I-95, Mystic, is a Colonial-style shopping center with more than sixty shops, restaurants, and a theater. There are free weekend concerts June through October. Call (860) 536-4941. Across the way bargain shop for clothes, toys, crafts, and more at **Mystic Factory Outlets,** Coogan Boulevard (860-443-4788).

Mystic's nearby neighboring towns offer these attractions:

Groton

Groton is about 5 miles west of Mystic.

Take the time to tour the historic ship *Nautilus* and the **Submarine Force Museum** (860-694-3174 or 800-343-0079). The self-conducted tour aboard the world's first nuclear-powered ship is free. The *Nautilus* was built in Groton by General Dynamics and launched in 1954. You see the torpedo room, officers' and crew's living and dining areas, and the attack center. The museum has submarine memorabilia, including a model of Captain Nemo's *Nautilus* from Jules Verne's *20,000 Leagues Under the Sea*. There are also working periscopes and a fascinating display of submarines dating from the Revolutionary War and midget submarines from World War II. The library, however, is open only to researchers.

New London

New London is about 9 miles west of Mystic.

The whaling industry once thrived here, and you can relive some of the glory by strolling through the downtown historic district, which comprises **Whale Oil Row,** an area of Greek Revival homes, and surrounding areas. **Nathan Hale Schoolhouse,** Union Plaza (860-443-7949), is where this Connecticut hero taught before he enlisted in Washington's Army.

The **U.S. Coast Guard Academy,** Route 32, New London (860-444-8270), one of four military institutes in the United States, trains young men and women to command ships in this multifaceted service. The USCG *Eagle*, a 1936 bark used in training, is the only square-rigger in government service and has led the tall ships parade in New York Harbor for the last twenty years. When in port, the ship is open to the public in the afternoons. During the fall and spring semesters, dress parades occur on Friday afternoons and are likewise open to all. The *Eagle* is impressive, especially so after seeing and learning about tall ships at the Mystic Seaport. The Visitors Pavilion and Museum are open daily May to October.

The Science Center of Eastern Connecticut, 33 Gallows Lane, New London (860-442-0391), is a relatively small facility (9,000 square feet) adjacent to the Connecticut College campus and arboretum. Most of the displays are appropriate for young grade school children. At the saltwater touch tanks, kids handle shells and horseshoe crabs; at the glassed-in honey beehive, kids view the busy tunnels of hive life; and by pressing buttons, kids hear songs of the area's birds such as hooded warblers and the Northern oriole. The nature trails connect to the Connecticut College Arboretum. Older children, however, might be bored with this low-tech exhibit.

The eclectic collection of the **Lyman Allyn Art Museum,** 625 Williams Street, on the Connecticut College campus, New London (860-443-2545), includes paintings by the Connecticut Impressionists and Hudson River School artists, early New England portraits, and eighteenth-century furniture, as well as tribal arts from Africa and the Americas and decorative arts from Asia and India. What most children like here is the **dollhouse** display that takes up one wall. This huge Victorian dollhouse has rooms upon rooms of furnishings. The details include tiny cards in the parlor and miniature needlepoint rugs on the floors.

Family Saturday programs are held two or three times a month. Past classes for preschoolers ages four to six have focused on storytelling and discovering how Victorian children played, and for ages seven and older classes have involved making shadow puppets and multicultural masks.

SPECIAL EVENTS

Fairs and Festivals

The *Mystic Discovery Guide* has a complete calendar of events. Here are some annual festivities.

June. Mystic/Noank Library Fair includes a plant, food, and book sale.

July. Sailfest, New London, international food, music, arts and crafts. Blessing of the Fleet, Stonington Borough, includes Saturday night lobster feast and band and Sunday parade.

August. Mystic Outdoor Art Festival, downtown.

October. Columbus Day Weekend. The Annual Chowderfest is held in the Mystic Seaport boat shed. Sample featured New England foods such as apple fritters, apple cider, wine, and, of course, the many varieties of chowder. Nineteenth-century tall ships are also open for visitors' curiosity, and the 1908 steamboat *Sabino* cruises passengers down the Mystic River.

WHERE TO STAY

You'll find listings of lodgings in the Chamber of Commerce's *Mystic Discovery Guide* and in the *Mystic and More* guide. Be sure to reserve in advance. The area has a mixture of guest houses and motels; some of the inns have age restrictions. **Covered Bridge Bed and Breakfast Reservation Service** (860-542-5944) offers a wide range of selections in the state. **Nutmeg Bed and Breakfast Agency** (860-236-6698) has 170 Connecticut listings. Although both registries specialize in romantic lodgings, each service has some accommodations suitable for families.

A large motel with an outdoor pool is the **Days Inn** (860-329-7466 or 800-DAYS INN) in Mystic. Other possibilities for families include the following.

The Comfort Inn, 48 Whitehall Avenue, Mystic (860-572-8531 or 800-228-5150), offers convenience, good prices, complimentary continental breakfast, and comfortable rooms (but there is no restaurant on property). Parents may be interested in knowing that this property offers free shuttle service to and from the Foxwoods casino. The corridors are interior, so the facility feels more like a hotel than a traditional motel.

The Inn at Mystic, U.S. Route 1 and Connecticut Route 27 (860-536-9604 or 800-237-2415), situated on fifteen acres, offers a range of accommodations in several buildings. Children like the grounds with its fountain, tennis court, and pool. The best rooms are in the Georgian Colonial-style main building. The comfortable motel units are decorated with American reproduction furniture.

The Mystic Hilton, 20 Coogan Boulevard, Mystic (860-572-0731), is across the street from the popular Mystic Aquarium and Institute for Exploration. The Hilton has an indoor pool and a restaurant on site. **The Steamboat Inn,** 73 Steamboat Wharf, Mystic (860-536-8300), overlooking the Mystic River, is a nice alternative for those who want to stay in town but not at a traditional chain motel or hotel. Furnished with period antiques and reproductions, all of the rooms have sitting areas. Children over six years old are welcome.

Taber Inne and Suites, 66 William Street, Mystic (860-536-4904), situated on three acres, is a handy option for families. The seven buildings feature standard motel units, as well as suites and one- or two-bedroom town houses. Most of the town houses have fireplaces, balconies, refrigerators, kitchenettes, and waterviews. Children six years and older are welcome in the town houses; in the other units, children of all ages are welcome.

Randall's Ordinary and Restaurant, P.O. Box 243, Route 2, North Stonington (860-599-4540), takes its name from the Colonial word for tavern. Situated on twenty-seven acres, this property gives your family acres to stroll. There are gardens, nature trails, and such farm animals as oxen and burrows. Kids like getting apples and carrots from the kitchen to feed these critters. There are three rooms above the restaurant in the John Randall House, which dates to 1685, and twelve rooms in the Jacob Terpenning Barn, which was moved to this site from New York. Furnishings are a mixture of American antiques and Ethan Allen reproductions. Parents should be warned that to reach some rooms you must climb winding staircases, which could be difficult or dangerous for young children. The barn rooms have telephone and televisions. The restaurant cooks 90 percent of dinners over an open hearth fireplace. Children—and adults—find this interesting to watch. Popular entrees are the grilled roast duck and salmon.

The Elms, 27-37 Ocean Avenue, Crescent Beach (860-739-5545), is a historic 1889 waterfront inn with its own private beach. Rooms have both private and shared baths.

Where to Eat

The Chamber of Commerce's *Mystic Discovery Guide* details a number of area restaurants. These are some good choices for families.

Kitchen Little, Route 27, Mystic (and Kitchen Little in the Village in Stonington), is the place to go if your family loves breakfast. You'll probably have to wait in line for the creative egg dishes and pancakes. Light lunches served, too; (860) 536-2122. Where to get locally caught lobster and other seafood specialties? Follow the crowds to **Abbott's Lobster in the Rough,** 117 Pearl Street, Noank (ten minutes south of Mystic). If the weather is nice, sit outside at picnic tables that overlook the Sound; (860) 536-7719. **Two Sisters Deli,** 4 Pearl Street, Mystic (860-536-1244), serves tasty sandwiches with catchy names (such as Big Sister's Midnight Snack) and delicious desserts. And, yes, there is such a place as **Mystic Pizza**—in fact, there are two: one is on West Main Street in Mystic (860-536-3700); the other is in North Stonington (860-599-3111).

Bee Bee Dairy Restaurant and Ice Cream Parlor, 33 West Main, Mystic (860-536-4577), is a good choice for families looking for moderately priced meals. The Bee Bee serves up such basic fare as hamburgers, grilled cheese, spaghetti and meatballs, and seafood dinners. The restaurant has wooden booths and tables with ersatz Tiffany lamps. Leave room for the peppermint ice cream and sundaes, local favorites. The breakfast menu is served all day.

Seamen's Inne, Mystic Seaport, Mystic (860–536–9649), has a mellow air, with well-spaced tables and not too much nautical and nineteenth-century decor. At lunch the salads (tuna, lobster, etc.) are good finds on a hot day. Hearty eaters can order babyback ribs, chicken, and steak. Hamburgers are there for the children, as well as a kids' menu that features pbj and grilled cheese sandwiches and a kid's portion of chowder. The Sunday brunch is popular with locals. Reservations are recommended.

SIDE TRIPS

- **The Valley Railroad Company,** 1 Railroad Avenue, P.O. Box 452, Essex (860–767–0103), offers an easy way to enjoy the scenery. Authentic 1920s coal-fired steam trains depart from the depot in Essex. For an extra charge you can sit in the restored "Great Republic," a first-class Pullman coach with mahogany paneling and swivel chairs. Options include a seventy-five-minute round-trip ride through the wooded Connecticut River Valley and a one-way trip to Deep River Landing, where you board a replica of a nineteenth-century paddle wheel boat for a seventy-five-minute cruise on the Connecticut River back to the depot in Essex. Along the way you pass the Gillette Castle and other scenic sites. Together, the train and boat ride take about two and a half hours. There is no eating on the train, but the boat has a snack bar. It's probably wise to bring your own snacks just in case your children don't like what's being served.
- If you're heading to New York from Mystic, take a break and stop by the **Barnum Museum,** 820 Main Street, Bridgeport. (Take I-95, exit 27 in Bridgeport.) This lively place is housed in a restored original building provided by showman and circus impresario Phineas Taylor (P. T.) Barnum in 1893 as a home to town historical and scientific societies. Barnum was a local boy, born in Bethel, Connecticut. Among the highlights: a hand-carved scale model of Barnum's "Greatest Show on Earth," a re-created library from Barnum's first Bridgeport mansion, a simulation of Tom Thumb's Bridgeport home, a Punch and Judy Show (Barnum was the first to introduce the puppets to American audiences), plus an exhibit devoted to clowning. One section of the building houses temporary exhibits. Call (860) 331-1104 for information.

For More Information

Mystic Chamber of Commerce, P.O. Box 143, 28 Cottrell Street, Mystic 06355 (860-572-9578), provides information and literature. You may also stop by the **Information Center at Mystic,** Olde Mistick Village (860-536-1641). A map and guide of Mystic and the surrounding towns are available from Connecticut's Mystic and More! P.O. Box 89, 470 Bark Street, New London 06320 (860-444-2206 or 800-TO-ENJOY).

Emergency Numbers

Ambulance, fire, and police: 911

Twenty-four-hour pharmacy: CVS, Long Hill Road, Groton;
(860-446-0912)

Mystic Pharmacy, 17 East Main Street (860-536-8615), is open from
8:00 A.M. to 8:00 P.M. weekdays and 8:00 A.M. to 6:00 P.M. weekends

Poison Control: (800) 343-2722

Twenty-four-hour emergency room: Lawrence and Memorial Hospital,
365 Montauk Avenue, New London, about 9 miles from Mystic;
(860) 442-0711

WASHINGTON, D.C.

In Washington, D.C., prepare to have fun and to feel proud, as our nation's capital is a city that belongs to all Americans. Even after more than 200 years, the city of Washington still sparkles. Pierre L'Enfant, the French architect who planned this city of wide avenues and open spaces, paved the way for a city of heroic proportions.

Spring is an especially good time to visit the nation's capital, for the city blooms with tulips and azaleas, and with any luck, you might catch the famous cherry blossoms. An autumn stroll through Rock Creek Park serves as a wonderful respite to life in the fast lane. Winter in Washington is lots of fun, too. After touring many of the museums' special exhibits, take the whole family ice skating on the Mall. And summer can be fun, but it's hot and humid.

GETTING THERE

Air travelers touch down at one of three airports in and around the District of Columbia. **Ronald Reagan (Washington) National Airport** is the closest to downtown, about 4.5 miles, or fifteen minutes away. Metrorail, Metrobus, and taxi service are available from the airport. **Washington Dulles International Airport,** approximately 26 miles from downtown, is a forty-minute drive, although during rush hour, the time and charges can increase significantly.

Baltimore/Washington International Airport (BWI), approximately 28 miles to downtown Washington, D.C., is about a fifty-minute drive in nonrush-hour traffic. Amtrak trains (202-383-3067 or 800-USA-RAIL) and the Maryland Commuter train line (MARC 800-325-7254) run frequently from BWI to Union Station in Washington.

For those traveling from major East Coast cities, including Boston, New York, Philadelphia, and Baltimore, taking Amtrak is a convenient way to access Washington. Trains pull into the beautifully restored Union Station, First Street and Massachusetts Avenue, NE, a complex with many boutiques, restaurants, and movie theaters.

Washington, D.C.

AT A GLANCE

▶ Visit Smithsonian Institution museums

▶ Walk through the Capitol and the White House

▶ See the Jefferson, Lincoln, Vietnam, Korean, and FDR memorials

▶ Tour the National Zoo

▶ Take in a play at Ford's Theatre

▶ Discover the Declaration of Independence at the National Archives

▶ Washington, D.C., Convention and Visitors Association, (202) 789-7000; www.washington.org

GETTING AROUND

An exciting town, Washington remains a manageable destination. Since the Mall acts as the tourist hub, the must-see sites can be navigated more easily than in most cities. In pleasant weather and with a solid pair of sneakers, you can see the sights by walking from Capitol Hill, along the Mall, with its museums, to the memorials.

To get to other parts of the city, **Washington Metropolitan Area Transit Authority's** (WMATA) **Metrorail,** the city's amazingly clean and safe subway, is your best bet. It's easy to navigate, with five color-coded subway lines—Orange, Red, Blue, Yellow, and Green—that cover much of the city and surrounding suburbs. Obtain Metro maps at the Visitors Center, 1212 New York Avenue, NW, or at any Metro station. Call (202) 789-7000. Up to two children ages five and under may ride free with a paying passenger. If you're darting all over the city, on any day except holidays, a One Day Pass allows unlimited travel after 9:30 A.M. WMATA also operates an extensive bus system. Call (202) 637-7000 for route and fare information.

Because public parking is scarce and parking lots fill up quickly, avoid driving downtown. You'll wind up frustrated. A popular and easy way to get around is to climb aboard either the **Old Town Trolley** or the **Tourmobile.** (See Special Tours.)

WHAT TO SEE AND DO

Museums

The largest and arguably most popular museum complex in the world, the **Smithsonian Institution** (www.si.edu), is in Washington, D.C. Begun in 1846 with a $500,000 donation from British scientist James Smithson, the Smithsonian complex today consists of sixteen facilities, including the National Zoo. Fourteen of the properties are in Washington, D.C. The other two facilities, the **Cooper-Hewitt Museum** and the **National Museum of the American Indian,** are in New York City.

The **Smithsonian Institution Building,** 1000 Jefferson Drive, SW (202-357-2700), the first to be completed in 1855, is affectionately called "the Castle" because of its architecture. Besides housing administrative offices, the building serves as the Smithsonian Information Center. Come here first to get oriented, find out about special exhibits, and plan your museum visits.

It's not likely that you'll be able to visit every one of the Smithsonian museums, and if by some chance you did, you surely wouldn't spend enough time to do them justice. Your best bet is to choose a few that most interest you. The Smithsonian complex includes **The Arts and Industries Building,** 900 Jefferson Drive, SW; **The National Museum of American History,** Constitution Avenue between Twelfth and Fourteenth Streets, NW; **The Museum of Natural History,** on Constitution Avenue at Tenth Street, NW; **The Freer Gallery** (Asian Art), Twelfth Street and Jefferson Drive, SW; **The Arthur M. Sackler Art Gallery** (Asian Art), 1050 Independence Avenue, SW; **The National Museum of African Art,** 950 Independence Avenue, SW; **The Hirshhorn Museum and Sculpture Garden,** Independence Avenue at Seventh Street, SW; **The National Air and Space Museum,** Seventh Street and Independence Avenue, SW; **The Renwick Gallery** (American Crafts), Seventeenth Street and Pennsylvania Avenue, NW; **The National Museum of American Art,** Eighth and G Streets, NW; **The National Portrait Gallery,** Eighth and F Streets, NW; the **Anacostia Museum,** 1901 Fort Place, SE; the **National Zoo,** 3001 Connecticut Avenue, NW; and **The National Postal Museum,** 2 Massachusetts Avenue, NE. All can be reached by telephone at (202) 357-2700. For a recording of daily events, call (202) 357-2020.

The **Arts and Industries Building,** 900 Jefferson Drive, SW (202-357-2700; www.si.edu), was completed in 1881. Kids love the elaborate carousel out front and will, undoubtedly, demand money to ride it. The museum, which hosts changing exhibits, is home to **Discovery Theater** (202-357-1500), the Smithsonian's children's theater program. The company hosts imaginative plays, puppet shows, and storytelling

Capital Children's Museum

When you're on Capitol Hill, take the time to visit the nearby **Capital Children's Museum,** 800 Third Street, NE (202–675-4120). Don't be put off by its bleak location, Nek Chand's Fantasy Garden outside the museum hints at the fun awaiting you inside. Chand, a Native American folk artist, created murals and several hundred life-size and miniature figures of men, women, children, and animals from discarded objects such as bicycle parts, fabric scraps, and broken jewelry. The robed figures—some with shimmery turbans and others with colorful, flowing caftans—herd sheep, move donkeys, and scatter ducks.

Inside the museum there's lots to do. Preschoolers can shop for groceries, grind chocolate to make their very own mug of hot cocoa in the Mexican Village, and crawl through a sewer, drive a school bus, and slide down a pole into a big red fire truck in the City Room. Children six and older can create their own cartoons at the Animation exhibit and mix special concoctions to make slimy stuff at the CMA Chemical Science Center. At the new JAPAN exhibit, they can ride a bullet train, take tea in a Tatami room, and shop for Kimonos.

sessions aimed at kids in preschool through grade 12. Reserve ahead for the performances, which are generally every other Saturday at 11:30 A.M. and 1:00 P.M. Tickets cost about $5.00.

The National Postal Museum, 2 Massachusetts Avenue, NE (www.si.edu), is dedicated to the history and development of the United States mail service. Here you can trace the route of the Pony Express; decide whether it's best to route a letter by land, rail, or sea; climb aboard a stagecoach; research your direct mail profile; and create your own greeting card. Learn about direct mail marketing in **What's in the Mail for You;** find out about the birth and proliferation of airmail in **Moving the Mail**—real 1920s airmail planes hang from the atrium ceiling; read actual letters sent home by soldiers in the **Art of Cards and Letters;** trace the development of the envelope in Undercover: Evolution of the American Envelope; and discover how stamps are printed in Stamps and Stories. You can peruse some of the more than 55,000 stamps on display and find out about interesting mail oddities.

What's the strangest package ever mailed? It was May Pierstroff, a four-year-old, on February 19, 1914. Her parents wanted her to visit her grandparents, but no one wanted to pay the train fare from Grangeville to Lewiston, Idaho. Her parents attached 53 cents postage to a tag around May's coat and sent her off. She traveled in the train's mail compartment and was delivered to her grandparents. Soon after the post office created rules forbidding the mailing of people.

The **National Museum of Natural History,** Constitution Avenue at Tenth Street, NW (www.si.edu), presents wonders of another kind. In the **Fossil Hall** the 80-foot-long skeleton of *Diplodocus,* the largest land animal to have existed, renders kids as well as adults wide-eyed. Peruse the bony remains of such fear-inspiring beasts as the *Stegosaurus,* and in the Ice Age Hall, the woolly mammoth. A gigantic African bush elephant is your host at the front door, and check out the 45.5-carat Hope diamond. Visit the **Insect Zoo,** where glass tanks, filled with beetles, bees, and scorpions, buzz, chirp, and whir. Watch centipedes wriggle, and if you time it right, help feed the friendly tarantula—he professes a fondness for crickets. Also check out the **Discovery Room,** a hands-on learning space for children four and older. Call ahead to find out when it's open.

The **National Museum of American History,** Constitution Avenue between Twelfth and Fourteenth Streets, NW (www.si.edu), details "everyday life in the American past." The exhibit After the Revolution focuses on the daily lives of eighteenth-century Americans. At **First Ladies: Political Role and Public Image,** learn how these women felt about their role and see their inaugural ball gowns. Kids like the locomotives in the **Railroad Hall,** the exhibit on the machines that sparked the industrial revolution, the coin collection in the exhibit **Money and Medals,** the Foucault pendulum, Oscar the Grouch from *Sesame Street,* and Archie Bunker's chair from *All in the Family,* among many other items of historical and popular interest. Watch as conservators restore the American flag that inspired Francis Scott Key to write "The Star-Spangled Banner." The museum is a good place to let your kids browse for hours, stopping briefly at whatever catches their fancy. Allow time to shop at the extensive gift and bookstore on the lower level, among the best of all the Smithsonian museums' shops.

The most popular museum of them all is the **National Air and Space Museum,** Seventh Street and Independence Avenue, SW (www.si.edu). Chronicling the story of flight, the museum presents a galactic lineup of aircraft, including such stars as the Wright brothers' *Kitty Hawk Flyer,* Charles Lindbergh's *Spirit of St. Louis,* John Glenn's *Friendship 7,* and the *Apollo 11* command module. Walk through the Skylab orbital workshop to touch a moonstone, see a lunar module, and discover just how little room astronauts have in space. Allow time for the museum's forty-minute movies, and stop in the gift shop for some astronaut ice cream on the way out.

The **Freer Gallery of Art,** Twelfth Street and Jefferson Drive, SW (www.si.edu), houses a renowned collection of Asian art and works by nineteenth- and early-twentieth-century American artists, as well as an often overlooked wonder—**the Peacock Room,** the only interior-design scheme by noted artist James McNeill Whistler. Walk in here and you and your kids will be intrigued by the intricate peacocklike designs. The museum has a children's guide to this room.

Don't skip this museum, as the swirls, patterns, and colors of Asian art delight kids. The gift shop, which has the city's best collection of children's books about Asia, also sells *The Princess and the Peacock,* a wonderfully illustrated kids' book about Whistler and the Peacock Room. With **ImaginAsia,** a free children's activity program, kids and their adult companions search the galleries for specific works, then come back to a classroom to create their own related art project. With Art of the Brush, for example, kids observe a calligrapher, locate the Chinese characters in displayed scrolls, and craft their own Chinese New Year's greeting. Programs are usually offered several times a month on Saturday or Sunday. Once a month, generally on Saturday, a staff member reads a children's story celebrating Asia. Call ahead for program times.

The Arthur M. Sackler Art Gallery, the Freer's sister museum, exhibits objects from Asia and the Near East from ancient times to the present. Chinese ritual bronzes, Buddhist and Hindu sculpture, and Persian and Indian paintings and manuscripts are displayed, but the kid favorite is the **Taj Mahal Emerald,** a glittery green gem weighing 141.13 carats.

Government Buildings

The Capitol, First Street between Independence and Constitution Avenues, NE (202-225-6827), sitting majestically atop the Mall's gentle rise, lends a commanding presence to the city. Inside, the building reveals a richness of intricate decoration complete with elaborate frescoes, murals, paintings, and mosaic tiles. Tours, which depart every five minutes from 9:00 A.M. to 4:30 P.M., start at the Rotunda. No guided tours are offered on Sunday.

In the main complex check out **Statuary Hall,** the old meeting chamber of the House of Representatives, which is lined with bronze and marble statues of two of each state's notable personages (some have spilled over into adjacent hallways). Children not only love finding their state's designee but also giggle at discovering the "secret of the whisper."

VIP Tours

A **VIP ticket** ensures you'll get in, although you'll still have to wait in line. Free VIP tickets are available for tours of the **White House,** the **Capitol,** the **Federal Bureau of Investigation,** the **John F. Kennedy Center,** and the **Bureau of Engraving and Printing.** Contact your senator or representative months in advance, as the number of tickets for each congressional office is limited. Write or phone, giving the number of tickets needed and the dates required.

The White House

At the **White House,** 1600 Pennsylvania Avenue, NW, more of the official rooms that dominate the public images of power come into view. As you walk through these carefully decorated spaces, you can imagine the pomp and flourishes of formal Washington. A VIP pass from your representative (ask as far in advance as possible) gains you entrance into one of the less crowded and more informative guided tours that depart from 8:00 to 10:00 A.M. Tuesday through Saturday. The regular tours (10:00 A.M. to noon Tuesday through Saturday) take you through the same rooms, although the crowds are continuous and the information from the guides less detailed.

To eliminate the long lines and waits, the National Park Service operates the **White House Visitors Center,** located at the U.S. Department of Commerce, 1450 Pennsylvania Avenue, NW (202-208-1631). Come here for free, same-day timed tickets to tour the White House. The center also has educational videos and gift items. Open 8:00 A.M. to 5:00 P.M. daily; from Memorial Day to Labor Day, extended hours are from 7:00 A.M. to 7:00 P.M.

But, alas, many kids find furniture boring. To stir interest, and to pick your favorite items to gaze at, purchase *The White House: An Historic Guide* before your tour. Published by the White House Historical Association, the book features color photographs and lots of details about furniture, paintings, and china. (Available at bookstores or by mail from the White House Historical Association, 740 Jackson Place, NW, Washington, D.C. 20506 (202-737-8292).

Because of an architectural anomaly, discussions on one side of the room could be overheard across the floor at the spot where John Quincy Adams sat at his desk. Legend has it that Adams owes some of his political acumen to this eaves-dropping.

When the House or Senate is not in session, line up before or after your tour for a peek at these august rooms. To view these chambers when elected officials hold sway, obtain a pass ahead of time from your representative or senator.

In the **Jefferson Building,** across the street from the Capitol, at First and East Capitol Streets, SE, is the **Library of Congress** (202-707-8000—general information; 202-707-5000—visitor's information; 202-707-5458—tour information). Comprising three entire buildings, it is reputed to be the world's largest library, containing more than 110 million items in 460 languages. Although there are 16 million volumes in the collection, there are also 2 million recordings, more than 12 million photographs, more than 4 million maps, and more than 46 million personal papers, documents, and manuscripts. Except for members of Congress and certain government officials, no one may check items out of the library; you read the material on site.

The reading room, which is open to any researcher eighteen years and older, is a sweep of mahogany desks set off by cream and red-hued marble pillars and archways. An intricate grand dome tops the space. Check out Treasures of the Library Congress, rotating exhibits of special items from the library's collection.

The **John Adams Building** houses part of the collection, as does the **James Madison Memorial Building,** which features temporary exhibits, the National Digital Library Visitor's Center and the **U.S. Copyright Office.** Your kids might be interested in the small display of original items submitted for copyrighting, such as the first Bert and Ernie puppets, Ken and Barbie dolls, baseball cards, and a speech by Martin Luther King Jr. With hungry kids, head to the cafeteria on the sixth floor of the Madison Building; it's open to the public after 12:30 P.M.

Watch money being printed at the **Bureau of Engraving and Printing,** Fourteenth and C Streets, SW (202-874-3188 or 874-3019; www.washington.org). The bureau designs, engraves, and prints U.S. securities, including paper currency and Treasury bonds, as well as assorted items for the federal government, such as White House invitations and identification cards, plus about 25 billion postage stamps per year. You'll see presses churning out $1 bills (8,000 sheets of thirty-two notes each are printed per hour), learn the composition of currency (75 percent cotton and 25 percent linen), and see money being trimmed and scanned for imperfections. Free samples aren't given away, but you can buy sheets of uncut (nonnegotiable) bills and baggies of shredded money. Tours are Monday to Friday 9:00 A.M. to 2:00 P.M. Line up early for same-day tickets.

See the documents that helped establish our country at the **National Archives,** Eighth Street and Constitution Avenue, NW, (202-501-5400; www.washington.org). The Declaration of Independence, the Constitution, and the Bill of Rights are exhibited in glass helium-filled cases and lowered each night into a storage vault.

The tour of the **Federal Bureau of Investigation,** J. Edgar Hoover Building, E Street between Ninth and Tenth Streets, NW (202-324-3447; www.washington.org), details the history and goals of the FBI. You'll see weapons confiscated from such gangsters as Al Capone and Bonnie and Clyde, walk past posters of the Bureau's ten most wanted criminals, and peer into the DNA laboratory and the Firearms Unit. The tour ends with a bang as the agent fires a real gun at a target. Same-day free tickets for the tour go quickly. Be sure to line up before 8:30 A.M.

The **National Gallery of Art,** 600 Constitution Avenue, NW (202-737-4215), is a gift to the eye. This museum consists of two buildings: the classically inspired West Wing, designed by John Russell Pope, and the East Wing, a dramatic asymmetrical trapezoid, designed by I. M. Pei. The museum houses a world-class collection of paintings, sculpture, and graphic arts from the Middle Ages to contemporary times. The huge **Calder mobile** suspended above the lobby of the East building especially charms children, as does the bold colors and lines of post-modern art. To turn the museum into an exciting treasure hunt for your kids, ask them to select several favorite postcards of paintings from the gift shop, or for those of you who are on-line, call up a painting from the Micro Gallery, the National Gallery's multimedia computer system. Then set out in search of the originals as you meander through the exhibits. Masterworks in the West wing include paintings by Leonardo da Vinci, Rembrandt, and Van Gogh.

The **United States Holocaust Memorial Museum,** 100 Raoul Wallenberg Place, SW between Fourteenth and Fifteenth Streets near Independence Avenue (202-488-0400; www.si.edu), tells the story of the Holocaust through a series of moving exhibits composed of actual artifacts. Because the main exhibits are likely to elicit strong emotions, these are recommended for kids ages eleven and older. For ages eight and above, visit Remember the Children: Daniel's Story, an exhibit dedicated to the 1.5 million children who died in the Holocaust. This exhibit, told from a child's point of view and using interactive exhibits, traces Daniel's experience of the Holocaust from a happy childhood to a concentration camp survivor.

Because the U.S. Holocaust Memorial Museum is so popular, admission to the permanent exhibit is only by timed tickets. Free passes, distributed first-come, first-served, are available daily at 10 A.M. Show up at the Fourteenth Street entrance by 8:30 A.M. Each person in line may obtain up to four tickets. Pro-Tix, (800) 400-9373, sells passes in advance for a nominal charge.

Historic Sites, Monuments, and Memorials

Monuments and memorials adorn the city, part of the nation's homage to its heroes. **The Washington Monument,** Constitution Avenue at Fifteenth Street, NW (202-426-6841; www.washington.org), a marble obelisk rising 555 feet and ⅛ inch, dominates the city's skyline. While the panoramic view from the top is among the best in town, the wait to board the elevator can stretch to hours. Free timed passes are required. The ticket kiosk on Fifteenth Street opens at 7:30 A.M. for same-day, first-come, first-served tickets. Advance tickets are available for a nominal charge from TicketMaster (202-432-SEAT or 800-505-5040). The scaffolding and fabric you see covering areas of the monument are part of a

A seventy-second elevator ride will take you and your family to the top of the Washington Monument.

multimillion-dollar restoration begun in January 1998 and scheduled to be completed in 2000. At times, the monument will be closed.

The Jefferson Memorial (202-426-6841; www.washington.org), adorns the south bank of the Tidal Basin. In spring you may find yourself surrounded by a sea of pink flowers if you are lucky enough to catch the famous cherry trees in blossom. The graceful, domed building reflects the architectural shape Jefferson used in designing Monticello, his Virginia home. Inside the columned rotunda, a 19-foot bronze statue of the statesman captures your attention. Passages from his writings, including quotations from the Declaration of Independence and the Virginia Statute of Religious Freedom, are engraved on the walls.

Like the Jefferson Memorial, the **Lincoln Memorial,** West Potomac Park at Twenty-third Street, NW (202-426-6841; www.washington.org), reminds the visitor of the leader's commitment to liberty. See sculptor Daniel Chester French's masterpiece at night, highlighted by the moon and subtle spotlights surrounding the monument. Seated, pensive, and brooding over the concerns of the Civil War, this Lincoln depicts a man burdened. Carved on the memorial's walls are excerpts of Lincoln's stirring Gettysburg Address and his second inaugural speech.

The Vietnam Memorial, Constitution Avenue and Henry Bacon Drive, NW (202-634-1568; www.washington.org), is perhaps the most moving monument in the city. As people walk along the path in front of the black granite monument set into the ground, they become quiet and contemplative, moved by the thousands upon thousands of names of that era's dead. Sometimes a mother or a child, or even someone the soldier never knew, leaves flowers, a flag, or a note next to their loved one's name. Few people walk away from this simple monument unmoved. Nearby, the **Vietnam Women's Memorial,** Twenty-first Street and Constitution Avenue, NW (202-426-6841; www.washington.org), is located in a grove of trees across from the Vietnam Memorial. This bronze statue depicts three servicewomen holding up one wounded soldier.

The Korean War Veterans Memorial, Independence Avenue at the Lincoln Memorial (202-619-7222; www.washington.org), consists of a black granite Memorial Wall etched with the faces of nurses, soldiers, chaplains, sailors, and others who served in the war, plus a sculptural group of nineteen soldiers. These haunting, 7-foot-high figures carry rifles and wear fatigues covered by ponchos. The lifelike group conveys the weariness and harsh realities of war.

At the **Franklin Delano Roosevelt Memorial,** 1850 West Basin Drive, SW (202-619-7222; www.washington.org), you walk through four outdoor sculpture courts, each depicting a different phase of FDR's four-term presidency. Among the artwork is George Segal's *The Breadline,* a realistic sculptural group of five men waiting in line for food. Older kids find the memorial illuminating, and younger ones like the waterfalls, fountains, and quiet pools.

Visit the **Frederick Douglass National Historic Site,** Cedar Hill, 1411 West Street SE (202-426-5961). Douglass lived here for much of the time he was in the city.

Virginia Attractions

At **Arlington National Cemetery,** Fort Meyer, across the Memorial Bridge (703-607-8052), see where America's military heroes, presidents, and other public figures have been honored, memorialized, and buried. This cemetery isn't just historical, however; there are often fifteen or more military funeral services a day, so don't be surprised if you come upon a service. Start at the visitor center near the Metro stop and obtain historical information, gravesite locations for notables, and information on **Arlington House** and the **Robert E. Lee Memorial.**

Visit the **Tomb of the Unknown Soldier** overlooking the Washington skyline. The tomb contains remains of unidentified soldiers from World War I, World War II, and Korea. The tomb itself is guarded twenty-four hours a day by the 3rd United States Infantry. Changing of the guard, a solemn and impressive ritual, occurs every half hour from April 1 through September 30, and every hour on the hour from October 1 through March 31. The guards change at two-hour intervals during night hours all year round.

The guard paces from his post to the crossway in twenty-one steps,

Newseum

The most interesting of Virginia's attractions for kids is the **Newseum,** 1101 Wilson Boulevard, Arlington (703-284-3544 or 888-NEWSEUM; www.newseum.org.) Opened in April 1997, this is the only hands-on museum dedicated to news. In the **Interactive Newsroom** kids (and adults) make choices about the day's top stories as announcers and work as investigative reporters. In the **Ethics Center** ponder the types of ethical dilemmas faced by journalists. In the **News History Gallery** learn about great news stories through artifacts and multimedia exhibits. The **Video News Wall** features copy from around the world, enabling visitors to compare how seventy different papers treat major stories differently. In the **Broadcast Studio** watch a real news program live and talk with visiting journalists.

At the **News Byte Cafe** you can grab a snack while browsing a news-related Internet site.

Freedom Park, adjoining the Newseum, honors "the spirit of freedom and the struggle to preserve it." The park's **Freedom Forum Journalists Memorial** honors reporters who have died in the line of duty. Icons of freedom displayed in the park include a 12-foot-high segment of the Berlin Wall; cobblestones from the Warsaw ghetto; a bronze casting of a South African ballot box from the 1994 election, the first one in which blacks were allowed to vote; a tin kayak used by a Cuban refugee to flee to the United States; and a bronze casting of Martin Luther King, Jr.'s jail cell door from his incarceration in 1963 in Birmingham, Alabama.

turning to pause while facing the memorial for twenty-one seconds. Turning once more, the guard pauses for another twenty-one seconds before repeating the process. "Twenty-one" represents the highest honor of salutation, matching the twenty-one-gun salute.

John F. Kennedy's gravesite has an Eternal Flame. If your children ask how the flame stays lit, tell them that there is a constantly flashing electric spark near the tip of the gas nozzle that relights the flame if it should go out due to rain or wind. **Jacqueline Kennedy Onassis** is buried here, and **Senator Robert F. Kennedy's** grave is nearby.

Additional graves of notables include those of **Lt. Commander Roger Bruce Chaffee,** U.S. Navy, Apollo astronaut, who perished while performing test operations for the Apollo 1 space mission; **Lt. Colonel Virgil I. ("Gus") Grissom,** U.S. Air Force, Apollo astronaut, the second American in space on the Mercury mission, 1961, and first person to make two space trips on the two-man Gemini flight in 1965; the seven commingled remains of the astronauts who died aboard the **space shuttle Challenger** in 1986; **Oliver Wendell Holmes, Jr.,** Civil War veteran and Supreme Court Justice; **Rear Admiral Robert E. Peary,** U.S. Navy explorer; and **William Howard Taft,** President and Chief Justice of the United States.

Also of note is the **Women in Military Service for America Memorial,** at the entrance to Arlington National Cemetery (703-533-1155 or 800-222-2294; www.wimsa.org). This memorial, dedicated October 1997, is dedicated to all women who have served in and with the military in times of conflict and peace. The **education center and theater** portray the history of women in the armed forces beginning 220 years ago. Children may be surprised to learn that women played important roles as far back as the Revolutionary War. The **Hall of Honor** recognizes women who have given a significant sacrifice, such as those who were prisoners of war or died in service, and those who were recipients of the highest awards for service and bravery. The **Computer Registry** makes it possible to locate and view the records of friends and relatives who were or are servicewomen. Special tours for children are available upon request.

The **Marine Corps War Memorial,** Marshall Drive between Route 50 and Arlington National Cemetery (703-285-3094), commonly referred to as the **Iwo Jima Memorial,** is not far from the cemetery. The capture of Iwo Jima, a noted incident in World War II, was immortalized on film when news photographer Joe Rosenthal photographed five marines and one Navy corpsman raising the large American flag. This sculpture honors not only those marines who fought in World War II, but every marine who has died defending America since 1775.

For more military lore and lessons, visit the **Pentagon,** Arlington (703-695-1776). This five-sided building houses various offices of the Department of Defense. One of the world's largest office buildings, it covers twenty-nine acres and has 17.5 miles of corridors. Although reservations are not required for a tour, you do need to bring photo identification cards for members of the family over the age of sixteen. An introductory film explains the history behind the building. The tour of the many corridors includes the **Military Women's Corridor,** the **Flag Corridor,** and the **Hall of Heroes,** a listing of those who received the Congressional Medal of Honor. You'll also see some aircraft and a selection of the **Pentagon's Time-Life Art Collection.** Be forewarned: Kids might find this boring.

Green Spaces and Recreation

In summer take time to golf at **East Potomac Park Golf Course,** in the East Potomac Park, Ohio Drive at Haines Point, (202-863-9007). Near the Jefferson Memorial, this facility has an eighteen-hole course, a driving range, and a miniature golf course (202-488-8087).

When it's spring in Washington, enjoy the outdoors by foot, by bike, and by boat. Take the time to smell the flowers, literally, at the gardens surrounding the iron **Bartholdi Fountain,** Independence Avenue and First Street, NW (202–224–3121).

The **U.S. Botanic Garden,** First Street, SW (202–225–8333), is closed for renovation until 2000, when it reopens with a National Garden that will feature an Environmental Learning Center, a First Ladies Water Garden, a Rose Garden, a Showcase Garden, and a Butterfly Garden.

Dumbarton Oaks Park, Dumbarton Oaks, Thirty-first and R Streets (202–338–8278), located in Upper Georgetown, has a noted collection of pre-Columbian and Byzantine art. An oasis in busy and crowded Georgetown, the ten-acre terraced garden, with its more than 1,000 roses, seasonal flowers, trees, and fountains, is a real treat.

If you can, spend some time in **Rock Creek Park.** Contact the Rock Creek Park Office of the Superintendent, 5000 Glover Road, NW (202–426–6832). The park's miles of wooded trails and paths for horseback riding and bicycling run from the Potomac River by the Kennedy Center all the way north to the D.C.-Maryland border. On Saturdays and Sundays the long stretch of **Beach Drive** that hugs the creek from Broad Branch Road to Military Road, NW, is closed to traffic from 7:00 A.M. to 7:00 P.M. Join the locals who roller skate, bike, and stroll along this scenic stretch.

Horse lovers can saddle up and take scenic trail rides at the **Rock Creek Park Horse Centre,** 5100 Glover Road, NW, in Rock Creek Park (202–362–0117). Riders must be twelve years of age.

The **C&O Canal** and its towpath stretch for 184.5 miles from Georgetown in the District to Cumberland, Maryland. Stroll or bike this gently ascending path, or board a mule-drawn barge for a trip narrated by costumed interpreters. Barges operate from mid-April to mid-October. The ninety-minute trips originate at Georgetown (202–653–5844) and at the visitor center in **Great Falls Park,** Maryland (301–299–3613). The falls, not high but powerful, draw crowds. The farther away you walk from the visitor center, the more peaceful the scene becomes. A snack bar offers light fare for the hungry traveler.

A winter visit to the city wouldn't be complete without an ice-skating session on the Mall, an often overlooked capital splendor, Seventh Street and Constitution Avenue, NW. At **Pershing Park,** Fourteenth Street and Pennsylvania Avenue, NW, you can easily escape the cold in the grand Willard Hotel. If the weather is cold enough, take to the ice on the Mall's **reflecting pool.** Framed by the Lincoln Memorial and the Washington Monument, this rink exudes a special glory on a starry winter night. The **National Gallery Sculpture Garden** has an ice rink surrounded by world-class sculptures.

The National Zoological Park

The National Zoological Park, 3001 Connecticut Avenue, NW (202–673–4800—recording; 202–673–4717—reception desk; www.si.edu/natzoo), is a great place to spend a half-day. With 5,800 animals on 163 acres, there's lots to see. Highlights include:

- **Great Cats.** Follow the paw prints down a walkway that leads to the stars—four tigers and three lions. In Predators Alcove pet a life-size *Tyrannosaurus rex* skull and take a break at Tiger Kid's Stop, a shady spot with benches, a water fountain, and glass-fronted balconies for easy viewing of these kingly beasts.
- **Amazonia.** Experience a tropical rain forest complete with waterfalls, 300 species of plants, and a learning gallery.
- **Think Tank.** Watch trainers discover how orangutans think.
- **Cheetah Conservation Station.** Observe these powerful and graceful cats.
- **Reptile Discovery Center.** See slithery snakes and reptiles and gape at the Komodo dragon, the world's largest lizard.
- **Panda House.** Visit with Hsing-Hsing, the male panda donated by the People's Republic of China. (Ling-Ling, his mate, died.)
- **Invertebrates.** Learn about starfish, sponges, giant crabs, and other spineless creatures.
- **Grasslands.** Observe bison, prairie dogs, and many species of grasses and plants indigenous to the Great Plains of North America.

Contact the National Park Service's Office of Public Affairs of the National Capitol Region, 1100 Ohio Drive, SW (202-619-7222), for detailed information about the district's many parks.

Special Tours

D.C. has two fun options that take the weariness out of walking for small children. Buy a ticket for the **Old Town Trolley Tours** or the **Tourmobile.** Along its two-hour narrated tour, the **Old Town Trolley** (202-832-9800), makes stops throughout Washington, including at some hotels, making it easy to sightsee. After leaving the trolley, visitors can reboard for another stop along the route.

The **Tourmobile** (202-554-5100), offers a year-round narrated tour with fourteen stops, including the White House, Washington Monument, Smithsonian Museums, Arlington National Cemetery, and Mount Vernon. Riders are allowed to reboard and ride to other stops on the route.

Scandal Tours of Washington serves up an irreverent look at the sites of D.C.'s past and current scandals, a tour especially appreciated by parents and teens. This ninety-minute bus ride presented by a local comedy group, Gross National Product (GNP), careens past such infamous sites as the Vista Hotel, where former D.C. mayor Marion Barry was arrested, and the Tidal Basin, where former congressman Wilbur Mills splashed with "exotic dancer" Fanne Fox. On board, the Gross National Product actors bring the satire to life. From Memorial Day to Labor Day the tours are open to individuals. The rest of the year, GNP does the tour for groups only. Call ahead for reservations (202–783–7212).

The **Black History National Recreation Trail** is a self-guided walking tour that highlights several black history sites throughout Washington, D.C. See the Metropolitan A.M.E. Church, Frederick Douglass's home, Howard University, and more. For a pamphlet and additional information, call the National Park Service at (202) 619–7222.

Athletic families might enjoy a guided bicycle tour of the city. **Bike the Sites** (202–966–8662; www.bikethesites.com) covers approximately 8 miles in a leisurely fashion, with frequent rest and photo stops. Bikes and helmets are provided. Allow about three hours.

Theater, Music, and the Arts

The **John F. Kennedy Center for the Performing Arts,** New Hampshire Avenue, NW near D Street (202–467–4600 or 800–444–1324), offers a schedule of cultural, theatrical, and dance performances on six stages. The Kennedy Center is home to the National Symphony Orchestra, the Washington Opera, and the American Film Institute.

From fall through spring, the Kennedy Center hosts The Imagination Celebration, featuring plays, puppet shows, and dance theater geared toward children. When the **National Symphony Orchestra** (202–467–4600) presents a petting, kids can try a tuba, finger a flute, bang the drums, and test out other symphonic instruments before the symphony's child-friendly performance.

The **Shakespeare Theatre,** 450 Seventh Street, NW (202–393–2700), presents Shakespeare's plays as well as one or two other selections each season. This relatively small theater is the place to introduce your preteen to the classics. Children under five are not admitted.

Ford's Theatre, 511 Tenth Street, NW (202–347–4833 or 800–899–2367), is a family-oriented theater, featuring plays and musicals most of the year, including an annual Christmas showing of Charles Dickens's *A Christmas Carol.*

National Theatre, 1321 Pennsylvania Avenue, NW (202–628–6161 or 800–447–7400), hosts Broadway musicals and American premieres.

Arena Stage, Sixth Street and Maine Avenue, SW (202–488–3300), offers

Spectator Sports

The $160 million **MCI Center,** Seventh and F Streets, NW (202–628–3200; www.mcicenter.com), is home to the National Basketball Association's **Washington Wizards,** the **Washington Mystics,** the women's basketball team, and the National Hockey League's **Washington Capitals.** Sports fans might want to stop by even if they're not attending a game to visit the facility's shops, restaurants, and exhibits.

Watch previews of events and historic moments in sports and politics on the wall of video monitors, play trivia games, and have your face superimposed on a postcard with sports greats at the ArenaNets computer stations. At the 25,000-square-foot Sports Gallery view such memorabilia as a 1909 T206 Honus Wagner baseball card, valued at $675,000, and play virtual reality sports games.

The MCI Center also has an array of restaurants, eateries and shops, including the four-level **Discovery Channel Store,** 601 F Street, NW (202–639–0908; www.flagship.discovery.com). The educational material, games, and books are interestingly exhibited using multimedia and interactive displays. Shoppers "time travel" from the first floor, which deals with prehistoric items and things from deep beneath the earth's surface, to the top level, which covers the far reaches of the universe.

classics and comedies in the Fichlander, a theater-in-the-round, and new plays and special readings in the smaller Old Vat room.

In summer **Wolf Trap Farm Park for the Performing Arts,** 1551 Trap Road, Vienna, Virginia (703–255–1868), presents stars in jazz, country, folk, rock 'n' roll, and other types of music in an open-air setting. Besides reserved seats, you can opt for lawn space (arrive early). Bring a blanket and a picnic dinner and enjoy music under the stars. In September Wolf Trap presents an **International Children's Festival,** featuring puppet shows, plays, dance troupes, and craftspeople from around the world.

SPECIAL EVENTS

Festivals

January. Martin Luther King's Birthday. Every four years, attend the Inauguration Celebration.

February. Black History Month.

March. Smithsonian's Annual Kite Festival on the grounds of the Washington Monument.

March/April. National Cherry Blossom Festival. The White House Easter Egg Roll, for children ten and under.

May. Festival of the Building Arts, National Building Museum.

June/July. The Festival of American Folklife on the Mall.

July. The best and brightest Fourth of July. Celebrate independence with fireworks and the sounds of the National Symphony Orchestra near the Capitol.

September. The International Children's Festival, Wolf Trap Farm Park, Vienna, Virginia. Toss a disc around at the National Frisbee Festival.

October. Explore the Rose Garden and the South Lawn of the White House on the Garden Tour.

November. Veteran's Day remembrances at Arlington National Cemetery.

December. Lighting of the National Christmas Tree at the Pageant of Peace.

WHERE TO STAY

Washington, D.C., offers a wide range of accommodations for a variety of budgets. Visitors can choose from luxury hotels to more moderate accommodations. Some of D.C.'s best lodging buys are weekend hotel packages. These special room rates reduce prices as much as 30 to 50 percent.

When choosing lodging, look for a Metro stop within walking distance and an indoor pool for cooling off and reenergizing after a day full of walking.

Hotels that frequently run weekend packages include **Hyatt Regency Washington–Capitol Hill,** 400 New Jersey Avenue, NW (202-737-1234 or 800-233-1234); **Loews L'Enfant Plaza,** 480 L'Enfant Plaza, SW (202-484-1000), one of the only city hotels that accepts pets; **Hotel Washington,** Fifteenth Street and Pennsylvania Avenue, NW (202-638-5900), just one block from the White House; **Washington Hilton,** 1919 Connecticut Avenue, NW (202-483-3000 or 800-HILTONS); and the **Four Seasons Hotel,** 2800 Pennsylvania Avenue, NW (202-342-0444).

For reduced rates every night of the week, call **Capitol Reservations,** 1201 K Street, NW (202-452-1740 or 800-VISIT-DC). This reservation service advertises discounts of approximately 30 percent at seventy area hotels, all in safe neighborhoods. **Washington D.C. Accommodations,** 2201 Wisconsin Avenue, NW (202-289-2220 or 800-554-2220) also offers hotel discounts.

For all suite properties, some of which feature kitchenettes, consider **Embassy Suites Hotel-Downtown,** 1250 Twenty-second Street, NW (202-857-3388 or 800-EMBASSY); **Embassy Square,** a Summerfield Suites Hotel, 2000 North Street, NW (202-659-9000); **Carlyle Suites,** 1731 New Hampshire Avenue, NW (202-234-3200); and **Capitol Hill Suites,** 200 C Street, SE (202-543-6000).

Budget-conscious families can save money in summer by staying in a **dormitory at Catholic University** in the residential community of Brookland (202-319-5277). The rooms (some as inexpensive as $45 per night) often come with access to great recreational facilities such as Olympic-sized pools, tennis courts, golf courses, and basketball courts. Because most rooms sleep two, bring sleeping bags for the kids.

WHERE TO EAT

Washington has a number of good restaurants located in all sections of town. **Union Station,** 50 Massachusetts Avenue, NE (202-371-9441), just north of the Capitol, offers a vast food court on the lower level, where even the pickiest eater will be satisfied. The **Old Post Office Pavilion,** Pennsylvania Avenue and Twelfth Street (202-289-4224), features an open-air food court in its renovated central courtyard. Here you combine history and good eats, and there's often live music. Go for lunch or stop in for a homemade ice cream cone at **Scoops Homemade Cones.**

For inexpensive Tex-Mex, check out the **Austin Grill,** 2404 Wisconsin Avenue (202-337-8080). Pizza lovers will find a creative twist and a tasty crust at **Pizzeria Paradiso,** 2029 P Street (202-223-1245). **Pizzeria Uno,** 3211 M Street, NW (202-695-6333), is another favorite for deep-dish Chicago-style pies, as well as burgers and pasta.

A favorite spot for teens: **The Hard Rock Cafe,** 999 E Street, NW (202-737-7625), features rock memorabilia along with burgers and such. For film buffs and the star-struck, **Planet Hollywood,** 1101 Pennsylvania Avenue, NW (202-783-7827), serves a similar menu, but the setting features movie memorabilia.

Sequoia, in Georgetown along the Potomac River, 3000 K Street, NW (202-944-4200), has indoor and outdoor dining plus great views of the Washington harbor and the Kennedy Center.

The Bombay Club, 815 Connecticut Avenue, NW (202-659-3727), offers good Indian fare in a comfortable club setting. **Clyde's,** 3236 M Street, NW (202-333-9180), a longtime gathering spot for college students and twentysomethings, serves salads, sandwiches, pasta, crab cakes, and grilled items. If you want to eat dinner at **Houston's,** 1065 Wisconsin Avenue, NW (202-338-4312), arrive early. Known for its barbecued ribs and chicken, the restaurant also serves salads, fajitas, and burgers.

McCormick & Schmick, 1652 K Street, NW (202-861-2233), serves good seafood, as does **Legal Sea Foods,** 2020 K Street, NW (202-496-1111). Kids like Legal's fish-shaped cheese ravioli.

At the Mall it's best to eat at the museum cafes and cafeterias. These are most crowded during the peak lunch hours, so eat early or snack on some popcorn and wait until two o'clock or so. The *Washington Post's Sunday Magazine,* and the *Washingtonian* frequently review restaurants.

SIDE TRIPS

Monticello

From D.C. it's easy to visit Thomas Jefferson's **Monticello** (804-295-8181), 125 miles away and just 3 miles southeast of Charlottesville, Virginia. See for yourself how the house reflects Jefferson's passions, architectural genius, inventions, and love of gardening. Step outside to the eighteen acres of gardens, re-created from Jefferson's personal records. There are horticultural exhibits and plant sales at the Thomas Jefferson Center for Historic Plants, and on Saturdays in summer, you can take a wildflower walk or a planting workshop, for which you must preregister.

Show yourself around Mulberry Row, the workplace of the laborers and the site of woodworking shops, slaughterhouses, and smokeshops.

Old Town Alexandria

With its centuries of history, its legendary tales, and its sophisticated restaurants and shops, Old Town Alexandria makes for an enjoyable outing that is merely across the Potomac River. First, stop by the visitor center at the **Ramsay House,** 221 King Street, and stock up on brochures about Alexandria's boutiques and history.

The best way to explore Old Town is by walking. Stroll along King, Cameron, Queen, and Duke Streets, names that harken back to the town's colonial past.

Visit **Gadsby's Tavern,** in the Old City Tavern and Hotel, 138 North Royal Street (703-548-1288), the pub often frequented by the Marquis de Lafayette, James Madison, and Thomas Jefferson, and take the tavern museum tour. Drop by **Robert E. Lee**'s boyhood home, 607 Oronoco

Mount Vernon

The home of our nation's very first president, George Washington's **Mount Vernon** is just 16 miles outside Washington; (703-780-2000). The property is accessible by car or by Metrobus; (202-637-2437). You may even get there by boat in the summertime by calling *Spirit of Mount Vernon* at (202) 554-8000. Get to know Mr. Washington, the farmer, as you learn of his cultivation of tobacco and wheat. Inside the mansion see Martha's porcelain tea service, the grandiose, two-story-high dining room, and paintings of Washington area landscapes as interpreted by eighteenth-century artists. Meander through the gardens, and enjoy a respite while admiring the trees that George Washington himself so adored.

Street (703-548-8454), a stately Federal house. See one of the gathering places of the merchants, the **Carlyle House,** 121 North Fairfax Street (703-549-2997), a sandstone manor dating to 1753. If you plan on touring many properties, consider purchasing a block ticket.

Also of interest is the **Alexandria Black History Resource Center,** 638 North Alfred Street (703-838-4356). Follow the walking brochure to black historic sites, which include streets where the first free blacks lived.

Stop by the waterfront **Torpedo Factory Art Center,** 105 North Union Street (703-838-4565), the 1918 manufacturing site of World War II torpedo shell cases where 160 professional artists not only work at their craft but display their wares.

For a river view board the ***Admiral Tilp,*** 205 The Strand (703-548-9000), for a forty-minute narrated tour.

Additional day trips worth a stop are **Baltimore, Annapolis** (see Baltimore chapter), and **Philadelphia** (see Philadelphia chapter).

FOR MORE INFORMATION

Contact the **Washington, D.C., Convention and Visitors Association,** 1212 New York Avenue, NW (202-789-7000, www.washington.org).

Several free periodicals serve as good references for current exhibits and special happenings for families. *Potomac Children,* a newspaper published ten times a year, P.O. Box 151544, Chevy Chase, Maryland 20815 (301-656-2133), has a calendar of events. *Washington Parent* appears six times a year and focuses on happenings around town and offers informative articles, although much of this information may be more useful to residents than visitors. Contact the **Parent Connection,** 5606 Knollwood Road, Bethesda, Maryland 20816 (301- 320-2321).

Emergency Numbers

Ambulance, fire, and police: 911

Children's National Medical Center, 111 Michigan Avenue, NW; (202) 745-5000

George Washington University Medical Center Emergency Room, 901 Twenty-third Street, NW; (202) 994-3211

Poison Control Center: (202) 625-3333

Twenty-four-hour pharmacies: CVS Drug, 6-7 Dupont Circle, NW; (202) 785-1466; CVS Drug, 1121 Vermont Circle, NW; (202) 628-0720

ACADIA NATIONAL PARK, MOUNT DESERT ISLAND, AND BAR HARBOR

Formed millions of years ago by the jagged edges of Ice Age glaciers, the area that became **Acadia National Park** offers dramatic coastal scenery. Most of Acadia National Park is on Mount Desert Island, once a popular summer resort for the wealthy. George Dorr and other influential citizens bought plots of land to preserve the area in the 1900s, then convinced the federal government to take over the land. In 1916 President Woodrow Wilson created the Sieur des Monts National Monument. With the addition of more land in 1919, the name of the area was changed to LaFayette National Park, making this the first national park east of the Mississippi. In 1929 the park's name was again changed to Acadia National Park. The town of **Bar Harbor** is the gateway to Acadia National Park.

Acadia National Park features classic Maine scenery of rocky coasts, granite cliffs, and mountains. The park, occupying more than half of Mount Desert Island as well as several offshore islands including Isle au Haut and Baker Island plus the Schoodic Peninsula, offers 22 square miles of mountains, valleys, and lakes bracketed by the Atlantic Ocean. While the park's premier season is summer, winter visitors can cross-country ski, snowmobile, ice fish, and hike. Early fall, when the summer crowds have departed, is one of the best times to visit.

GETTING THERE

Acadia National Park is 161 miles northeast of Portland, Maine. The **Hancock County/Bar Harbor Airport,** Trenton, has daily flights from Boston on Colgan Air (800–272–5488 or 207–667–7171)

In summer **Greyhound** (207–945–3000) has service between Bangor

Acadia National Park and Bar Harbor
AT A GLANCE

▶ Explore a classic Maine landscape of sea-splashed rocky coasts

▶ Look for whales, osprey, and eagles on day cruises

▶ Sea kayak through habitats of harbor seals and porpoises

▶ Hike isolated trails on Isle au Haut

▶ Acadia National Park (www.nps.gov), Hulls Cove Visitor Center (207-288-3338); Bar Harbor Chamber of Commerce (800-288-5103).

and Bar Harbor. **The New England Transit Company** (207-772-6587) has bus service between Boston and Bar Harbor from mid-June to Labor Day.

If driving, follow Route 3 from Ellsworth onto Mount Desert Island. If arriving from southern Maine, avoid the traffic along coastal Route 1 by taking the turnpike to Bangor, then taking I-395 to Route 1A south into Ellsworth.

The **Bluenose Ferry** operates between Bar Harbor and Yarmouth, Nova Scotia. Contact the CN Marine Reservations Bureau, P.O. Box 250, North Sydney, Nova Scotia B2A 3M3, Canada (800-341-7981—United States or 207-288-3395). Daily service is available from late June to late September; three times per week in fall and spring and twice weekly in winter.

GETTING AROUND

A car is essential. Rentals are available at the airport and in Bar Harbor.

WHAT TO SEE AND DO

Acadia National Park

With its classic Maine landscape of beaches and sea-splashed rocky coasts, **Acadia National Park** ranks seventh in popularity among national parks, attracting more than 2.7 million visitors each year. The peaks of the **Mount Desert Mountains** dominate the park; **Mount Cadillac** at 1,530 feet is a park highlight, the highest point on the East Coast. Most visitors who are short on time drive the **Park Loop Road** to the summit of Mount Cadillac. Although this short trip will give you a taste of Acadia, try to spend more time off the road, hiking, bicycling, and enjoying the scenery away from the crowds.

The park charges an entrance fee for visitors. Passes are valid up to a week after purchase. In addition, there are also annual passes and discount permits for seniors and disabled citizens.

As in many other national parks, children age eight and older in summer can earn a **Junior Ranger** badge. The educational specialist at Acadia, however, has developed a similar program for children seven and younger, affectionately referred to as the **"junior junior ranger program."** For each age group, children need to purchase a book of activities for a nominal fee. By completing these activities and attending a ranger-led program, kids earn their badge.

For more information, check out the National Park Service Web site at www.nps.gov. Or visit the Thompson Island Information Center, Route 3 (207-288-3411), and 7.5 miles farther on, the Hulls Cove Visitor Center (207-288-4932). The park's headquarters are on Route 233 between Bar Harbor and Somesville (207-288-3338).

GETTING AROUND THE PARK

Between 1915 and 1933 philanthropist John D. Rockefeller, Jr., financed the building of more than 50 miles of **carriage roads** designed to provide paths for bicyclists, hikers, horseback riders, and carriages without interference from motor vehicles. At any given time, some of the carriage roads may be closed for repairs.

Scenic Drive

The park's most popular road, the 27-mile **Park Loop Road** (including the Mount Cadillac ascent), connects Mount Desert Island's lakes, mountains, and seashores, affording great views. A good place to begin the tour is at the **Hulls Cove Visitor Center.** To avoid traffic, begin this tour early in the day. Be sure to get out of your car to walk the footpath that winds alongside the road and also to hike some trails.

The following are some interesting sites along the **Park Loop Road.** About 2 miles from the Hulls Cove Visitor Center is **Sieur des Monts.** Nearby are gardens, a nature center, and a museum. The one-acre **Acadia Wild Garden,** about 5.6 miles on Park Loop Road from the Hulls Cove Visitor Center, has a path that's easy for children to follow as well as more than 400 species of plants native to Acadia. The garden's twelve sections correspond to the park's habitats and include the plants native to woods, meadows, mountains, heaths, beaches, and bog. The garden's meadow plot with its variety of wildflowers is especially nice.

Special Tours

- **National park tours** (207–288-3327) The two-and-a-half hour tours begin from Bar Harbor, making stops at Cadillac Mountain, Sieur des Monts Spring, and Thunder Hole.
- **Guided nature walks for children.** The Hull's Cove Visitor Center sponsors walks for children ages five to twelve (accompanied by an adult). Guides lead young explorers and teach compass and map-reading skills. To reserve ahead for these popular, free tours, call the center's reservation line (207–288-5262) at least four days in advance.
- **Carriage rides. Wildwood Stables** (207–276-3622) offers a choice of horse-drawn carriage rides along the carriage roads, including one to Jordan Pond for afternoon tea. Children enjoy this old-fashioned bumpy ride.
- **Ferry rides to Baker Island.** The Islesford Ferry Company (207–276-3717) leads four half-hour cultural and natural history trips to the Baker Island Lighthouse in July and August.
- **Islesford Historical Cruise** (207–276-5352). This two-and-three-quarter-hour trip features a boat ride across Somes Sound to Little Cranberry Island. A park ranger leads the island walk and the visit to the **Islesford Historical Museum,** featuring a collection of artifacts and documents on Mount Desert Island's nautical heritage.
- **Bass Harbor cruise.** Departing from Bass Harbor twice a day in July and August, this two-hour cruise has a ranger aboard who talks about the seals and the lobster traps you see.
- **Whale-watching cruises.** The **Bar Harbor Whale Watch Company,** Bluenose Ferry Terminal, Route 3, Bar Harbor (207–288-2386, 800-WHALES 4) has three-hour trips on board the *Friendship IV,* a 92-foot catamaran, from late May to mid-October.
- **Whale Watches Inc**. (207–288-3322 or 207–244-5882) offers two- and four-hour trips May to October. Along with whales, you might see eagles, osprey, and porpoises. For those who like sailing, this company offers a two-hour schooner cruise along Acadia's rocky shores.

At the **Nature Center** (207–288-3338) children can look at animal displays and pick up guidebooks and brochures on the park's wildlife. In the park's logbook, children can record the critters they have seen. Down a woodland path from the nature center is the **Abbe Museum of Maine Indian Artifacts** (207–288-3519). Displays tell visitors about the Native Americans who first inhabited this area. The collection includes pottery, bone and stone tools, quill jewelry, beads, a birchbark canoe, and a wigwam.

Also on Park Loop Road, about 10 miles from the Hulls Cove Visitor Center, is the 2-mile-long **Ocean Trail** leading to **Sand Beach,** a pebbly stretch open to the public and monitored by lifeguards from Memorial Day to Labor Day. The water, though, rarely gets above 55 degrees and generally is too cold for even the heartiest swimmers.

Farther along Park Loop Road, **Thunder Hole** at high tide offers the awesome sight of incoming surf shooting into the air through a rock crevice. Just south of Thunder Hole are the scenic **Otter Cliffs,** 100 feet of pink granite. Continue on Park Loop Road until you see wooden stairs just before Hunters Head. These lead to **Little Hunters Beach,** a picturesque rocky cove with crashing waves.

You pass **Wildwood Stables,** offering horseback and carriage rides, on the way to **Jordan Pond,** a scenic glacier-carved body of water flanked by Penobscot Mountain to the west and Pemetic Mountain to the east. Look to the north and you'll see the **Bubbles,** a pair of rounded mountains.

The **Jordan Pond House** (207-276-3316) may be crowded, but it's also a nice place to pause for tea and treats. Easy hiking trails here are the **Jordan Pond Nature Trail,** a 1-mile loop from the parking lot, and the longer **Jordan Pond Shore Path,** which circles the pond for 3.3 miles. Rugged hikers in the mood for some uphill paths can take the **Bubble Rock Trail,** a 1-mile path that ascends the Bubbles.

About 5 miles farther on Park Loop Road is the turnoff that leads to the summit of **Cadillac Mountain.** At the top on a clear day you can see all of Acadia National Park, as well as the waters of **Frenchman Bay** and **Blue Hill Bay.**

Somes Sound

Somes Sound, which bisects the eastern and western halves of Acadia National Park, is the only fjord on the east coast of the United States. The mountains rise up dramatically from this glacier-carved gorge. To see these sights from your car, drive Sargent Drive, off Route 198.

The Western Region of Mount Desert Island

Less visited, this region offers more quiet (although that's a relative term in Acadia's prime summer season). To get there, follow Route 233 and Route 198 west, then turn left onto Highway 102. Follow to **Echo Lake,** Highway 102, the best place in the park to go swimming. Patrolled by lifeguards in season, this freshwater lake is warmer than the Atlantic.

Farther south on Route 102A is **Seawall,** a natural seawall created by the pounding surf that is a good spot to look for seabirds. Continue on Route 102A to the **Ship Harbor Nature Trail,** a scenic and easy 1.3-mile loop. Just a bit farther is the **Bass Harbor Lighthouse** located on Mount

More Outdoor Activities:
Bicycling, Kayaking, Rock Climbing, and Hiking

- **Bicycling.** Acadia is a terrific place to bring your bike, or rent one from stores in nearby Bar Harbor. Although bicycling is permitted along Park Loop Road, because of traffic it's preferable to pedal along the scenic but bumpy gravel carriage roads, which are closed to cars.

  Off-road biking, especially on hiking trails, is strictly prohibited. Bicyclists are required to wear helmets. A bicycle trail guide is available at the Hulls Cove Visitor Center.

  The **Bar Harbor Bicycle Shop,** part of the **National Park Activity Center,** 137–141 Cottage Street, Bar Harbor (207-288-0342), rents and sells bicycles and equipment year-round. They have children's bikes, children's bicycle seats, and trailers so you can pull your kids along.

- **Sea kayaking. National Park Sea Kayak Tours** offers guided sea kayaking mid-May to Labor Day. Beginners are welcome. There is a minimum height requirement of about 4 feet, 8 inches (generally age ten) for a solo kayaker, but ask about taking younger children in a tandem kayak. Groups are limited to twelve. The company does a variety of trips, but most popular is the half-day (four-hour trip). Routes vary. You might see harbor seals, bald eagles, or porpoises.

- **Rock climbing. Acadia Mountain Guides,** part of the **National Park Activity Center,** 137–141 Cottage Street, Bar Harbor (207-288-0342), offers rock- and ice-climbing instruction and guided outings. Beginners are welcome.

- **Hiking.** Trails that are good for families with younger children and beginning hikers are the **Cadillac Summit**, a paved 0.3-mile loop that begins from the Cadillac Summit Parking area, and the **Ocean Trail**, a 3-mile path with coast and cliff views that can be accessed from Sand Beach or the Otter Point parking areas. Most of the **carriage roads** offer routes that are relatively easy, although some stretches are uphill.

  With older, more adventurous children, try moderate trails such as the **Bowl Trail,** a 1.4-mile path that begins 100 feet north of the Sand Beach parking area; the **Gorham Mountain Trail,** a 1.8-mile route from the Gorham Mountain parking area that ascends this oceanside mountain; and the longer **Champlain Mountain Trail,** a 2.2-mile circuit that begins at the Bear Brook parking area.

  Acadia National Park has several strenuous trails as well. Check with a park ranger for suitability and conditions.

Desert Island's southernmost point. The lighthouse, built in 1858, is now fully automated.

Isle au Haut

You can avoid Acadia's crowds by basing your stay at **Isle au Haut,** an island 15 miles southwest of Mount Desert and accessible only by a forty-five-minute ride on a mail boat. In summer two boats depart from Stonington, on Deer Isle (207-367-5193). Families with preteens and teens who like to hike and camp should consider this trip. Trails on Isle au Haut lead through dense woods and along cliffs.

If you don't want to camp, Isle au Haut is a good day trip away from the crowds. In July and August one boat goes to the town's landing and another arrives at **Duck Harbor.** What many visitors do is take the mail boat to the landing and hike the 5 miles to Duck Harbor, then return on the mail boat from Duck Harbor. Check the schedule; the last boat often departs around 5:30 P.M.

Potential summer campers who want to obtain a permit for one of the handful of spaces on Isle au Haut enter a lottery. Obtain an application by calling (207) 288-3338 or by writing Acadia Ranger Headquarters, P.O. Box 177, Bar Harbor 04609. State your preferred camping dates (three-night maximum), send a deposit (call and ask how much), and mail the application, postmarked April 1 or soon after. Camping is allowed May 15 to October 15.

Schoodic Peninsula

The **Schoodic Peninsula,** the only part of Acadia National Park connected to the mainland, attracts fewer visitors than does Mount Desert Island. From Bar Harbor it takes about an hour by car to reach the Schoodic Peninsula, which is off Route 186. A 6-mile-long road leads through the park. Don't miss **Schoodic Point** at high tide when the surf, unbroken by offshore islands, pounds the rocks.

Bar Harbor Region: Sea Life

The area has three separate aquariums focusing on regional sea life. The **Oceanarium/Lobster Hatchery,** 1 Harbor Place, Bar Harbor (207-288-2334), focuses on lobster hatching, explaining the lobster's life cycle. The **Mount Desert Oceanarium,** Route 3, (207-288-5005), focuses more on lobsters and the lobster industry. Come aboard a lobster boat, talk with real Maine lobstermen, and learn about lobster traps and buoys. Other sea life includes seals swimming in a 50,000-gallon tank and marsh critters that might be seen in a walk through the Thomas Bay Marsh.

In Southwest Harbor is the **Mount Desert Oceanarium,** Clark Point Road (207-244-7330). The touch tanks here with horseshoe crabs, sea cucumbers, and starfish are great for younger children. There are also exhibits on whales and fishing gear.

Note: Reduced admission combination tickets are available for all three museums.

Whales are the focus of the **Bar Harbor Whale Museum,** 52 West Street, Bar Harbor (207-288-2339). Admission is free.

Children enjoy the many hands-on exhibits at the **Natural History Museum at College of the Atlantic,** Route 3, Bar Harbor (207-288-5015), including the touch tanks full of turtles, tadpoles, and other island natives. There's also a "Whale on Wheels" project, which lets children assemble a whale skeleton from scratch. Daily lectures for the whole family are given at 11:00 A.M.

WHERE TO STAY

Camping in Acadia

Blackwoods is the only campsite in the park that is open year-round. From June 15 to September 15, reservations are a must. Contact the **National Park Reservation Service** (800-436-PARK). Reservations are taken up to five months in advance. Another option is camping at **Seawall** (open May through September) near the southern tip of the islet. Accommodations are first-come, first-served. Campsites at **Isle au Haut** are distributed by lottery (see "Isle au Haut" above).

Staying in Bar Harbor

Bar Harbor offers more than 2,500 guest rooms, from bed and breakfasts to motels and hotels. Reserve well ahead for the busy months of July and August. For accommodation information, contact the **Bar Harbor Chamber of Commerce,** P.O. Box 158, 93 Cottage Street, Bar Harbor 04609 (207-288-5103); www.acadia.net/bhcc. Also call the **Northeast Harbor Chamber of Commerce** (207-276-5040) and the **Southwest Harbor Chamber of Commerce** (207-244-9264).

Overlooking the village green, **Acadia Hotel,** 20 Mount Desert Street, Bar Harbor (207-288-5721), has a wraparound porch and pleasantly decorated guest rooms. One has a kitchenette. At **Atlantic Oakes By-the-Sea,** Route 3, Bar Harbor (207-288-5801 or 800-33-MAINE), all rooms have water views, although accommodations in those buildings farther away from the water cost less. Children like the pebbly beach and the tennis courts as well as the outdoor and indoor swimming pools. In addition to bed-and-breakfast facilities, this property has hotel rooms, fourteen efficiency units, and two apartments—a two-bedroom and a five-bedroom—which are rented on a weekly basis.

Bar Harbor has many motels that offer clean accommodations for families. Among these is **Bar Harbor Quality Inn,** Route 3 and Mount Desert Street (207-288-5403 or 800-282-5403). This typical Quality Inn, with exterior corridors, is about a half mile from downtown Bar Harbor. Children like the outdoor heated pool as well as the televisions in the rooms. Some efficiency units are available. **Best Western Inn,** Route 3, Bar Harbor (207-288-5823), also has drive-up units with exterior corridors but is in a quieter area than the Quality Inn. **The Park Entrance Oceanfront Motel,** Hamor Avenue, Route 3, Bar Harbor (207-288-9703 or 800-288-9703), is on ten acres near an entrance to Acadia National Park. The property has a pebble beach on Frenchman Bay as well as a heated pool, a picnic area, and volleyball and basketball courts. Suites and kitchenettes are available.

In Seal Cove

Seal Cove Farm, HCR 62, Box 140, Mount Desert (207-244-7781), is a farmhouse that dates back more than one hundred years. It offers three spacious rooms, one with private bath. Breakfast is included. Children are welcome to help feed the ducks, sheep, turkeys, chickens, and goats.

In Southwest Harbor

The 112-year-old **Claremont,** Claremont Road, Southwest Harbor (207-244-5036), has a turn-of-the-century feel. There are twenty-four rooms in the main building, many with spectacular views of the water or of Mount Cadillac. There are also a number of cottages, each with a living room and fireplace. The common rooms and a game room filled with books are pleasant. The dining room (jacket and tie are required) serves good food. Guests can also use the croquet, badminton, and tennis courts, as well as the rowboats. Every August the hotel holds the Croquet Classic.

WHERE TO EAT

In Acadia

Jordan Pond, Park Loop Road, Acadia National Park (207-276-3610). A park tradition for almost one hundred years, the restaurant at Jordan Pond offers everything from afternoon tea on the lawn to dinner by the fire. The location is splendid, and the food is okay. Even if you don't dine here, you're welcome to stroll the grounds.

In Bar Harbor

Cafe Bluefish, 122 Cottage Avenue, Bar Harbor (207-288-3696). The dark wood furnishings and mismatched linens and china give this restaurant a funky feel. The menu features an array of chicken, seafood, and vegetarian dishes. Entrees such as mushroom bean Stroganoff and seafood strudel make this place a haven for those who don't eat red meat.

Freddie's Route 66, 21 Cottage Street, Bar Harbor (207-288-3708). This is the place if you're nostalgic for the 1950s. The decor includes a Seeburg jukebox, a soda fountain, and memorabilia and period gas stations. The menu features seafood and other diner-style entrees such as roast turkey and chicken. Children's plates are also available.

Island Chowder House, 38 Cottage Street, Bar Harbor (207-288-4905). This casual eatery has reasonable prices on seafood. Good choices are the soups and seafood pasta. Chicken and steak are also available.

A friendly but noisy place, **Miguel's Mexican Restaurant,** 51 Rodick Street, Bar Harbor (207-288-5117), has good Mexican food at reasonable prices. Locals like the tacos, the blue corn crab cakes, and the shrimp fajitas. **Jordan's Restaurant,** 80 Cottage Street, Bar Harbor (207-288-3586), a simple place, offers basic food such as burgers, grilled cheese, and chicken, plus homemade soups and chowders.

Northeast Harbor Area

In Maine you have to have lobster. On Somes Sound at **Abel's Lobster Pound,** Route 198, 5 miles north of Northeast Harbor (207-276-5827), the prices are fair, the lobster is good, and you can eat indoors or outside at the picnic tables.

SIDE TRIPS

Head south to **Portland** to see the oldest lighthouse in the state, **Bath** to tour the Maine Maritime Museum, the **Kennebunks** for a family beach vacation (see Kennebunkport chapter), and **Freeport** for the scores of outlet shops.

FOR MORE INFORMATION

The **Bar Harbor Chamber of Commerce,** P.O. Box 158, 93 Cottage Street, (207-288-5103 or 800-288-5103), is open year-round and provides information on sights and accommodations. The **Mount Desert Chamber of Commerce** (207-276-5040) operates a seasonal information site on the town dock.

Acadia National Park

A good source for maps, information, and audiocassette guided tours of Acadia is the **Hull's Cove Visitor's Center,** (207-288-3338), open May to mid-October. Watch the brief film introducing visitors to the park and obtain a schedule of seasonal activities. For year-round general information, call (207) 288-3338. For **National Park Service naturalist activities,** call (207) 288-5262. Also, check out **Acadia National Park** online, www.nps.gov.

For **road and weather information,** call (207) 288-3338. For **camping information,** contact the **National Park Reservation Service** (800) 436-PARK.

Emergency Numbers

Emergencies in Acadia National Park: (207) 288-3369

Emergencies outside the park: 911

Mount Desert Island Hospital, Bar Harbor: (207) 288-5081

Park Rangers: (207) 288-3369 or (207) 288-3360

Bar Harbor Police: (207) 288-3391 non-emergency

Mount Desert Police: (207) 276-5111 non-emergency

KENNEBUNK AND THE KENNEBUNKPORT AREA

Kennebunk and **Kennebunkport**, known collectively as the Kennebunks, have been attracting summer visitors for centuries. In the 1700s the Abnaki Indians came to these shores for summer fishing and hunting. Before the Revolutionary War, shipbuilding was already an industry in Kennebunk along the Mousam River. From 1800 to about 1850 more than 1,000 wooden schooners, cargo vessels, and clippers were built in the area's fifty shipyards. Here, as in other New England ports, wealthy sea captains built impressive homes, many of which still grace Kennebunkport's streets. After the Civil War shipbuilding became less important, and the region gained prominence as a summer vacation spot for the affluent from Boston and New York. By 1907 thirty grand hotels had been constructed in Kennebunk and Kennebunkport.

Today the Kennebunks and the surrounding towns still attract large numbers of vacationers who come for the sea breezes, the beach, and boating. The Kennebunks comprise four distinct communities. Kennebunk is where many shipowners and shipbuilders originally settled. Across the Kennebunk River is Kennebunkport, a bustling beach town whose center, Dock Square, features upscale boutiques and restaurants. Ocean Avenue, which winds along the water, sports many lavish houses, including Walker's Point, the summer home of former president George Bush and his family.

Cape Porpoise, along Route 9 east about 4 miles from downtown Kennebunkport, is a small fishing village complete with lighthouse and dock. Farther east off Route 9 is **Goose Rocks Beach,** a village of private homes and a few rental properties fronted by a calm, wide beach. If you have young children and want a quiet getaway, consider basing your Kennebunk/Kennebunkport stay at Goose Rocks Beach.

The Kennebunks

AT A GLANCE

- ▶ Explore scenic Maine beaches
- ▶ Board whale-watching and lobstering cruises
- ▶ Tour the seashore Trolley Museum, one of about only twenty in the United States
- ▶ Trek through the area's nature preserves
- ▶ Kennebunk-Kennebunkport Chamber of Commerce, (207) 967-0857; www.kkcc.maine.org

GETTING THERE

Kennebunkport is 30 miles northeast of Portsmouth, New Hampshire, 29 miles southwest of Portland, Maine.

The **Portland Jetport,** thirty minutes from Kennebunkport, is served by Delta Airlines, Continental, US Airways, United Airlines, and Northwest Airlink. You can also fly into Boston's **Logan Airport,** approximately ninety minutes from Kennebunkport, is served by many major airlines.

The Kennebunks are off I-95. Take the Maine turnpike to exit 2 or exit 3. From exit 2, Wells, take Route 109 east to Route 1 north to Route 9 east. From exit 3, take Route 35 east to Kennebunk.

The **Coastal Connection** (207-282-5408) is a seasonal public transportation system operated through the Southern Maine Intermodal Transportation Advisory Committee from late June to Labor Day. The Coastal Connection links five communities along Route 1—Kennebunk/ Kennebunkport, Wells, Ogunquit, York, and Kittery/Eliot.

GETTING AROUND

A car is convenient, but be prepared for traffic in town and for a shortage of parking spaces. Take advantage of the **Intown Trolley,** Kennebunkport (207-967-3686), which operates from 10:00 A.M. to 7:15 P.M.; last tour at 6:30 P.M. With its wood and polished brass, the trolley is charming. It's also convenient. The trolley driver delivers a brief history of the area and points out such "attractions" as former president George Bush's house and Spouting Rock (when the waves hit this rock formation, a spout of water shoots up). The trolley departs from town on Ocean Avenue and stops at the Nonantum Resort, Colony Hotel, Shawmut Inn, Rhumb Line Motor Lodge, Franciscan Monastery, Kennebunk Beach at Narragansett, Sundial Inn, and the Kennebunkport Beach Improvement Association. One fare is good all day.

Bicycling avoids the parking problems. The pedaling is easy, since the area is mostly flat. Your family can rent bikes at the **Cape-Able Bike Shop,** Town House Corners, Arundel Road, Kennebunkport (207-967-4382 or 800-220-0907 in Maine). Choose from mountain bikes, twenty-one-speed bikes, BMX, cross-terrain, and tandems. Kid trailers, three-wheelers, baby seats, and all frame sizes are available.

WHAT TO SEE AND DO

Beaches
The beaches, which range from quintessential rocky coasts to sandy shores, are what really draw families to the area. The first thing to know is that although the beaches are free, there is a charge for a parking permit. During the week, purchase these at the town halls in Kennebunk and Kennebunkport. On weekends when the town halls are closed, purchase a permit at the police station, Crow Hill, Route 9 toward Cape Porpoise. Local lodging establishments also sell beach passes. You can avoid the hassle of parking by biking, walking, or taking the Intown Trolley.

The second thing to know is that this is Maine: The water is brisk, usually around 65 degrees. Little kids and teens seem to have no trouble splashing about; it's usually the adults who avoid getting in above their knees. But even if you don't get really wet, the sea breezes and the scenery are invigorating.

Kennebunk Area
Kennebunk and **Gooch's Beach,** along Beach Avenue, are long, wide strips of sand. These popular beaches are open 9:00 A.M. to 5:00 P.M., but they don't have lifeguards or rest rooms. The Intown Trolley stops across the street at Narragansett By the Sea, a condominium. Not far away is an area unofficially known as **Mothers' Beach** because for decades mothers with tots in tow have congregated here. Although the beach is just a moderate swath of sand, the surf here is mild and the water shallow. There is also a grassy area with a swing set. No lifeguards are on duty.

Parson's Beach (also called Parson's Way), Ocean Avenue, where the river feeds into the ocean, near the Colony Hotel, is fronted by a grassy

Cruises, Sails, Kayaks

An important part of the Kennebunk/Kennebunkport experience is to get out on the water. Whale watch, learn about lobstering, sail, and kayak.

- **Whale-watching.** The *Indian Whale Watch,* which leaves from Arundel Wharf, Ocean Avenue, Kennebunkport (207–967–5912), is a good choice for families.

  The 75-foot vessel holds up to seventy-two people, has an enclosed passenger house in case it's rainy or cold, and, like other whale-watching trips, heads to **Jeffrey's Ledge,** 20 miles off the coast of Maine, a prime whale-feeding ground. Because the cruise lasts four hours, the voyage is best suited for older kids and teens.

  The outing presents a classic Maine experience of swells, laughing gulls, and a seascape of lobster buoys, sails, and sun. Along with the captain's narration, a naturalist points out the marine life, which may include sharks, the smaller minke whales, and the big boys—finback whales that can be 80 feet long. Watch the "footprint" of the whale, the flat spot in the water where the whale last submerged, to get an idea of where it will come up next. It's tremendously exciting to see these gentle behemoths of the deep breach the surface and blow giant sprays of water 10 feet in the air.

  How many whales you see depends, of course, on the whales. But more often than not, you'll see at least one at Jeffrey's Ledge, and often many more.

  Young children are likely to get bored on a whale-watching cruise. Arrive early to claim the limited outside seats in the shade. On a hot day, or if your family is prone to seasickness, you want to be outdoors in the wind. Take seasickness precautions if needed. Cold soda and hot dogs are sold on board, but the prudent might want to bring their own snacks. Reservations are recommended.

- **Lobstering.** Two boats let you tag along to the traps. **Scenic Lobster Cruises Aboard *Second Chance,*** 4-A Western Avenue, Lower Village, Kennebunk (207–967–5507 or 800–767–BOAT), offers ninety-minute trips from July through August. The captain tells tales of Kennebunkport's prime as a shipbuilding center and teaches voyagers about the art and history of lobstering. A similar excursion is offered by **Lobster-boat Cruises,** Captain David Bond, P.O. Box 1093, Kennebunkport (207–967–2921).

(continued)

Cruises, Sails, Kayaks (continued)

The ninety-minute trips depart from the Nonantum Resort, Ocean Avenue, Kennebunkport. During the day reservations are taken at the Nonantum front desk. Fares are collected on board.

Six passengers are the maximum on board the 40-foot *Lion,* a self-proclaimed "rugged" example of a traditional Downeast work boat. Captain David shows you how lobsters are caught and relates facts of the region's maritime history.

- **Sailing.** Another Kennebunkport tradition is sailing. Two- to four-hour sail trips from Cape Arundel to Cape Porpoise are available on the **schooner *Lazy Jack,*** Schooner's Wharf, Ocean Avenue, Kennebunkport (207–967–8809), which departs from Schooner's Inn. Available end of May to mid-October.

The *Bellatrix* departs from the Nonantum Hotel, Ocean Avenue, Kennebunkport (207–967–8685), available mid-May through October.

The 37-foot ocean-racing yacht is available for charter sailing trips to Cape Porpoise and to spots near Walker's Point, former president George Bush's estate. Sail charters include free sailing instruction.

The Maine Sail School, Ocean Avenue, Kennebunkport (207–967–5043), also offers a variety of coastal cruises, half- and full-day charters, as well as sailing lessons.

- **Learning local lore. Maritime Productions,** Ogunquit (207–641–2313), brings to life local legends on scenic ninety-minute or two-hour cruises. The cast enacts tales of haunted lighthouses, wrecks, pirates, and ghost ships. Recommended for ages six and older.
- **Kayaking and canoeing.** Kayak Adventures, Paul J. Holop, Kennebunkport (207–967–0005 or 800–853–5002), launches guided ocean and river trips daily from the Shawmut Ocean Resort, May to September. Experienced paddlers can rent kayaks.

strip with benches. Locals come here to walk and admire the sunset. Swimming is discouraged. Parking for this beach is along Route 9.

Cape Porpoise/Goose Rocks Beach Area

Although officially part of the town of Kennebunkport, the postcard pretty village of **Cape Porpoise** is about 4 miles east of Kennebunkport's Dock Square on Route 9 and different enough in atmosphere to feel like an entirely separate place. Cape Porpoise offers the beach without Kennebunkport's bustle. The area even has a small dock complete with lobster traps and a view of a lighthouse. At Christmastime, Cape Porpoise gains fame for its unusual holiday "tree," a series of lobster traps with wreaths stacked in the shape of a mighty evergreen and generally displayed outside the firehouse.

To get to **Goose Rocks Beach,** continue on Route 9 east past the main part of Cape Porpoise to Dyke Road. Turn right on Dyke Road to King's Highway, then turn left and follow the road to the mile-long beach. Goose Rocks is the area's best beach for families with young children. The fine sand, calm surf, and long, gradual underwater slope give kids plenty of shore-side splashing; plus Goose Rocks is quieter than the bustling Kennebunks.

Preteens and teens who need to be in the middle of the action, however, might feel hopelessly marooned if you base your vacation here. The Intown Trolley doesn't stop here. Although bicycling to Dock Square is a definite possibility, it's really too much to do on a daily basis. With teens, a stay at Goose Rocks would likely have you driving them back and forth to Dock Square, a trip that easily gets tiresome.

Small enough to feel perfect for a quaint fishing village, which, of course, Cape Porpoise is, the village's dock has all the classic Maine elements—boats, stacked lobster traps, an eatery, and a view of the Goat Island Light that leads boats into the channel. Just park the car and walk around; your children, especially if they are new to the delights of New England, will like the atmosphere. You might even see fishermen unloading the day's catch.

Museums and Historical Attractions

Although the historical attractions aren't what drew your family to the Kennebunkport area, the region does offer some history. An easy way to get a sense of the Kennebunks is to drive the Ocean Avenue loop. This takes you past many gracious nineteenth-century homes and enables you to get a view of **Walker's Point,** the eleven-acre summer estate of former president George Bush and his family.

An area museum that's worth a visit is **The Seashore Trolley Museum,** Log Cabin Road, Kennebunkport (207–967–2800), open May to early November (weather permitting). Trolleys had their heyday from about the 1880s to 1930. This unusual museum, one of about twenty in the United States, preserves and restores trolley cars. Of the 200-plus car collection, approximately fifty are restored and on display. Grade-schoolers are enthralled by the whistles, bells, and benches. (Warn young ones that trolleys are noisy—they clang and hiss.) In addition to the depot, the museum has three car barns packed with trolleys from different periods and locales. Craftsmen may be in the process of restoring one of these old gems.

The Wedding Cake House is one of the most photographed homes in Kennebunk.

"Famous" trolley cars in the collection include Montréal's *Golden Chariot,* New Orleans' *Streetcar Named Desire,* and a San Francisco cable car. A highlight is the 2-mile trolley ride through the woods. In July the museum hosts the USA Trolley Parade, and in August there's an Olde Tyme Circus. Families can eat at the Trolley Fare snack bar or enjoy lunch in the picnic grove.

For those who want to see and learn something of Kennebunkport's history, visit **The Brick Store Museum,** 117 Main Street, Kennebunk (207–985–4802). The maritime history of Kennebunkport, and two of its most prominent families, the Lords and Barries, are detailed in this brick store and in the three adjacent nineteenth-century buildings comprising the museum. The museum is known for its crafts, arts, textiles, and archives. Rotating displays include the local works of authors and artists. The museum also offers ninety-minute Architectural Walking Tours of Kennebunkport's historic district, highlighting commercial and domestic architecture, and concludes with a tour of the Taylor-Barry House. Tours run from June to September.

Among the most photographed homes is the **Wedding Cake House,** Summer Street, Route 35, Kennebunk. The Wedding Cake House gets its name from the tale of the sea captain who had to leave his wedding before a "proper wedding cake could be baked." To atone, the captain built this ornately decorated house as a present to his wife. The house is private, but there is a gift shop in the carriage house.

Green Spaces

The **Franciscan Monastery and Grounds,** Beach Street, Kennebunkport, is a wonderful oasis. Although the monastery is not generally open for tours, the 200 acres of woods and gardens are open to the public. Winter 6:00 A.M. to 6:00 P.M. Summer 6:00 A.M. to 8:30 P.M. Free. The Lithuanian Franciscans purchased this property, a former estate, in 1947 and added chapels, a guest house, and thousands of plantings and flowers. Trails wind their way through the woods and overlook Kennebunkport Harbor and the river.

Wells, about 5 miles south of Kennebunk, has two nature preserves. **The Wells National Estuarine Research Reserve at Laudholm Farm** R.R. 2, Box 806, Wells (207-646-1555), consists of 1,600 acres of fields, forests, wetlands, and beach on the coast of southern Maine. This site, where the Merriland, Webhannet, and Little Rivers meet the Atlantic Ocean, is home to many endangered species, including black ducks, peregrine falcons, and piping plovers. The public portion of the reserve centers on **Laudholm Farm,** a 250-acre historic saltwater farm, the last remaining one in the area. Seven miles of trails run through salt marshes and woodlands and near coastal dunes. The Sunday tour, geared to families with children, meanders through a variety of habitats, from fields and forests, to rivers, marshes, estuaries, and sand dunes, and leads to the ocean.

The **Reserve Discovery Program** makes it inviting for families to explore the area. Special trail guidebooks are available for children for each of the five trail loops. Kids ages nine to eleven can enroll in the Junior Researchers Program, a two-week morning camp that gives children the opportunity to explore the reserve trails with a teacher. The Advanced Junior Researcher Program is a two-week day camp for children ages eleven to thirteen.

The Rachel Carson National Wildlife Refuge, R.R. 2 Box 751, Wells (207–646-9226), open sunrise to sunset year-round, is administered by the U.S. Fish and Wildlife Service. The 4,800 acres of salt marsh, upland habitats, and barrier beach is a haven for more than 250 species of migratory and resident birds. At various times of the year, you can see Canada geese, black ducks, and green winged teal, as well as shore birds, gulls, terns, and songbirds. The 1-mile interpretive nature trail is wheelchair accessible (and good for strollers).

Where to Eat in Wells: Locals like the **Maine Diner,** Route 1 North (207–646–4441), which serves breakfast, lunch, and dinner. A friendly and affordable eatery, it is known for its chowder.

Camps and Classes

The **Kennebunkport Beach Improvement Association** (KBIA), Kennebunk (207-967-2180), offers children's activities throughout the summer. Children ages three to eighteen can participate in swimming, sailing, rowing, fishing, golf, tennis, arts and crafts, photography, and sand castle building. A beach picnic is offered weekly.

The Maine Sail School, Ocean Avenue, Kennebunkport, (207-967-5043), offers a variety of coastal cruises, half- and full-day charters, and sailing lessons for adults and teens.

Shopping

Kennebunkport Area. Most of the "action" in town takes place around **Dock Square,** Kennebunkport. A monument "to our soldiers and sailors" forms part of a traffic circle that seems always jammed with cars in summer. The nearby buildings house a variety of T-shirt shops, galleries, boutiques, and eateries. The ones listed below are just a sampling. Many of Dock Square's shops are open daily in summer but have erratic hours or are closed out-of-season. When in doubt, call ahead.

The sign outside **Kennebunkport Book Port,** 10 Dock Square, Kennebunkport (207-967-2815), reads ICE CREAM, CANDY, CHILDREN, BARE FEET, SHORT HAIR, LONG HAIR, NO HAIR, CATS, DOGS, AND SMALL DRAGONS ARE WELCOME HERE ANYTIME. Enjoy browsing in this store, which specializes in books on Maine and the sea but also sells a range of popular titles. There's a good children's section as well. A small sitting area on the staircase landing and helpful handwritten notes with recommendations from staff make this an inviting place.

The Good Earth, Ocean Avenue, P.O. Box J, Kennebunkport (207-967-4635), is a pottery cooperative selling decorative stoneware, cooking, and serving pieces. **Shoot the Moon,** Ocean Avenue, Dock Square (207-976-2755), offers an unusual collection of pottery, handcrafted jewelry, and other items. At **The Whimsy Shop,** Dock Square, Kennebunkport (207-967-5105), you'll find luxurious throws from Kennebunk weavers, pottery from Maine and New England, and handcrafted birds by Will Kirkpatrick.

The Mole Hole, Village Quay, Route 9, Kennebunkport (207-967-4037), has much for children, including wind chimes, a Wee Forest Folk Mice Collection, Little Soul Dolls, and other handcrafted items. **Animal Instinct,** Ocean Avenue, Kennebunkport (207-967-5825), sells plush animals, including stuffed lobsters.

The **Village Confectionery,** Lower Village, Mole Hole Shops, Kennebunkport (207-967-4572), offers a large assortment of gourmet chocolates, Maine salt water taffy, fudge, jelly beans, and other sweets. **The Jack &**

Jill Shop, 38 Main Street, Kennebunk (207-985-7211), has been in business for more than twenty-five years, selling brand-name children's clothes for infants to size 14 for girls and size 20 for boys. **Mainely Quilts,** 108 Summer Street, Kennebunk (207-985-4250), sells old and new quilts.

You've heard the commercials; now you can visit the store. **Tom's of Maine Natural Living Store and Factory Tours,** Lafayette Center, Kennebunkport (207-985-3874), has tours every Monday and Thursday at 11:00 A.M. and 2:00 P.M. from the second week in June through Labor Day. Throughout the rest of the year tours are offered on Wednesday at 11:00 A.M. Reservations are suggested. Tom's of Maine is a store where "natural" is the main ingredient in products. Tom and Kate Chappell moved to Maine twenty-five years ago to start living a simpler life with a deeper connection to the land. To meet their desire for natural foods and products, they developed their own, including their own natural personal care products. Tom's of Maine is most famous for its natural toothpaste, available at health food stores throughout the United States, but at Tom's of Maine you'll find gift products and clothing, too.

Cape Porpoise/Goose Rocks Beach Area. At the **Cape Porpoise Lobster Company,** Pier Road (207-967-4268 or 800-967-4268), you can buy that really fresh Maine souvenir for the folks back home. This combination seafood market and fried food take-out ships lobster overnight to all fifty states and sells fresh clams, haddock, mussels, scallops, and shrimp ready to cook. *Downeast* magazine has labeled their ready-to-eat lobster roll one of the best in Maine.

Christmas House on Cape Porpoise, Pier Road (207-967-4111), open daily April 1 through December 22; January and February by appointment. You can't miss this charming Christmas collectibles shop—look for the red sleigh out front. The store sells handcrafted ornaments and figures created by artists from across the United States and from other countries. As befits a shop where Santa would feel comfortable, the atmosphere is cheery and the selection wide. Especially nice when we visited were the Tweedledee, Tweedledum, and Alice in Wonderland ornaments, plus the hand-carved caroler dolls.

Other Attractions
The Maine Aquarium, Route 1, Saco (207-284-4511), tries hard, but it will most likely disappoint all but the youngest children. Older kids (and adults) who have visited large aquariums in big cities such as Boston and Baltimore won't find the moderate size tanks or the variety of marine life here impressive. That said, preschoolers and young grade-school children interested in the underwater world can still become wide-eyed at the marine life. Several exhibits display Maine fish, including largemouth

Amusement and Water Parks

Saco's three amusement parks attract children and teens looking for good, clean fun. While a visit along this busy strip is far from anyone's vision of a quiet Maine idyll, children soak up the fun here. It's convenient that the Cascade Water and Amusement Park and Funtown USA are adjacent and that Aquaboggan Water Park is just a few more miles up the Route 1 strip.

Cool off at **Cascade Water and Amusement Park,** Saco (207-284-6231), open mid-May to Labor Day. Kids like the water slides and the pool, and little ones enjoy kiddie bumper boats and a climbing area with a rope bridge and tunnels. You can also challenge each other to go-carts and mini-golf. Next door, **Funtown USA,** P.O. Box 29, Route 1, Saco (207-284-5139), keeps kids happy with grand prix race cars, skid cars, water slides, a wave pool, bumper boats, mini-golf, and a toddlers' splash and play. Older children and teens like this place, as do young ones. The kiddie ride area has ten attractions for tykes, including mini-bumper boats, a train, swings, and a merry-go-round. Especially nice for parents is the free admission to the park. You pay only for the rides. This is great for little kids who may just want to sample a few rides, have a snack, and go home. Funtown's eateries offer the usual array of fast-food burgers and pizza.

Aquaboggan Water Park, Route 1, Saco (207-282-3112), open daily late June through Labor Day, keeps kids splash happy with water slides, pools, a toddler area, and mini-golf.

bass and yellow perch found in Maine lakes, trout from the state's rivers, and, of course, lobster from the Casco Bay area. Two seals swim in an open tank about the size of a backyard pool, the touch tank has starfish to handle, and other tanks feature moray eels, sharks, and some tropical fish. If you do visit, time your trip to coincide with feeding time for the sharks and seals, 11:00 A.M., 1:30, and 3:00 P.M.

Another plus for small children is the free petting zoo outside. Ducks waddle around a pond, and a small red barnyard houses sheep and a black goat. Picnic tables are outside. In the summer, a daily lobsterbake is open to the public.

Theater
The Arundel Barn Playhouse, Arundel (207-985-5552), presents comedies, drama, and musicals, as well as children's programs.

SPECIAL EVENTS

February. Winter Carnival Weekend.

March. Annual Kennebunk and Kennebunkport Home and Food Show.

May. Cook's Tour—Kitchens by the Sea.

June. Bed-and-Breakfast Inn and Garden Tour.

July. Casco Bay Concert Band and Annual Fourth of July Picnic on the Green.

August. Annual Teddy Bear Show.

September. Annual Fiddle Contest and Old Time Country Music Show.

December. Christmas Prelude.

WHERE TO STAY

Kennebunkport Area

Cabot Cove Cottages, P.O. Box 1082, 7 South Main Street, Kennebunkport (207-967-5424; www.cabotcovecottages.com), open mid-June to mid-September, offers fifteen one- and two-bedroom units, all with kitchen facilities. The cottages are within walking distance of the beach and Dock Square. **Idlease & Shorelands Guest Resort,** P.O. Box 769, Route 9, Kennebunkport, (207-985-4460; www.vrmedia.com/idlease/), is a family bargain within minutes of Parson's Beach. For large families and reunions the management will arrange horseback riding, basketball, yard games, and horseshoes. There is an outdoor swimming pool.

The Maine Stay Inn and Cottages, 34 Maine Street, P.O. Box 500A, Kennebunkport (207-967-2117 or 800-950-2117; www.MaineStayInn. com), is a true find—a well-appointed inn that welcomes families with children. Listed in the National Register of Historic Places and located in the Historical Preservation District of Kennebunkport, the Maine Stay is an 1860 Italianate-style house decorated with a mix of period antiques and comfortable pieces.

The owners have two daughters and understand families. The Maine Stay has a jungle gym and a croquet set on the lawn, as well as lounge chairs in the garden. The parlor is welcoming without being fussy; children and adults feel free to sit here. Children's books are available along with adult selections. Afternoon tea and lemonade and cookies are served. A full breakfast is served every morning. Families and guests staying in the cottages can request breakfast delivered to their room. All the rooms are air-conditioned, and each has a television.

The **Rhumb Line Motor Lodge,** 41 Turbos Creek Road off Ocean Avenue, Kennebunkport (207-967-5457 or 800-33-RHUMB; www. rhumblinemaine.com) is a hybrid, more than a motel but not a full-scale resort. The two-story building set on four acres has comfortable, good-sized rooms with interior corridors. The rooms all have air-conditioning, televisions, refrigerators, and night lights. First- floor rooms have a patio, and second-floor rooms have balconies. The building is angled so that each room has a view of the pool, a convenience for parents who want to watch their kids play. There is a grassy area for impromptu soccer games, and a basketball hoop is nearby. Another plus: The Intown Trolley makes regular stops here, so you can forgo the beach traffic hassles. Closed January. Rates include continental breakfast.

Campgrounds

Salty Acres Campground, Route 9, Kennebunkport (207-967-2483), open mid-May to Columbus Day, has sites for tents and RVs. Some sites have water and sewer hookups. There are hot showers, flush toilets, and a dumping station, as well as a kiddie pool, playground, and adult pool.

Cottage/Apartment Rentals

To get the most room for your money, rent a cottage or an apartment. There are several rental agencies, including Sand Dollar Real Estate (207-967-3421). The Kennebunk/Kennebunkport Chamber of Commerce (207-967-0857 or 800-982-4421) also has listings.

Cape Porpoise/Goose Rocks Beach Area

Nestled among the gracious homes opposite Goose Rock Beach is the **Tides Inn By-The-Sea** and **Tides II,** 252 Goose Rock Beach, Kennebunkport (207-967-3757), open mid-March to mid-October; reservations accepted January 1. The Tides Inn By-The-Sea is only one of two commercial properties along the beach; the other is the general store. This friendly yellow Victorian building has a second-floor porch and a great view of the sea. There is no air-conditioning, but because this is Maine, you probably won't miss it.

The hallways and the room doors are decorated with paintings of flowers and seascapes. The rooms, although not large, are comfortably furnished with a combination of such Victorian pieces as oak bureaus, rockers, and wicker headboards plus sturdy collectibles. Families can choose the one-week apartment stay or opt for a weekend in a designated family room. Number 7, one of the family rooms, has a double bed plus two twin beds. The Tides II contemporary apartments come equipped with kitchenettes and a view of the ocean. The inn also operates a restaurant serving breakfast, dinner, and lighter fare.

WHERE TO EAT

Kennebunkport Area

Kennebunk does have a five-star restaurant, **The White Barn Inn,** 37 Beach Street, Kennebunkport (207-967-2321).

This is not the place to take children unless they are well-behaved teens who enjoy fine dining and unless you feel comfortable spending a good deal of money. Price-fixed dinners average around $60 per person.

Grissini, 27 Western Avenue, Kennebunkport (207-967-2211), serves reasonably priced Italian fare, including a variety of pastas and pizza. The menu at **Alisson's,** 5 Dock Square, Kennebunkport (207-967-4841), includes nachos, beef stew in a bread bowl, and sandwiches. At the **Breakwater Restaurant and Inn,** Ocean Avenue, Kennebunkport (207-967-3118), the sunporch with its ocean view is a favorite dining room. Locals recommend the lobster crepes, the broiled sea scallops, and the prime rib.

A ten-room inn, **The Green Heron,** 126 Ocean Avenue, Kennebunkport, (207-967-8961), is open to the public for breakfast. Some locals swear that the blueberry buttermilk pancakes are the best in town. *Note:* Credit cards are not accepted; bring cash.

For picnic fare and take-out items check out **Chase Hill Bakery,** 9 Chase Hill Road, Kennebunkport (207-967-2283), which has a variety of breads, breakfast items, and delectable desserts. The **Port Lobster Seafood Market,** P.O. 729, Ocean Avenue, Kennebunkport (207-967-5411), sells fish, shellfish, and lobster, as well as clam chowder and lobster and seafood rolls. The market will prepare a travel pack of your favorite sole, haddock, crabmeat, lobster tails, live lobsters, salmon, or clams to take home with you.

Cape Porpoise/Goose Rocks Beach Area

The Lobster Pot, 62 Mills Road, Route 9, Cape Porpoise (207-967-4607), has little atmosphere but lots of family-friendly spirit, including moderate prices. The restaurant consists of one big room with long tables and ceiling fans. Children are given crayons to color the lobsters on their menu. For lighter fare, choices include tuna rolls, lobster rolls, and hamburgers, any of which would satisfy child-size appetites. Lobster Pot specialties include baked stuffed haddock and steamed lobster. Because of its informal atmosphere, good food, and reasonable prices, The Lobster Pot is a good place to come for your seafood family feasts.

Nunan's Lobster Hut, 50 Mills Road, Route 9, Cape Porpoise

(207-967-4362), looks more like a shack than a popular restaurant, but the locals swear by this place. Savor authentic Maine seafood such as fish chowder, lobster, and steamed clams at moderate prices.

Opposite Goose Rocks Beach are the **Tides Inn By-The-Sea** and **The Sandy Bottom Pub,** Goose Rocks Beach, Kennebunkport (207-967-3757). The Tides Inn By-The-Sea offers a main dining room and a pub. Enjoy the ocean views with your homemade breakfast of French toast or Timber Island crab cakes on an English muffin. For dinner, choose from such entrees as grilled filet mignon, grilled vegetable lasagna, and seafood fettucine. The Sandy Bottom Pub has lighter fare, including the inn's well-known crab cakes and steamers as well as hamburgers and barbecued chicken wings.

SIDE TRIPS

- **Freeport** has scores of outlet shops, **Portland** has the oldest lighthouse in the state, **Boothbay Harbor** has a scenic coastline, and, farther up the coast, **Acadia National Park** offers the rugged scenery of cliffs, ocean, and woods.

- With just five rooms, the **Telemark Inn** in Bethel offers the intimacy of small group explorations in the **White Mountains National Forest.** Book a multisport package at this plain but comfortable inn and you can hike, mountain bike, canoe, and llama trek by day, but come back each night to a comfortable lodge. Follow creeks through fern beds to swimming holes and beaver dams. Paddle Umbagog Lake in search of moose and mountain bike to waterfalls. Each adventure sports a kid-friendly pace, with lots of pauses and snacks plus a picnic lunch. At night gather round a campfire for tepee parties, storytelling, and stargazing.

  For those who've fallen in love with the llamas, the Telemark Inn offers three-day-two-night llama treks. Steve Crone, the owner, is great at teaching kids, even those as young as five, to lead these intelligent and gentle animals. Because the llamas carry the gear, trekkers walk into the backcountry without the burden of heavy backpacks.

  In the winter the Telemark Inn offers cross-country skiing and dog jorring (dog sledding without the sled). Call (207) 836-2703, or visit their Web site at www.maineguide. com/bethel/telemark.

FOR MORE INFORMATION

The **Kennebunk-Kennebunkport Chamber of Commerce,** P.O. Box 740, Kennebunk (207-967-0857; www.kkcc.maine.org), offers information on attractions and lodging. The information booth at 173 Port Road (before Lower Village) is open daily from 9:00 A.M. to 5:00 P.M. from Memorial Day to Columbus Day. The **Kennebunkport Information and Hospitality,** near Dock Square (207-967-8600), is also open Memorial Day to Columbus Day.

Note: Public restrooms are located at Dock Square (next to Ben & Jerry's).

Emergency Numbers

Emergency: 911

Kennebunk Police (non-emergency): (207) 985-6121

Kennebunk Fire Department (non-emergency): (207) 985-7113

Kennebunkport Police and Kennebunkport Fire Department (non-emergency): (207) 967-3323

Twenty-four-hour care for minor or major emergencies: Southern Maine Medical Center, Medical Center Drive, Biddeford; (207) 283-7000. Also, the Kennebunk Walk-in Clinic, Route 1 North, Kennebunk (207-985-6027), offers walk-in service

BALTIMORE

Baltimore, nicknamed "Charm City," has lots to recommend it, including personality. With its dazzling Inner Harbor, relatively new but old-style baseball stadium, top-notch art museums, the winding waterfront of Fells Point, and lots of ethnic neighborhoods, Baltimore is very different—but no less alluring—than its neighbor, Washington, D.C., less than one hour away. Instead of a planned, grand design for the ages, Baltimore exudes a down-to-earth hominess that adds charm to the historic sites, children's attractions, and educational museums.

GETTING THERE

The **Baltimore/Washington International Airport** (410-859-7100) is a fifteen-minute drive from downtown Baltimore. The BWI Airport Van Shuttle (410-859-7545) takes visitors to many Inner Harbor hotels for reasonable rates. Taxis are also available.

Amtrak trains stop at Baltimore's Penn Central Railroad Station, North Charles Street, between Oliver and Lanvale Streets. Call (800) 872-7245. For day trips to points between Washington, D.C., and Baltimore during the week, including Camden Yards and Penn Station, the MARC commuter train (800-325-RAIL) offers inexpensive service and frequent departures.

Bus travelers arrive at the Greyhound/Trailway terminals, 210 West Lafayette Street, and the Baltimore Travel Plaza. For information call (410) 744-9311.

By car Baltimore is easily reached by I-95 from the north or south, and I-70 and U.S. 40 from the west.

GETTING AROUND

Much of Baltimore, including the newly renovated waterfront and Fells Point, can be visited on foot. For cold days and weary feet, however, there are several transportation possibilities. To avoid the challenge of navigating the many one-way streets in Baltimore by car, visitors should consider the **Metro,** a limited subway system that runs until midnight, or the

Baltimore

AT A GLANCE

▶ Enjoy a charming, down-to-earth city with lots of personality

▶ Explore the National Aquarium in Baltimore and the Maryland Science Center

▶ Climb aboard trains at the B&O Railroad Museum

▶ Discover four first-rate art museums

▶ Take in professional sporting events—baseball (Orioles), football (Ravens), lacrosse (Thunder), and soccer (Blast)

▶ Baltimore Area Convention and Visitors Bureau, (410) 837-4636 or (800) 282-6632

Mass Transit Administration (MTA) bus lines, which run twenty-four hours. MTA offers a one-day Tourist Passport for unlimited travel downtown. For fare and route information, call (410) 539-5000.

The **Water Taxi** (410-563-3901 or 800-658-8947) is an enjoyable way to reach points along Baltimore's Inner Harbor, including Fells Point, Little Italy, and the Aquarium. Inexpensive all-day passes are available for adults and children.

A car is also handy. Driving around Baltimore is simple, as street signs are easy to read and routes are marked. The trick to remember is that many of Baltimore's main streets are one-way.

WHAT TO SEE AND DO

Inner Harbor Attractions

If you have limited time in the city, head for the Inner Harbor, where many of the family attractions are located. Park the car—you can walk to everything. You will easily find a day's worth of attractions if not more.

Maryland Science Center, 601 Light Street (410-685-5225), entertains all ages with its hands-on exhibits. At the exhibit on Maryland's Chesapeake Bay, look at tiny baby crayfish under a microscope, and find out about the life of a blue crab. The Hubble Space Telescope opens kids' eyes to the skies, while Energy Place lets them use their bodies to generate electricity.

Take young children, ages two to seven, to K.I.D.S., a room with blocks,

Port Discovery

This new $32-million children's museum (35 Market Place; 410–727-8120) immerses kids in its hands-on exhibits and adds more kid fun to the already appealing Inner Harbor. Geared to children ages six through twelve, the museum is the first to have exhibits designed with the assistance of the Walt Disney Company's Imagineers. Highlights include:

- **KidWorks.** Three stories of ropes and bridges to climb. The higher you go, the harder the climb and the more brain-teasing obstacles to solve.
- **Adventure Expeditions.** A Nile journey fraught with close encounters with cobras and mummies. Dig through an archeological site to find Pharaoh's treasures.
- **Baffled Family House.** Rooms with crazy angles that appear to swallow up family members.
- **R&D Dreamlab.** A real workshop that has power tools kids can use to construct their own inventions.
- **Television Studio.** Enables kid directors, actors, and writers to produce their own news shows.

play areas, and appropriate hands-on items. The Davis Planetarium's sky show will leave your kids starry-eyed, and any of the educational, but usually entertaining, movies at the IMAX Theater are a big hit since the screen is five stories tall. After a ten-year hiatus, the Rooftop Observatory is now open every Thursday night for families to come view the stars through a seventy-one-year-old telescope. The programs at both the planetarium and the IMAX theater are included in the price of admission.

What's an Inner Harbor without some maritime lore and actual ships? Baltimore has three noteworthy vessels that the curious can board. The **Baltimore Maritime Museum,** Pier 3, Pratt Street (410-396-3854; www.livingclassrooms.org), is a floating museum that consists of three ships: the 1940s submarine U.S.S. *Torsk,* the Lightship *Chesapeake,* and the Coast Guard cutter the *Taney,* the last remaining ship to have survived the attack on Pearl Harbor. All are open for self-guided tours. The *Torsk* submarine is distinguished for sinking the last Japanese warship in World War II. A walk through these narrow corridors lets kids know just how cramped life under the sea can be. The *Chesapeake*'s beacon lantern served as a floating lighthouse in areas where rocks or shoals made the construction of a stationary lighthouse impossible. Quarters were tight here, too, and talk was often punctuated by the blast of foghorns.

The U.S. frigate *Constellation* returns to the Inner Harbor Constellation

Dock in June 1999. This National Historic Landmark, the first commissioned ship of the U.S. Navy, launched in 1797.

For some pure play try **Art Links Baltimore,** off Key Highway, Inner Harbor at Rash Field, next to the Science Center (no phone). The artist-designed holes at this miniature golf course feature such regional themes as a crab feast, a Preakness winner's circle, and Edgar Allan Poe's Nevermore.

For a literal overview of Baltimore, check out the view twenty-seven stories up at the Top of the World observation level and museum in the **World Trade Center,** 401 East Pratt Street (410-837-4515). The museum features exhibits on the port and the city's history and economic development. Top of the World often holds special events geared to kids, especially around holidays. Activities include puppet shows, storytelling, and face painting. Call ahead to check out the schedule.

Now that you've seen the top, try a bottoms-up view at the **Baltimore Public Works Museum and Streetscape,** 751 Eastern Avenue at Fallsway (410-396-5565). Housed in the Eastern Avenue Pumping Station, a plant that originally processed the city's sewage, the museum demonstrates the city's public utility services from street lighting to trash removal to plumbing. The brightly colored outdoor Streetscape gives an insider's glimpse of the workings beneath the city streets. Children enjoy picking out the underground phone lines, water, and gas pipes by color. An activity center for ages three to ten, Construction Site, is open on weekends and by request.

Isaac Myers Shipyard, Inner Harbor, is Baltimore's first black-owned and -controlled shipyard, established after the Civil War by Isaac Myers. Visit the historic beginnings of the man who went on to establish the National Labor Union for blacks in 1869.

Also in the Inner Harbor, **The Power Plant**—an actual headquarters of a former power plant—is being transformed into a nightlife and entertainment complex. The structure is already home to the Hard Rock Cafe, ESPN Zone (see Where to Eat), and Barnes & Noble. More restaurants and stores are expected to open soon.

Museums and Historic Baltimore Sites

In addition to the prosperity brought to the city by its port, Baltimore grew because of its railroad. With the laying of the Baltimore and Ohio tracks at the Mount Clare station in 1827, the city solidified its importance as a commercial distribution center.

Often overlooked is the **B & O Railroad Museum,** 901 West Pratt Street (410-752-2490; www.borail.org), located at the site of the former Mount Clare Station. It's worth a stop, especially if toy trains, tracks, and thoughts of steaming around the countryside in a locomotive keep your child, or the child within you, happy.

National Aquarium in Baltimore

This world-class aquarium alone merits a trip to Baltimore's Inner Harbor. Highlights include:

- **Wings under Water.** The largest ray exhibit in the world, featuring cow-nose, blunt-nose, and other types of rays.
- **The Open Ocean.** (a.k.a. the Shark Tank). Home to sand, tiger, nurse, and sandbar sharks, as well as other ferocious and ferocious-looking fish.
- **South American Rain Forest.** A showcase for a wealth of plant and animal life, including parrots, sloths, and even a piranha.
- **Marine Mammal Pavilion.** This 1.2-million-gallon pool is where you'll find beluga whales and bottle-nosed dolphins.
- **Maryland: Mountains to the Sea.** An up-close look at local creatures such as bullfrogs, soft-shell turtles, flounder, and blue crabs.

- **Atlantic Coral Reef.** This 335,000-gallon tank is home to schools of rainbow-colored fish.

The aquarium's **Amazon River Forest** exhibit, depicting the seasonal flooding of the Rio Negro, is scheduled to open in March 2000. The aquarium also features special limited-time exhibits such as **Venom: Striking Beauties,** which showcases poisonous aquatic and terrestrial creatures from Africa, Australia, and South America, including the taipan (the world's most dangerous snake), black mambas, tarantulas, and the deadly blue-ringed octopus.

Contact the aquarium for the latest on current and upcoming exhibits. National Aquarium in Baltimore, Pier 3, East Pratt Street; (410) 576–3800; www.aquar.org.

Upstairs this museum displays a priceless collection of model trains, including a Lionel freight set from the 1920s and some rare locomotives. Enjoy the elaborate display of tracks that wind through a replica of a 1940s city and of Maryland's mountains. Downstairs—save that for last—is the real thing, restored trains in an authentic roundhouse. As you listen to the taped sounds of whistles, chugs, and clanking, climb on and ogle such railroad darlings as a mail car, a caboose, and a big "mountain hauler."

After you explore the museum's three buildings, take a train ride to the nearby **Mount Clare Mansion.** Dating back to about 1756, this Georgian estate was home to Charles Carroll, founder of the Baltimore and Ohio Railroad.

The **Star-Spangled Banner Flag House and Museum,** 844 East

Three of the friends you will meet at the National Aquarium in Baltimore.

Pratt Street at Howard Street (410-837-1793), is the home of Mary Pickersgill, the woman who sewed the flag that flew over Fort McHenry, Pickersgill, a widow, paid nearly $200 of her own money to purchase the 400 yards of material for the 30-by-42-foot flag, the largest in the world at the time. Working more than 1,000 hours, she received $405.90 for sewing this flag and another, smaller version. The receipt is showcased in the museum. The museum hosts a variety of monthly events, including open-hearth cooking demonstrations. Hands-on activities for kids, such as unrolling a full-size version of one of the original flag stripes, are scattered throughout the tour. If you're in the area around Flag Day (June 14), stop by for the hilarious Star-Spangled Banner Singing Contest, open to contestants of all ages.

For more history, visit **Fort McHenry,** Fort Avenue (410-962-4299). The American flag flying here after a long night of British attack in 1814 inspired Francis Scott Key to write the words to *The Star-Spangled Banner.* Visitors can explore the fort restored to its pre–Civil War appearance, walk o'er the ramparts, and see where the British invaded. From Memorial Day through Labor Day, there's shuttle boat service to the fort from Baltimore's Inner Harbor. Ask the museum about the special children's programs available year-round that give kids an idea of what it was like to be a soldier in 1814. On certain Sundays during the summer, visitors are treated to military tattoo ceremonies featuring patriotic music and military drills. Ranger programs, providing guided walks through the fort and human interest stories, are led during the summer months from 10:30 A.M. to 4:30 P.M. A Fort McHenry "must-do," visitors can help guards fold a full-size replica of the Star-Spangled Banner.

Baltimore is an industrial city, and its laborers—garment workers, oyster canners, printers, and others—come to life in the **Baltimore Museum of Industry,** 1415 Key Highway (410-727-4808). Housed in a former 1870 cannery, the hands-on exhibits teach kids about the labor in these laborers' days. Kids feel the muscle it took to operate a printing press, sample a foot-operated sewing machine, and—against a sweatshop display—see a photo of the real women who worked cramped together at their machines. At Children's Motorworks kids join a scaled-down assembly line learning firsthand about the benefits, and boredom; at the Cannery they take part in shucking and canning oysters in a simulated 1883 factory.

The kid-friendly **Maryland Historical Society,** 201 West Monument Street (410-685-3750), offers history-related activity sheets, lots of hands-on activities, and a Child's World gallery featuring antique toys.

Several famous people associated with Baltimore have historic sites in the city. Budding journalists may want to breeze through the **H. L. Mencken House,** 1524 Hollins Street (410-396-1149), home to the outspoken journalist Henry Louis Mencken, "The Sage of Baltimore." This nineteenth-century row house is furnished with Mencken's belongings and presents a short film on his life and works.

Westminster Hall and Burying Ground, West Fayette and Greene Streets (410-328-7228), is where Edgar Allan Poe and his wife, first cousin Virginia Clemm, are buried. Many other notable Marylanders rest here as well. Tours are conducted the first and third Friday evening and Saturday morning each month with prior reservations. The **Edgar Allan Poe House,** 203 North Amity Street (410-396-7932), where Poe lived from 1831 to 1835, is open with abbreviated hours.

Another Baltimore legend is represented in Charm City. The **Babe Ruth Birthplace,** 216 Emory Street (410-727-1539), features exhibits on George Herman "Babe" Ruth as well as famous Orioles. Scheduled to open in 1999, the **Baseball Center,** Camden Station Passenger Terminal Building at Oriole Park at Camden Yards (no phone), will pay homage to baseball and to the Babe with exhibits. Computer and laser technology will enable visitors to stand in a batter's box and swing at a pro's best curve or fast ball. Part of the station's corridor will be decorated to resemble a 1920s railroad car of the kind the Babe used to ride to games.

The town's new specialty museum, the **Dr. Samuel D. Harris National Museum of Dentistry,** 31 South Green Street (410-706-0600), is on the University of Maryland at Baltimore campus. Artifacts include George Washington's dentures and the dental instruments used to treat Queen Victoria.

Art Museums

Baltimore Museum of Art, Art Museum Drive between Charles and 31st Streets (410-396-7101), is the city's premier art museum, featuring the Cone Collection, with outstanding works by Matisse, Picasso, and Cézanne, plus an entire wing devoted to modern art. Besides these paintings—and the gift shop—kids seem to enjoy the Arts of Africa, specifically the masks, and the Cheney Miniature rooms, whose scaled-down furnishings depict lifestyles from the seventeenth to the nineteenth century and are guaranteed to elicit an "ooh" from anyone who appreciates miniatures.

Besides its permanent collection the museum is noted for its frequent, top-quality shows. Call and see what's being featured, and inquire about children's classes, often scheduled on weekends.

The **Walters Art Gallery,** 600 North Charles Street (410-547-9000), boasts more than 30,000 items in its collection, which spans 5,000 years. Some kid-pleasing highlights include Byzantine silver and jewelry, an extensive arms and armor collection, jewelry by Fabergé, and an extensive Asian arts wing at **Hackerman House,** 1 West Mount Vernon Place. Some children love the delicate swirls, patterns, and colors of these works in porcelain and lacquer.

The **Black American Museum,** 1765-69 Carswell Street (410-243-9600), presents changing exhibitions of contemporary black Americans and third world artists.

Your kids might like to see the innovative works at the **American Visionary Art Museum,** 800 Key Highway and Covington Street (410-244-1900), a museum that was designated by Congress to feature the "best in self-taught, 'outsider,' or visionary artistry." Past exhibits have focused on divine flight and unique wood sculpture celebrating earth and the spirit. The Wildflower/Sculpture Garden is a kid-pleaser, with its wedding altar created from woven tree limbs and its great whirligig. Exhibits vary in quality.

Zoos

The Baltimore Zoo, Druid Hill Park (410-366-5466), boasts a large colony of African black-footed penguins, an elephant compound, an African watering hole, and a chimp forest, plus a nice children's zoo. Take the kids for a lesson on Maryland's habitats at the children's zoo, which features replicas of five Maryland ecosystems. On the first Saturday of every month, kids under age twelve are admitted free.

Performing Arts

Baltimore has an abundant selection of theaters. Among the choices are the **Theatre Project,** 45 West Preston Street (410-752-8558), featuring national touring groups; the **Morris A. Mechanic Theatre,** Hopkins Plaza, Baltimore and Charles Streets (410-752-1200), which presents Broadway hits; and **Center Stage,** 700 North Calvert Street (410-332-0033), home of the state theater of Maryland, which hosts repertory and original shows. Go to the **Fells Point Cafe,** 723 South Broadway Street (410-327-8800), for audience-participation theater, which may include improvisation or mystery theater. **The Arena Players,** 801 McCulloh Street (410-728-6500), feature mainly African-American productions, and the **Children's Theater Association,** (they perform at the Baltimore Museum of Art, too), 100 West 22nd Street (410-366-6403), hosts children's productions.

The **Baltimore Opera Company** performs at the Lyric Opera House, 140 West Mount Royal Avenue (410-685-0693). The Baltimore Museum of Art is home to the **Maryland Ballet,** Art Museum Drive (410-467-8495). The **Baltimore Symphony Orchestra** plays at Joseph Meyerhoff Symphony Hall, 1212 Cathedral Street (410-783-8000). The **Chamber Music Society of Baltimore** presents monthly concerts at Meyerhoff Auditorium, the Baltimore Museum of Art, Art Museum Drive (301-486-1140).

Shopping

At **Lexington Market,** 400 West Lexington Street (410-685-6169; www.lexingtonmarket.com), grab some lunch. This is the country's oldest continuously operating market, where 140 merchants offer fresh seafood, including Maryland crab cakes, meats, cheeses, wines, and anything else you can imagine. **Harborplace,** at the corner of Light and Pratt Streets, offers more than 150 shops, eateries, and restaurants in two pavilions. When you tire of browsing, enjoy the water view from the terraces.

Tours

Several creative tours in Baltimore are worth a try. The **Insomniac Tour** run by Baltimore Rent-A-Tour (410-653-2998) is a fun tour of the city at night for adults and teens, but it's offered only for large groups. Call for more information and reservations. **Trolley Tours** of downtown Baltimore run daily in the warmer months. Also call Baltimore Trolley Tours (410-724-0077).

Available harbor and boat tours include the *Baltimore Patriot I* and *II* (410-685-4288), the **Clipper City/Baltimore's Tall Ship** (410-539-6277), and **Harbor Cruises** aboard the *Bay Lady* and *The Lady Baltimore* (410-727-3113).

SPECIAL EVENTS

Sporting Events

Oriole Park at Camden Yards, 333 Camden Street (410-685-9800), is open from April to October for Baltimore Oriole baseball games. Built in 1992, the park mixes an old-stadium feel with modern amenities. Be sure to purchase tickets in advance for this popular summer activity.

The **Preakness,** one jewel in racing's Triple Crown, is run in May, Pimlico Race Course, 5101 Park Heights Avenue, Baltimore (410-542-9400).

The **Baltimore Ravens** play at a brand-new stadium. The 69,400-seat **NFL Stadium** at Camden Yards, adjacent to Oriole Park at Camden Yards, has the biggest scoreboards in any sporting venue. The site awaits a corporate sponsor for an official new name. Call 410-481-SEAT or 800-551-SEAT for ticket information, or contact the Baltimore Ravens, 1101 Russell Street (410-230-8000).

Festivals

January. Baltimore on Ice.

February. Celebrate Black History Month at city sites.

March. Annual Street Performers Auditions, Inner Harbor. Public Works Museum Open House for Archeology Week.

April. Mayor's Easter Egg Hunt, Druid Hill Park.

May. Preakness Stakes horse race at Pimlico Race Course with a week-long celebration throughout the city, including a parade.

June. National Flag Day Celebration at Fort McHenry.

July. July Fourth Celebration at the waterfront.

September. Baltimore Book Festival.

October. Baltimore on the Bay, the annual family festival of the city's maritime heritage. Annual Fells Point Fun Festival. Kids on the Bay, a waterside children's festival.

November. Baltimore's Thanksgiving Parade from downtown to the Inner Harbor. Hottest winter.

December. Noontime Christmas concerts all month long, except on Sundays, at Lexington Market. Parade of Lighted Boats at the Inner Harbor. Christmas at Harborplace. Baltimore's New Year's Eve Extravaganza, a nonalcoholic celebration geared toward the entire family and ending with fireworks over the harbor.

WHERE TO STAY

The Inner Harbor is a practical area to stay in since much of Baltimore can be visited on foot from here. Among accommodation possibilities are the **Holiday Inn–Inner Harbor,** 301 West Lombard Street (410-685-3500), and **Baltimore Marriott Inner Harbor,** 110 South Eutaw Street (410-962-0202). Ask about the Marriott's Two for Breakfast package. Try **Harbor Inn at Pier 5,** 711 Eastern Avenue (410-539-2000). The **Harbor Court Hotel,** 550 Light Street (410-234-0550) on the harbor, offers a Baltimore on Ice wintertime package that lets children stay for free. The **Hyatt Regency at the Inner Harbor,** 300 Light Street (410-528-1234), has easy access to Harborplace and the Convention Center, plus special packages for families. The **Stouffer Renaissance Harborplace Hotel,** 202 East Pratt Street (410-547-1200), is a convenient lodging. The **Omni Inner Harbor,** 101 West Fayette Street (410-752-1100), offers seasonal family packages, often with discounted attraction tickets and $1.99 children's menus. The **Sheraton Inner Harbor,** 300 South Charles Street (410-962-8300), also features seasonal packages.

The **Brookshire Inner Harbor Suite Hotel,** 120 East Lombard Street (410-625-1300), is an all-suite hotel. The **Comfort Inn** at Baltimore's Mount Vernon, 24 West Franklin Street (410-727-2000), is located near the Walters Art Gallery.

For reservations in bed and breakfasts that welcome children, call **Amanda's Bed and Breakfast Reservation Service,** 1428 Park Avenue (410-225-0001). The **Biltmore Suites,** 205 West Madison Street (410-728-6550), is an all-suite property in the Mount Vernon historic district.

WHERE TO EAT

Baltimore is a great place to taste the Chesapeake Bay region's seafood specialties, among them crab cakes, steamed crabs, steamed shrimp, and fresh oysters. Suggestions for family-friendly restaurants include **Phillips,** 301 Light Street (410-685-6600 or 410-327-5561), for seafood near the Inner Harbor. If you're looking for lunch at the Inner Harbor, the fast-food eateries at **Harborplace,** Pratt and Light Streets (410-332-4191), offer enough choices to please any picky eater. An amphitheater features free entertainment.

Wayne's Bar-B-Que, in the Pratt Street Pavilion (410-539-3814), has spicy wings and pork barbecue. Also in the pavilion is **Tex-Mex Grill** (410-783-2970), which features fajitas and burritos, the chain restaurant **Pizzeria Uno** (410-625-5900), with its Chicago-style deep-dish pizza, and **Planet Hollywood** (410-685-STAR), the movie-themed eatery.

For burgers and rock 'n' roll, check out **Hard Rock Cafe,** in the Power Plant, Inner Harbor, 601 East Pratt Street (410-347-7625). Also in the Power Plant is **ESPN Zone** (410-685-3776), a family sports-themed restaurant with big-screen TVs and interactive video games. Baltimore's ESPN Zone is the first of its kind in the nation. Expect these restaurants to open in other U.S. cities in the near future.

Little Italy, 6 blocks east of the Inner Harbor, is the place to be for authentic Italian food in one of the oldest neighborhoods in the city. Try out **Velleggia's,** 829 East Pratt Street (410-685-2620) or **Sabatino's,** 901 Fawn Street (410-727-9414). For seafood in Fells Point, locals like the **Fishery,** 1717 Eastern Avenue; (410-327-9340). If you're downtown and just want a sandwich, get one at **Lenny's Deli of Lombard Street,** 1150 East Lombard Street (410-327-1177).

Baltimore's official *Quick Guide* offers a comprehensive list of restaurants.

SIDE TRIPS

Annapolis

About an hour away from Baltimore, Annapolis, at the picturesque junction of Chesapeake Bay and the Severn River, is a worthy day trip. Settled in 1649, much of the city has been designated a National Historic Landmark District. Stroll along its narrow streets, admiring the architecture and the shops, and grab a bite to eat. A kid-pleaser is a tour of the bay. Several are available, from the forty-minute harbor tour aboard the *Harbor Queen* to the seven-and-a-half-hour tour aboard the *Bay Cruise,* which passes the city landmarks en route to the Eastern Shore town of St. Michaels. For tour information contact **Chesapeake Maritime Tours,** city dock at Main Street (410-268-7600).

Be sure to tour the **U.S. Naval Academy,** bordered by King George and Randall Streets (410-263-6933). Established in 1845, the Academy's museum in Preble Hall exhibits flags, ship models, and war relics. In warm weather watch the cadets muster in front of Bancroft Hall at noon. Older children may like visiting the historic houses, such as the eighteenth-century **Hammond-Harwood House,** 19 Maryland Avenue, with its period pieces.

Before leaving the city take some time to romp at the **Neuman Street Playground,** an eclectic collection of climbing apparatus surrounded by green spaces for running.

Greenbelt

This Washington, D.C., suburb has **NASA's Goddard Visitor Center,** Greenbelt, Maryland (301-286-8981), where you can educate the family about space exploration at interactive exhibits created for children. Highlights include a Manned Maneuvering Unit, in which kids capture satellites in space, and a reproduction Gemini capsule with a mock take-off recording. Rockets are launched on the first and third Sundays of each month, and weekly grounds tours run every Thursday afternoon.

For additional day trips to points along the Eastern Shore, see the chapter on Washington, D.C. For a free Maryland Travel Kit, call (800) 543-1036.

FOR MORE INFORMATION

Visitor Information Centers

The Baltimore Area Convention and Visitors Association (BACVA), 100 Light Street, 12th floor (410-837-4636 or 800-282-6632; www.baltimore.org), will soon move to a new location on the west shore of the Inner Harbor. Contact the Chamber of Commerce (410-269-0642) or the Department of Recreation and Parks (410-396-7900).

To avoid lines, order tickets right at the BACVA from **Baltimore Tickets** (410-752-8427 or 888-BALT-TIX). Here you can buy discount ticket packages or tickets to specific attractions, such as the National Aquarium in Baltimore, Baltimore Zoo, Maryland Historical Society, and Baltimore Orioles. Open Friday to Sunday, 10:00 A.M. to 4:00 P.M.

Need to make a dinner reservation? BACVA volunteers will be happy to help you. Take a look at their on-hand selection of menus from some of Baltimore's most popular eateries.

Senior citizens will find the Waxter Center for Senior Citizens helpful. Call (410) 396-1341. Persons with disabilities can get referrals and information from the **Handicapped Services Coordinator** at the Mayor's Office (410-396-1915) or from the **Disabilities Information and Assistance Line** (410-752-DIAL). The Easter Seal Society of Central Maryland has published a Baltimore guide for travelers with disabilities, Bright Lights, Harbor Breezes. For a copy call (410) 335-0100.

Emergency Numbers

Ambulance, fire, and police: 911

Block's Pharmacy, Baltimore Street at Linwood Avenue, is open from 9:30 A.M. to 9:00 P.M. Monday–Saturday and from 10:00 A.M. to 2:00 P.M. on Sundays; (410) 276-2312

Johns Hopkins Hospital Emergency Room: (410) 955-5000

Maryland Poison Center: (410) 528-7701

BOSTON

Ever since a group of Revolutionaries dumped tea in the Boston harbor, the city has held a special fascination. Despite the busy, big-city ambience, Boston is eminently family friendly, offering an uncommon mix of history, museums, and fun. Don't miss the opportunity to visit here with your kids, whether you tour on a family getaway or take the kids with you as part of a business trip.

GETTING THERE

Most major domestic and international airlines, as well as several regional carriers, provide service to **Logan International Airport,** about 3 miles from downtown Boston.

Traffic in the morning and evening rush hours can significantly lengthen the time it takes to reach town from the airport, thus increasing taxi fares. One way to beat the traffic is to take the **Airport Water Shuttle.** The seven-minute trip—kids will love the ferry ride—departs from the airport to Rowes Wharf, downtown, and from downtown to the airport, every fifteen minutes Monday through Friday from 6:00 A.M. to 8:00 P.M. and every thirty minutes Friday from 8:00 A.M. to 11:00 P.M., Saturday from 10:00 A.M. to 11:00 P.M., and Sunday from 10:00 A.M. to 8:00 P.M. No service is available on holidays. Call (800) 23-LOGAN for more information.

If you're traveling light, consider taking the subway. The **MBTA** (Massachusetts Bay Transit Authority) Blue Line stops at the airport. Check out the MBTA's Web site at www.mbta.com for more details on public transportation including commuter rail, subway, bus, and water shuttle service.

Amtrak trains (800–USA–RAIL) service Boston, arriving at South Station, on the Red "T" line, and Back Bay Station, on the Orange "T" line. Commuter trains link Boston with the suburbs. For information on the MBTA Commuter Rail or "T" customer service, call (617) 222-3200.

Another airport note: When awaiting departures, be sure to stop by the airport's Kidport, a free play space for kids with climbing equipment for wee ones and several computer terminals for older kids.

Boston

▶ Walk the Freedom Trail

▶ Visit more than a dozen hands-on, kid-oriented museums

▶ Contact Greater Boston Convention and Visitors Bureau, at (617) 536–4100 or (888) SEE–BOSTON to receive a free travel planner, a family-friendly pass, and a "Kids Love Boston" guide

GETTING AROUND

The only time your children will be bored in Boston is when you're stuck in traffic. Take to the streets, not as the early Revolutionaries did to protest taxes, but to avoid the often clogged roads and to savor the city. Whenever possible, walk, or take the subway, known as the **"T."** Reasonably safe during the day—as in any city, be vigilant and use common sense —the "T" gets you around quickly and inexpensively. Divided into Red, Green, Orange, and Blue lines, the fares depend on the number of zones traveled. The **Visitor Passport** gives you unlimited travel within Boston for three or seven days. Obtain a passport at the Visitor Information Centers (see For More Information), or call the T Customer Service Center at (617) 222–3200.

WHAT TO SEE AND DO

Museums

Forget about dry-as-dust exhibit halls with a look-but-don't-touch rigidity. Boston's museums offer lots of family fun.

At **Children's Museum,** 300 Congress Street (617–426–8855), there's something for every kid, from preschoolers to teens.

Kids four years and under enjoy **Playspace,** where they can climb in cars, build with blocks, and enjoy a variety of other activities. At **Science Playground** such simple acts as spinning tops and plates teach kids about scientific principles. **Teen Tokyo** introduces American youths to their Japanese peers. Learn about the life of a Japanese student by stepping into a subway car and standing on the footprints that show you just how packed the place gets. Your child can browse through *manga* (popular comic books), listen to Japanese rock 'n' roll, and compare fashions.

The museum's latest exhibit is **Arthur's World.** Based on the popular PBS show and author Marc Brown's book series, the exhibit includes a Backyard Sleepover with real tents, and Arthur's World TV, featuring footage from *Arthur* shows and technology that allows children to appear on a TV screen as characters in Arthur's World. The **New Balance Climb,** a two-story indoor climbing sculpture, has tunnels, towers, and planks for kids to climb up, down, and across.

Be sure to check out the **Computer Museum,** 300 Congress Street (617–426–2800; www.tcm.org). This place proves that computers aren't just for "nerds." The easy-to-follow programs let you and your kids enjoy such instant creativity as designing a virtual fish, releasing it into the 2,200-square-foot Virtual Fish Tank, and watching as it combats schools of angry predators. Kids can have their picture taken with the original R2-D2 from *Star Wars* and parents can sample the latest in children's multimedia software displayed in the Best Software for Kids Gallery. While kids love the place, parents, especially those from the precomputer generation, may have even more fun gaining familiarity with the programs and possibilities through play. Your children may have to tear you away from the terminals.

Nearby is the **Boston Tea Party Ship and Museum,** Congress Street Bridge, Boston; (617–338–1773). For grade-school kids who have undoubtedly heard of the Boston Tea Party, boarding this replica of the ship involved in that famous incident is fun. Costumed guides retell the tale.

Easily accessible via the "T," the **Museum of Science,** Science Park, (617–723–2500; www.mos.org), gets mixed reviews. Skip the anemic rain forest and the deadly dioramas of marshes complete with mounted birds looking as bored as the viewers. Go directly to the must-see galleries. These include **Science in the Park,** featuring more than eighteen playground activities that teach Newton's laws of physics, **Seeing Is Deceiving,** which explores how the human brain deals with sensory overload, and **Discovery Center,** which provides preschoolers with a playroom featuring hands-on water activities and a creature habitat at kids' eye level. The Discovery Center's fabulous view of Boston can be enjoyed through the center's many periscopes and special lenses. One of the liveliest spaces is **Seeing the Unseen,** which renders the world of fleas, termites, tadpoles, shrimp, and other tiny creatures visible through high-powered microscopes.

The **Theater of Electricity** will snap, crackle, and pop you into attention. Here the world's largest Van de Graaff generator produces bolts of lightning as the guide explains the phenomenon. Instructive with a flash of Frankenstein eeriness, the show is loud and flamboyant. Young children may be frightened, but older ones will be fascinated. Since the museum also features an **Omni Theater** plus a **planetarium** with both laser and sky shows, plan to spend several hours on-site. For those interested in weekend education courses the museum offers a variety of Saturday programs, including a trip outside in the summer to discover edible wild plants. Call (617) 589-0300 for course information.

The New England Aquarium, Central Wharf (617-973-5200; www. neaq.org), while not large, opens a window on some watery wonders. You'll love watching the lazy sea turtles float, the sharks swim swiftly, and the schools of fish wriggle by in the big, central tank. Feeding time is especially interesting. The Aquarium Medical Center is an ER for aquatic creatures, starring a battle-scarred piranha, a wounded garter snake, a sea horse with gas, or whatever critter becomes ill that day. Through windows visitors not only observe a working diagnostic and treatment center but can talk to the staff. The veterinarians and technicians explain procedures and discuss slides via microphones, video microscopes, and monitors. Called the first extensive, interactive care unit at a zoo or aquarium, the medical center wows kids—and adults—with high-tech procedures such as ultrasound for a sea raven or a CAT scan for a penguin. Past emergency room dramas featured a turtle obtaining a cast for his shell, a cowfish taking an eye exam, and an orphaned and malnourished seal pup gulping a much needed "squid shake."

The aquarium's new west wing has changing exhibits. An IMAX theater will be completed by 2000.

Be sure to visit the sea lions in the **Discovery,** the floating pavilion next door. Guthrie, a 650-pound performer, puts on quite an educational show four times daily, as he swims, dives, "talks," and teaches kids about recycling. There is also a new outdoor harbor seal area.

The **Museum of Fine Arts,** 465 Huntington Avenue (617-267-9300) has noted collections of Asian art, American decorative arts, and nineteenth-century French works. Newly installed galleries, Egyptian Funerary Arts and the Art of the Ancient Near East, explore the ancient worlds of Egypt and Babylon. Objects on display include exquisite gold jewelry and thirteen mummies, the museum's biggest kids' attraction.

The **Sports Museum of New England** is located at the Fleet Center, 150 Causeway Street, Boston (617-787-7678). This museum has three theaters that offer films and facts on great moments in New England sports history from high school through professional sports. There is also an exhibit at 25 Shattuck Street in Lowell, Massachusetts (978-452-6775).

Markets, Historical Markers, Parks

From the aquarium it's an easy walk to **Faneuil Hall Marketplace.** The ranger talk about the historic liberty speeches delivered here isn't likely to rouse your children, but the rows upon rows of shops, stalls, and eateries

Special Tours

- **Whale-watching.** From April through October get ready to yell "thar she blows" when you spot one of these magnificent leviathans breaching the waves. Two places that book whale-watching tours in the city are A.C. Cruise Line, 28 Northern Avenue, Boston (617-261-6633 or 800-973-5281), and the New England Aquarium, Central Wharf, off Atlantic Avenue (617-973-5277 or 800-973-5281).

- **Black history.** Grab a *Black Heritage Trail* brochure for a self-guided tour of fourteen Beacon Hill historic sites including the memorial to the 54th Regiment. Guided tours are available by appointment (617-742-5415).

- **Walking tours.** Boston By Foot offers walking tours May through October. Boston By Little Feet is the company's family walking tour for children six to twelve and their parents. Although reservations are not required, call (617) 367-2345 or (617) 367-3766 (recorded message) for schedule and rates.

in the nearby markets will. This place offers cheap eats for lunch and limitless possibilities for parting with some allowance money for souvenirs.

From Faneuil Hall follow the red path that details some of the best parts of the **Freedom Trail,** including Paul Revere's house and the Old North Church. There's something about Paul Revere's house that renders this famous personage real. Looking at the furnishings and rooms helps round out the life of this Revolutionary as father, provider, and silversmith. The 3-mile Freedom Trail, which passes by sixteen historic sites from the Colonial and Revolutionary eras, starts at the Boston Common.

Across from the Common is the **Public Garden,** a great take-a-break place. The ponds, swans, and brass ducklings, kept shiny by so many little bottoms saddling them, offer a pleasing city oasis. Plan to picnic or at least play a while here.

The seventy-two-acre **Franklin Park Zoo,** Franklin Park, off Blue Hill Avenue (617-442-2002), located in beautiful Franklin Park, offers some easy outdoor time. Preschoolers like the farm animals at the Petting Zoo, and everyone seems to enjoy the African Tropical Forest, a zoo highlight with leopards, antelope, and gorillas.

Television history was made at **The Bull & Finch Pub,** 84 Beacon Street (617-227-9600). The outside of this pub served as the model for *Cheers*. While Norm and Sam are nowhere to be seen, parents can have a beer and buy their kids a T-shirt with the Cheers logo. Upstairs, there's a

A ride on the swan boats in Boston's Public Garden will delight every member of the family.

more formal restaurant. While kids are welcome, the prices may be high for some family budgets.

Performing Arts
In addition to the Boston Ballet, the Boston Symphony, the Boston Pops, and several theaters, check the schedule for the Boston Children's Theatre, the New England Hall, 225 Clarendon Street (617-277-3277). The engaging performances are by children for children.

More Useful Numbers
BOSTIX Ticket Booth, Faneuil Hall (617-423-4454; fax 617-423-2131), offers tickets to entertainment and cultural events. Open Tuesday to Saturday 11:00 A.M. to 6:00 P.M., Sunday 11:00 A.M. to 4:00 P.M. BOSTIX also sells half-price tickets for same-day performances.

SPECIAL EVENTS

Boston is not only a town that loves its sports but a place that knows how to celebrate. When phone numbers are not listed, for detailed information on festivals and celebrations, contact the Greater Boston Convention and Visitors Bureau at (617) 536-4100 or (888) SEE-BOSTON; www.bostonusa.com Here are some highlights.

Sporting Events
The old Boston Garden has been replaced with the **Fleet Center,** 150 Causeway Street (617-624-1000). The center has expanded by nearly 5,000 seats and is much more family friendly. The food and rest rooms that were an embarrassment to the city in the old building are not a concern in the new. The Fleet Center continues to host the city's hockey team, the **Bruins,** from October through March, and the basketball team, the **Celtics,** from October through May. The **Red Sox,** the American League baseball team, play at Fenway Park, 4 Yawkey Way, April to October. For ticket information, call (617) 267-8661; to charge tickets (617) 267-1700. For TDD (617) 236-6644. Football fans wanting to root for the **New England Patriots,** Foxboro Stadium, Route 1, Foxboro, should call (800) 543-1776 or (800) 828-7080.

For three days during the World Cross-Country Championship Weekend in March, star athletes compete in track-and-field events. In April the world-famous **26-mile Boston Marathon** takes runners from Hopkinton to Copley Square, Boston. Grab some oranges and water, and enjoy cheering on the participants (617-236-1652). In October line the shores of the Charles River for the renowned rowing event, **Head of the Charles Regatta** (617-536-4100).

Festivals

January. First Day Celebration. Japanese New Year Festival at the Children's Museum.

February. Chinese New Year Celebration, Boston's Chinatown. Celebrate Boston Family Week, held during President's Day week, with museum events citywide.

March. St. Patrick's Day Weekend and Parade, Faneuil Hall Marketplace. New England Spring Flower Show, Bayside Expo Center.

April. Return of Swan Boat, Public Garden. Run in the Boston Marathon on Patriot's Day or celebrate Patriot's Day Weekend with reenactments of Paul Revere's Ride, and the Battles of Lexington and Concord at Old North Church.

May. Ducklings Day Parade, Boston Common. Boston Kite Festival, Franklin Park.

June. Annual Teddy Bear Picnic and Sing-Along, Boston and suburbs.

July. The Harborfest-Explanade Celebration includes July 4 fireworks and a Boston Pops outdoor concert.

August. Italian Festivals, North End.

September. Arts Boston Festival brings indoor and outdoor cultural events citywide.

October. Head of the Charles Regatta, Charles River. Halloween Festivities, including the Fright Night train from Boston to Salem.

November. First Thanksgiving Dinner, a traditional sit-down holiday dinner held at Plimoth Plantation, Plymouth Massachusetts.

December. Ice Skating at Frog Pond, Boston Common. Tree Lighting and Carol Singing, Boston Common and Prudential Building. First Night, citywide events held on New Year's Eve day and night (buttons—your entry to all First Night events—cost $10).

WHERE TO STAY

The easiest way to see the city with kids is to stay at a well-located hotel near a "T" stop in a good walking neighborhood. Call the Boston CVB for accommodation brochures and information on the latest family packages available. Remember that hotels always have lower rates on weekends; ask for these. Several hotels offer kids' amenities.

Suite accommodations give families more room for the money. The centrally located **Fairmont Copley Plaza Hotel** (617-267-5300; www.fairmont.com) frequently offers family-friendly packages. **The Four Seasons Hotel Boston** (617-338-4400; www.fourseasons.com) offers a

"Weekend with the Kids" package that includes use of a VCR, children's movies, and an executive suite with sitting area. For families of up to five people, the luxurious **Ritz-Carlton Hotel** (617-536-5700; www.ritzcarlton.com) offers the "Junior Presidential Suite Retreat," featuring a two-bedroom suite complete with books, toys, and a play area. Suites at **Doubletree Guest Suites** (800-222-TREE or 617-783-0090; www.doubletreehotels.com) consist of a living area with pullout couches, a coffeemaker and refrigerator, a television, plus a bedroom with a second television and a bathroom.

Boston has several **bed and breakfast** registries. Try the **Bed and Breakfast Agency of Boston** (617-720-3540 or 800-CITY-BNB) for town houses, studios, and condominiums. **Host Homes of Boston** (617-244-1308) offers guest rooms in town homes and houses in Boston and its nearby suburbs.

WHERE TO EAT

It's not just baked beans, chowder, and Boston cream pies—though these can be very good here. Boston has lots of good restaurants. **Faneuil Hall Marketplace** offers many spots for quick and cheap eats. Nearby, **Ye Olde Union Oyster House,** 41 Union Street (617-227-2750), open since 1862, is well known for its seafood and pastas. The crowds at **No-Name Restaurant,** 15½ Fish Pier (617-338-7539), attest to the popularity of this inexpensive seafood place. **Boodle's,** 40 Dalton Street (617-266-3537), in the Back Bay area, has burgers, salads, and sandwiches. Adventurous kids might like **Casablanca,** 40 Brattle Street (617-876-0999), for its crab cakes, chili, and couscous. **Legal Sea Foods** with three downtown locations, 35 Columbus Avenue (617-426-4444), 800 Boylston Street (617-266-6800), and 100 Huntington Avenue (617-266-7775), is a great place to get your fill of New England clam chowder. It also has kid-friendly menus featuring fish-shaped cheese ravioli.

Two inexpensive family choices are **Zuma's Tex-Mex Cafe,** 7 North Market Street (617-367-9114), a casual restaurant serving good Southwestern fare; and the **Milk Street Cafe,** 50 Milk Street (617-542-2433), a kosher restaurant that draws locals in with its tasty soups, sandwiches, and salads.

The Official Guidebook of the Greater Boston Convention and Visitors Bureau lists many area restaurants.

SIDE TRIPS

Boston can serve as the hub of a great family foray. **Lexington** and **Concord** offer more Revolutionary history, and in **Salem** the Salem Witch Museum and the Witch House will intrigue kids. Farther north try the beaches at **Parker River Refuge,** Newbury; **Plum Island; Newbury-town;** and **Good Harbor Beach,** Gloucester.

FOR MORE INFORMATION

The **Greater Boston Convention and Visitors Bureau** offers many free maps, brochures, seasonal travel planners, and accommodation guides. The GBCVB also produces *Kids Love Boston,* $3.25, a big-type guide with pleasing illustrations aimed at elementary-school kids. Get one of these ahead of time so that your child can help plan your visit, a good way to ensure cooperation. For more information, including a guide to accommodations, call the bureau: (617) 536-4100 or (800) SEE-BOSTON.

Visitor information centers: Boston Common Information Center, 146 Tremont Street (617-536-4100), open Monday–Saturday from 8:30 A.M. to 5:00 P.M. and Sunday from 9:00 A.M. to 5:00 P.M. Prudential Information Center, Prudential Plaza, 800 Boylston Street (617-536-4100), is open Monday–Saturday from 9:00 A.M. to 6:00 P.M. National Park Service, 15 State Street (617-242-5642), is open daily from 9:00 A.M. to 5:00 P.M. Cambridge Discovery, Harvard Square, Cambridge (617-497-1630), is open Monday–Saturday from 9:00 A.M. to 6:00 P.M. and Sunday from 1:00 to 5:00 P.M.

The Boston Parents Paper, P.O. Box 1777, Boston 02130 (617-522-1515; www.parentsplus.com). This monthly publication lists special events and resources for families and features the area's best calendar listings for children. Browse among the advertisers for kid-oriented shops and services. The publication is free at more than 1,000 locations.

Persons with disabilities can get referrals and information from **The Information Center for Individuals with Disabilities,** Fort Point Place, 27–43 Wormwood Street, Boston 02210; (617-727-5540).

For Boston Parks & Recreation, call (617) 725-4505. You can reach the National Historical Park Visitor Center at (617) 242-5642.

Emergency Numbers

Ambulance, fire, and police: 911

Boston Police: (617) 247-4200

Children's Hospital Emergency Room: (617) 735-6611

Poison Hotline: (617) 232-2120

Twenty-four hour pharmacy: Phillips Drug Store, 155 Charles Street, Boston; (617) 523-1028 or (617) 523-4372

CAPE COD

C ape Cod, a 70-mile stretch of land separated from the Massachusetts mainland by the Cape Cod Canal, is an idyllic seaside getaway. These days the Cape attracts more family visitors than any other New England destination except, perhaps, Boston. There is good reason for it's popularity. A Cape Cod family vacation is an old-fashioned beach-and-fishing-hole interval made glorious by the scenery. It is days spent beachcombing and nights spent stargazing. On a Cape Cod vacation, you can enjoy clear ponds and wild, running surf, bike past cranberry bogs, hike along high, windswept dunes, dig in clam flats, examine tide pools and crab holes, and look for breaching whales off the coast. The Cape is divided into two diverse sections: The **Upper Cape** is closer to the mainland and highly developed; the **Lower Cape,** with Provincetown at its tip, is quieter and includes much of the **Cape Cod National Seashore,** established to protect the area from commercialism. Cape Cod consists of fifteen towns plus a number of villages. Those who want to be close to nature may consider a cottage or camping in the more isolated Wellfleet-Truro-Eastham area of the Lower Cape. Families who want nearby conveniences and attractions—and great beaches—however, prefer the Upper Cape. The West Yarmouth-West Dennis area, for instance, at the Cape's geographical center, has the best family beaches and is close to the shopping and conveniences of Hyannis. Heading west it's just one hour to the recreational area surrounding the Cape Cod Canal; on the east an hour's drive leads to the beautiful National Seashore.

GETTING THERE

Barnstable County Airport, Hyannis (508-775-2020), is served by Delta Connection to Boston and by Continental Airlines and the commuter line Colgan Air, from Newark.

Bonanza (800-556-3815) runs frequent buses from Boston and Logan Airport to Bourne, Falmouth, and Wood's Hole, plus daily service from New York, Danbury, Hartford, Albany, Springfield, and Providence to Hyannis and Wood's Hole. **Plymouth & Brockton Company** buses

Cape Cod

AT A GLANCE

▶ Relax on oceanside beaches and calm bayside coves and tidal pools

▶ Tour the Cape Cod National Seashore with its dunes, marshlands, waves, and wildlife

▶ Take a whale-watching cruise

▶ Bicycle on the Cape Cod Rail Trail

▶ Cape Cod Chamber of Commerce, (508) 362-3225; Web site: www.capecodchamber.org

travel to and from Boston, Logan Airport, Plymouth, Provincetown, and towns in between. Call (508) 775-5524 or (800) 328-9997 (Massachusetts) for schedules.

By car the Cape can be accessed two ways: Routes 495 and 195 converge to become Route 25, which leads to the Bourne Bridge, and Route 3, which leads to the Sagamore Bridge. It's about a two-hour drive (less if the traffic is light) from Boston to the bridges.

Bay State Cruises (617-723-7800) runs passenger vessels between Boston and Provincetown in the summer.

GETTING AROUND

Driving, sometimes a slow process, is the main form of transportation. There are three highways: Mid-Cape Highway (Route 6) is the fastest but has no water view; Route 28 goes along the south shore and is slow and highly trafficked; Route 6A provides scenic views of the north shore.

Public transportation: **RTA (Regional Transit Authority)** runs buses from the commuter parking lots at the Sagamore Bridge to Wood's Hole. Call (508) 385-8311 for schedules. Provincetown has a public shuttle bus (508-487-3353) that serves Provincetown and Herring Cove Beach from late June to early September.

Ferry service includes Hy-Line (508-778-2602) during summers to Martha's Vineyard and Nantucket from Hyannis. Steamship Authority (508-477-8600) operates year-round from Wood's Hole to Martha's Vineyard (the shortest route on the Cape, it takes forty-five minutes) and from Hyannis to Nantucket. In the summer these ferries also run from the Vineyard to Nantucket, returning to Hyannis. Island Commuter (508-548-4800) heads to the Vineyard from Falmouth Harbor.

Cape Cod Canal's service roads are great for biking, walking, and jogging. You'll also find three bicycle trails within the Cape Cod National Seashore. See the Cape Cod visitor's guide for trail details and bike rental companies.

WHAT TO SEE AND DO

More Beaches
Every town on the Cape has saltwater beaches; some also offer sandy beaches on lakes or ponds. Towns charge parking fees and some require beach stickers. Some families with young children prefer the **bay beaches** because the lack of waves makes swimming and wading easier for little ones. On calm days, the ocean beaches are irresistible.

Upper Cape
The oceanside beaches on the Upper Cape are not as spectacular as those farther out, and they're generally more crowded, but they have plenty of action and attitude. **Craigville Beach,** on Nantucket Sound between Centerville and Hyannisport, is wildly popular, especially among teenagers; the water is warmer than is usual on beaches this side of the Cape, and there is some surf.

In Hyannis, **Veterans' Park Beach,** a 600-foot stretch of fine sand on placid Lewis Bay, is popular with young families because it is protected and has a playground and shady picnic area. Nearby **Kalmus Park Beach,** which rounds a point in Lewis Bay, offers calm waters for young children in the cove and good **windsurfing** for teens and adults on the ocean side.

In West Yarmouth, **Sea Gull Beach** draws a crowd of teenagers and young singles; there are also dunes and a playground. Perhaps the best beach for families is **Sandy Neck Beach,** a 6.5-mile-long barrier beach of sea grass and dunes that shelters Barnstable Harbor from Cape Cod Bay. Much of the beach is pebbly underfoot, but the calm waters and tide pools more than make up for it—just be sure the kids bring beach sandals and stay off the dunes, which are fragile. All the above-mentioned beaches have lifeguards, rest rooms, a bathhouse, and food, and each charges a parking fee.

Lower Cape: Bayside Beaches
One of the charms of the Cape for children is finding wildlife underfoot just about everywhere. This is particularly true at the Outer Cape's **bayside beaches,** whose calm, warm waters and teeming tide pools draw

many families with children under twelve. Preschoolers with a pail and shovel can amuse themselves trapping minnows and trying to trick hermit crabs out of their shells. Send your older children on a scavenger hunt for clam shells, skate eggs, starfish, snails, and the best find of all—big, brown horseshoe crabs.

The bayside beaches are town-run, and there are typically fees for nonresidents to park. Especially nice are **Corporation Beach** in Dennis and **Skaket Beach** in Orleans, a half-mile stretch of grainy sand that becomes a vast tidal flat at low tide; there are lifeguards, rest rooms, and a concession stand.

Serious clamming is hard work best left to teenagers with big appetites. But even six- to eight-year-olds can dig enough clams to steam open before dinner, and any child who can make it over the rocks can gather mussels when the tide is out. For steamers, try the flats off the **Orleans Town Landing** on Pleasant Bay, at the Route 28 bridge just north of the Harwich line. For mussels, try **Hemenway Landing** in Eastham and the rocks along the breakwater at the west end of Provincetown.

More Outdoor Adventures

Berry picking. Wild blueberries, raspberries, beach plums, and grapes are plentiful in summer on public lands, where they may be gathered for free; or visit a berry-picking farm. For strawberries head to **Namskaket Farm,** on Route 6A in East Brewster.

Exploring the woods. **Nickerson State Park.** Just off Route 6A in Brewster, this cool and leafy refuge covers more than 1,900 acres of pine woods and sparkling swimming ponds. The woods are full of wildlife, none of it ferocious except the mosquitoes; chipmunks, raccoons, deer, foxes, skunks, and muskrats are seen regularly, as are many migratory birds. The 1.5-mile-long Goose Pond Trail winds through uplands and salt marsh.

Nickerson offers 418 campsites, 250 of which are available by reservation; the others are first come, first served. There is no fee for day use, and the park's 8-mile-long **bicycle trail** connects to the Cape Cod Rail Trail, which cuts through the park south of Route 6A.

The park's eight freshwater "kettle ponds," carved out by glaciers as they retreated from Cape Cod more than 10,000 years ago, are the park's stars. Fish for trout in four of the ponds, motorboat on **Cliff Pond,** and, with little kids, play in **Flax Pond,** whose long, shallow stretch of water is great for toddlers who like to splash. On shore try catching frogs and toads and in the next cove, Jack's Boat Rentals has pedal boats, canoes, kayaks, sunfishes, and sailboards. Flax Pond has a woodland setting and shade but enough rocks in the fine sand to necessitate beach sandals. The under twelve set gathers at the park's **Nature Center** for crafts

Cape Cod National Seashore

Cape Cod National Seashore, a 44,000-acre preserve, stretches 40 miles from Chatham to Provincetown. The National Seashore is a landscape of breaking surf, rippling beach grass, dunes, and salt marshes.

The Seashore comprises fifteen named beaches; six are managed by the Park Service, the others by the towns in which they lie. All but two, however, are oceanside beaches with rough surf. Enjoy walking along the dune line and beachcombing, but unless your kids are teens and strong swimmers, it's best to save swimming for the calm, bayside beaches.

Nauset Beach, in Orleans, a long stretch of sand with a limitless horizon, is a great place for sandcastle building, kite flying, long walks, and swimming when the water is relatively calm. There are lifeguards and more parking than at most beaches.

Marconi Beach, South Wellfleet, is better for younger swimmers, especially when there is shade created by the shadows of the dunes.

Cahoon Hollow Beach, a town-managed beach in Wellfleet, with its wood-paneled station wagons, beachside bar, and lithe young surfers, looks for all the world like a southern California beach bum's dream and has a similar laid-back-but-edgy energy. Teenagers beg to come

here. There are lifeguards.

At the end of the Cape, just past the Province Lands Visitors Center, is glorious **Race Point Beach,** the Park Service's 8-mile stretch of high dunes and breaking surf.

At the **Gull Freshwater Pond,** Wellfleet, you won't find crowds. At the **Wellfleet Bay Wildlife Sanctuary,** off Route 6, (508–349-2615), there are organized bird-watching walks, canoe trips, and the Goose Pond Trail, a mile-long path.

Ranger programs include many excellent activities for families with children. Besides the Story Hour (for children four to ten) and a more hands-on Discovery Hour (for children eight to twelve), there are **canoe trips** on Nauset Marsh and Pilgrim Lake, as well as **mountain biking treks** and **sunset campfires,** when rangers sing songs and tell ghost stories between discourses on local history and ecology. Many of the best ranger programs are **hikes,** including hour-long beach walks at Nauset Light Beach, Marconi Beach, and through Province Lands. Wonderfully thrilling for older children are the **night walks,** which begin at 8:00 P.M. and continue well after dark through most of the summer. The night walk from Race Point Beach is especially exciting, as it re-creates a night watch

(continued)

Cape Cod National Seashore *(continued)*

performed by the old shipwreck patrols.

Adventurous older children should sign up for the twice-weekly **orienteering program.** There are also eleven **self-guided trails.** All but three are less than a mile long. **Buttonbush Trail,** a quarter-mile-long trail, beginning at the Salt Pond Visitor Center, is an "all senses" boardwalk trail that has a guide rope and braille text; sighted visitors are encouraged to walk it blindfolded, an unusual opportunity that most children love. Difficult but rewarding is **Great Island Trail** (6 or 8 miles round-trip, depending on which way you go), which takes hardy hikers along the shores of what was once a whalers' rendezvous.

For information, call the Park Service's two visitor centers: **Salt Pond Visitor Center,** Eastham (508-255-3421), and Province Lands Visitor Center, **Province-town** (508-487-1256).

One caution: Deer ticks, which are found all over Cape Cod, are especially common in this area, where they cling to beach grass and hide in the low scrub that borders trails. These ticks can carry Lyme disease, a serious and debilitating disease. Ask a ranger for a pamphlet detailing precautions *before* setting out.

programs that include building bird feeders and weaving dream catchers. Nickerson offers a **Junior Ranger Program,** open to children ages eight to fifteen. For campsite reservations, call (508) 896–4615; for other information call (508) 896-3491.

Outings with the Cape Cod Museum of Natural History, Brewster. The museum, popular with younger children, houses a collection of reptiles, amphibians, and fish in a two-story building set on eighty-two acres. The best things are the special activities. Sign up for an owl prowl, a sunset canoe trip, a stargazing walk, an overnight stay at the Monomoy lighthouse or a family cruise on Nauset Marsh. But the big crowd pleaser is "We Eat Too!," a program that lets kids watch turtles, snakes, and frogs munch their lunch.

Riding on a Glider, Cape Cod Airport, Marstons Mills. The pilot tailors the rides to the interests and bravery of passengers: chasing seagulls with the younger children, doing roller-coaster effects with the adventurous ones, or turning upside down. These are two-person gliders, but parents may ride with younger children (to about age ten) or two middling-sized kids can share a seat. The view from above is amazing, taking in all of Cape Cod, the Islands, and Boston. **Cape Cod Soaring Adventures** (508-540-8081) offers sight-seeing flights lasting from twenty to forty-five minutes.

Freshwater fishing. The Cape's lakes and ponds offer bass, trout, pickerel, and perch, and sometimes salmon or sunfish. Children under fifteen don't need fishing licenses, but everyone else does; you can get them at the town halls. No license is needed for **surf fishing** or **salt-water fishing** of any kind, which sometimes lands striped bass and bluefish right from the swimming beaches. Older children might want to go out **sport fishing** with the grown-ups on one of the many charter boats that chase tuna, swordfish, bass, and blues from Ocean Street Dock (in Hyannis), Rock Harbor (in Orleans), and MacMillan Wharf (in Provincetown).

Crabbing. Always a favorite among young children. Any child with a hand line and a chicken bone can manage from the little bridges over the Herring River, Bass River, and other tidal rivers on the south shore.

Bicycling. The **Cape Cod Rail Trail** offers 25 miles of paths from South Dennis to Wellfleet. The Rail Trail is level enough for training wheels and tricycles, and the landscape is pure Cape Cod: scrubby oaks and kettle ponds, beach roses and salt marsh, cranberry bogs and pitch pine forests. Road crossings are well marked for both bicyclists and motorists. There are many access points along the trail; the Eastham trailhead, near the Salt Pond Visitors Center in the Cape Cod National Seashore, is a popular starting point, as is **Nickerson State Park,** in Brewster, which has 8 miles of trails of its own. From the park, older children can head to **Punkhorn Parklands,** an 800-acre tract of Brewster conservation land off Run Hill Road, where there's good **mountain biking.**

On the Inner Cape, the best trails are the **Shining Sea Bikeway,** which runs 3.5 miles from Falmouth to the busy harbor at Woods Hole, and the two **Cape Cod Canal service roads.** The latter trails are great stop-and-start paths, just right for younger riders who can pause to watch the freighters and tugboats and yachts as they make their way through the canal. The service roads run about 7 miles each; there are clearly marked access roads on both sides of the canal.

Museums and Attractions

Although the Cape isn't teeming with museums with kid appeal, there are a number of kid-friendly attractions. The museums are generally low-key and best for rainy days or as part of a general sight-seeing tour.

The breaching of a whale off Cape Cod will thrill family members of all ages.

Bourne. Trading Post Museum, Aptucxet Road; (508) 759-9487. If you're near the Bourne Bridge, stop by the Pilgrim trading post, one of the first in North America. Its claim to fame: It was reconstructed in 1930 on the original site with original materials. President Grover Cleveland's private railroad is also on the premises, as are a windmill, herb gardens, and picnic area.

Brewster. Located mid-Cape on the bay side, Brewster has charming nineteenth-century homes built by sea captains, antiques shops, art galleries, a summer day camp for ages seven to seventeen (508-896-3451), and the following attractions:

Bassett Wild Animal Farm, Tubman Road; (508) 896-3224. Take the kids on hayrides and pony rides, and see a variety of birds and wildlife in natural surroundings. There's a picnic area, too. **Cape Cod Museum of Natural History,** Route 6A; (508) 896-3867. The museum has two floors of indoor exhibits and special family programs. **New England Fire and History Museum,** Route 6A; (508) 896-5711. This large collection of antique fire-fighting equipment and memorabilia includes eye-catching exhibits: a Victorian apothecary shop, a blacksmith shop, and an interesting diorama of the Great Chicago Fire of 1871. The museum is open late May through Columbus Day. **Stoney Brook Mill,** Stoney Brook Road, grinds corn Thursday, Friday, and Saturday afternoons during July and August. Young kids will be intrigued, and they should like the small museum upstairs.

Whale-watching and Scenic Cruises

Whale-watching is a favorite family adventure on Cape Cod from April through October, when humpbacks, right whales, minke whales, and finback whales feed in the plankton-rich Stellwagen Bank, 4 miles off Provincetown.

A whale watch can be a thrilling experience for children when they see whales arcing out of the water or swimming under the boat. A marine naturalist accompanies every Cape Cod whale watch, so the trips are educational, too. But before you go, size up your children and their limits. Sunburn, seasickness, crankiness in crowds, or a bad case of the fidgets can swamp the fun pretty quickly, and most Cape Cod whalewatching trips last about three and a half hours. Children under eight may be happier ashore.

Most whale-watching excursions leave from **MacMillan Wharf,** in Provincetown; *Dolphin Fleet* (800–826-9300),

the *Portuguese Princess* (800–442-3188), and *Provincetown Whale Watch, Inc. (Ranger V)* (800–992-9333) are all good operators. At **mid-Cape,** try *Hyannis Whale Watcher* (800–287-0374), which leaves from Barnstable Harbor.

Many **scenic cruises** are offered in Cape Cod Bay, the Cape Cod Canal, Nantucket Sound, Bass River, Pleasant Bay, and out of the south shore harbors. **Sunset cruises** are especially nice for families after a long day of running around, **catamaran trips** are popular during the day, when the boats can be moored for swimming and snorkeling, and **schooner trips** appeal to older children who can lend a hand with the sails. For more information check the brochures at the visitor centers or inquire at the docks in Falmouth, Hyannis, South Yarmouth, Chatham, Wellfleet, and Provincetown.

Chatham. **The Railroad Museum,** Depot Road (no phone) in a restored 1887 depot features thousands of train models, old railroad equipment, and a 1910 New York Central caboose that visitors can walk through. Allow time for the **Veterans Field Playground** across the street, one of the best on the Cape.

Falmouth. This picturesque town on Route 28 on the Cape's southwestern tip has the **Cape Cod's Children's Museum,** Falmouth Mall (508-457-4667). Exhibits include a wooden train to climb on, two whisper dishes, a star show in summer, a puppet stage, a room that catches your shadow, and an exhibit that raises a hot air balloon with the heat from a toaster. The mall has a movie theater and many, many shops where older children and teenagers can entertain themselves separately.

Hyannis. Yes, it's congested and suburbanized, but it's also a transportation and shopping hub and boasts **Cape Cod Potato Chips,** Breed's Hill Road in Independence Park; (508) 775-7253. This probably will make a bigger impression on your kids than most museums. On weekdays, watch the hand-cooking process that results in these tasty tidbits. Then visit the gift store to sample some chips and, of course, buy a bag or two.

Mashpee. Cape Cod is where the Pilgrims first encountered the **Wampanoag Indians**, with whom they worked out a careful sharing of the land. That story and many of its Native American characters (Squanto, the corn giver, for instance, and Massasoit, the great sachem), are familiar to all children old enough to have fumbled through a Thanksgiving play.

The **Mashpee Wampanoag Indian Museum,** Route 130, (508-477-1536), is a small museum staffed by present-day Wampanoag, many of whom live in this part of the Cape. The most compelling exhibits, in the front room, quietly chronicle the Puritans' resolute colonization of Cape Cod's native peoples. These exhibits—which include an Indian-language Bible, Europeanized clothing, and an astonishing painting of an Indian missionary at work—probably won't interest younger children although they make a very moving cautionary tale for grown-ups.

In the back room a series of old-fashioned, rather decrepit exhibits and dioramas hold younger children's attention. The moth-eaten stuffed squirrel gets petted by every child under ten, and the arrowhead case is well smudged by little hand- and noseprints.

Adjacent to the museum parking lot is a pretty, willow-lined stream with a **fish ladder,** where children can watch the herring run in spring and early summer. It's a nice place for a **picnic.**

Summer visitors can get a rousing glimpse of contemporary Native American life at the **Wampanoag Pow wow,** held every year around the Fourth of July in Mashpee. A powwow is an amazing spectacle for anyone who attends one, but children especially appreciate the exhibition dancing performed by Native Americans in full regalia—deerskins, feathered headdresses, turtle-claw armbands, and shimmering jingle dresses. Food vendors offer everything from fry bread to buffalo chili and sassafras tea, while craftspeople hawk mostly jewelry. There is also an excellent **clambake.** For information, call the Mashpee Chamber of Commerce (508-477-0792).

Provincetown. "P-town," the tip of the Lower Cape, has beautiful beaches, sand dunes, shops, and galleries. This colorful artistic colony also is the site of the first Pilgrim landing and boasts the Cape's most visited attraction: **Pilgrim Monument and Provincetown Museum,** off SR 6 on High Pole Hill; (508) 487-1310. If your kids are energetic, climb the stairs and ramps to the top of the 252-foot tower honoring the Pilgrims, which provides splendid views of the town and harbor. You won't be disappointed by the museum, which contains lots of intriguing things: *Mayflower* memorabilia, ship models, items taken from nearby shipwrecks, old toys, scrimshaw, figureheads, and an old fire engine made by an apprentice of Paul Revere.

Sandwich. Located on the bay in the Upper Cape, charming Sandwich, the oldest town on the Cape, was the site of one of the country's largest glass factories during the nineteenth century. **The Sandwich Glass Museum** at 129 Main Street (508-888-0251) displays this beautiful vintage glass, but most kids will be ready to bolt in under five minutes. (Instead, they may prefer seeing the glassblowing demonstrations at **Pairpont Crystal** near the Sagamore Bridge; 508-888-2344 or 800-899-0953.)

One attraction that will appeal: **Heritage Plantation,** Grove and Pine Streets (508-888-1222). Pack a lunch (there are picnic grounds, plus a windmill, outside) and plan to spend some time here. Take a ride on the restored 1912 carousel then see the antique and classic cars in the Round Stone Barn. The antique miniatures at the military museum are appealing. There's also an art museum, although the large Currier & Ives exhibit will leave most kids bored. The seventy-six acres of trails and gardens offer a nice respite. If you came foodless, The Dan'l Webster Inn in town serves three meals.

Another Sandwich attraction: **Yesteryears Doll Museum,** at the corner of Main and River Streets (508-888-1711). If there's a doll lover in the family, stop to see the lovely vintage dolls, dollhouses, and miniatures. In East Sandwich don't miss **Green Briar Nature Center,** 1 Discovery Road (508-888-6870). Besides the natural history exhibits inside, there are two reasons to stop at the center: the lovely fifty-seven-acre Briar Patch Conservation Area's nature trails and the Green Briar Jam Kitchen, where you can tour an old-fashioned kitchen to see jams, jellies, and preserves made in the traditional way. In the summer the demonstrators use an unusual sun-cooking method. Call for days when the kitchen is in operation.

West Yarmouth. ZooQuarium, Route 28, West Yarmouth (508-775-8883), features glass tanks housing specimens of mostly local fish and pond life. Outdoors, there are live animal demonstrations and an unshaded zoo area that features a couple of porcupines, sheep and llamas, two pigs, a crow and an owl, deer, miniature horses, and the like. The main attraction is the **sea lion show** (held five times daily in summer, four times daily in the off-season), but it's mostly unimpressive, with an elderly, blind harbor seal who does little but wolf down fish and a California sea lion who barks and balances a ball on her nose. The closing act is cute; several children from the audience get wet, fishy kisses from the sea lion. Far more interesting is the extensive **shell collection** in the main building, but its typewritten labels are so old and faded they can scarcely be read.

Woods Hole. The **National Marine Fisheries Aquarium**, 166 Water Street, (508-548-7684), is much more worthwhile and entertaining. Woods Hole is home to some of the finest marine biological research in the United States (both the Woods Hole Oceanographic Institution and the Marine Biological Laboratory are here), and this aquarium, run by a subagency of the U.S. Department of Commerce, is a hands-on, science-is-amazing kind of place. Children squeal over the exhibit tanks, which contain some of the ugliest fish you've ever seen: odd, mucky-looking individuals with horns and fins, a toothed species, and one with glittering blue eyes. Upstairs, there is a group of **touch tanks** where youngsters may handle lobsters, sea stars, horseshoe crabs, whelks, and other species—even hauling them out of the tanks to examine them under a big, table-mounted magnifying glass.

Several ventures-for-hire emphasizing marine education also operate out of Woods Hole. Among them is the very good "discovery cruise" sponsored by **OceanQuest** (800-37-OCEAN) aboard the *Tiger Shark,* a 60-foot **oceanographic research vessel** docked just below Water Street. (This is also the operator chosen by the Cape Cod Children's Museum for its marine biology trips.) Young "oceanographers for the day" get experience hauling plankton nets, operating a bottom grab, reading a hydrometer, and investigating sea life under microscopes during the ninety-minute cruise.

Shopping

You'll find antiques shops, galleries, and country stores throughout the Cape. If you need some basics, stop at Falmouth Mall, Route 28, open seven days. It has major stores, such as Bradlees, specialty shops, and a cinema. Bargain shop at Cape Cod Factory Outlet Mall, off exit 1, Route 6, Sagamore. Kids' stores include Toy Liquidators, Carter's Childrenswear, OshKosh B'Gosh, and Bugle Boy.

Performing Arts

The **Harwich Junior Theatre,** Division Street, West Harwich (508-432-2002), has been putting kids on stage (with adults in the grown-up roles) since 1952. The plays are meant for children, and are drawn from fairy tales, fables, Maurice Sendak stories, and similar sources. The audience gets to hiss at the bad guys and sing songs now and then; a jester warns about scary parts. The company also offers many **summer theater classes** in such things as creative movement, musical theater, stagecraft, and playwriting. Visitors may apply.

Imagine!, (508-362-6333) shares a playhouse with the Barnstable Comedy Club, Route 6A, Barnstable Village. Children act and crew in sixteen summer performances of such plays as *Alice in Wonderland* and *The Velveteen Rabbit.* Imagine! also has summer classes.

The Mimsy Puppets (508-432-1279), a longtime Cape Cod puppet troupe in the Dennis and Brewster area, brings a collection of plush puppets performing nursery stories. It's the kind of performance that typically ends with a bunny hop. Farther down Cape, the **Wellfleet Periwinkle Players** (508-349-0330), sponsored by the Wellfleet Recreation Division, put on very ragged but charming performances in an elementary school gym.

Several professional adult theaters, such as the **Cape Cod Melody Tent,** Hyannis (508-775-9100), and the venerable **Cape Playhouse,** Dennis (508-385-3838), also stage children's productions in summer, as does the **Cape Rep Outdoor Theater** (508-896-1888), which has its stage in a pine and oak grove off Route 6A in Brewster, an especially nice venue for families.

SPECIAL EVENTS

Check with the Cape Cod Chamber of Commerce for details on these annual fairs and festivals and obtain the calendar of events.

April. Brewster in Bloom, daffodil festival.

July. Barnstable County Fair, with rides, exhibits, and food.

September. Harwich Cranberry Festival, weeklong event with food tastings, band concerts, parade, craft show and sale, and more.

Thanksgiving through New Year's Eve. Christmas on Cape Cod, series of events including choirs, orchestras, caroling on the green, tree lightings, and more.

WHERE TO STAY

Make reservations early. If you're stuck, the information booths located throughout the Cape can also help with accommodations. The following, all on the Upper Cape, represent the variety of accommodations available for families.

The Breakers, 61 Chase Avenue, Dennisport, (508–398–6905), has minisuites and two-bedroom two-bath efficiencies. The heated pool faces the ocean, and there's a private beach. Lower rates midweek.

Cranberry Cottages, 785 State Highway, Eastham (508–255–0602 or 800–292–6331), offer a friendly family atmosphere with lots of things to do in the nearby area, including miniature golf, whale-watching, and beach-combing. The two-bedroom housekeeping cottages offer cable TV, fully equipped kitchenettes, and pull-out sofa beds. The smaller one-bedroom cottages don't have housekeeping and have a three-person maximum.

Kalmar Village, Route 6A, North Truro (508–487–0585), is a good choice if you want to get to the surf without having to drive there—there's a 400-foot private beach and a large outdoor pool with a slide. Most of the lodgings are cottages (with kitchenettes, full housekeeping, and up to three beds), but there are also some efficiency units and motel rooms for smaller families. Another plus is the fact that the cottages are right along Route 6A, the perfect place for a scenic Cape drive.

Lighthouse Inn, West Dennis (508–398–2244), has cottages on seven oceanfront acres, a restaurant, plus tennis, pool, miniature golf, a private beach, and supervised activities for ages two and up in July and August.

New Seabury Resort and Conference Center, (508–477–9111 or 800–999–9033), midway between Falmouth and Hyannis, features 160 villas spread out over 2,000 oceanfront acres, with pool, golf, and tennis. A summer program keeps ages four and up busy, and there's a center for teens.

WHERE TO EAT

What would a visit to Cape Cod be without a lobster dinner? Consult *The Cape Cod Times,* the local daily paper, for restaurant listings. On the Lower Cape the self-service **Bayside Lobster Hutt,** Commercial Street, Wellfleet Center, is in an old oyster shack and offers inexpensive, fresh Cape seafood. Upper Cape locals love **Joe Mac's,** Taunton Avenue, Dennis. It's not fancy, but families feel at home (there's a game room for kids), and the menu includes everything from pizza to lobsters. **Hearth 'n Kettle Family Restaurant** chain serves affordable, traditional food at locations in Centerville, Orleans, South Yarmouth, Hyannis, and Falmouth. These restaurants are accessible for patrons in wheelchairs.

Box Lunch of Cape Cod, Route 6, North Eastham, and six other locations (508–255–0799), makes picnicking easy with a big selection of "roll-wiches," yummy fillings rolled up tight in soft, flat pita bread. Ingredients range from avocado and sprouts to roast beef and cheese. The "kid-wiches," including "Piglet" (ham and cheese) and "Boring" (three melted cheeses), are ample and wonderfully tidy in their pita wrappers; chips and drinks round out the meal. Box Lunch now has six stores on the Cape (the other stores are in Falmouth, Hyannis, South Dennis, Brewster, East Orleans, and Provincetown). Most locations have a separate breakfast menu, and some sell newspapers, beach toys, and other sundries.

The Lobster Claw, Route 6A (next door to the fish market), Orleans (508-255-1800), has won plenty of "Best Family Restaurant" awards. In midsummer it is a very busy place, serving more than 700 customers a day. The long wait for a table passes pleasantly in the upstairs Surfboat Lounge, which has a TV. Downstairs, a gift shop draws a crowd of young mischief makers with squeaky lobster toys and other ridiculous souvenirs. The decor runs to fishing nets, and the food is best when it's beachy. The steamers are abundant and sweet and the onion rings chewy. There's a respectable chowder, but skip the beef, which too often arrives overcooked and oddly damp.

Serena's, 545 Route 6 (about a mile past the Wellfleet Drive-In), South Wellfleet (508-349-9370), is a grown-up restaurant that puts up nicely with children, and the kid touches are truly inspired. Two basketball hoops in the parking lot draw a crowd of show-offs, both young and old. Young children get a basket of crayons and *Where's Waldo* books to pass the time at the table, and a slice of watermelon comes in place of salad with the kids' meals. Seafood can be had both plain and fancy—everything from baked scrod and steamed lobster to seafood fra diavolo. There are some meat dishes, mostly parmigiana, and a selection of pasta dishes with tasty and inventive sauces, including a good one that pairs artichokes and tomatoes, but the pasta itself is undistinguished. The decor is blessedly grown-up, with paneled walls, pitchers full of wildflowers, and lighting low enough to hide the watermelon seeds strewn about the table.

Check out the **Sundae School Ice Cream Parlor,** 210 Main Street, East Orleans (508-255-5473); also in Dennisport. With six Ben & Jerry's on Cape Cod, it would seen unnecessary to list another ice cream parlor, but the Sundae School makes ice cream and frozen yogurt so rich and tasty that it draws crowds.

The 1799 **Barnstable Tavern & Grille,** Route 6A in Barnstable Village, across from the courthouse (508-362-2355), is more adaptable than most historic eateries to different levels of family chaos. Yes, there are flowers on the tables and the TV in the bar is likely to be tuned to an equestrian event, but real kids can eat hot dogs here, too. Families with antsy individuals should head outdoors to the streetside cafe, which serves from the same menu. The food is good tavern fare; the big draw is the Black Angus steaks. This is a good place to eat supper before seeing a play at the Imagine! children's theater, which is right across the street.

The Flume, Lake Avenue, off Route 130, Mashpee (508-477-1456), is run by Wampanoag Indians; more important, however, is the terrific food. Located in the woods near the Mashpee Wampanoag Indian Museum, the restaurant displays Native American beadwork and artifacts, along with historical photographs of local families. The menu is mostly homey; it includes pot roast, chicken pie, a lot of local seafood, and a Portuguese dish of beans, rice, and sausage. Children can order smaller portions of any entree or select from the appetizer menu.

Salty's Diner, 540 Main Street (Route 28), West Yarmouth (508-790-3132), is a campy, sand-on-the-floor kind of places. The service is T-shirted and cheerful, and the astonishing collection of mounted fish, seashells, buoys, folk art, neon signs, and other things will keep the kids well occupied until the food comes. Hard-core diner fans can get meat loaf, liver and onions, and other specials, but this diner cares about seafood. The chowder is creamy and bacony, the swordfish is tasty, and even the fried fish is sweet. The bad news is that the diner is very stuffy on hot nights, but you can take your meal out on the patio, where the seating is family-style. "Awesome!" reads a child-written entry in the guest book. *Note:* Salty's does a brisk business at the bar, which some parents may frown on, but designated drivers drink their nonalcoholic beverages on the house.

SIDE TRIPS

American history comes alive in Plymouth, about halfway between the Cape and Boston. **Plimouth Plantation,** a 1627 village, is an interesting place where costumed residents reenact daily life in New Plymouth. Adjoining the village is **Hobbamock's Homesite,** which features the Wampanoag Indians of southeastern New England and their culture. Step aboard *Mayflower II,* a reproduction of the ship that brought the Pilgrims to Plymouth in 1620. For more information call (508) 746-1622. Stop by to see **Plymouth Rock,** Water Street (which, with its portico protection is not very imposing). Another day, take a passenger ferry to explore the splendid beaches and picturesque towns of **Martha's Vineyard,** only forty-five minutes from Woods Hole. (See Getting Around.)

FOR MORE INFORMATION

The main office of the Cape Cod Chamber of Commerce, exit 6 off Route 6, Hyannis 02601 (508-362-3225), has helpful brochures including a free *Kids on the Cape* booklet. In addition to the main location, other offices are located at exit 5 off Route 3 South approaching the Sagamore Bridge and Route 25 East on the approach to the Bourne Bridge.

For a complete Massachusetts vacation kit, which includes Cape Cod, call the Massachusetts Office of Travel and Tourism at (617) 727-3201 or

(800) 447-MASS, or visit their Web site at www.mass-vacation.com. Great Dates in the Bay State is a recorded list of statewide events, updated biweekly; call (800) 227-MASS (Northeast only).

Emergency Numbers

Ambulance, fire, and police: 911

Hospitals: Cape Cod Hospital, 27 Park Street, Hyannis, well marked from all exits; (508) 771-1800. A smaller facility is Falmouth Hospital, 100 TerHeun Drive, Falmouth; (508) 457-3524. The twenty-four-hour emergency rooms at these two hospitals are jammed in the summer. If you have a lesser emergency, you may get faster service at one of the many walk-in clinics scattered throughout the Cape that are listed in the phone directory. Most keep standard office hours.

Poison Control: (800) 682-9211 from the Cape

Most of the CVS pharmacies located on Cape Cod are open twenty-four hours daily in summer.

NEW BRUNSWICK

N ew Brunswick, an Atlantic province, shares a common border with Maine, but once you enter the area you know you're not in New England anymore. Of the approximately 34,000 Loyalists who fled America for Nova Scotia at the end of the revolution, more than 14,000 settled in present-day New Brunswick. This Loyalist fervor is alive and well in some quarters, although American tourists are graciously welcomed (bygones are indeed bygones). There's a French influence as well in the eastern and northern sections, where descendants of the Acadians, or French settlers, still reside.

New Brunswick is a beautiful province, bordered on the east by the Gulf of St. Lawrence and on the south by the Bay of Fundy. It offers rocky coasts, lush green countryside, and several interesting cities. The Fundy Coast and the Saint John River Valley are of special interest because of their proximity to the United States and their many offerings for families. If you have time to explore more, however, try to sample all of New Brunswick's delightfully diverse districts.

GETTING THERE

The main commercial airports, in Fredericton, Moncton, and Saint John, are served by major Canadian airlines and Northwest Airlines, which operates to and from Boston.

VIA Rail serves much of this area. For information and reservations, call (800) 561-3952.

SMT Eastern Limited is a regional bus service that has links to bus routes in other provinces and in the United States. Call (506) 648-3500.

Coastal Transport Limited ferry to Grand Manan leaves from Blacks Harbour, just off Route 1. Call (506) 642-0520. Marine Atlantic's ferry to Digby, Nova Scotia, leaves from Saint John. For general information, call (506) 636-3606; for central reservations, call (800) 341-7981.

New Brunswick can be reached from Maine via I-95, which turns into the Trans-Canada Highway, Route 1, in New Brunswick.

New Brunswick

AT A GLANCE

▶ Explore rocky coasts, lush countryside, and an eclectic cultural mix

▶ Drive the Fundy coast and the River Valley

▶ See the famous reversing falls

▶ Visit a 300-acre historical Loyalist community at King's Landing Historical Settlement

▶ Information Centres, (506) 460-2191 and 460-2129; www.gov.nb.ca/tourism

GETTING AROUND

Public buses are available in the larger cities. Fredericton issues tourist parking passes for all visitors, permitting free parking at all municipal parking meters and parking lots for three days. Obtain them from the Information Centre at City Hall or during the summer at the Legislative Assembly and the highway information center.

WHAT TO SEE AND DO

Fundy Coastal Drive

This beautiful stretch of coast boasts the highest tides in the world, due to the shape and dimensions of the bay. Approximately every twelve hours and thirty minutes, one hundred billion tons of ocean pour in from the open Atlantic, a quiet but steady swirl. *Note:* Bay waters are cool, so be prepared for a brisk dip. East of Moncton the waters are warmer.

If you're entering the area from Maine, the coastal city of **St. Stephen** will be your first stop. Downtown traffic is usually bumper to bumper, but stop at the Information Center for maps, literature, and advice. Next, head to the **Ganong Chocolatier Shop,** 73 Milltown Boulevard (506-465-5611). There you can watch chocolate-dipping demonstrations and see the world's tallest jelly bean display. The world's first candy bar was supposedly created at the Ganong candy factory in 1910. You can tour the factory, on the outskirts of town, during the annual Chocolate Festival in August. Nearby, Oak Bay is one of the province's fourteen supervised beaches.

The sea caves at St. Martin's, a short drive from New Brunswick, are great places to explore.

Your next stop, **St. Andrews-by-the-Sea,** is where you will want to stay for a while. At the tourist information center on the way into town, get maps and walking-tour brochures. Many of the gracious homes date to the 1880s, and some to the 1700s. Some Loyalist settlers who came here during the American Revolution dismantled their homes and brought them over in barges to reassemble here. In this charming town on the shores of Passamaquoddy Bay, whale-watching tours leave from the town wharf. Some additional local sights your family will like follow.

Atlantic Salmon Information Center, Route 127 (506–529–3000). True, it doesn't sound fascinating, but you'll be surprised how much you and the kids will learn. Walk along the nature trail by the stream that shows the fish in their natural environment. A coloring book detailing the salmon's life cycle is for sale.

Huntsman Marine Science Centre and Aquarium, Brandy Cove (506–529–1202). This aquarium is a must-see, with a Please Touch Tank, harbor seals, and interpretive displays.

Nearby, high over the bay in a lovely setting, sits the historic **Blockhouse,** once used to keep watch in case of invasion by sea. You can go inside to have a look around; a guide will answer questions.

Heading east, you arrive at **Saint John,** on the Bay of Fundy at the mouth of the Saint John River. This is Canada's oldest city and New Brunswick's largest. If you're driving here in the morning, watch out for the thick fog that is a trademark of this area. Saint John (not to be confused with Saint John's, Newfoundland) is full of surprises and family pleasures. An industrial city and international seaport, Saint John has undergone major restoration in recent years. Today the **Market Square Waterfront** complex, with its hundred-year-old brick facade, is a charming area of shops, boutiques, and restaurants. Historic walking tours are led by costumed guides daily in July and August. Tours leave from Barbour's General Store, Market Slip, restored and stocked with goods from the years 1840 to 1940.

Another family-friendly highlight is **Saint John City Market,** 47 Charlotte Street; it is believed to be the oldest building of its kind in use in Canada. Stop at a cafe or buy snacks of fresh cheese, baked goods, produce, maple syrup, and other goodies. Often indigenous people sell handwoven baskets here.

Let your kids try dulse, the local sea-vegetable specialty gathered from rocks along the Bay of Fundy and dried in the sun. While an acquired taste, the locals love it, and some prefer it to popcorn. The Market is closed Sundays.

Rockwood Park, in the middle of the city, covers 2,200 acres, so plan to spend some time here. The freshwater lakes offer supervised swimming, canoeing, and paddle boating. Visit the zoo and children's petting farm, enjoy the hiking and jogging trails, and try the bumper boats and miniature golf. The park also has camping and trailer facilities.

Canada Games Aquatic Centre, 50 Union Street (506-658-4715), just across from Market Square, is a find. This modern facility features two huge warm-water, shallow leisure pools, separated by an island with a double looping water slide. There's also a competition pool and two exercise rooms. Visitors pay a small fee.

Aitken Bicentennial Exhibition Center (ABEC), 20 Hazen Avenue (506-633-4870), is a colorful and lively arts and sciences museum. It features ScienceScape, a permanent children's gallery.

Fort Howe Lookout, Main Street (North End), is a blockhouse that formerly protected the harbor. Although you can't go inside, the grounds offer a great view of the city and port.

Reversing Falls

Reversing Falls is a natural phenomenon occurring where the Saint John River empties into the Bay of Fundy. The falls are really below the water: Explain this to the kids first, or else they might be disappointed. During low tide, tidal waters drop 14.5 feet below river levels, causing the full force of the 450-mile river to crash through a narrow gorge into the harbor. As the tides rise in the bay, the river waters gradually calm and actually reverse in direction as the bay waters rise above them. To get the most out of this sight, try to observe the falls twice on the same day: at or near high and low tides. For a short interpretive film explaining, but not actually showing, the phenomenon, go to the rooftop theater at the Reversing Falls Tourist Information Center (506-658-2937). It's at the west end of the Route 100 bridge that crosses the river.

Loyalist Settlement at King's Landing

Don't miss **King's Landing Historical Settlement,** 23 miles west of Fredericton, off the Trans-Canada Highway (Route 2) at exit 259 (506–363–4999 or 800–561–0123). A visit to this nearly 300-acre re-created Loyalist settlement circa 1790–1870 will be a high point of your family's stay in the area. The setting, high above the Saint John River, is stunning: green and lush, with winding dirt roads, open expanses of farmland, and woods. You can—and should—hitch a ride aboard a horse-drawn wagon: There's much to cover here and lots of walking. The village buildings, which were brought from nearby, include houses varying from plain and simple to utterly grand, a church, a one-room schoolhouse, a general store, a tavern and inn, a blacksmith shop, and a bakery. The smell of baking, the sights of men tilling the fields and women weaving, the sounds of children playing are all part of this wonderful experience. Costumed interpreters include children age nine and older who take part in a five-day live-in **Visiting Cousins** program, which transforms them into children of the 1800s. After a visit your kids may want to come back and participate. Special theme weekends, such as the Scottish and Harvest festivals and the agricultural fair, add zest to this well-done settlement. There's a self-service restaurant as well as the full-service King's Head Inn.

River Valley Scenic Drive

Northwest of Saint John is **Fredericton,** the provincial capital. Called the "City of Stately Elms," it is situated along the picturesque Saint John River. Fredericton is small, very walkable, and a pleasant place to spend some time before or after you visit the Fundy Coast. At one time an important military center, much of its historic past remains. The *Fredericton Guide* has a suggested walking tour, and some sites may pique your kids' interest. Your best bet: Take the walking tours led by historically costumed guides who offer dramatic commentary. Call City Hall information at (506) 460-2129.

A riverfront pathway ideal for strolling stretches along the green, starting at the Sheraton Inn and extending to the Princess Margaret Bridge. Stop in at the **Fredericton Lighthouse Museum.** As you walk to the top level, a variety of interactive exhibits describe the history of the region. The view is lovely on a clear day. Call (506) 459-2515 for information.

Fredericton has lots of inviting, green spaces, including **Odell Park,** where landscaped paths lead to geese, ducks, and deer, and a lovely arboretum. **The Mactaquac Provincial Park,** just outside town on Route 105, is the largest recreation park in the province, with more than 1,400 acres of open land and forest. The two supervised beaches are a draw for families, as are the self-guided nature trails, an eighteen-hole golf course, camping facilities, and a restaurant. In winter the park is popular for its skating, sledding, snowmobiling, cross-country skiing, and horse-drawn sleigh rides. Call (506) 363-4747 or 363-4925 for information.

Your kids will enjoy the **Changing of the Guard,** which takes place July and August in Officers' Square and at City Hall, Tuesday through Saturday. The sentry changes every hour on the hour. The guard was formed in 1793. Call City Hall information for details. **The Guard House,** Carleton Street, appears as it was in 1866, when the Fifteenth Regiment was in residence. In summer guards wearing the regiment's red-coated uniforms give tours.

The Legislative Assembly Building, Queen Street, is very British and quite majestic. Even young kids will say "wow!" when they see the throne (speaker's chair), set on a dais in the Assembly Chamber under a canopy bearing a carved royal coat of arms. You can visit the chamber while the legislature is in session, although chances are your kids will appreciate it more when it's empty. Call (506) 453-2527 for information.

On Saturday mornings visit the **Boyce Farmers Market** (506-451-1815), just behind the Old York County Jail, between Regent and Saint John Streets. Farmers and their wares, artisans, and craftspeople make this a colorful place to linger, browse, and buy.

For a change of pace visit the nearby **Woolastook Park** (506-363-5410), 15 miles west of Fredericton on Route 2, the Trans-Canada Highway. Your kids will like the giant water slides, wading pool, beach, minigolf, and nature trails.

Performing Arts

Fredericton Outdoor Summer Theater, downtown on the lawn of Officers' Square, features theater-in-the-square seven days a week from July 1 to September 6. The Square is also the setting for the July and August Summer Music Concerts, held weekly at 7:30 P.M. Call (506) 461-2191 for information on both programs. In Saint John, the **Classical Music Summer Sounds Concerts** at Centenary Queen Square, United Church, Princess Street, are held Tuesdays at 8:00 P.M. Call (506) 634-8123. The city also has free **Outdoor Concerts,** mid-June to late July, at King's Square, featuring a variety of performers; (506) 658-2893.

Shopping

New Brunswick is well known for its crafts—from folk art to dolls to pottery and metal. The Department of Economic Development and Tourism publishes a *New Brunswick Craft Directory* that lists studios, boutiques, and outlets. Fredericton, with the highest concentration of craftspeople, is known as the pewter-smithing capital of Canada.

SPECIAL EVENTS

Fairs and Festivals

Contact the individual tourist associations for information on the following festivities.

Late June–early July. Festival International de la Francophonie offers music, art, dances, literature, and food indigenous to the francophone culture; (506) 395-9746.

The Salmon Festival, in conjunction with Canada Day celebrations, features children's activities, picnics, a circus, giant bingo, a beer garden, and, of course, a salmon dinner; (506) 789-2808.

July. Loyalist City Festival reenacts the 1783 Loyalist Landing. There is an authentic eighteenth-century military encampment, pageants, parades, and fireworks; (506) 634-8123.

August. Celebrate Acadian culture at the Festival Acadien with a variety of activities such as concerts, exhibitions, and the Blessing of the Fleet; (506) 726-2688.

Chocolate Festival with pudding-eating contests, candy treasure hunts, a cookie-decorating contest, and chocolate Olympic games; (506) 465-5616.

September. Atlantic Balloon Festival, hot-air balloon rides, helicopter rides, and parachute demonstrations.

Harvest Jazz and Blues Festival; (506) 455-4523 or (888) 622-5837

WHERE TO STAY

New Brunswick has a free, in-province reservation system, Dial-A-Nite, available at provincial tourist information centers (shown at major entry points on the New Brunswick Highway map). The system enables travelers to make advance reservations directly with hotels, motels, inns, outfitters, farm vacations, and many privately owned campgrounds. Here are some picks for families.

Fredericton

Lord Beaverbrook Hotel, 659 Queen Street (506-455-3371), is conveniently located. It has been here for years and is still perfectly comfortable. There's a nice family restaurant, and the kids will like the indoor pool.

Sheraton Inn Fredericton, 225 Woodstock Road (506-457-7000 or 800-325-3535), is the city's newest. Located on the banks of the Saint John River, the hotel has 223 rooms, with fourteen suites. Indoor and outdoor pools, tennis courts, a family restaurant, and free parking are some of the offerings.

Near King's Landing, in Prince William, the **Chickadee Lodge** (506-363-2759), is a cozy log bed and breakfast by the river, set back from the Trans-Canada Highway. You have to share a bath, but the rooms are clean and comfortable. This is a good place to stay if you're en route or spending the day at King's Landing: otherwise, you're basically in the middle of nowhere.

The Carriage House Inn, 230 University Avenue (506-452-9924 or 800-267-6068), a three-story Victorian home in downtown Fredericton, welcomes children even though it is decorated with antiques.

St. Andrews-by-the-Sea

The Algonquin, 184 Adolphus (506-529-8823 or 800-441-1414), is a large and luxurious Canadian Pacific resort with a pool, golf, tennis, biking, and more. In July and August there's a supervised program for a fee for ages five to twelve from 10:00 A.M. to 4:00 P.M.

The A. Hiram Walker Estate Heritage Inn, (506-529-4210), built in the grand style of 1912, has been restored to its original elegance. The former home of the Hiram Walker distillery family is situated on eleven acres in the heart of town. Friendly, efficient service, combined with elegant grandeur, will make your visit truly memorable. All rooms have private baths.

Saint John

Delta Brunswick, 39 King Street (506-648-1981 or 800-268-1133), has a great downtown location, indoor pool, and family restaurant with a kid's menu. An unsupervised Children's Creative Centre is open from 6:00 A.M. to 11:00 P.M. with games, movies, and toys.

Shadow Lawn Inn, 3180 Rothesay Road (506-847-7539), is located in the quaint town of Rothesay, 13 kilometers from Saint John and ten minutes from the airport. This understated elegant Victorian inn offers nine luxurious rooms, beautifully furnished with antiques; private baths.

WHERE TO EAT

In Fredericton stop by the Tourist Information Centres to look through the menu binders. In-the-know locals in Saint John congregate at **Reggie's Restaurant,** 26 Germain Street (506–657–6270), famous for its bagels and smoked meat from Montréal , hearty breakfasts, and inexpensive lunches that include clam and fish chowders, lobster rolls, and bagel burgers. Indeed, lobster is everywhere: In summer even McDonald's serves McLobster sandwiches, although this isn't the best way to sample this seafood delight. **Keystone Kelly's,** in Saint John's Market Square Complex (506–634–0616) has a menu to please all, with Italian, Mexican, and Canadian cuisine.

SIDE TRIPS

There's lots to explore east of Saint John. On your way to **Moncton,** detour on Route 111 to **St. Martin's** and explore the long stretch of beach and sea caves (but note the tide schedules first). There are twin covered bridges at the harbor and a tourist information center. As you drive east, you're entering the Southern Shores District, home of **Fundy National Park** (506–887–2000), on Highway 114 between Saint John and Moncton. Hike, fish, boat, beachcomb, or take part in nature interpretation programs. Kiosks in the park have information about special activities for kids ages six to twelve, campfire programs, and entertainment, which takes place at a natural amphitheater. Salt water is piped in from the Bay of Fundy and heated for the swimming pool. Lodging is available in the park's hostel or in nearby Alma.

The lively city of **Moncton** has great family appeal. At **Magnetic Hill,** Mountain Road, just off the Trans-Canada Highway on the northwest outskirts of town, cars appear to coast uphill and water seems to flow upwards. Set your car in neutral and feel it coast uphill backwards; trained staff is there to help you experience this optical illusion.

Magnetic Hill's Wharf Village has enough attractions to encourage families to stay the day: **Mountain Magic Water Park** (open mid-May to mid-October), **Magnetic Hill Zoo,** an outdoor concert center, mini-steam engine rides that transport visitors around the complex, crafts and souvenir shops, and **Wharf Village Family Restaurant.** Across from the complex, the **boardwalk** has go-carts, miniature golf, batting cages, fishing, and other attractions. For information on Magnetic Hill attractions, call (506) 853–3590.

In downtown Moncton's **Bore Park,** just off Main Street, twice daily, the Bay of Fundy tides rise up to 30 feet in little over an hour, creating a wave known as the Tidal Bore. The town of **Dieppe,** which adjoins Moncton's eastern borders, boasts the **Crystal Palace,** 499 rue Paul, a huge indoor amusement park with roller coaster, carousel, playground areas, games of skill, a science center with twenty-nine interactive exhibits, and lots more. The complex also includes four cinemas, a food court, McGinnis Landing Restaurant, and a Best Western hotel (506–858–8584 or 800–528–1234). Call (506) 859-4FUN for Crystal Palace Information. For complete information on the area, contact the City of Moncton, 655 Main Street, Moncton, New Brunswick, EIC IE8 (506–853–3590).

FOR MORE INFORMATION

Fredericton has two Tourist Information Centres: Trans-Canada Highway near Hanwell Road, exit 289 (506–460–2191), and City Hall, corner of Queen and York (506–460–2129). Saint John has several Tourist Information Centres around town. For information contact the Visitor and Convention Bureau, P.O. Box 1971, Saint John E2L 4L1 (506–658–2990). Tourism New Brunswick can be reached at (800) 561–0123; www.gov.nb.ca/tourism. The province maintains Tourist Information Centres at major entry points.

Emergency Numbers

Ambulance, fire, police, and poison control in Fredericton: 911. Police, fire, and rescue squad in Saint John: 911

Poison control in Saint John: (506) 648–7111. Elsewhere, consult the front of the phone book

Twenty-four-hour emergency room in Fredericton: Dr. Everett Chalmers Hospital, Priestman Street; (506) 452–5400

Twenty-four-hour emergency room in Saint John: Saint John Regional Hospital, 400 University Avenue; (506) 648–6000

Shopper's Drug Mart is a provincewide chain of pharmacies open late and on Sundays. In Saint John the store at 57 Landsdowne Place is open from 8:00 A.M. to midnight, seven days a week

JACKSON AND THE MOUNT WASHINGTON REGION

Jackson and the Mount Washington Region—North Conway, Bartlett, and Waterville Valley—in the heart of the White Mountains, offer a splendid array of outdoor family activities. In winter Jackson comes alive; it's a noted cross-country ski area. Gliding through a snowy forest is great fun, and the slow pace, perfect for admiring icicles and looking for deer tracks, allows for easy conversation with your kids. From Jackson it's an easy drive to several downhill ski areas that feature quality children's programs. In fall the woods fill with brilliant reds, oranges, and yellows. In summer the mountains offer miles of trails for horseback riding and hiking, and clear streams for fishing and wading. One cautionary note: Avoid the region during black fly season. While the time period and the intensity of the infestation vary with the weather, generally these insects invade for three weeks from late May to mid-June. For anglers the black flies bring some of the season's best fishing, but most visitors will want to avoid the woods during this time. (Some seasoned campers swear that Avon's Skin So Soft, in addition to its other attributes, repels these pests.) So before booking in late May to mid-June, check with the locals first.

GETTING THERE

Portland Jetport (207-775-5726), about ninety minutes southwest of Jackson in Portland, Maine, is the closest major airport and is serviced by most major domestic airlines. Other airports include Manchester Airport in New Hampshire (603-624-6556), about 100 miles southeast of the region, Boston's Logan Airport (617-561-1800 or 800-23-LOGAN), 140 miles to the south; and the Eastern Slope Regional Airport in Fryeburg, Maine (207-935-2800), about twenty-five minutes from North Conway.

By bus, Concord Trailways (800-639-3317) runs a daily route from Boston, arriving in Jackson about 9:00 P.M.

Jackson and the Mount Washington Region

AT A GLANCE

▶ Explore the 750,000-acre White Mountain National Forest

▶ Ski cross-country and downhill

▶ Hike trails that wind through the mountains

▶ Canoe, kayak, and mountain bike

▶ Ride a train up the highest peak in the continental United States.

▶ Jackson Chamber of Commerce, (603) 383–9356; Mount Washington Valley Visitors Bureau, (603) 356–5701 or (800) 367–3364; Jackson Chamber of Commerce, (603) 383–9356; Mount Washington Valley Visitors Bureau, (603) 356–5701 or (800) 367–3364

For those traveling by car, Jackson and the surrounding towns are easy to locate off I-93. From Boston it's a three-hour drive into Jackson, taking 1-95 to Portsmouth, New Hampshire, then Spaulding Turnpike and Route 16 to North Conway, and into town. Avoid the North Conway traffic, which can be formidable, by taking West Side Road at the first light in Conway to River Road, then taking Route 16 or Route 302.

GETTING AROUND

A car is an absolute necessity, although families should bring their bicycles as well.

WHAT TO SEE AND DO

Because most area attractions use post office boxes and route numbers instead of numbered street addresses, route numbers are listed here. Call the attractions if you need more specific directions.

Mountain Magic

Hiking. With more than 250 trails in the **White Mountain National Forest's** 750,000 acres, there's a great variety of paths for all ability levels. City kids especially appreciate the feathery green and cool woods.

For some easy adventure with younger kids, try these under-one-hour round-trip trails. Wear your bathing suits on the 0.4-mile hike to **Gibbs Falls** on the **Crawford Path,** which starts 13.9 miles west of Silver Springs Country Store and Campground, Bartlett. The road ascends slightly, and then there's a steep descent to the falls. Another easy hike, the Diana's Bath 0.4-mile trail, takes you along a babbling brook to a series of small cascades and shallow pools.

Other popular hikes include the **Crystal Cascade/Tuckerman's Ravine,** Mount Washington. The 0.75-mile round-trip hike starts from the AMC Pinkham Notch Camp, Route 16, north of Jackson, and leads to the waterfall. If you continue on to Tuckerman Ravine, 4.8 miles, three hours round trip, you'll see splendid views of Mount Washington. The trail to **Arethusa Falls,** Crawford Notch State Park, Bartlett (603-374-2272), begins from the parking lot on the west side of Route 302, Crawford Notch. Follow the north bank of Bemis Brook to the falls, the highest in the state, cascading from 200 feet. From the south side of Hurricane Mountain Road, North Conway, take the **Black Cap Mountain** trail for 1.5 miles, one hour round trip. Rewards include an exceptional view of the valley.

For hiking that's a bit more challenging, good for hardy elementary school kids and teens, try this two-hour round-trip hike. **Winniweta Falls** is a 2.1-mile relatively easy hike that begins 3.1 miles north of Jackson's Covered Bridge. The trail crosses Ellis River, meadows blooming with wildflowers, and ascends for the last fifteen minutes as you near the 40-foot falls.

Obtain hiking information from the Mount Washington Valley Visitor Bureau and the Jackson Chamber of Commerce (see For More Information). The Silver Springs Country Store and Campground, Route 302, Bartlett, New Hampshire 03812 (603-374-2221), sells a tip sheet of "Twenty of the Most Rewarding Hikes in the White Mountains" for a nominal fee.

The **Appalachian Mountain Club** (AMC), another reliable source of information, has its main headquarters at Pinkham Notch, Mount Washington. Call (603) 466-2721 or (603) 466-2725 for trail information and (603) 466-2727 for workshop and family vacation package information. The AMC offers quality trail maps and advice, plus lectures and workshops for children and adults. Learn about flora and fauna, bushwhacking, bug and birding, and wild edibles. Many workshops include an overnight stay in one of the AMC area huts. Families new to hiking might consider a beginner backpacking and camping weekend workshop. If that's too long, try an AMC Family Discovery day hike for 4 miles of fun. AMC activities operate year-round. In fall follow a waterfall tour, in winter sample snowshoeing, and in early spring go maple sugaring.

Adventures abound in the majestic White Mountains.

For those who want to enjoy Mount Washington but only want a limited amount of walking, sign on for an AMC Alpine Garden Tour. Guides drive you to the top of Mount Washington, then lead you on a hike through the Alpine Garden and back up to the summit for your van ride back down. Call (603) 466-2727.

Eastern Mountain Sports (EMS), Main Street, North Conway (603-356-5433), also organizes guided hikes on weekend mornings from June through September.

Canoeing/Kayaking/White-water Rafting. Canoe outfitters **Saco Bound,** Route 302, Center Conway (603-447-2177 or 447-3801), make it easy to enjoy a lazy paddle on the Saco River, combining sunning, swimming, and picnicking. Follow the current for 43 miles if you go the distance, or take a shorter trip. Saco Bound provides equipment, instructions, and even a guide for a daylong trip on Tuesdays and Thursdays in July and August. Call ahead. For a more exciting ride, try springtime white-water rafting. Most excursions include a steak barbecue lunch and time to swim and explore the river and surroundings.

The **Appalachian Mountain Club** (AMC) organizes a two-day canoe and camping trip to Lake Umbagog. Call (603) 466-2727 for more information.

Biking. For older children and adults, mountain biking offers a challenge along with some spectacular views. **The North Conway Athletic Club** (603-356-5774) organizes mountain bike outings and suggests good routes. Bike rentals are available at the Joe Jones Shop

Scenic Drives and Views

In summer and fall these mountain drives offer eye-popping vistas.

- The **Mount Washington Auto Road,** Route 16, Pinkham Notch, Gorham (603–466-3988), is famous. Take your car 8 winding miles to Mount Washington's summit; at 6,288 feet, it's the highest in the northeastern United States. The drive is worth the view, but only if you're comfortable with steep, winding roads as the grades average 12 percent. If the sky is clear, you can see six states; if not, you can still see the Sherman Adams Summit museum with its slide show, **Home of the World's Worst Weather.** The locals are not kidding, either. Be sure to dress warmly, for this hour-long trip to the top of Mount Washington is known for its winds and quickly changing weather. To access the auto road, take Route 16 about 8 miles south of Gorham to Glenn House, which is open mid-May to mid-October.

- **Kancamagus Highway,** Route 112, runs 35 miles from Conway to Lincoln. Stop for a picnic at Lower Falls (6.7 miles from Conway) and an easy hike through the Rocky Gorge 8.4 miles from Conway. The short walk from the parking lot at Sabbaday Falls, 14.9 miles from Conway, leads you by cascading falls. With any luck you'll spot some moose taking a splash at Lily Pond (18.1 miles from Conway). Cool off at the Wilderness Trail, 28.8 miles from Conway. The trail from the parking area leads you along a suspension bridge to a spot with good river swimming.

- Children love the **Conway Scenic Railroad,** Main Street, North Conway; (603–356-5251 or 800–232-5251). This one-hour ride in an antique coach departs from an 1874 railway station and chugs along through Bartlett and into Crawford Notch. Reserve in advance during the fall foliage season. Open from May to October.

- **Mount Washington Cog Railway,** Route 302, Bretton Woods (603–278-5404 or 800–922-8825, ext. 7), an 1869 steam-powered train, takes you to the top on a three-hour trip over rough and rugged terrain. The railroad track is the second steepest in the world. Reservations are recommended; open May through October.

- **Wildcat Mountain Gondola,** Route 16, Pinkham Notch (603–466-3326), offers a fifteen-minute ride to the top of the 4,100-foot Wildcat Mountain. Bring a bag lunch for a summit picnic, explore the surrounding trails, then ride back down. The gondola is open mid-May through mid-October.

(603-356-9411) and the Sports Outlet (603-356-3133), both in North Conway.

Off Road Cycling Adventures, P.O. Box 2055, North Conway 03869 (603-356-2080), creates customized one- to five-day guided trips for adults and children eleven years and older. In summer both **Attitash Bear Peak** and **Bretton Woods** open their lifts to mountain bikers. At Attitash Bear Peak cyclists get off at the midpeak station. The trails down are intermediate and advanced. Bring your own bike or rent one. Adult and junior sizes are available. At Bretton Woods a quad lift takes bikers to trails for various abilities. Bretton Woods is a good choice for beginner mountain bikers, who can practice at the area's two terrain gardens. The natural terrain obstacles in the beginner's area help novices gain confidence, and the jumps, water ditches, and logs in the advanced area enable pros to fine-tune their techniques.

More Warm-Weather Fun

Parks. **Echo Lake State Park,** Route 302, North Conway (603-356-2672), is a good family day trip with its swimming area for children, picnic tables and grills for lunch or a barbecue, and trail that circles the lake. You can even rent a boat. The park is open June through Labor Day.

Fishing. With forty-five lakes and ponds as well as 650 miles of streams in the region, the Mount Washington Region is an angler's delight. Good spots include the Wild and Saco rivers as well as Basin Reservoir and Russell Pond. A state license is required for nonresidents over twelve, and certain restrictions apply. Call the New Hampshire Fish and Game Department at (603) 271-3421 for more information.

Tennis. **New England Tennis and Hiking Holidays,** Mount Cranmore Recreation Center, North Conway (603-356-9696 or 800-869-0949), organizes hiking and tennis vacations, including meals and lodging at local inns or at condominiums. While not catering to families, the programs are suitable for parents and teens.

Golfing. Appreciate the beauty of the mountains from the valley golf courses. Duffers have their choice of three public eighteen-hole courses in the area: **North Conway Country Club** (603-356-9391), **Hale's Location Country Club** (603-356-2140), and the **Wentworth Resort Golf Club** (603-383-9641).

Additional Attractions

Story Land, Route 16, Glen (603-383-4293) is a must-see if you have preschool children or young grade-schoolers. They will love the come-to-life Mother Goose settings complete with child-size buildings and recognizable characters. Humpty Dumpty—sitting on a wall, of course—greets you. Rest on a bench, and Little Miss Muffet's spider comes and sits beside you. Walk into Peter, Peter, Pumpkin Eater's house, and visit the Old Woman in the Shoe. Drift by the castle on a swan boat, get sprayed by a gentle raft ride, or sit in a Polar Coaster, where the seats resemble walruses. Story Land is great low-tech fun for little kids. It's open from June through October.

Next door, open mid-May to mid-October, is **Heritage New Hampshire,** Route 16, Glen (603-383-9776). Explore local history, beginning with a 1634 English village from which the ship *Reliance* sailed to Portland. Visitors "see" President George Washington, learn about the effects of the Industrial Revolution in New Hampshire, and come back to the present on a simulated train ride through Crawford Notch at peak foliage.

Less educational but also fun is the **Attitash Bear Peak Alpine Slide and Outdoor Amusements,** Route 302, Bartlett (800-223-SNOW). Choose the fast track or a slower one. The park also offers a scenic chairlift ride to the top of the mountain and plenty of space for a countryside picnic. It's open from May through October.

Somewhat hokey, but fun for younger kids, are Santa's Village and Six Gun City. **Santa's Village,** Route 2, Jefferson (603-586-4445), is Santa's summer home. Tots delight in their visit with Santa's helpers and with the big guy himself. Christmas-theme attractions include a kiddie roller coaster, a Yule Log water flume, animals to pet, and two shows—the Jingle Jamboree and the Live Tropical Bird Show. At **Six Gun City,** Route 2, Jefferson (603-586-4592), see the Wild West of the White Mountains complete with a frontier village, a bank robbery, and a sheriff and outlaw shoot-'em-up. Kids may even earn a deputy's badge. At the Frontier Show, hear stories of this hard-knock life; at the Miniature Diamond B Ranch, pet miniature goats, burros, and horses. Amusements include a miniature golf course, water slide, and boat rides. Open from mid-June to Labor Day.

In fall, bite your way into some of the area's edible wonders: crisp apples. Pick your own bushels at several area orchards, including **Hatch Orchard** in Center Conway; (603) 447-5687.

Winter Fun

Horse Logic Hay and Sleigh Rides, Route 116, Jackson (603-383-9876), bundles you into its cozy carriage and takes you through Jackson's scenic winter landscape.

Downhill Skiing. Mount Washington Valley is home to several family-friendly ski areas. It's a great place to learn how to ski (ask about Learn to Ski packages).

Attitash Bear Peak, in Bartlett (603–374–0946 or 800–233–SNOW), has something for all ages, beginning with an Attitots ski program for ages one to three and continuing up to an Attiteens racing program. Lift tickets for kids cost less with a pay-what-you-ride system and a Sunday kids-pay-their-age deal.

Waterville Valley, New Hampshire, offers comprehensive ski programs for kids, child care for wee ones, a family-friendly atmosphere, and a variety of packages. Often kids ski free midweek, so ask. Choose to stay in condos, bed and breakfasts, or lodges. In summer the ski area offers attractively priced family packages and lots of activities. For information call (800) 468–2553. (See Where to Stay.)

Bretton Woods, Route 302, Bretton Woods (603–278–5000 or 800–232–2972) is actually a good place for families with grade-school children new to the sport. The thirty trails here are mostly beginners, with several intermediate and a few advanced runs. Besides the downhill trails, Bretton Woods has a snowboard park, 90 kilometers of groomed terrain for cross-country skiing, and a recreation center with an indoor pool, a racquetball court, a sauna, exercise equipment, and a game room. Night skiing is available on weekends and holidays.

The Bretton Woods nursery has programs, including arts and crafts and storytelling, for children ages two months to three years old. The Hobbit Ski School teaches children ages four to twelve.

King Pine, Route 153, East Madison (snow phone: 800–367–8897; lodging reservations: 800–FREE–SKI), is actually the winter guise of Purity Spring, a year-round resort. There are only seventeen downhill trails on thirty-five acres at King Pine, most of them beginner. In addition to downhill skiing, King Pine offers 25 kilometers of cross-country skiing at the Knee-Hi Ski School for ages four to seven. Lessons are taught at three different levels, according to ability, not age. All-day weekend programs are also available for eight- to four-year-olds. During school vacations (December, February, and March) there is also a special Youth Vacation Ski Camp. For more information, call 800–414–CAMP.

For nonskiers in your clan, Purity Spring offers ice skating on an indoor lighted rink, snowboarding, snowshoeing, and dog-sledding outings.

Cross-Country Skiing. Jackson has been rated one of the four best places in the world to cross-country ski because of the abundance, quality, and variety of trails. Besides 600 kilometers of groomed trails, the area frequently offers a special reduced-rate bed-and-breakfast ski package midweek. As you glide from inn to inn, the trails take you near covered bridges, over snowy fields, and along creeks. Several of the lodgings welcome children. For package information call **Country Inns in the White Mountains,** P.O. Box 2025, North Conway 03860 (800–562–1300).

The **Jackson Ski Touring Foundation,** Jackson (603-383-9355), makes sure that more than 90 miles of trails in the village of Jackson and throughout the White Mountain National Forest are groomed. Trails are marked by ability, and maps are available from the center. Ski rentals and lessons are available at the Jack Frost Nordic Shop.

Another big center is the **Mount Washington Valley (MWV) Ski Touring,** Intervale (603-356-9920), a similar organization that offers 65 kilometers of groomed trails. Special events include a Holiday Cookie Fest, when skiers go from inn to inn tasting holiday cookies, and, in late February, a chocolate festival.

The **Appalachian Mountain Club,** Route 16, Pinkham Notch (603-466-2727), offers its hiking trails for cross-country skiing.

Ice Skating. When you tire of the snow, take to the ice at public rinks in Jackson Village as well as in Conway and North Conway Villages. If you didn't bring your own skates, rent them at Ski and Sports Shop, North Conway (603-356-9411).

Shopping

North Conway, with more than 200 outlets, is perhaps New Hampshire's most famous off-price shopping mecca. Not only do the factory shops offer discounted merchandise but New Hampshire's lack of sales tax adds to the savings.

North Conway's discount stores stretch for blocks along Route 16. If you have time for only one place, head to **Settler's Green Outlet Village Plus,** (603-356-7031), which offers more than thirty shops. Set back from the road and designed to look like a mock New England town instead of another strip mall, this shopping area is among the most pleasant to browse and also has some of the area's nicest shops. Teens like Banana Republic, Bugle Boy, and the J. Crew Factory Store. For the little ones, snap up the deals at Carter's Childrenswear. For outdoor enthusiasts and that oh-so-comfortable casual look, try Eddie Bauer and American Eagle Outfitters. Most stores have savings from 20 to 50 percent off catalog or retail prices. **Cafe Zum Zum** is a good snack stop, and the **Sweetery** sells old-fashioned New England fudge. Parking is easy, and to make shopping even easier, this outlet center has a Sheraton Inn.

Adjacent to Settler's Green is the **L.L. Bean Factory Store,** Routes 16 and 302, (603-356-2100), with an array of camping and sporting goods. Next door is a well-placed **Friendly's,** Route 16 (603-356-6108), a moderate-priced restaurant known for its sundaes. A **MacDonald's,** Route 16, is just up the street.

Keep the car parked and walk across the street to the **Tanger Outlet**

Center, Route 16 (603-356-7921), where you can browse off-price deals on such brand names as Liz Claiborne and Calvin Klein. Another **Tanger Outlet Center,** Route 16, a few blocks away, features a **Corning Revere Clearance Center** for housewares and for kids an **OshKosh B'Gosh** store. Don't miss the **village of North Conway,** which has more charm than the strips of outlets as well as some nifty boutiques and specialty stores. Children like browsing in **Zeb's General Store,** Main Street, (800-676-9294), which proclaims that it sells "absolutely positively 100 percent New England products." Peruse candles, wood work, bags, gourmet food such as salsa and vinegar, and other items. Overindulge with fudge, cranberry chutney, Vermont's Finest chocolate golf balls, maple syrup, and kids' favorites such as "chocolate cow plops," gummy worms, and giant jawbreakers.

SPECIAL EVENTS

For more information on events listed, call the Mount Washington Valley Visitor Bureau at (603) 356-3171 or (800) 367-3364.

January. Jackson Skiing Legends, Black Mountain, features a vintage-attire ski race and a classic film festival.

February. Family Frolics Week at Mount Cranmore, North Conway. Wildcat Silly Slaloms and kid's special events week, Wildcat Mountain. Winter Carnival, King Pine Ski Area, with races, barbecues, and fireworks.

March. Spring Carnival, Mount Cranmore, North Conway. March Madness at King Pine Ski Area, family fun for all ages.

April. Easter Bunny Express aboard Conway Scenic Railroad.

May. Wildquack River Race Festival, Jackson Village. Race your duck in the stream or join in the Quackers Parade.

June. Conway Village Festival. Mount Washington Auto Road Climb to the Clouds, road race and celebration.

July. Fourth of July Carnival, North Conway, has face painting, fried dough, and rides galore.

July/August. Sunday night outdoor band concerts in North Conway.

August. Attitash Equine Festival, Attitash Mountain, Bartlett, is a world-class riding show that also includes a children's playground, pony rides, and food fest.

September. Railfans' Day, Conway Scenic Railroad, celebrates old trains. White Mountain Jazz and Blues Festival, Conway.

WHERE TO STAY

After a day full of mountain air and activity, come home to a cozy New England inn or condominium. Here are some that are family friendly and have hiking and cross-country skiing trails just out the back door. Be sure to ask about weekend or other family packages.

Attitash Mountain Village, across from the Attitash Bear Peak slopes, has one-, two-, and three-bedroom units, some of which have kitchenettes. For reservations call the **Attitash Travel and Lodging Bureau** (800–223–SNOW).

Christmas Farm Inn, Route 16B above the village, Jackson (603–383–4313 or 800–HI–ELVES), pleases younger ones with its game room, sauna, outdoor pool, and year-round Christmas decorations. A small sitting room off the main parlor features a child-size rocking chair, as well as puzzles, games, and a television.

Ellis River House, Route 16, P.O. Box 656, Jackson (603–383–9339 or 800–233–8309), is a turn-of-the-century farmhouse overlooking the Ellis River. From April through July the stream is stocked with trout, and the outdoor pool is available all summer. In winter the famed Jackson cross-country ski trails are literally out your door. The decor is country Victorian. Rooms combine Oriental rugs, floral wallpaper, calico pillows, and lace runners on bureaus. The effect is welcoming and not too fussy. There are four family suites for extra space. Cribs and high chairs are available, and the breakfast room has a refrigerator and microwave for guests' use, a nice touch for families who want to serve snacks to young children. Children twelve and under stay free with parents.

The **Eagle Mountain Resort,** Carter Notch Road, Jackson (603–383–9111 or 800–966–5779), has a nine-hole golf course that becomes a cross-country ski area in winter. Other features include a health club, an outdoor pool, and tennis courts. **The Wentworth Resort Hotel,** Route 16A at Carter Notch Road, Jackson (603–383–9700 or 800–637–0013), is right in the heart of Jackson and offers sixty-two rooms. The cross-country ski trails start nearby, and the property features an outdoor ice rink in winter and an outdoor pool in summer. In warm weather try your skill at the eighteen-hole golf course and on the tennis courts. At the **Four Points Hotel,** Route 16 at Settler's Green, North Conway (603–356–9300 or 800–648–4397), kids under twelve stay and eat for free. The **Nordic Village Vacation Resort,** Route 16, Jackson (603– 383–9101 or 800–472–5207), offers one- and two-bedroom rental condominiums.

The Mount Washington Valley offers a reservation service. Call (800) 367–3364 for more information. Also, **King Pine** (see page 121) has lodging packages. Call for more information. For additional lodging suggestions contact the **Jackson Lodging Bureau** (800–866–3334).

In winter **Waterville Valley,** New Hampshire, has comprehensive ski programs and child care; in summer the area offers boating, tennis, horseback riding, a sports center, and a daily activity program for kids ages three to five, six to eight, and nine to twelve. Family activity packages get the gang going with daily tennis clinics, hikes, and aerobic classes, as well as mountain biking, roller blading, and boating. Choose to stay at a variety of inns, lodges, or condominiums. For information call (800) 468-2553.

Two of our favorite properties in Waterville Valley are **The Black Bear Lodge** and **The Golden Eagle Lodge.** Since both are served by Waterville Valley's free shuttle, you don't have to drive to the slopes or the village. **The Black Bear Lodge,** Snowsbrook Road. (603-236-4501 or 800-468-2553), offers one-bedroom suites that accommodate from four to six people and come equipped with a kitchen. Like a hotel, there is a twenty-four-hour front desk, which is nice for families, just in case any late-night assistance is needed. The Black Bear has an indoor/outdoor pool (although it's small), a hot tub, and a video arcade. On some evenings the property shows children's films such as *Pinocchio.* The decor of the suites focuses more on sturdiness than aesthetic appeal. Sofas pull out into beds that can accommodate two small children. **The Golden Eagle Lodge,** Snowsbrook Road (603-236-4174 or 800-468-2553), is reminiscent of an Adirondack lodge, with its two-story lobby and shingle, log, and stone facade. The inn offers one- and two-bedroom units, each with kitchen facilities. There is a twenty-four-hour desk and an indoor pool.

There are several town house and condominium communities near the Waterville Valley complex. Contact **Resort Condominium Rental,** Valley Road, P.O. Box 379 (603-236-4101 or 800-556-6522), and **Windsor Hill Condominiums,** Jennings Peak Road (603-236-8321 or 800-343-1286).

Bretton Woods Motor Inn, Route 302, Bretton Woods (603-278-1500 or 800-258-0330), is managed by the same company as the Mount Washington Hotel & Resort (see below). Open year-round, this facility is just ¼ mile from the Bretton Woods ski area. In ski season a free shuttle transports you to and from the ski area. The rooms have televisions, and the facility has an indoor pool and a restaurant (open for breakfast and dinner), all pluses for families. The same company also books the **Townhomes at Bretton Woods,** one- to five-bedroom accommodations, and the 1896 **Bretton Arms,** an upscale Victorian inn.

The **Country Inn at Bartlett,** Route 302, Box 327, Bartlett (603-374-2353), is a homey and friendly house built in 1885 and surrounded by tall pine trees. Rooms in the main house are decorated with collectibles and some antiques. Families will find more space in the cottages, which have cable TV, private baths, and small porches. Some cottages have kitchenettes. There are reduced-price packages. Children under twelve stay free.

Mount Washington Hotel & Resort, Route 302, Bretton Woods (603–278–1000 or 800–258–0330), is a grand dame hotel, with its colonnaded porch and mile-long drive. Surrounded by 18,000 acres of national forest, the hotel offers golf, hiking trails, and great views of the peaks of the White Mountains. Built in 1902, this hotel has the panache of that era. However, it lacks some modern amenities. Rooms do not have televisions or air conditioning, and the once-grand lobby can look a bit sparse. The resort features twenty-seven holes of golf, tennis courts, a swimming pool, horseback riding, and mountain bike rentals. Open Memorial Day to mid-October. With the installation of a heating system, sections of the hotel are now also open in winter. Rates include breakfast and dinner daily.

From July through Labor Day the King of the Mountain Kids Kamp at the Mount Washington Hotel & Resort for ages five to twelve offers activities daily from 9:00 A.M. to noon, 1:00 to 4:30 P.M. and 7:00 to 9:00 P.M. The program continues on Saturdays and Sundays in September to mid-October. The family chambers—two bedrooms connecting through a bath—give families space and privacy. Staying here all depends on how comfortable your family feels roaming a vast turn-of-the-century hotel.

The 1785 Inn, Routes 16 and 302, 3582 North White Mountain Highway (603–356–9025 or 800–421–1785), not only is one of the oldest buildings in the valley, but has one of the best views of Mount Washington and houses one of the area's nicest restaurants for both atmosphere (romantic and subdued) and food (continental). The dinner prices reflect the quality, however, so take only sophisticated older children here for meals. This charming inn welcomes children of all ages as overnight guests.

The rooms have a Victorian country flare. There are spool beds, white iron and brass beds, wicker chairs, oak rockers, and always a quilt. Although the front faces a noisy road, the grounds feature an outdoor pool and playground. In winter, just step out the door to get on the Mount Washington Valley cross-country trail.

WHERE TO EAT

Try a smoked chicken and tortilla salad or a plain hearty New York sirloin at **The Christmas Farm Inn,** Black Mountain Road, Jackson (603–383–4313). Taste a Reuben Express or a Turkey Trolley at **Glen Junction,** Route 302 in Glen (603–383–9660), where a toy train chugs around the room on a track on the wall. For seafood **Snug Harbor,** Route 16, North

Conway (603-356-3000), is the place with fried and baked regional fish and a little pirates kid's menu. **Elvio's,** Main Street, North Conway Village (603-356-3307), has the best pizza in town, featuring thin-crust, thick-crust, and/or white varieties. **I Cugini,** Route 302, Bartlett (603-374-1977), has particularly good soup, pasta entrees, and a menu tailored to children's appetites.

Horsefeathers, Main Street, North Conway (603-356-2687), serves up good family eats. Signature items include pastrami sandwiches with roasted peppers, New England clam chowder, and chicken pot pie. The kids' menu is good too, with Jurassically shaped chicken strips and spaghetti, plus desserts such as worms and dirt (chocolate pudding with cookie crumbs and gummy worms).

Yankee Food Works, Route 302, Bartlett (603-374-6223), features sandwiches and snacks. Seating is available on an outdoor deck. Live entertainment is offered on Friday and Saturday nights. A take-out menu is available.

The Red Parka Pub, Route 302, Glen (603-383-4344), is a favorite spot after a day on the slopes. Skis dating to the 1930s decorate the place, and a patio provides outdoor dining. The menu features steak and prime rib, as well as seafood, poultry, and an extensive salad bar.

The **Appalachian Mountain Club,** Route 16, Pinkham Notch Gorham (603-466-2721), offers dinner get-togethers after a long day's hike. Dinner begins at 6:00 P.M., and don't be late. The menu changes daily. Call in advance for reservations.

After a trip on the Cog Railway, stop at **Fabyans Station,** next door, Route 302, Bretton Woods (603-846-2222), in the old railroad depot. They offer hearty burgers and sandwiches. For dessert ice-cream lovers have **Ben & Jerry's Scoop Shop,** Norcross Place, North Conway (603-356-7720).

SIDE TRIPS

There is no shortage of side trips from the Jackson area. **Portland, Maine,** is ninety minutes southeast, and **Boston** is two and a half hours south. (See the Boston chapter.)

Portsmouth offers **Strawberry Banke,** P.O. Box 300, Portsmouth, New Hampshire 03802 (603-433-1100). This museum includes more than forty houses that trace the development of the area from 1630 through the 1950s. Kids love the Colonial and Federal furniture and artifacts. The museum is open May through October and on weekends in December for a candlelight stroll. Portsmouth also features **The Children's Museum,** 280 Marcy Street, 03801 (603-436-3853), where there's hands-on fun for little ones.

FOR MORE INFORMATION

Call the **Mount Washington Valley information line** (877-WHT-MTNS or 948-6867) for lodging and activities. **Jackson Chamber of Commerce,** P.O. Box 304, Jackson (603-383-9356 from New Hampshire and Canada; 800-866-3334 from elsewhere), publishes a free visitor's travel guide and will book reservations for you. **Mount Washington Valley Visitor Bureau,** Box 2300, North Conway (603-356-5701 or 800-367-3364), publishes the *Mount Washington Valley Visitor Guide.* For information on recreational facilities, including biking and hiking trails, contact the **White Mountain National Forest** at P.O. Box 638, Laconia 03247 (603-528-8721). Also check with the **Trails Bureau, New Hampshire Division of Parks and Recreation,** P.O. Box 856, Concord 03301; (603-271-3556, parks or 603-271-3627, recreation services).

Tourist information booths are located in Jackson Village as well as North Conway and Conway villages. For specific locations call the visitor's numbers listed above.

Check out the local happenings with *The Mountain Ear* (603-447-6336), the Mount Washington region's weekly newspaper. For a twenty-four-hour weather line call (603) 447-5252.

Emergency Numbers

Ambulance, fire, and police in Conway and North Conway: 911

Ambulance and fire in all other towns: 1-539-6119

Health-Net information line: (800) 499-4171

Memorial Hospital emergency room, Route 16, North Conway; (603) 356-5461

Poison Control: (800) 562-8236

Police in Bartlett: 1-539-2234

Police in Jackson and Glen: (800) 552-8960

There is no twenty-four-hour pharmacy. A convenient pharmacy is CVS Pharmacy, Shaw's/North Way Plaza, Route 16, North Conway; (603) 356-6916.

CAPE MAY

C ape May, New Jersey, a born-again beach town, boasts a historic district with colorfully restored Victorian houses: Turreted, gabled, bay-windowed, and laced with gingerbread, these houses are a treat to the eye.

Although the emphasis in town is clearly on romantic getaways for couples, several properties welcome children. The beach, the nearby nature preserves, and the friendly feel of the town make it a great place for families, provided you choose the right accommodations.

How the town came to be is an interesting story. The rich and the famous flocked to Cape May in its nineteenth-century heyday. Arriving by steamboat and railroad from Philadelphia, Baltimore, and Washington, political leaders such as Millard Fillmore, Franklin Pierce, Abraham Lincoln, and Ulysses S. Grant shook off the rigors of politics for sand and surf on Cape May's shores. Along these once-wide beaches, Louis Chevrolet and Henry Ford raced their automobiles. John Philip Sousa played at Congress Hall, one of the grande dame hotels, and Wallis Simpson, the future Duchess of Windsor, debuted at the Colonial Hotel on Ocean Avenue. In 1891 Benjamin Harrison took over Congress Hall, making it his summer White House.

Spurred by such high-society tourism, entrepreneurs built hotels such as the Mount Vernon, which, though it burned just before its official opening, offered 2,000 rooms and stretched for blocks along the Atlantic. In 1878 a disastrous fire destroyed many of these grand hotels, particularly in the West End. The locals, hurriedly rebuilding for the coming summer season, eschewed costly and difficult-to-build large hotels for three-story Victorian "cottages" with plenty of spare rooms for summer guests. These now grace the streets of Cape May, still offering bed-and-breakfast in rooms filled with Victorian antiques. In elaborately draped parlors, afternoon tea is almost always served.

At the turn of the century, Atlantic City's modern accommodations had stolen Cape May's place in the sun, and the town experienced a gradual decline. But in the 1960s when urban renewal planners began tearing these old Victorian dwellings down to make way for modern motels, preservationists rallied. After a protracted fight in the early 1970s, Cape

Cape May

AT A GLANCE

▶ Discover a restored beach town with Victorian flair

▶ Watch thousands of hawks and other birds in fall

▶ Walk through nature preserves

▶ Stay in turn-of-the-century bed-and-breakfast inns

▶ Greater Cape May Chamber of Commerce,
(609) 884-5508; Mid-Atlantic Center for the Arts,
(609) 884-5404; www.capemaymac.org

May was designated a historical district. Restoration then began in earnest, and cottages formerly partitioned into boarding houses and apartments were born again as elegant guest homes.

GETTING THERE

Traveling by land from Washington, D.C., take either of two routes to Cape May: I-95 over the Delaware Memorial Bridge to Route 40 east, to Route 55 south, to Route 47 south, to U.S. 9 into Cape May; or travel on I-295 to U.S. 322 south, to Route 55 south, to Route 47 south, to U.S. 9 into Cape May.

The Cape May–Lewes Ferry runs daily between Cape May and Lewes, Delaware. Kids really enjoy this boat ride because it offers a welcome break from being cooped up in a car. The ferry terminal is on U.S. 9, 3 miles west of the southern terminus of the Garden State Parkway. For schedule information call (800) 64-FERRY; or visit www.capemaylewesferry.com.

From New York City take the Garden State Parkway south to Mile Marker 0 into Cape May.

From Philadelphia take the Atlantic City Expressway to the Garden State Parkway south, which is exit 75. Follow to Mile Marker to Cape May.

GETTING AROUND

The best ways to see Cape May are by foot or by bicycle. Self-guided tour maps outlining walking tours of Cape May are available at the Washington Street Mall's information booths. **Surrey Bicycles,** a four-seated bike

You and your family can climb the 199 steps to the top of the Cape May Point Lighthouse . . . the view will not disappoint.

with a canopy-hood—perfect for the family—can be rented at Victorian Village Plaza's **Village Bikes,** Lafayette and Elmira Streets; (609) 884-8500. Carriage, trolley, and guided walking tours also originate at the Washington Street Mall. Call Cape May Carriage Company (609-884-4466).

The Mid-Atlantic Center for the Arts (MAC)

The Mid-Atlantic Center for the Arts (MAC) (609-884-5404; www. capemaymac.org), a multicultural organization, hosts an array of activities, including music festivals, house tours, and crafts fairs. Every Thursday in July and August, MAC presents the Cape May Kids Playhouse, Convention Hall, 714 Beach Drive, an evening of juggling, music, and comedy geared to families. MAC publishes a weekly information guide, *This Week in Cape May.*

WHAT TO SEE AND DO

Nature: Beaches and Birds

Miles of beach lure summer crowds. The **beach** along **Beach Avenue** offers families the typical delights of sun and sand. Come early, as these shores get really crowded. Pick a spot and bring or rent a beach umbrella. Collect starfish, great cream-colored whelks, giant horseshoe crab shells, and driftwood. A time-honored tradition is strolling along the boardwalk and munching such beach delights as pizza and fries.

Fall, with smaller crowds, quieter beaches, and water temperatures still warm enough for swimming, may be the best time to enjoy this historic beach town. Additional autumn attractions include the annual Victorian Week, a ten-day celebration of the Victorian lifestyle that begins Columbus Day weekend every October. Each fall the birds come by the tens of thousands to Cape May, funneling through here for food and rest before crossing Delaware Bay and continuing south. The beaches afford a perfect vantage point for such spectacular sights as a phalanx of Canadian geese in precise formation above the gray-blue surf, or thousands of hawks gliding on warm air currents before swooping down on their prey.

For unobstructed views of the sunset be at **Sunset Beach,** foot of Sunset Boulevard, Cape May Point (for directions, call 609-884-7079). As the sun slips below the horizon, the Sunset Beach Gift Shop plays a tape of Kate Smith singing "God Bless America." Arrive early so that kids can scour the sands for "Cape May Diamonds," translucent quartz pebbles once prized by the area's Kechemeche tribe. Be sure to wear beach shoes as the sand is rocky.

Besides the beachfront near the heart of town, two areas offer less crowded beaches and, in fall, the best spots for birding: **Cape May Point State Park** and the **Cape May Migratory Bird Refuge,** a stretch of beach and dunes along Sunset Boulevard.

Cape May Point State Park—take Sunset Boulevard to Lighthouse Drive—has 195 acres of nature trails, wooded areas, and a half-mile of beachfront. Check out the station headquarters for a modest display of birds and shells and for the schedule of beginner bird walks and demonstrations of hawk banding.

Walk along the boardwalk trails (wide enough for wheelchair access and strollers) through clusters of red cedars and shrubs to ponds where,

Nearby Nature

- **The Nature Center of Cape May,** 1600 Delaware Avenue (609–898–8848), has exhibits on wetlands, birds, and shellfish and a starfish petting pool. On their Harbor Safari, guides pull a net through shallows.
- The **Cape May County Park and Zoo,** Route 9, Pinelane (609–465–5271), houses more than 250 species of animals. Located just 7 miles north of Wildwood via the Garden State Parkway, the zoo is an easy day trip, guaranteed to make little (and not so little) ones smile with delight. A highlight is the fifty-five-acre African savannah. From an overlook watch giraffe, zebra, ostrich, and antelope roam over the grasslands. Along the walkway listen to the mynah birds chatter. Other zoo highlights include a bear habitat, a reptile house, lions, tigers, and cougars. Bring a picnic lunch and spend several hours. After visiting the zoo, take time to enjoy the tennis and basketball courts and the nature trail.
- Don't miss **Leaming's Run Gardens and Colonial Farm,** 1845 Route 9 North, Cape May Courthouse, New Jersey 08210, about 14 miles north of Cape May (609–465–5871). Open mid-May to mid-October, this place offers thirty acres of beautifully sculpted, tranquil gardens and fern-carpeted woods.

Allow at least ninety minutes, preferably longer, to follow the winding path through each of twenty-five settings, carefully planted with colorful annuals and graced with lily ponds, gazebos, and benches shaded by tall trees. By June the roses are best, and in October it's still warm, but the leaves are turning. The gardens, set above a forest bed of soft cinnamon ferns, each illustrate a color theme or solve such common gardening problems as hillsides and too much shade.

This kind of "education" is easy on the eyes. The English Cottage Garden pops into color with 140 varieties of flowers; the Serpentine Garden (demonstrating how to plant in a long narrow area) winds its way to the lake in a burst of red salvias; the Knoll Garden, with its wild flowers, illustrates planting at different levels; and the reflecting pond laced with water lilies demonstrates how to use water to mirror flowers.

This is a garden for relaxing and sharing a pleasant moment. Just to be sure, there are signs urging you to PLEASE LOOK BACK, RELAX HERE, and WATCH FOR HUMMINGBIRDS.

Another surprise is the occasional sound of roosters at the Colonial farm here that re-creates the world of Thomas

(continued)

Nearby Nature *(continued)*

Leaming, the whaler who originally settled this property in 1706. The farm has a one-room log cabin, a barn with roosters, and a dooryard garden planted with such typical Colonial crops as cotton, tobacco, peanuts, okra, pumpkin, and squash. The gardens end at the Cooperage, one of the largest dried-flower shops in the East.

especially in fall, snowy egrets hover like angels, and herons seem to walk on water. A special fall treat is the sight of thousands of hawks. A hawk-watch platform adjacent to the parking lot provides a good observation point for those with young children too weary to wander, or climb the abandoned World War II concrete bunker that juts out into the ocean. This, incidentally, is a good place to glimpse the falcons gliding on an updraft.

For more information on birding, contact the **Cape May Bird Observatory,** New Jersey Audubon Society, 705 East Lake Drive, P.O. Box 3, Cape May Point 08212; call (609) 884-2736 or 884-2626 (the hotline) for the latest information.

Victorian Architecture

If you're a fan of whimsical architecture, be sure to stroll along Columbia Avenue, Hughes Street, Perry Street, and Ocean Avenue past some gaily painted dowager queen hotels. Sit on the serpentine porches of the surviving grand properties—the Chalfonte, Congress Hall, and the Colonial —or rest in a wicker rocker on the back veranda of an elegant bed and breakfast and take in a view from the past.

The **Emlen Physick House,** 1048 Washington Street (609-884-5404), Cape May's only Victorian house museum, is open for tours. Built in 1879, this home has the elaborate furnishings of its eccentric and wealthy resident, Dr. Emlen Physick. A weekly tour offered throughout the year is "The Doctor is In." A costumed actor in the character of Dr. Physick takes visitors on a tour of the house. In July and August there are weekly tours geared for children.

SPECIAL EVENTS

Festivals, Theater, and Cultural Events

April. Tulip and Harbor Festival. The trolleys offer a great vantage point that's easy on little feet. Family Street Fair with children's entertainment and Dutch dancing.

May. Cape May Music Festival, a six-week-long festival that showcases the talents of noted soloists and musicians. Almost all of the festival's numerous concerts are held at Congress Hall, Beach Drive at Perry Street.

June. An old-fashioned Victorian fair with Victorian games and pastimes, crafts and antiques vendors.

July–August. The **Cape May Kid's Playhouse** and the **Vintage Film Festival** offer entertainment for both young and old.

October. During Victorian Week this town throws a Victorian fete. Enjoy vaudeville shows, a fashion show, an antiques fair, walking tours, and old-house restoration workshops.

November. During Victorian Holmes Weekend Cape May is the setting for amateur sleuths to solve Sir Arthur Conan Doyle's Sherlock Holmes mysteries.

December. Christmas Lights Trolleys tour the decorated streets.

WHERE TO STAY

Some of the best bets for family lodging in Cape May are the motels, apartments, suites, and condominiums, as well as a handful of bed-and-breakfast inns that welcome families. Book as far in advance as possible, as Cape May is a very popular summer spot. Be advised that most of the charming bed-and-breakfast inns do not really welcome children. In addition, many of these inns, in keeping with the period, either don't have air-conditioned bedrooms or have only one or two at most. Don't believe that stuff about cross-breezes and fans. Without this modern convenience in summer, you will be either hot or very hot. If this matters, ask ahead of time and find a lodging that accommodates your needs. Some inns, such as the Queen Victoria, are open year-round; others close for the season in November.

An Italianate 1863 grande dame, **The Southern Mansion,** 720 Washington Street (609-884-7171; www.southernmansion.com), occupies almost a block, a rarity for Cape May. Enclosed by a 150-year-old hedgerow, the lawn provides privacy plus a safe place for kids to play. The rooms, whether in the main house or in the recently built annex, feature custom-made armoires to hide the television, Victorian bureaus and rockers, private baths, and air-conditioning. The sunroom, with its wall of windows, patina of fine wood, and hanging ferns, provides a welcoming place to enjoy the full breakfast that is included in the room rate. Downstairs there's a ballroom, and the inn hopes to be able to build an indoor pool. Like many of Cape May's properties, The Southern Mansion caters to couples seeking a romantic getaway, but the hosts are friendly and the inn welcomes well-behaved children ages eight and older.

Among the family-friendly properties offering apartment suites are **Heritage House,** 680 Washington Street (609-884-3338); **Patricia's Guest House** (609-884-9211; www.capenet.com/capemay/patricia); **Regent Beach,** beachfront condominiums, 10 Congress Street (609-884-5049); **Antoinette's Guest Apartments,** 717 Washington Street (609-898-0502; www.capenet.com/capemay/antointt); **Cliveden Cottage,** 709 Columbia Avenue (609-884-4516 or 800-884-2420); and the **Dormer House Bed and Breakfast,** 800 Columbia Avenue (609-884-7446 or 800-884-5052), which has one- and two-bedroom apartments with kitchens.

Goodman House, 118 Decatur Street (609-884-6371), one half block from the beach, also offers rental apartments with kitchens. Goodman House is home of the **Dollhouse and Miniature Museum of Cape May** (open seasonally).

The Virginia Hotel, 25 Jackson Street (609-884-5700 or 800-732-4236), is a restored Victorian inn. Families feel especially comfortable in the five rooms that come with sleeper sofas. All twenty-four rooms have down comforters, televisions, private baths, and VCRs. Children under ten stay for free, and rates include a complimentary continental breakfast. Although the dining room at the Virginia is nonsmoking, the rooms allow smokers. If you need a smoke-free room, be sure to ask for one.

Motel-type properties that welcome families include the **Camelot Motel,** 103 Howard Street (609-884-1500). Only 50 yards from the beach, the Camelot has two-bedroom efficiencies complete with kitchenette. The **Atlas Inn and Beach Resort,** 1035 Beach Drive (888-285-2746) has both a pool and restaurant, while **Avondale by the Sea,** Beach Avenue and Gurney Street (609-884-2332 or 800-676-7030), has a pool and provides continental breakfast (no restaurant). Both Atlas Inn and Avondale have efficiency apartments.

If you're traveling to Cape May with young children, a good bet is the **Chalfonte Hotel,** Box 475, 301 Howard Street (609-884-8409; www.chalfonte.com). The Chalfonte has special two-bedroom apartments and separate dining facilities for kids six years old and under. Parents can enjoy a romantic dinner while their kids eat and then play with newfound friends supervised by college-age counselors.

The Queen Victoria, 102 Ocean Street (609-884-8702), a nicely appointed bed-and-breakfast with Edwardian antiques, welcomes children and offers cot rentals for the little ones but has a limited number of rooms for families. According to the owners, this bed and breakfast has comfortable and functional antique furniture "sturdy enough to plunk down in, relax, and put your feet up on." Families may prefer the

Queen's Hotel, Ocean and Columbia Streets (609-884-8702), operated by the same family. More of a boutique lodging, this property's rooms all have private baths, refrigerators, coffeemakers, televisions, and telephones.

Built in 1879, **Congress Hall,** Beach Avenue and Perry Street (609-884-8421), one of Cape May's grand old hotels, is undergoing renovation and is scheduled to reopen in 2000.

WHERE TO EAT

In high season—summer and during fall's Victorian Week—book your dinner reservations ahead; otherwise, the lines and the wait can be long.

For an Italian dinner, try **God Mothers,** 913 Broadway (609-884-4543). **Bodacious Bagels,** Beach and Howard Streets (609-884-3031), offers eat-in or take-out bagel sandwiches and salads. The **Ocean View Restaurant,** Beach Drive and Grant Avenue (609-884-3772), is open for breakfast, lunch, and dinner and serves diner fare. **McGlade's,** 722 Beach Drive (609-884-2614), features seafood and American cuisine. **Henry's** oceanfront (609-884-8826), offers family fare. **The Mad Batter,** 19 Jackson Street (609-884-5970), is a lively place with an eclectic menu.

For fine dining, families with older children should try either **The Ebbitt Room,** in the Virginia Hotel, 25 Jackson Street (609-884-5700), or **The Washington Inn,** 801 Washington Street (609-884-5697). The crab cakes at The Washington Inn are among the best in town.

SIDE TRIPS

Preteens and teens may urge you to spend some time at **Wildwood,** a bustling beach town. Wildwood, along with attracting its share of college students and twenty-somethings, makes families feel at home. The beach is wide, the waves are manageable, and the 2-mile boardwalk comes replete with eateries, arcades, and amusements.

As any beach town aficionado knows, half the fun is enjoying the scene off the sand, and Wildwood's **boardwalk** is perfect. For kids the arcades and rides proffer a wonderland of fun; for parents it's a nostalgic stroll. Unlike the re-created midways being built at theme parks across the United States, Wildwood presents the real thing: T-shirt shops, saltwater taffy, arcade games of skill, and lots of boardwalk snacks. Treat the kid in you, along with those with you, to such time-tested beach fare as funnel cakes, pizza, and cotton candy.

You'll get nothing but "wows" from your kids when they see the **Ferris wheel at Mariner's Landing Pier** (Schellenger Avenue and the boardwalk). The largest in the East Coast at 156 feet high, this whirling bit of wonder serves as Wildwood's unofficial fun symbol. **Dinosaur Beach Adventure Theme Park** (Juniper Avenue and the boardwalk), at the former Hunt's Pier, sports rides based on these popular, prehistoric critters. Blast off in an inner tube pushed along by a jet spray of water; board a jeep for a safari ride through a jungle populated with high-tech, animated dinosaurs; and shriek with delight at the 40-foot drop on the log flume. Little kids aren't forgotten, either. They can dig for fossils, fly high on a Dragon Jet and Tilt, and take a spin on the carousel.

Your children will undoubtedly want to make the fun park rounds. Roller-coaster enthusiasts find life's ups and downs thrilling on the **Great Nor'easter at Morey's Pier** (Twenty-fifth Street and the boardwalk), a suspended looping coaster that swirls you at speeds up to 55 mph. Both Morey's Pier and Mariner's Landing Pier feature a **Raging Waters Theme Park** for those who want more than ocean waves. Slide, slither, wiggle, and float, as well as get splashed and sprayed, at these kid-pleasing places. Although young children find pint-size pools and sprays at both parks, the **Raging Waters Theme Park at Morey's Pier** sports an expanded kiddie section themed to pirates.

Festivals, all free and all season long, add to the family fare. Two favorites include the **East Coast Stunt Kite Championships,** in late May, and the **Annual National Marbles Tournament,** in late June. At the kite display children grow wide-eyed at the high-flying maneuvers from team ballets to top-speed tricks. At the marbles matches kids gain inspiration (not to mention moves) from watching their peers ages eight to fourteen compete for scholarship money. Days when these hotshots aren't playing, your kids are free to try their skill on the ten permanent marbles rings, just another of Wildwood's bows to family fun.

In September, Wildwood hosts the Professional Rodeo Cowboys Association Western rodeo. Watch calf roping, trick riding, broncobusting, and bull riding.

Besides boardwalk browsing, sandcastle building, and swimming, a time-honored tradition is to get out on the water. Several companies offer **whale- and dolphin-watching cruises.** While you should be ready to yell "Thar she blows," you're more likely to encounter schools of playful dolphins than the great behemoths of the deep. Boats include the *Cape Dinner Cruise* (609–523–0888) and the speedboat the *Silver Bullet* (609–522–6060).

The Wildwood area offers more than 12,500 rooms in motels, hotels, and condominiums. For families, especially those with young children who want beachside access and more quiet than constant activity, **Wildwood Crest,** south of the boardwalk area, may be more appropriate. The **Reges Oceanfront Resort** (the beach at 9201 Atlantic Avenue; 609–729–9300) offers rooms with kitchenettes, an adult and kiddie pool, and some organized children's activities in season. Several rental agencies can book stays at homes and condominiums. For properties in Wildwood contact **Oceanside Realty** (4500 Atlantic Avenue; 609-522-3322); for Wildwood Crest contact **Century 21** (5604 Pacific Avenue; 609-522-1212). The Tourism Authority publishes a calendar of events (800-WW-BY-SEA). The Chamber of Commerce (609-729-4000) and the Hotel and Motel Association publish lodging guides (800-786-4546).

Board the Cape May–Lewes ferry for a trip to Lewes, Delaware, another beach town. Within several hours of Cape May, you can be in Philadelphia or the Brandywine Valley, Pennsylvania. (See the appropriate chapters.)

FOR MORE INFORMATION

For more information on Cape May, New Jersey, contact the **Greater Cape May Chamber of Commerce,** P.O. Box 556, Cape May, New Jersey 08204 (609-884-5508). For information concerning upcoming Cape May activities and cultural events, contact the **Mid-Atlantic Center for the Arts (MAC),** P.O. Box 340, 1048 Washington Street, Cape May, New Jersey 08204 (609-884-5404; www.capemaymac.org).

Emergency Numbers

Ambulance, fire, and police: 911

Poison Control: 911

Twenty-four-hour pharmacy and around-the-clock medical attention: Burdette Tomlin Hospital, Cape May Courthouse, exit 10 off Garden State Parkway; (609) 463-2000

Hospital: The Burdette Tomlin Memorial Hospital is 11 miles away; (609) 463-2000.

CATSKILL AND SHAWANGUNK MOUNTAINS

Mention the word *Catskills,* and many people still envision the large hotels in Sullivan County where families from New York City once flocked by the carload. Few of those resorts exist today, and the ones remaining have changed with the times, offering more than shuffleboard and handball.

There's much more to this area than stereotypes. The Catskill Mountains cut across four counties, each with its own personality: Ulster in the east, Sullivan in the south, Greene in the north, and Delaware in the west. The 386,000 acres of unspoiled state-owned Catskill Forest Preserve and the 705,000 acres of privately and state-owned Catskill Park offer a variety of simple, natural pleasures: miles of hiking and skiing trails, plus creeks and streams for fishing, canoeing, and tubing. Much of this pristine area is in western Ulster and southwestern Greene counties, although Sullivan and Delaware counties have their share of natural places as well.

The Shawangunk Mountains are located west of the Hudson River, in New York's Hudson Valley. No one knows for sure what Shawangunk means, but one thing that's for certain is the authentic pronunciation. Locals say "Shong-gum" and so should visitors. The Shawangunk mountains have a rich history of such rural industries as barrel-hoop making, huckleberry picking, and rock quarrying for millstone. Today, the mountain range is preserved for daytime recreational use and is a haven for hikers, rock climbers, and snow shoers. Local author Marc B. Fried has written several nature and folk history books about the area. Check out his latest, *Shawangunk: Adventure, Exploration, History and Epiphany from a Mountain Wilderness,* for a more detailed history of the area.

Whether your lodging choice is simple, fancy, or in-between—and there's a wide selection of each—the Catskill and Shawangunk Mountains

Catskill and Shawangunk Mountains
AT A GLANCE

▶ Enjoy canoeing, kayaking, fishing, and tubing

▶ Ski at Hunter Mountain and Windham

▶ Stay at family-friendly resorts

▶ See more then 2,000 animals at Catskill Game Farm

▶ Tourist information, (518) 943-3223

afford your family a wonderful opportunity to get in touch with the outdoors any time of the year. The What to See and Do section includes some attractions in Ulster, Sullivan, and Greene counties—in addition to just hiking and enjoying the scenery—that you might enjoy during a stay in the area. Delaware County, largely rural, also provides beautiful scenery, particularly during fall.

Note: Avoid hiking during hunting season in areas that allow hunting. Ask the state parks and tourist offices about safety precautions.

GETTING THERE

The area is served by a number of commuter and regional airlines, with limousine service to Albany International, New York City's JFK and La Guardia airports, and Stewart Airport in Newburgh. Commuter flights are available from Stewart Airport to Sullivan County International Airport in White Lake (914–583–6600).

Amtrak currently doesn't serve the Catskills. Closest stops: Rhinecliff and Hudson, New York (800–USA–RAIL). Adirondack Trailways, Trailways, Short Line, and Mountain View serve various areas of the Catskills. By car the Catskills are accessed via exits 16 through 21B of I-87, the New York State Thruway. The Route 17 "Quickway," beginning at exit 16, stretches westward to Lake Erie, passing through Sullivan and lower Delaware counties.

GETTING AROUND

Some Catskill cities have their own local bus service, although vacationers invariably rely on their cars to get around.

Consider taking a canoe trip on the Delaware River when you visit the Catskills.

WHAT TO SEE AND DO

Ulster County

Hiking. More than one-third of northwestern Ulster County lies within the **Catskill Forest Preserve,** which starts just west of the city of Kingston. The southern part of the county is in the **Shawangunk Mountains,** officially not part of the Catskill Mountains. But because this is also a popular vacation destination, attractions and lodging in the Shawangunk area are included here. The Hudson River runs along Ulster's eastern boundaries. A good place to start a tour is the **Minnewaska State Park** (10 miles west of New Paltz on U.S. 44 and U.S. 55; 914-255-0752). This park offers miles of hiking trails, some leading to waterfalls.

Attractions

Swimming. Visit the **Village of Saugerties'** sandy public beach on Esopus Creek, at the bottom of Hill Street. A lifeguard is on duty from July Fourth weekend through Labor Day; (914) 246-2321.

Opus 40 and the Quarryman's Museum, High Woods, Saugerties (914-246-3400), is an environmental sculpture made of tons of finely fitted bluestone and constructed over thirty-seven years by sculptor Harvey

Fite. The creation spreads over more than six acres. You and the kids can walk through, around, and over it, past pools and fountains, and up to the monolith that is the summit of the work. Summer concerts of jazz, folk, and classical music are held on selected evenings. Fite's collection of tools (many hand-forged) and furnishings from a quarryman's household (stove, cupboard, and handmade dominoes) are housed in the museum. Open from Memorial Day to November 1, but call first; some Saturdays are reserved for special events.

Southeast of Woodstock the city of **Kingston,** along the Hudson River, was a leading nineteenth-century maritime center. At the Historic Rondout area—a revitalized nineteenth-century waterfront community with shops and restaurants—those days are relived. See the **Hudson River Maritime Museum,** 1 Rondout Plaza (at the end of Broadway) (914-338-0071). The small museum tells the story of the Hudson through models, artifacts, photographs, and paintings. Exhibits change often. In the outdoor area antique vessels are displayed. Visiting vessels, such as the sloop *Clearwater,* are often tied up at the museum's bulkhead. The *Indie II* excursion boat leaves for a ten-minute cruise to the Rondout II Lighthouse, where you can climb to the top for river views. The museum, open from May to October, has a number of special events including the Shad Festival each May. Shad and shad roe are served along with music, puppet shows, and boat rides. The September Harvest Festival features crafts, harvest food, music, and boats.

Across the street is the **Trolley Museum,** 89 East Strand; (914-331-3399). The big draw is the excursion ride that runs 1.5 miles along the tracks of the old Ulster & Delaware Railroad to picnic grounds on the Hudson shores. The museum displays trolley, subway, and rapid-transit cars. Open Memorial to Labor Day.

Shawangunk Area of Ulster County
Widmark Honey Farms, Route 44–55, 2 miles west of Gardiner (914-255-6400), has been producing honey on this working farm for more than one hundred years. Along with honeybees and livestock, the farm has three American black bears that wrestle and perform in ninety-minute shows from May to October, on Saturday, Sunday, and holidays

---

Tubing on Esopus Creek

Tubing is a great way for older kids and adults to enjoy the Esopus Creek, located within the Catskill Forest preserve. Town Tinker Tube Rental has a substation at The Lodge at Catskill Corners, 3 miles east of Phoenicia, where kids ages twelve and older can rent tubes and equipment. (Head protection and life vests are required for everyone under fourteen.) The novice section of the creek is about 2.5 miles, or about a two-hour trip, and features one set of fast-moving rapids at the beginning. After that enjoy a slow, winding ride through gorgeous scenery. Call (914) 688-5553; www.towntinker.com.

Woodstock

Woodstock, just west of Saugerties, is at the foot of Ohayo and Overlook Mountains in the Catskill range. A brochure of area attractions, including hiking trails, is available from the Chamber of Commerce, P.O. Box 36, Woodstock 12498 (914–679-6234). Stores that sell area hiking maps include the **Golden Notebook,** 29 Tinker Street (914-679-8000), which also has a children's book and cassette annex.

Woodstock is known for the 1960s music festival, although that didn't take place here. The festival was already named when the original deal fell through, and the site was relocated to Sullivan County.

Woodstock—a community of writers, musicians, artists, and craftspeople—is worth a stop.

Browse in the shops on and around Tinker Street. Don't miss **Tinker Toys of Woodstock,** 5 Mill Hill Road. Then take the kids for a romp in the **Woodstock Wonderworks,** a community-built playground at the elementary school, Route 375. The complex, open to the public when school isn't in session, features tunnels and mazes, a dragon slide, a Viking ship, a guitar car, and picnic tables.

Just outside Woodstock, you'll find **Kenneth L. Wilson State Park,** Wittenberg Mountain Road, Mount Tremper (914–679-7020). A sandy beach on the park's shallow lake is perfect for tots. Nearby, marked trails wind through the woods. There are rest rooms, a picnic area, and overnight campsites by reservation.

at 3:00 P.M. The farm and apiaries are open all year. You can taste free honey and pet goats, calves, and lambs. Picnicking is allowed.

Winter pleasures include **Belleayre Mountain Ski Center,** NY–28, Highmount (914-254-5600), the county's largest downhill area. It's open Thanksgiving weekend to the end of March. The lower mountain is for beginners and novices. A nursery caters to ages eight weeks to twelve years (reservations suggested), and SkiWee lessons for ages four to twelve are available on weekends and holidays. Anyone purchasing a ticket gets a free lesson. Some 6.2 kilometer of ungroomed cross-country trails are free. Lessons are available.

Sullivan County

This southwestern Catskill county, bordered on the west by Pennsylvania, has some of the big hotels and resorts long associated with these mountains. There are also more simple lodgings and plenty of family-friendly activities. The *Sullivan County Travel Guide* suggests several different driving tours; one includes the county's famous covered bridges.

This county was the site of the **Woodstock Festival,** held in Bethel. If your teens consider this a historic site, then drive by for a look. The farm is located off Route 17B on Hurd Road. The site is being developed into a concert venue with events throughout the summer. Call the Gerry Foundation (914–295–2716) for information.

You'll be close to the 1,409-acre **Lake Superior State Park** in Bethel, on Duggan Road, between Routes 17B and 55. This lake has a nice, sandy beach, lifeguards, and rowboat rentals, and allows fishing and picnicking. Call (914) 583-7908, ext. 5002.

In the northern half of the county is **Apple Pond Farming Center,** Hahn Road, Calicoon Center (914–482–4764). Call for reservations. This is a working farm; all equipment is pulled by horses. On the horse-drawn wagon tour, you meet sheep, goats, lambs, and several breeds of horses. As you ride through the fields, you hear about farming in olden days. The farm is open year-round, so depending on when you visit, you may see wool spinning, beekeeping, or maple syrup-making. There are hayrides in the summer and sleigh rides in the winter. There's a picnic area. A guest house is available by the weekend or week; reserve in advance. Because this tour involves walking through fields, strollers aren't appropriate.

In the southern half of the county, stop at the **Fort Delaware Museum of Colonial History,** Route 97, Narrowsburg (914–252–6660). This is a no-frills (but interesting) re-creation of the first settlement in the upper Delaware River Valley in 1754. Costumed interpreters explain how these wilderness dwellers survived. The stockaded settlement comprises log dwellings, a blacksmith's shop, a weaver's shed, armory, pens for animals, and the fort. Demonstrations of spinning, candle dipping, and musket and cannon firing are held frequently. Open from Memorial Day weekend through Labor Day, there are a variety of special events in July and August.

Cruise the Hudson River

Rondout Landing is the departure point for Hudson River cruises aboard the excursion ship *Rip Van Winkle* from May through October. Two-hour sight-seeing tours of river estates and lighthouses are included, as are all-day sojourns down to West Point Military Academy in Orange County. The West Point round trip takes seven hours and doesn't stop, except to let off one-way passengers, so unless your kids love cruising, opt for the shorter tours. The boat has a snack bar on board. Reservations are suggested for evening music cruises, which feature local country and western or rock 'n' roll bands. Call (914–255–6515 or 800–843–7472). For more information, contact Ulster County Tourism, 244 Fair Street, Kingston (914–340–3566 or 800–DIAL-UCO; www.co.ulstetiny.us).

More Outdoor Activities—Sullivan County

- **Canoeing and kayaking.** Paddle along the Delaware River. Several outfitters offer rentals, including **Kittatinny Canoes & Rafts,** Route 97, Barryville (800–FLOAT–KC); **Lander's River Trips,** Route 97, Narrowsburg (800–252–3925); and **Wild and Scenic River Tours & Rentals,** Route 97, Barryville (800–836–0366), which also offers tubing and family canoe and kayak trips.
- **Bicycling.** Pedal through the countryside on a weekly guided bicycle trip with the **Bicycle Club of Sullivan County** (914–794–3000, ext. 5010). Trips offered April through October.
- **Horseback riding.** Ride through the woods with **Hadley Riding Stables,** Old Liberty Road, Monticello (914–434–9254). While waiting to saddle up, children can feed goats, lambs, and ducks at the barnyard zoo. Young kids go on pony rides, and ages seven and older can try trail rides. **Arrowhead Ranch,** Cooley Road, Parksville (914–292–6267), offers trail rides on 1,000 acres as well as lunch and overnight trips.
- **Fishing. Eldred Preserve Resorts,** Route 55, Eldred (800–557–FISH), has two lakes stocked with rainbow, brook, and golden trout as well as bass. Boats can be rented.

Eldred also offers sporting clays and shooting instruction.
- **Fly-fishing.** Roscoe is reputedly the birthplace of American fly-fishing. At **the Catskill Fly Fishing Center and Museum,** Livingston Manor (914–439–4810), kids can take fishing lessons during Environmental Camp in July. The museum details the history of the sport.
- **Downhill skiing and snowboarding. Holiday Mountain Ski Area,** Box 629, Monticello (914–796–3161), has fifteen slopes and offers night runs.
- **Cross-country skiing. Liberty Parks and Recreation,** at Hanofee Park, Liberty (914–292–7690), has eighty-six acres of trails plus ice skating.
- **Eagle Spotting.** Sullivan County is the winter home to more than one hundred bald eagles. The **Eagle Institute,** at 1905 Williamsbridge, (914–965–7777), offers guided eagle watches. Ask about the children's festival.
- **Soaring.** From Wurtsboro Airport, at 50 Barone Road, Wurtsboro (914–888–2791), take off and glide over the valleys in a sailplane.

For more information, contact the Sullivan County Visitors Association, Monticello (914–794–3000, 800–882–CATS; www.co.sullivan.ny.us.sctg).

Minisink Battlefield, Minisink Ford, SR-97 west to Route 168 (914-794-3000, ext. 5002). This is the site of the 1779 battle in which American militiamen were massacred by Tories and Mohawk Indians sympathetic to the British. Three flat interpretive nature trails wind through woodlands. Across from the entrance is the 1848 Roebling's Suspension Bridge, the oldest in America, created by John Roebling of Brooklyn Bridge fame.

Greene County

This northern Catskill county offers a variety of ethnic and music festivals, scenic trails, one hundred waterfalls (many with natural pools for swimming), and appealing family attractions. The town of **Catskill,** just off the New York State Thruway in the eastern central part of the county, has several of particular interest.

One of the favorites is **Catskill Game Farm,** off Route 32 (518-678-9595). Families have been coming here for generations, and the appeal is obvious: 2,000 animals, including bears, tigers, lions, and performing acts such as monkeys that juggle and elephants that dance. Buy crackers to feed deer and llamas at the petting zoo, or bottle feed small baby pigs and lambs. A train heads from the petting zoo to the birdhouse. Have lunch either at the snack bars or the picnic area, and stay the day. Open Memorial Day to Labor Day.

Another popular attraction is **Clyde Peeling's Reptiland,** Route 32 (518-678-3557). Your kids will either be totally fascinated or completely repelled by the approximately one hundred reptiles ranging from little garden snakes to big king cobras. Open Memorial Day to Labor Day.

Elsewhere in the county you'll find **Zoom Flume Waterpark,** Shady Glen Road, East Durham, northwest of Catskill (518-239-4559). This is the Catskills' largest waterpark. There are waterslides, bumper boats, and other attractions. Open Memorial Day to Labor Day.

North-South Lake Public Campgrounds, County Route 18, Haines Falls, southwest of Catskill (518-589-5058 or 357-2234). This New York State-run recreation area has two sandy beaches on either end of the lake, plus boat rentals and fishing. Hike in the surrounding woods; one trail

Giant Kaleidoscopes

A giant, walk-in kaleidoscope housed in a silo is the centerpiece of **Catskill Corners,** P.O. Box 300, Route 28, Mt. Tremper (914-688-2451; www.catskillcorners.com). Lean back or lie on the floor to see the light and mirror show "America: The House We Live In," a rapid succession of images, from Pilgrims to patriots, presidents to Elvis Presley, accompanied by music. The noise may scare younger kids, but grade-schoolers are likely to say "wow" to the spectacle. Also on site are a Museum of Light Sculptures; Scopeworld, an interactive display of kaleidoscopes; the Kaatskill Kaleidostore, which sells an array of these magic tubes; Festival Marketplace, featuring works by Woodstock area artists; plus the Spotted Dog Firehouse Restaurant.

Ski Greene County

- **Hunter Mountain,** New York Route 23A, Hunter (518–263–4223 or 800–FOR–SNOW). This three-mountain complex covers forty-six slopes and trails. Machine-made snow keeps the place open from November through April, and a snowtubing park with six chutes offers off-the-ski-trail fun. A Peewee program for infants up to age five combines child-sitting with skiing for the older tots. At Ski-Wee Frostyland ages five to twelve learn to ski on weekends and holidays from 9:30 A.M. to 3:30 P.M. (reserve). The mountain has ethnic and music festivals and the Sky Ride, with views of the Northeast from the Catskills' longest and highest chairlift. Call for a summer schedule.

- **Sky Windham,** Route 23 West, Windham (518–734–4300 or 800–729–SKIW, 800–729–4SNO). Ski on twin mountain peaks with thirty-three trails. The Children's Ski School offers half- or full-day programs that include activities for non-skiers ages one to seven, for preskiers age three, for ages four to seven at Mini-Mogul Skiers, and two- or five-hour sessions on weekends and holidays for Mogul Master Skiers ages eight to thirteen. Reservations with full payment required. Area lodging can be reserved through the Lodging Service (800–729–SKIW).

For more information, contact Green County Tourism, Catskill (518–943–3223).

leads to the scenic Kaaterskill Falls. Call (800) 456–CAMP for reservations from April to October.

Delaware County

Largely rural Delaware County, which includes the western slopes of the Catskill Mountains, offers 11,000 acres of reservoirs for fishing and thousands of acres of forests for hiking. State parks include Bear Spring Mountain, Walton (607–865–6989); Beaver Kill, Downsville (607–363–7501); East Branch State Forests, Downsville (607–363–7501); Little Pond State Park, Turnwood (914–439–5480); and Oquaga Creek State Park, Masonville (914–439–5480).

Bike along the former railbed of the Catskill Mountain branch of the Delaware and Ulster Railroad. The **Rails-to-Trails** route extends from Kingston to Oneonta. The western section begins at Bloomville and passes through the villages of Hobart and Stamford, then parallels Route 23 along the Bearkill Stream to Grand Gorge, Mile Post 19. For tougher trails, head to the **Ski Plattekill Mountain Biking Center,** Cold Spring Road, Roxbury (607-326-3500; www.plattekill.com). Beginner trails are wide with gentle slopes, and advanced routes are narrow and steep.

Hike a portion of the 19-mile **Catskill Scenic Trail,** an especially good path for younger kids. The mostly flat paths follow the former rail tracks of the New York Central Railroad.

Enjoy a scenic train ride aboard the **Delaware and Ulster Rail Ride,** Route 28, Arkville (914-586-3877 or 800-225-4132). The one-and-three-quarter-hour trip winds through the Catskill Mountains. Theme rides add to the fun; kids especially like the train robbery outings.

Drive across **covered bridges** that cross the Delaware River. **Fitches Bridge** crosses the West Branch 2 miles north of Delhi. The **Hamden** bridge is on Route 10 on the left side of the road as you drive from Delhi to Walton. The bridge in **Downsville** is at the outskirts of the village, along routes 206 and 30. You can take photos from the riverbank, but this bridge doesn't allow cars.

Tour the **Hanford Mills Museum,** Routes 10 and 12, East Meredith (607-278-5744 or 800-295-4992), a working saw- and gristmill. The site has a Fitz overshot waterwheel, a gasoline-powered engine and dynamo, and a farmstead.

For more information, contact the **Delaware County Catskills Chamber of Commerce,** 114 Main Street, Delhi (800-642-4443; www.delawarecounty.org).

Performing Arts

In Ulster County, Kingston's **Ulster Performing Arts Center,** 601 Broadway (914-339-6088), features Broadway plays suitable for families, concerts ranging from symphony to rock, and second-run movies for reasonable prices. **Shadowland Theatre,** Ellenville (914-647-5511), has a professional company in residence performing Broadway-style productions, musicals, and children's plays from June to October.

In summer the **Nutshell Arts Center Gallery,** Route 52, Lake Huntington (914-932-8708), offers a weekend chamber music series. **The Delaware Valley Opera** performs at the **Tusten Theatre,** Bridge Street, Narrowsburg (914-252-7576). The **Forestburgh Playhouse,** 55 Forestburgh (914-794-2005 or 914-794-1194—after June 1), offers musicals and mysteries, as well as the **Young Audience Festival at Forestburgh,** original musical productions for ages five to twelve.

SPECIAL EVENTS

Ballgames, Fairs, and Festivals

At **Baxter Stadium,** Mountaindale (914–436–GAME), you can watch the **Catskill Cougars,** a minor league baseball team, and the **New York Diamonds,** part of the United States Women's Baseball League.

Contact individual tourist offices for more information on festivals in their area.

May. Woodstock–New Paltz Arts and Crafts Fair, New Paltz, Ulster County; Shad Festival, Maritime Museum, Kingston, Ulster County.

July. Fourth of July celebrations in Village of Ellenville, City of Kingston, New Paltz, and Saugerties in Ulster County. St. Joseph's Italian Festival, New Paltz, Ulster County.

August. Ulster County Fair, New Paltz. Antique and Classic Boat Show, Rondout Landing, Kingston, Ulster County.

September. Woodstock–New Paltz Arts and Crafts Fair. Garlic Festival, Saugerties.

July–October. A variety of ethnic and music festivals at Hunter Mountain, Greene County; with food, crafts, and entertainment.

August. Delaware County Fair, Walton. Old Franklin Day, Franklin, Delaware County, features crafts, flea markets, and activities.

October. Annual Apple Festival, Hensonville, Greene County.

WHERE TO STAY

Fancy resorts, simple motels, bed-and-breakfast inns, cabins in the woods: The Catskill and Shawangunk Mountains have them all. Each county tourist office can supply a listing of lodgings. Here are a few to give you an idea of what's available for families.

Ulster County: Catskill

Frost Valley YMCA, Frost Valley Road, Claryville (914–985–2291). This splendid place is closed in late June (except Father's Day weekend) and in July and August, when it becomes a summer camp, but the facility is open the rest of the year to the public. Accommodations include some grand rooms in the "Castle," once the home of the industrialist who owned this property, where you share the house (and baths) with other guests. Lodges, much like motel accommodations, and basic cabins are also available. Everyone eats family-style in the main dining hall. When you check in, obtain a schedule of events, which include Junior Naturalist programs,

Shawangunk Mountains Family Resorts

- **Mohonk Mountain House,** Lake Mohonk, New Paltz (914-255-1000 or 800-772-6646—from area codes 212, 516, or 718). This historic Victorian resort, situated on 7,000 acres of nature preserve, offers specialty, themed weekends fall through spring. During January's What's in the Winter Woods, you and your kids learn about forest animals and winter night skies; during the March Family Festival, listen to storytellers and join in singalongs.

  When not busy with events, hike in the woods; if it's cold enough, skate on the frozen lake or the pond. When it snows, enjoy cross-country skiing and snowshoeing. On weekends a modified kids' program operates for ages three to twelve. From Memorial Day to Labor Day, there are programs for ages two to seventeen. Baby-sitting is available at an extra charge. The rates include three meals a day. The rooms, remember, are not "hotel modern." Rather than glitz, you have lots of Victorian oak and fireplaces.

- **Pinegrove Resort Ranch,** Lower Chestertown Road, Kerhonkson (914-626-7345 or 800-346-4626). This year-round dude ranch caters to families by offering day-long activities at an all-inclusive price. The rooms, like the resort, are plain but comfortable. Located on 500 acres between the Shawangunk Mountains and the Catskill range, this ranch guarantees guests one instructional ride a day. If there's room, you can sign up for more. From 10:00 A.M. to 5:00 P.M. every day, a nursery cares for kids up to two years old, and a day camp keeps kids ages three and up happily busy feeding llamas, singing on hayrides, and riding ponies. Children under age seven learn to ride in the corral, and kids over seven go on trail rides with adults. Evening entertainment includes square dancing, scavenger hunts, and family games. The price includes three meals a day, an all-day snack bar, rides, and entertainment. Rates are half-price for children four through sixteen, and kids under four stay for free.

crafts, group hikes, and orienteering. There are also hayrides and singalongs. Enjoy rowing, swimming in a pond, bicycling, and square dancing, as well as cross-country skiing and sledding in the winter.

Sullivan County

The Concord Resort Hotel, Kiamesha Lake (800-431-3850), formerly one of the big Catskill hotels, has closed. Sheraton Hotels has purchased the property and, after extensive renovations, will open it as a hotel in 2002.

Kutsher's Country Club, near Monticello (914-794-6000 or 800-431-1273), is another of the old-style resorts that has been trying to woo a new generation by promoting its kids' programs. These include a nursery for young ones, programs for ages three to five and six to nine, plus some activities for preteens and teens. With 450 rooms and more than 1,200 acres, Kutsher's is big. This Catskills' fixture offers tennis, golf, snowtubing and tobogganing, and nightly entertainment. For additional lodging information, call the Sullivan County Visitor Associates (800-882-CATS).

Greene County

Balsam Shade Farm, Route 32, Greenville (518-966-5315; www.balsamshade.com), is a casual, country family lodging with a pool, tennis court, hiking trail, and lovely mountain views. The farm has nightly entertainment and three meals served daily with farm-grown vegetables.

Albergo Allegria, Route 296, Windham (800-6-ALBERGO; www.AlbergoUSA.com), is a hospitable Victorian bed-and-breakfast that welcomes families. Albergo Allegria offers Belgian waffles or gourmet omelettes (among other delicious foods) in the outdoor cafe. If you happen to stay during the ski season, warm yourselves by the fireplace during the Après Ski on Saturdays, when complimentary hot cider and hot chocolate are served.

Scribner Hollow Lodge, Route 32A, Hunter (519- 263-4211), has a rustic atmosphere with scenic Catskill views, sauna and Jacuzzi, an outdoor heated swimming pool, all-season tennis courts, and an indoor spa/pool.

Sunny Hill Resort and Golf Course, Route 32 or 82, Greenville (518-634-7642), has 200 acres of open spaces and private woods as well as Lake Loree. The resort offers an eighteen-hole golf course, a video game room, tennis courts, and an outdoor swimming pool.

WHERE TO EAT

Each county's travel guide offers dining listings. In Greene County **La Conca D'Oro,** 440 Main Street, Catskill, serves good northern Italian food (518-943-3549). **Red's,** Route 9W, West Coxsackie (914-731-8151), is known for its fresh seafood.

Club 97, Route 97, Callicoon (914-887-5941), offers great family dining, with an available children's menu, serving dishes from Italian to seafood to prime rib, plus homemade desserts.

Eldred Preserve Restaurant, Route 55, Eldred (914-557-8316), is open every day from June to August; specialties include fresh trout and continental cuisine. Reservations are suggested in summer and fall.

SIDE TRIPS

Wherever you stay, take a side trip to explore adjacent Catskill counties (Greene County, for instance, is about forty-five minutes north of Kingston). From Delaware County drive north to Cooperstown in adjoining Otsego County to the **National Baseball Hall of Fame** (607-547-9988). Most of Ulster and Sullivan counties are less than ninety minutes from New York City.

FOR MORE INFORMATION

Tourist Information in Greene County, Thruway exit 21, Catskill (518-943-3223), is open seven days a week, or call (800) 542-2414. For Ulster County, call (800-DIAL-UCO). Sullivan County has two Information Center Cabooses. The first, on Broad Street, Roscoe, is also a mini railroad museum, open Memorial Day to mid-October. The Livingston Manor Caboose, exit 96 off Route 17, is open July and August on Friday, Saturday, and Sunday. You can also call (914) 794-3000, ext. 5010, or (800) 882-CATS. Delaware County Chamber of Commerce, 97 Main Street, Delhi, New York 13753; (607) 746-2281 or (800) 642-4443.

Emergency Numbers

Since we're covering a wide area, we've listed county sheriff numbers.

Greene County
Sheriff: (518) 943-3300; emergency 911

Catskill Community Care Clinic, 159 Jefferson Heights, Catskill: (518) 943-6334

Greene Medical Arts Center: (518) 943-1505

Ulster County
Sheriff: (914) 338-0939; emergency 911

Kingston City Hospital, 396 Broadway: (914) 331-3131

Sullivan County
Sheriff: (914) 794-7100; emergency 911

Community General Hospital has two branches: one on Bushville Road, Harris, in the center of the county (914-794-3300), and one in Callicoon, in the west, Route 97 (914-887-5530).

Regional

Poison Control: (914) 353-1000 or (800) 336-6997 (from 518 and 914 area codes)

There are no twenty-four-hour pharmacies in the area. A number are open seven days a week, such as CVS, Route 9W, King's Mall, Kingston (914-336-5955), 9:00 A.M. to 9:00 P.M., Monday through Saturday, closing at 6:00 P.M. on Sunday. Some pharmacies post emergency numbers on their front doors for after-hours assistance.

LAKE GEORGE

The Lake George, New York, area offers families a rare combination—hundreds of thousands of acres of woodlands, ponds, and lakes plus a first-class family hotel, the Sagamore Resort, in Bolton Landing. The 32-mile-long Lake George is part of upstate New York's Adirondack Park, six million acres of private and state-owned land, approximately 60 percent of which is wilderness. These forests, islands, and mountains provide families with ample opportunities to enjoy the fall foliage

The first thing you must do, however, especially if you approach the lake from the south, is to have faith. You must believe that there are undeveloped parcels beyond the village of Lake George, a town choked with motels, cottage colonies, eateries, and souvenir shops. Just a short drive north takes you to Bolton Landing, a less built up town, and beyond that you find quiet lakeside villages, natural shoreline, and thickly wooded mountains.

GETTING THERE

The closest airport to Lake George is Albany International Airport (518–869–9611), some 50 miles away. Car rentals are available at the airport.

Adirondack Trailways (800–225–6815), runs buses to Lake George, Glens Falls, Tupper Lake, and Lake Placid from Albany, with connections to New York City. In Lake George the bus stops at the Mobil Station, 320 Canada Street (518–668–9511). Greyhound travels from New York to Glens Falls, 10 miles away, stopping at All Points Diner, 21 South Street (518–793–5052). To reach Lake George passengers must hook up with an Adirondack Trailways bus, which leaves from the Coopers Cave Restaurant on Hudson and Elm; (518–793–5525).

Amtrak's *Montréaler* train stops at nearby Fort Edward; however, this small town provides no direct transportation to Lake George. You can take a local bus from Fort Edward to Glens Falls, then transfer to another bus for Lake George (June to Labor Day only). Call Greater Great Falls Transit (518–792–1085).

Lake George

AT A GLANCE

► Hike scenic woodland trails

► Boat on 32-mile-long lake surrounded by green mountains

► Explore Fort Ticonderoga, a reconstructed eighteenth-century fort

► Warren County Tourism Department, (800) 365-1050, ext. 5100 or (518) 761-6366; www.visitlakegeorge.com

The village of Lake George is located off the Northway, I-87, near the junction of U.S. 9 and SR 9N, which travels north along the lake's western shore.

GETTING AROUND

A car is a must, as there's no public transportation within the Lake George area. Boat-rental facilities are located at various points along the lake (see the *Warren County Travel Guide* for specific locations). Lake George Village offers trolley rides daily from Memorial Day to Labor Day. Call (518) 792-1085 for schedule and stops.

WHAT TO SEE AND DO

Museums and Historical Sights

Most people are so busy having fun in Lake George that they don't seem to notice the scarcity of museums. (We don't consider the House of Frankenstein Wax Museum on Canada Street a "museum" in the true sense of the word.) Many museums are small ones dedicated to local history and not terribly interesting to kids. Two area attractions do fill the bill, however.

The International Arts and Culture Association (IACA), 277 Glen Street, Third Floor, Glens Falls (518-793-2773), has fun interactive exhibits for kids of all ages. The museum also displays children's art from around the world.

Fort William Henry Museum, Beach Road and Route 9 entrances; (518) 668-5471. Will be interesting to your kids if they have seen or read James Fennimore Cooper's *The Last of the Mohicans*. They'll especially appreciate this restored Colonial fortress, which played an integral role in

A narrated cruise around Lake George aboard the Minne-Ha-Ha *is a great way to take in the scenery.*

the French and Indian War. Costumed guide-historians conduct tours during July and August. The musket and cannon firings and demonstrations of musketball molding and grenadier bomb-tossing appeal to school-age kids and teens, although younger ages may wince at the noise from the firings. For some reason the dungeons and stockades are always the most popular exhibits with kids. During late spring and early fall, audiovisual displays take the place of the guides.

Beaches

A listing of area beaches appears in the *Warren County Travel Guide*. **Million Dollar Beach,** on the southern shore, east of U.S. 9 on Beach Road (518-668-3352), is the town's largest and best suited to families, with a lifeguard, bathhouse, picnic facilities, and volleyball nets. Parking fee.

Boaters can explore the lake's many islands, some with sandy beaches. A permit is required to picnic on Lake George Islands. Call the Department of Environmental Conservation (518-623-3671).

Scenic Drive

The one-hour trip from **Lake George to Hague** is a convenient length for kids and provides good views, especially during fall's leaf-peeping season. From Bolton Landing follow Route 9N over Tongue Mountain to Silver

Hiking around Lake George

Whatever type of trail you and your kids want to try—nature or hiking, easy or strenuous—you'll find it in or near Lake George. The Adirondack Mountain Club (800–395–8080) publishes *An Adirondack Sampler* in two volumes, with easy to moderately difficult hikes and backpacking trips of Warren County and Adirondack Park.

Easy nature trails through pines and hardwoods are just part of the attraction of **Crandall Park International Trail System,** south of Glens Falls on Route 9. Bring a picnic, Frisbee, and fishing poles and spend the afternoon. Also available are a fishing pond, tennis and basketball courts, baseball field, and playground. A Fit-Trail has wooden exercise stations.

Prospect Mountain's entrance to its splendid hiking trail is on Montcalm Street, Lake George. Ages eight and up should be game for the moderate climb to the 2,100-foot summit for splendid views of the Adirondacks, Vermont's Green Mountains, and New Hampshire's White Mountains. If that's too strenuous, take the 5.5-mile scenic highway to the parking lot, then ride the "viewmobile" to the summit.

The Adirondack Mountain Club's *Kids on the Trail! Hiking with Children in the Adirondacks,* by Rose Rivezzi and David Trithart, details trails and hiking tips. The book is available in bookstores and through the Adironack Mountain Club (800–395–8080).

Bay. The road cuts through woods, then leads past wide lake views to the mountain lookout. Another good pick is the **Prospect Mountain State Parkway,** a 5.5-mile drive to the 2,030-foot summit.

History

Fort Ticonderoga (518–585–2821) is about 30 miles north of Bolton Landing. Built in 1755, by the French and called Carillon, the fort was taken by the British in 1759 and renamed Ticonderoga, an approximation of a Native American name. The star-shaped fortress is notable for events in May 1775 when Ethan Allen and the Green Mountain Boys, along with Benedict Arnold (who was still a loyal soldier then), seized the fort in the first American victory in the battle for independence. The fort is strategically located on Lake Champlain where it meets Lake George, an important early transportation route.

What you see is a full-scale reconstruction from the fort's ruins, a project begun privately in 1908 by the Pell family. The thick stone walls and battlements punctuated by cannons make it easy for kids to envision Revolutionary sieges. At various times the "Place of Arms," or interior parade grounds where soldiers once practiced drills, comes alive with the marching beat of a fife and drum corps. Docents and costumed interpreters answer questions. The surrounding barracks house a museum that tells the history of the region and the fort. Although the exhibits are noninteractive displays of artifacts, children should find enough of interest, especially if they're curious about early weapons and soldiers. Among the kid-pleasing items are circa 1720 muskets, cases of powder horns, and a room of eighteenth century halberds and swords, all looking fiercely ominous.

Bring a picnic lunch and take your time here. On the property there is an eatery offering drinks and a limited selection of sandwiches and snacks. Even young children will appreciate the bucolic view of the surrounding mountains and the peaceful lake.

Special Tours

The best way to explore the lake is by boat. Several companies offer cruises. As the boats pull farther away from shore, the wave runners diminish, eventually disappearing, leaving you with views of mist-shrouded islands that dot the lake and the scenic, less developed eastern shore. These quiet stretches of water make it easy to imagine how impressive and important the lake was to the Native Americans and first settlers.

The Sagamore Resort offers two-hour sightseeing cruises aboard the *Morgan;* a luncheon buffet is optional. South of the Sagamore, the boat cruises by several of the mansions remaining from what was dubbed Millionaire's Row. These gracious homes are remnants of Lake George's heyday from the 1880s through the 1920s when the country's wealthy gathered on these shores.

Both **Lake George Steamboat Cruises** (518–668–5777 or 800–553–BOAT) and **Lake George Shoreline Cruises,** Kurosaka Lane (518–668–4644), offer daily narrated sight-seeing cruises.

Mountainaire Adventures (800–950–2194) features guided walking tours, and **Overlook Tours, Inc.** (518–742–1735) and **Historical Makers** (518–668–5755) offer historical and environmental tours. (See also Getting Around for trolley rides in Lake George Village.)

More Attractions

Aqua Adventure Water Slide, Route 9, Queensbury (518–792–8989). Splash, loop, and curve down water slides at this park. A kiddie pool and play area are on site.

Great Escape and **Splash Water Kingdom Fun Park,** Route 9 (518–792–3500). When your family wants to play at amusement parks, the state's largest is the place. Enjoy one hundred rides, shows, and attractions, such as Noah's Sprayground Water Area, Raging River Raft Ride, the Comet Roller Coaster, and the Boomerang and Bobsled.

Magic Forest, Route 9 (518-668-2448). Younger kids may prefer this smaller, calmer park to Great Escape. With twenty-five rides, a Fairy Tale area, and Santa's Hideaway, this small park is just right for tots.

Rodeos are held at three area ranches weekly in summer: **Painted Pony Rodeo,** Lake Luzerne (518-696-2421); **1,000 Acres Ranch and Rodeo,** Stony Creek (518-696-2444); and **Ridin-Hy Ranch and Rodeo** (518-494-2742). (See Where to Stay.) For a list of area stables, consult the *Warren County Travel Guide.*

Shopping
Bargains abound in Warren County's more than eighty factory outlets, most located in what's known as the **Million Dollar Half-Mile** Factory Outlet Strip (take I-87 exit 20, then north on Route 9). **Aviation Mall,** I-87, exit 19, in Queensbury, is the area's largest mall and rents strollers.

Performing Arts
Lake George Dinner Theatre, Holiday Inn Turf at Lake George, features Broadway show performances by professional Equity actors. Call (518) 668-5781 for program information. Renowned artists perform at **Luzerne Chamber Music Festival** (518-696-3892).

Adirondack Theater Festival French Mountain Playhouse at the Lake George RV Park, Route 149 (518-798-7479), offers children's workshops, solo performers, and more in June and July.

Thirty miles away, the **Saratoga Performing Arts Center** has top-named performing arts companies, such as the New York City Ballet and the New York City Opera, as well as popular entertainers. Call (518) 587-3330 for schedules.

SPECIAL EVENTS

Sporting Events
Adirondack Red Wings hockey team plays at the Glens Falls Civic Center, Route 9 (Glen Street); (518) 798-0202.

Adirondack Lumberjacks, AAA baseball at Glens Falls, East Field, Dix Avenue; (518) 743-9618.

Fairs and Festivals
February. Warren County comes alive with winter carnivals. Lake George usually celebrates on weekends with a variety of races, including one in which participants pull full-size outhouses (yes, outhouses). For

the kids: Olympic games, clowns, contests, and Georgie the Snowman. The Warren County Tourism Department can provide specific dates, as well as sites and listings of cross-country ski centers.

July–August. Family concerts at Shepard Park, Lake George; Thursday night fireworks.

August. Warren County Fair, Fairgrounds, Warrensburg. Family Festival Week, Shepard Park, Lake George, with entertainers, crafts, games, and more.

September. Hot Air Balloon Festival, Glens Falls–Queensbury.

October. Gore Mountain's Foliage Festival, with music, food, parade, and entertainment for kids. World's Largest Garage Sale, Warrensburg, has the town outfitted with vendors, garage sales, crafts, entertainment, and more.

WHERE TO STAY

If your family likes being in the middle of the action, the commercial strip of wall-to-wall motels on Route 9 will do. To appreciate the true beauty of the area, however, venture somewhat beyond. A complete chart of accommodations, ranging from rustic cabins to luxurious resorts, is included in the *Warren County Travel Guide* available from the Tourism Department (800-365-1050, ext. 5100). Family-friendly possibilities include the following.

Cresthaven Resort Motel, Lake Shore Drive, Route 9N (518-668-3332), is spread out on thirteen acres, with its own 300-foot sandy beach. Choose from log cabins, cottages, or efficiencies. A kiddie pool, game room, playgrounds, grills, and picnic tables are tailor-made for families.

Roaring Brook Ranch and Tennis Resort, 2.5 miles south on Route 9N, (518-668-5767), has one indoor and two outdoor pools, horseback riding, five tennis courts, and a playground, plus a children's counselor in July and August. Families appreciate the coin laundry on premises.

Ridin-Hy Ranch Resort is on 800 acres on Sherman Lake, Warrensburg (518-494-2742). This year-round resort offers all-inclusive vacation plans. There's an indoor pool, beach, and playground area, and rodeos are held throughout the summer.

The **Sagamore Resort,** 800-358-3585, sits on its own 70-acre island in Lake George, just half a mile from the village of Bolton Landing. Originally built in 1883, the historic property, with its sweeping lawn and prominent lakeside locale, was an important part of Lake George's era as a summer gathering spot for the country's wealthy.

The property, which underwent a $75 million refurbishment in 1985, offers families a pampering, if pricey, retreat. For parents, the spa offers a variety of treatments and the fitness center has an ample array of work-out equipment plus a pretty lake view. The resort has its own golf course and tennis center. In the fall, the indoor pool is a prime gathering spot for kids. In the summer the Teepee Club, the kids' program, operates daily; in the fall and winter there are supervised activities for ages four to thirteen on Saturday from 8:00 A.M. to 4:00 P.M. and from 5:00 to 9:00 P.M.

The main hotel has one hundred rooms and suites. A series of lodges, some along the lake, offer an additional 240 rooms, some of which are suites with living areas, kitchenettes, and one or two bedrooms. The Teepee Club is housed in Lodge 4, so if your children are young, you may want to pick a room or suite near that building.

Problems: With lots of boats and locals on wave runners, the lakefront at the resort is noisy. It has limited space for lake swimming.

Treasure Cove, Diamond Point, 4 miles north of town (518-668-5334), is directly on the lake, with its own private sandy beach. Stay in two- or three-bedroom cottages, some with fireplaces. Two pools, a playground, lawn games, and row- and motorboats add to the appeal.

WHERE TO EAT

With more than 275 restaurants in the area, your family need never go hungry. For restaurant listings check out the *Lake George Guide,* a weekly tourist paper available around town. When your taste for fast food begins to fade, try **Log Jam** (518-798-1155), 4.5 miles south on U.S. 9 at the junction of 149. This casual place has a rustic, log-cabin feeling and serves solid American fare, with a children's menu available. **Mario's Restaurant** (518-668-2665), .25 mile north on U.S. 9 and SR 9N, dishes out large portions of chicken, beef, seafood, and veal. It also features a children's menu and valet parking. For older kids with sophisticated palates, or for a parent's night out, try the nouvelle American cuisine at **The Trillium** in the Sagamore Resort, Bolton Landing (518-696-4430). This highly rated restaurant doesn't come cheap, but it's truly a fine dining experience.

SIDE TRIPS

The touring possibilities in the Lake George area are numerous. The *Warren Country Travel Guide* offers some appealing possibilities.

Adirondack Park

If you decide to head northwest and explore the more remote parts of Adirondack Park, keep in mind that many mountain highways can be slow going, albeit scenic, so don't plan too much for one day. Two interpretive visitor centers offer indoor and outdoor exhibits and year-round programs about Adirondack Park. One is in Paul Smiths, New York, northwest of Lake Placid on SR 30, 1 mile north of SR 86 (518-327-3000); the other is in Newcomb on SR 28N, 14 miles east of Long Lake (518-582-2000). Blue Mountain Lake, northwest of Lake George, is home to the Adirondack Museum on SR 28N/30; it's worth a stop. The indoor and outdoor exhibits reveal area history and culture in an interesting way and include Adirondack guide boats, log hotel, blacksmith shop, and posh private railroad car. Open summer to mid-October, this is a splendid trip during the peak foliage period. Call (518) 352-7311 or 352-7312 for hours.

Lake Placid

You'll see some of the best scenery on the way to Lake Placid (I-87 north to exit 30; follow Route 73 west). The village, on the shores of Mirror Lake and Lake Placid, hosted the 1932 and 1980 Winter Olympics, and the game sites and facilities are open to visitors. Depending on the ages and stamina of your kids, you can either visit individual sites or purchase a complete self-guided auto tour package. Included are chairlift rides to the summit of Whiteface Mountain (site of the 1980 alpine events), a trolley ride to the mile-long bobsled and luge runs, and visits to the Olympic Center ice complex and the Olympic Jumping Complex, where U.S. Ski Team freestyle aerialists polish their techniques in summer by jumping off ramps into a pool of water. For information call the Olympic Regional Development Authority (518-523-1655 or 800-858-7782—Eastern Canada, 800-462-6236—United States).

In winter Lake Placid is a haven, and heaven, for snow enthusiasts. **Whiteface Mountain** offers the greatest vertical drop in the East, varied terrain, plus a play-and-ski program for ages three to six and a ski school for ages seven to twelve. In addition, there's a nursery for tots ages one to six.

The **Mt. Van Hoevenberg Cross-Country Center,** a ten-minute drive from Lake Placid, features 50 kilometers of groomed trails, including novice, intermediate, and expert loops. Next door to the center, try the bobsled and luge runs. The bobsled ride is generally offered Tuesday through Sunday from 1:00 to 3:00 P.M. Sign up for the luge ride Saturday and Sunday from 1:00 to 3:00 P.M. In addition, the **Jackrabbit Trail** offers nearly 25 miles of cross-country skiing that links the towns of Keene, Lake Placid, Saranac Lake, and the High Peaks region. Obtain a map from the Adirondack Ski Touring Council, P.O. Box 843, Lake Placid, New York 12946 (518-523-1365).

For more sports visit **Mirror Lake,** where Eric Heiden claimed five gold medals in 1980. Skate indoors at the Olympic Center or outdoors at the Olympic Oval. For something different try tobogganing and dogsledding across the lake.

For a schedule of winter events and ski conditions, call (518) 523-1655 or (800) 462-6236 in the United States, (800) 858-7782 in Eastern Canada. For Lake Placid lodging reservations, call (800) 44-PLACID, (800) 447-5224.

Wilmington

Santa's Workshop in Wilmington will delight preschoolers. Families have been coming to this nonglitzy attraction for generations to meet Santa at his home and workshop, pet his live reindeer, go on the rides (including a miniature railroad), and see puppet shows. For a taped message of the park schedule, call (518) 946-7838.

FOR MORE INFORMATION

Warren County Tourism Department, 1340 State Route 9, Lake George; (518-761-6366 or 800-365-1050, ext. 5100; www.visitlakegeorge.com). Drop by the office or phone for a *Warren County Travel Guide* and other helpful information. Information on Adirondack Park can be obtained from Department of Conservation, 50 Wolf Road, Albany, New York 12233 (518-457-3521). For the entire Adirondack Region, call (800) ITS-MTNS. If you're heading to Lake Placid, lodging and sight-seeing information can be obtained from **Lake Placid/Essex County Visitors Bureau,** Olympic Center, Lake Placid 12946 (518-523-2445 or 800-44-PLACID).

Emergency Numbers

Ambulance, fire, and police: 911

Glens Falls Hospital, 100 Park Street, Glens Falls: (518) 792-3151
    (it has a twenty-four-hour emergency room)

Poison Control: (518) 761-5261

There are no twenty-four-hour pharmacies open to the public.

NEW YORK CITY

I f your family loves the energy and excitement of a big-city vacation, there's no place like New York. The good news is that New York is now known as "the Comeback City," for it leads the nation in crime reduction. Along with a 41 percent drop in crime since 1993, New York is also sprucing up many tourist areas, most notably Forty-second Street.

If possible, come in spring, fall, or at Christmas, when the city is at its finest. But even sizzling summer comes with merits: Many New Yorkers head for the hills on the weekends, leaving behind a less crowded city.

Check with the New York City Convention and Visitors Bureau (212–484–1222) for special city passes and money-saving packages such as the **CityPass Attraction Booklet.** This booklet gives you discounted admission to six of Manhattan's top sights: the American Museum of Natural History, Empire State Building Observatories, Intrepid Sea-Air-Space Museum, Metropolitan Museum of Art, Museum of Modern Art, and Top of the World Trade Center.

GETTING THERE

New York is served by three airports: John F. Kennedy International (JFK), about 15 miles from mid-Manhattan; LaGuardia, about 8 miles; and Newark (NJ) International, about 16 miles. Buses, limousines, and taxis are available at all three. Yellow medallion metered taxis are the most convenient mode into Manhattan if you're arriving with kids and baggage. Avoid the limousine drivers who appear near the baggage areas soliciting fares; instead, arrange service through Ground Transportation.

You can avoid street traffic altogether by taking the ferry from LaGuardia Airport, **New York Waterway** (201–902–8700 or 800–533–3779) and **Harbor Shuttle** (800–54–FERRY) offer commuter ferry service from the airport to the upper East Side and a few other locations. The ferries, which are comparable to taxis in cost, are quicker than a cab ride.

Amtrak (800–USA–RAIL) and a number of commuter trains arrive at either Grand Central Terminal, Forty-second Street and Park Avenue, or Penn Station, between Thirty-first and Thirty-third Streets and Seventh

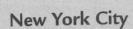

New York City

AT A GLANCE

► Browse in some of the best museums in the world

► Spend the day in Central Park

► Visit Ellis Island, the Empire State Building, and the World Trade Center

► See a Broadway show

► New York Convention and Visitors Bureau, (212) 484–1222 (to speak with an information counselor) or (800) NYC-VISIT (to order a brochure); www.nycvisit.com

and Eighth Avenues. The newly renovated Grand Central Terminal has been restored to its former glory. There are chandeliers, marble balustrades, and don't forget to look up at the brilliant constellations on the sky ceiling. Taxi stands and public transportation are available at both stations.

Greyhound, Trailways, and other long-distance and commuter buses use the Port Authority Bus Terminal, between Fortieth and Forty-second Streets and Eighth Avenue. Taxis line up at the front entrance.

Manhattan is an island entered via bridges, tunnels, parkways, and expressways. The New York Thruway (Routes 287 and 87) leads to Manhattan's east and west sides. The New England Thruway (I–95) leads, via connecting roads, to all five boroughs: Queens, Manhattan, Bronx, Brooklyn, and Staten Island. The western entry is accessed by I–80, while the south is served by the New Jersey Turnpike (I–95), which leads to the Holland Tunnel in lower Manhattan, the Lincoln Tunnel in midtown Manhattan, or the George Washington Bridge in upper Manhattan.

GETTING AROUND

The streets in midtown Manhattan, where most hotels are located (Thirtieth and Sixtieth Streets from the East River to the Hudson River), are arranged in a grid, with streets running east and west and avenues north and south. Fifth Avenue separates the east from the west side. Once you figure out the avenues, New York is a surprisingly easy city to navigate; however, Lower Manhattan (with Greenwich Village, Chinatown, Little Italy, and the Financial District) doesn't adhere to this system. In midtown walking is often the best way to get around, particularly at rush hour. If you do drive or take a taxi, be aware of gridlock and leave yourself some extra time. At night exercise common sense and stay away from streets that aren't well lit or well trafficked.

Public buses require exact fare in change or metro cards, sold mostly in subway stations. Request a transfer upon boarding. This entitles you to a free ride on a connecting line. Some buses have maps in a receptacle near the driver. Maps may also be obtained near the entrance of some major library branches.

The subway system is fast and has been cleaned up extensively over the past few years. However, it's best to avoid the subways late at night. Tokens or Metrocards are sold by clerks near turnstiles, and children under 3 feet 8 inches ride free. Request a map. Information for both the subway and buses is available twenty-four hours a day by calling (718) 330-1234.

Taxis in New York are plentiful. Hail a cab on any street corner. Some taxi drivers may be annoying; if this is the case, feel free to step out and find another ride.

Double-decker buses, operated by Gray Line Tours, are a good idea for avid sight-seers. Although traffic may be a problem at times, the buses stop at almost all attractions and parks. There is a flat fare for unlimited riding during one or two days. Call (800) 669-0051, (800) 876-9868, or (800) NYC-BUSO.

WHAT TO SEE AND DO

Museums and Historic Sites

New York has some of the best museums in the world. Since you could literally spend days—even weeks—exploring them, the following list includes only those with special kid appeal.

What kid doesn't like dinosaurs? Make no bones about it; the **American Museum of Natural History,** Central Park West and Seventy-ninth Street (212-769-5100; www.amnh.org), has added two halls of these giants. The frames of such giants as *Tyrannosaurus rex* and *Apatosaurus* (formerly known as *Brontosaurus*) loom imposingly. Kids can finger the fierce nose horn of a *Triceratops,* flip through charts to find out how a dinosaur moves, walk about the skeleton of a *Barosaurus,* and check these giants' genealogy by using a computer.

Explore more skeletons in Mammals and Their Extinct Relatives, the largest exhibition of real fossils on view anywhere in the world. Fossil finds include the head and trunk of Effie, a baby woolly mammoth, a 57-million-year-old horse skeleton, and a block of Ice Age fossils from Agate Springs, Nebraska. Kids love working the interactive computers, which explain evolutionary changes, touching such fossils as the teeth of a

Hyracotherium (horse ancestor), and feeling the claw imprint of the *Amphicyon,* a bear relative. See the film in the mammal theater first, as it explains the system used to organize and group this exhibit.

There's lots more to see: the gems and mineral gallery, with one of the largest pieces of crystallized gold ever found; the largest meteorite ever retrieved (which you can touch); a herd of wild (mounted) elephants; a 1,300-year-old giant sequoia, and lots more. The Hall of Biodiversity features a re-creation of an African rainforest. Interactive computer stations identify more than 1,500 specimens, and a multiscreen video installation allows visitors to take a virtual tour of nine distinct ecosystems. At the Natural Science Center, kids can touch and explore fossils, shells, and other natural objects. The Naturemax Theatre boasts a four-story screen for interesting educational films.

Your kids will like the **Children's Museum of Manhattan,** 212 West Eighty-third Street (212-721-1234; www.cmom.org). While this doesn't rank with, say, Boston's Children's Museum, it has enough changing and permanent exhibits to keep kids of all ages busy. At Word Play, the museum's language-development exhibit for infants to age four, kids can chirp like birds in the Chatterbug Tree, sort words at the Post Office Pick-Up, and crawl through a twisting path at Explorer's Park. Kids ages five to eleven can find out about human systems at Body Odyssey, where they can crawl through a digestive system, slide into the lower intestines, zap body invaders, and find out why people belch. Older kids will head straight upstairs to the Media Center, where they can work a TV camera or sit behind the mike and read the news. The outdoor urban environment area encourages kids to think seriously about recycling. For younger kids the family learning center has an interactive Dr. Seuss exhibit, where kids can climb aboard the Cat in the Hat's clean-up machine or steer the boat in *Green Eggs and Ham.* There are also frequent supervised art activities. Special events and activities are constantly going on such as cultural performances in the theater, call for a schedule.

Go aboard the **Intrepid Sea-Air-Space Museum,** Pier 86, West Forty-sixth Street and Twelfth Avenue (212-245-0072). This 900-foot aircraft carrier is best appreciated by school-age kids and their parents who will love the freedom to roam about and explore. The carrier was used in World War II, during the Vietnam War, and as a space program recovery ship. Along with peering through a periscope and exploring the deck, kids can see the cockpit of the world's fastest jet, historic aircraft, an Army armored tank display, and the world's only nuclear missile submarine open to the public (guided tours available). Call about Saturday afternoon workshops and hours. Multimedia presentations are offered Wednesday through Sunday, from October 1 to March 31, and daily from April 1 to September 30.

Great Outdoor Spaces: Central Park

Smack in the middle of the city, Central Park extends south to north from Central Park South (Fifty-ninth Street) to 110th Street and from Fifth Avenue to Central Park West. Here you can:

- Fish (and release your catch) at the Harlem Meer, a lake at 110 Street and Fifth Avenue (212-860-1370)
- Ride a carousel in mid-park, Sixty-fourth Street (212-879-0244)
- Watch a puppet show at the Swedish Cottage Marionette Theater, mid-park (212-988-9093)
- Roller blade, guided by dance instructors (212-360-1311)
- Roller skate at the Wollman Rink, Fifty-ninth Street and Sixth Avenue (212-396-1010)
- Listen to storytellers every Saturday at 11:00 A.M., from June through September, at the Hans Christian Andersen statue, Seventy-second Street and Fifth Avenue (212-929-6871)
- Play at the Hecksher Playground, where you'll find a wooden bridge, sandbox, slides, seesaws, and swings.
- See polar bears, penguins, and sea lions at the Central Park Zoo, Central Park at Sixty-fourth Street (212-861-6030); and meander through an enchanted forest of bunnies, fish, turtles, and birds at Tisch Children's Zoo, designed for children six and under.

The **Jewish Museum,** 1109 Fifth Avenue at Ninety-second Street (212-423-3200), features four floors of exhibits, with frequently changing themes. Family workshops and special events make this a worthwhile place to visit. Older children like the audiotaped vignettes of European immigrants and the collection of ornate torah scrolls.

Liberty Science Center, Liberty State Park, New Jersey (201-200-1000), a hands-on science and technology museum across the river from Lower Manhattan, is easily accessible by ferry. Particularly pleased are Manhattanites who find the excellent **New York Hall of Science** in Flushing Meadows, Queens (718-699-1341), less convenient. Highlights include the E-Quest exhibition, where kids can create a geyser or a bubbling hot spring via hand-controlled water valves, and the Center's F-15 fighter jet trainer/simulator, a gift from the Air Force. Visitors can simulate a flying experience around regional landmarks, employing the same equipment used in Bosnia to train U.S. and NATO pilots. At Liberty Science Center, one floor of exhibits centers on the body. Kids love the pitch-black touch tunnel and labyrinth with mirrors and optical illusions. The environmental area includes a Bug Zoo and touch pool with horseshoe crabs. Older kids will love the kid-sized climbing wall. There's also a huge OMNIMAX theater, the largest in the country. An added plus: a fabulous view of Manhattan and the Statue of Liberty. A ferry leaves from the World Financial Center in lower Manhattan; call (800) 53-FERRY for information. People movers pick up passengers at the dock. Call the museum for other transportation options.

The **Lower East Side Tenement Museum,** 97 Orchard Street (212–431-0233), is dedicated to immigrants and their experience on the Lower East Side. It offers walking tours, dramatizations, media programs, and special exhibitions. Orchard Street, with its bargain shops—some "schlock," some name brands at hefty discounts—is an experience in itself. There's lots of local color in this area, and you're a short cab ride away from Chinatown and Little Italy.

Metropolitan Museum of Art, Fifth Avenue and Eighty-second Street (212–535-7710; www.metmuseum.org), is one of the world's greatest museums. The facility's enormity can overpower young ones, particularly during the crowded weekends. The key: Arrive early and focus on areas of particular appeal. Most kids are fascinated by the extensive Egyptian exhibits; wend your way toward the Temple of Dendur, housed in its own glass-enclosed wing. Nearby is the American Wing Garden Court, a peaceful place to sit and enjoy the stained glass (some of it by Tiffany), potted trees, and fountain. Off the court is the arms and armor area. In the second-floor Chinese Garden Court, watch fish swimming in pools and absorb the serenity of this magical place. In nice weather proceed to the pleasant rooftop sculpture gallery (it has its own elevator) with views of Central Park and the city. In the African Gallery, kids are fascinated by the fanciful masquerade masks of West Africa's Guinea Coast and the brass and ivory sculptures and adornments of the Benin collection. Kids may also like the renovated Greek galleries. Weekend family programs are free with admission and include short films and lectures; call for information.

You can combine a visit to the Jewish Museum with one to the **Museum of the City of New York,** Fifth Avenue at 103rd Street (212–534-1672). It's just 11 blocks north, a nice walk on a pleasant day. Don't miss *New York Toy Stories,* the museum's latest permanent exhibit. Highlights include antique carousel horses from Coney Island and a gallery featuring favorite characters from children's literature. Half of the museum is devoted to changing exhibits, and there are frequent family workshops tied to these exhibits and storytelling workshops every Saturday. There are also seasonal walking tours of the five boroughs. Families who like to walk are cordially invited.

The museum is directly across from the beautiful **Conservatory Gardens** in Central Park, called "The Secret Garden" by some. Stop in for a peek—but note that this part of the park is a bit more desolate than the lower part below Eighty-sixth Street, so don't stray off the main pathways.

For contemporary art, visit the **Museum of Modern Art,** 11 West Fifty-third Street (212-708-9480; www.moma.org). This museum bucks the trend and opens Monday, closing instead on Wednesday. Some kids enjoy the art here; others will be bored. The museum has a number of noted pieces by Matise, Picasso, and Miró. Aim for a Saturday visit, when guides host special tours to introduce families with kids ages five to ten to the important aspects of the museum's collections. On Saturday there are also workshops with games and activities, as well as a Family Films program that presents classic shorts.

The **Museum of Television and Radio,** 25 West Fifty-second Street (212-621-6600) houses an extensive collection of 20,000 radio and television program tapes listed in a computerized file; select one and watch or listen to it in a console booth. Because of reruns and cable TV, kids think they've seen it all, but there are some gems they'll never catch on Nick at Nite. Re-creating radio workshops for ages eight to thirteen are held on Saturdays during the school year. Kids read scripts and make sound effects to create their own classic show. Call (212) 621-6000 to reserve.

South Street Seaport Museum, Visitor's Center, 12 Fulton Street (212-748-8600), isn't just a museum, it's a 12-block historic district in lower Manhattan where your family can easily spend most of the day. Stop by the visitor's center for information on what's going on, as special events are scheduled frequently. At the children's center kids interact with special exhibits and take part in weekend workshops. A number of historic ships anchored here can be boarded. From early May to late September, sailing trips aboard the schooner *Pioneer* visit ports along Long Island Sound and offer views of he Statue of Liberty, Ellis Island, and the Manhattan skyline. Call (212) 748-8786 for reservations. Kids also enjoy strolling through the traffic-free, cobblestone streets lined with shops, restaurants, and inexpensive eateries.

One of New York's newest museums is the **National Museum of the American Indian, Smithsonian Institution,** 1 Bowling Green between State and Whitehall Streets (212-514-3700). On display are North, Central, and South American Indian artifacts. Kids can play with display artifacts such as Seneca corn husk dolls and Zapotec dance masks. Daily tours are led by Native Americans, and the museum maintains a video program and resource center geared specifically to children. If you're visiting in November, the museum's Harvest Ceremony, the Thanksgiving story told from a Native perspective, is the most popular program of the year.

New York Harbor Tours

The most impressive view of the New York skyline is from a cruise boat; kids like the fresh air, the seagulls (bring bread to feed them), and the water views. Some rides are seasonal so call ahead.

- **Staten Island Ferry** (718-727-2508). Since 1905 the ferry has taken passengers from Battery Park to Staten Island. It's the best ride in the city, and it's free.
- **New York's Fast Ferry** (800-693-NYFF). This is the quick trip from Staten Island to midtown.
- **WindSpirit** (888-946-3774 or 212-758-5323). This forty-passenger catamaran offers daily harbor cruises.
- **Express Navigation** (800-BOAT-RIDE or 908-872-2628). In seventy-five minutes this high-speed cruise takes you past the Statue of Liberty, Ellis Island, and the Empire State Building. For sports fans, there are weekend cruises to Shea Stadium to watch the Mets play baseball.
- **Spirit Cruises** (212-727-7768). These sleek ships offer dining, dancing, and theme cruises.
- **Circle Line** (212-563-3200). The three-hour cruise circles Manhattan Island (this could be a bit long for kids), and the two-hour Express Cruise showcases the sights of lower Manhattan.
- **OpSail 2000.** More than fifty nations are sending ships to participate in the largest gathering of tall ships and naval vessels in history. July 3 to 9, 2000, in New York harbor.

Attractions

So it's not the world's tallest building: Could you come to New York without seeing the **Empire State Building,** Thirty-fourth Street and Fifth Avenue (212-736-3100; www.esbnyc.com)? The view from promenades on the Eighty-sixth or 102d floor on a clear day is exhilarating. Thrillseekers will love the **New York Skyride** in the Empire State Building. Strap into your seat as this eight-minute motion flight-simulation film rockets you through NYC's biggest attractions. The Skyride is on the second floor of the Empire State Building and runs continuously seven days a week from 10:00 A.M. to 10:00 P.M. Combination tickets for the observation deck and the Skyride are available at a reduced price from the observation deck ticket office.

Farther up Fifth Avenue, **Rockefeller Center** (between Forty-seventh and Fifty-second Streets) has a sunken plaza where your family can ice skate in winter. **The benches at the Channel Gardens** on the Fifth Avenue side, with their always changing flower and plant arrangements, offer a pleasant place to sit and people-watch.

The **United Nations,** First Avenue at Forty-sixth Street, may be exciting for older kids (those under age five aren't allowed on tours). Free tickets to General Assembly and Security Council meetings are available on a first-come, first-served basis. Call (212) 963-7713. Downtown, the distinctive towers of the **World Trade Center** offer an observation deck; (212) 435-4170. Next door, the **World Financial Center** has shops, restaurants, a pleasing waterfront walkway, with a playground nearby, and free art and culture shows geared to kids. Kids can learn about bears and bulls on a thirty-minute tour of the **New York Stock Exchange** (20 Broad Street, between Exchange Place and Wall Street). The tour includes a ten-minute historical film, interactive activities teaching how to track stock information, and a tour of the trading floor. Tickets are distributed Monday through Friday beginning at 8:45 A.M. Arrive early, as tickets go fast.

"The Lady in the Harbor," the **Statue of Liberty National Monument,** is reached via Circle Line Ferry from Battery Park in Lower Manhattan. There's an American Museum of Immigration in the base. Call (212) 269-5755 for ferry information, (212) 363-3200 for Statue information. Summer crowds are endless; arrive early and expect lines. Likewise for the nearby **Ellis Island Immigration Museum,** where the Great Hall has been restored to its 1918-1924 appearance and houses galleries filled with memorabilia, an oral history recording studio, two theaters, and a wall honoring immigrants who passed through. Ellis Island is also reached via Circle Line ferry; a shuttle service runs between the two attractions.

Sports fans can see the locker rooms of the New York Knicks and the New York Rangers as well as catch the view from a luxury suite on a **Madison Square Garden Behind the Scenes Tour,** Madison Square Garden, Seventh Avenue between West Thirty-first and Thirty-third Streets (212-465-5800).

At **Chelsea Piers Sports and Entertainment Complex,** Hudson River between Seventeenth and Twenty-third Streets (212-336-6666), athletic families can play minigolf, swim, ice skate, play basketball, climb a wall, and practice batting.

Television fans can attend free tapings of shows, that is, if they are sixteen years or older. The best way to obtain tickets for *Late Night with David Letterman* is to write *six months* ahead to Late Show Tickets, Ed Sullivan Theater, 1697 Broadway, New York, NY 10019 (212-975-5853). For those persons who didn't plan ahead, the box office hands out one hundred standby tickets at noon on taping days. Only one ticket is given to each person, so don't send Mom or Dad to get them for the whole family. (Note that standby tickets don't guarantee admission.) Tapings are Monday through Friday at 5:30 P.M.

If you really plan ahead, you may get lucky and obtain free tickets to tapings of *Saturday Night Live*. Be part of the ticket lottery that is held each year at the end of August by mailing a postcard postmarked in August to Saturday Night Tickets, NBC, 30 Rockefeller Plaza, New York, NY 10112. Standby tickets are given out at 9:15 A.M. at NBC on the mezzanine level of the Forty-ninth Street side of Rockefeller Plaza. Again, these tickets are limited to one person and do not guarantee admission.

Performing Arts

Show your children the bright lights of Broadway by taking them to a musical extravaganza. To find out what's playing, call the **Broadway Line** (212-302-4111 or 888-BROADWAY) for a complete listing and description of Broadway and Off-Broadway shows and to book tickets. Other ticket services include **Tele-Charge** (212-239-6200 or 800-432-7250) and **TicketMaster** (212-307-4100 or 800 755-4000). If you're willing to wait in line (arrive early) you can save 25 to 50 percent on tickets for that day's shows by queuing up at the **TKTS** booth (Forty-seventh Street and Broadway in Times Square, or downtown at Two World Trade Center). Call (212) 768-1818 to hear what's available. **The Theater Development's Fund's Theater Access Project** (212-221-1103 or 212-719-4537 TTY; www.tdf.org), provides sign language interpreted performances of Broadway shows. **Hands ON** (212-627-4898 voice and TTY) offers the same service for off Broadway productions.

New York has many kids-only presentations and theater groups such as **TADA! Youth Ensemble,** West Twenty-eighth Street between Sixth and Seventh Avenues (212-243-6736). The **New Victory Theater,** 209 West Forty-second Street (tickets: 212-239-6200; schedules: 212-564-4222), presents plays, dances, films, and opera just for children. Consult the children's listings in the weekly *New York Magazine* for current performances. Seasonal treats include the **Marionette Theater,** West Seventy-ninth Street and West Drive (212-988-9093), which is held in the Swedish Cottage in Central Park. If you're here for the holidays, don't miss the Easter or Christmas shows at Radio City Music Hall, featuring the famous Rockettes (212-247-4777). For a behind-the-scenes tour of this grand theater, call (212) 632-4041.

Lincoln Center for the Performing Arts, 70 Lincoln Center Plaza (Broadway at Sixty-fourth Street), features multiple stages. The complex offers opera education workshops for families with children ages six to twelve prior to select weekend matinee performances (call 212-870-5643 for reservations). Every fall and winter the **Big Apple Circus** performs its one-ring act in a fully heated tent; no seat is more

Play Space

Chelsea Piers Sports and Entertainment Complex, Seventeenth to Twenty-third Streets, along the Hudson River on Piers 59 to 62 (212-336-6666). Manhattanites come to the piers to play and work out. Along with the 150,000-square-foot Sports Center, Chelsea Piers has Sky Rink, the city's only indoor, year-round ice skating rink; Roller Rinks, outdoor rinks for in-line and roller skating; the Field House, an athletic facility with a climbing wall for kids, a toddler gym, and batting cages, basketball courts, and an indoor soccer field; AMF Chelsea Piers Bowl, a forty-lane bowling alley; and the Golf Club, Manhattan's only year-round driving range. Chelsea Piers also houses television and fashion photography studios, sports retail shops, and three restaurants: the Crab House, the Chelsea Brewing Company, and Caffe Fammilia (serving pizza, pasta, and sandwiches). Spirit Cruises (212-727-7768) leaves from the pier for lunch, dinner, and moonlight cruises of New York harbor.

than 50 feet from the ring (call 212-268-2500 for tickets and information). The Lincoln Center also presents ongoing **Movies for Kids,** weekend screenings of high-quality family films (call 212-875-5610 for information). Additional programs to inquire about include Rush Hour tickets to the **New York Philharmonic** for teens, **Jazz for Young People** concerts, free performances of precollege Juilliard School performers, and the **New York City Ballet's** family matinee series.

Other performances with kid appeal are held throughout the year, and, of course, *The Nutcracker* ballet is a perennial Christmas sellout. If you come to see Lincoln Center during the day, the public library branch at the east end of the complex has a nice kid's reading room on the second floor. For more information call (212) 875-5350.

Carnegie Hall, Seventh Avenue at Fifty-Seventh Street (212-247-7800) has better acoustics than ever. Its varied schedule of classical, jazz, symphonic, Broadway show tunes, and other performances please a wide range of musical tastes. **The New Amsterdam Theater,** 214 West Forty-second Street (212-282-2900), is back in business after Walt Disney Company's multimillion-dollar renovations. The famous playhouse is worth visiting to admire the ornate decor and to appreciate its historical value. Kids will appreciate the popular stage production of *The Lion King.*

The **Ford Center for the Performing Arts,** Forty-second and Forty-third Streets (212-307-4550), joined together the Apollo and Lyric theaters, creating a 1,850-seat musical performance space.

Besides enjoying the view of New York's skyline, another reason to take the ferry to Staten Island is **Snug Harbor Cultural Center,** 1000 Richmond Terrace (718-448-2500). The Greek-Revival homes in this eighty-three-acre complex have been turned into concert halls, art galleries, and a children's museum.

Shopping

New York shopping is legendary, from the tony department stores to the bargains sold by street vendors. There are simply too many shopping opportunities to mention all or even many of them. Famous department stores include **Macy's,** Thirty-fourth Street and Broadway, among the largest stores in the world; **Bloomingdale's,** Third Avenue at Fifty-ninth Street; and **Saks Fifth Avenue,** at Fiftieth Street. At Christmas the animated displays in the department store windows are guaranteed to delight kids. Here's a quick list of just a few kid-pleasing stores.

F.A.O. Schwarz, 767 Fifth Avenue (212-644-9400), is an attraction as well as a store. This flagship of the chain is both fanciful and fun. Browse for stuffed animals of almost any variety, from cuddly dogs to a 9-foot-tall bear big enough to require his own den and house to go with it. The Bookmonster has shelves of kid-pleasing volumes, and the New York City section sports such souvenirs as a Statue of Liberty head dress. Call the store for a list of current special events, which may include celebrity book signings and presentations by Barbie doll designers.

At the **Warner Brothers Store,** Fifty-seventh Street and Fifth Avenue (212-754-0300), find out what's up. Kids love the three floors of trendy 'toon stuff, from T-shirts to plush toys. **The Disney Store,** 39 West Thirty-fourth Street (212-279-9890), is a kid-pleaser with its Walt Disney Company clothing, stuffed animals, video games, and collectibles. For comic collectibles as well as current funnies, the city has three specialty shops: the **Comic Arts Gallery,** Third Avenue between Fifty-sixth and Fifty-seventh Streets (212-759-6355); **New York Comics,** Broadway and Forty-eighth Street (212-956-1133); and **Village Comics,** Bleecker Street between Sullivan and Thompson Streets (212-777-2770).

Niketown, 6 East Fifty-seventh Street (212-891-6453), has CD-ROMS to help you choose the right pair of sports shoes from their more than 1,200 choices. If the wind's right and you've left your kite at home, buy one at **Big City Kite Company,** 1210 Lexington Avenue (212-472-2623).

Sports

New York fans are loyal to their teams. **Madison Square Garden,** Seventh Avenue between West Thirty-first and Thirty-third Streets (212-465-5800), is home to the **Rangers** for ice hockey and to the **New York Knicks** for men's basketball and the women's basketball team the **New York Liberty** (212-564-WNBA). For basketball tickets, call (212) 465-JUMP. For hockey tickets, call (212) 308-NYRS. The **Mets** play baseball at **Shea Stadium** (718-507-TIXX), and the **Yankees** have their baseball diamond at **Yankee Stadium,** the Bronx (718-293-6000). Football fans can watch the **Giants** and the **Jets** in **Giants Stadium,** the Meadowlands Complex, East Rutherford, New Jersey. Call (201) 935-8222 for Giants tickets (available only as season tickets, not for individual games) and (201) 935-8500 for Jets tickets. The **MetroStars,** New York's professional soccer team, plays at Giants Stadium (888-4-METROTIX), from March to October.

SPECIAL EVENTS

There's never a dull moment in the Big Apple. Check the Other Events listings in *New York* magazine and the Friday Weekend section in the *New York Times* for the latest happenings. Here's a sampling:

January. Chinese New Year celebration, Chinatown

February. Westminister Kennel Club Dog Show, Madison Square Garden

March–April. Spring Flower Show; Ringling Brothers Circus, Madison Square Garden; Easter Show, Radio City Music Hall; Macy's Flower Show, Macy's at Herald Square; Easter Parade, Fifth Avenue

May. Cherry Blossom Festival; Fifty-third Street Jazz Festival, Fleet Week, Intrepid; Ninth Avenue International Food Festival

June–August. Central Park Summer Stage; Free Shakespeare in the Park; Free Summergarden Concerts, the Museum of Modern Art; Free Summer Pier Concerts, South Street Seaport

July. Fourth of July festivities with Harbor Festival and fireworks, South Street Seaport and East River; New York Philharmonic, Central Park

August. Lincoln Center Out-of-Doors

September. Feast of San Gennaro, Little Italy; Third Avenue Street Fair; Book Fair, Fifth Avenue

October. Halloween Parade, Greenwich Village; Boo at the Zoo, International Wildlife Conservation Park (the former Bronx Zoo)

November. New York Marathon; Macy's Thanksgiving Day Parade

December. Lighting of giant Christmas tree, Rockefeller Center; Origami Christmas Tree, American Museum of Natural History; First Night, citywide

WHERE TO STAY

Located in the theater district the **New York Doubletree Guest Suites,** Forty-seventh Street and Seventh Avenue (212-719-1600 or 800-424-2900), offers a family-friendly Children's Center on the fourth floor. Rooms here have covers on electric outlets and plastic on furniture edges. If needed, the staff brings you diapers or other necessities. Also in the theater district, the **Millennium Broadway,** 145 West Forty-fourth Street (212-768-4400), offers upscale amenities. Ask about their lower weekend rates.

Loew's New York Hotel, 569 Lexington Avenue at Fifty-first Street (212-752-7000 or 800-23-LOEWS), has a Loew's Loves Kids program, which lets children under eighteen stay free with parents. The restaurant and room service feature kid's menus, kids get free ice cream dessert with any entree for kids, children under ten receive a gift bag upon check-in, and a second adjoining room is available at a discount. The **Grand Hyatt New York,** Park Avenue at Grand Central (212-883-1234 or 800-233-1234), has kid's menus in the restaurant and for room service. A second room for children is available at a discounted rate.

At any of the nine **Manhattan East Suite Hotels** (800-ME-SUITE), you get more room for your money. All the accommodations, from studio suites to four-bedroom units, feature kitchen facilities. **Le Parker Meridien,** 118 West Fifty-seventh Street (212-245-5000), is a well-appointed hotel in a midtown location. **The Mark,** Madison Avenue at East Seventy-seventh Street (212-744-4300 or 800-THE-MARK), is an uptown and upscale luxury hotel that combines the friendly feel of a small hotel with big hotel services and good-sized rooms, most of which have in-room refrigerators and a microwave—necessities for the all-important kids' snacks. The Upper East Side location puts you blocks from such New York City staples as Central Park and the Metropolitan Museum of Art.

Journey's End Hotels, 3 East Fortieth Street (212-447-1500 or 800-668-4200), offers limited services at lower than typical big-city rates. Other less expensive choices include the **Days Inn,** 440 West Fifty-seventh Street (212-581-8100 or 800-231-0405), where kids under seventeen stay free and those under twelve eat free as long as adults dine with them.

The beautifully redesigned **Barbizon,** 140 East Sixty-third Street (212-838-5700), offers guests eighteen and older complimentary use of the adjacent Equinox Spa, a first-class facility with a swimming pool, work-out areas, and classes. The rooms, however, are unusually small.

Don't forget to inquire about weekend deals at some of the upscale properties. Depending on the season you could be pleasantly surprised with a posh room at a good price.

WHERE TO EAT

New York has some of the finest restaurants in the world. *The Zagat Restaurant Survey,* available at bookstores, is a handy objective guide to New York eateries, with special headings for indicating eateries appealing to kids and teens. Here are just a few of our city favorites.

It seems all kids ten and up somehow gravitate to West Fifty-seventh Street, where they have a choice of the **Hard Rock Cafe** at 221 (212-459-9320), **Planet Hollywood** at 140 (212-333-7827) or **Motown Cafe** at 104, between Sixth and Seventh Avenues (212-581-8030), which has soul food and the world's biggest record. All have incredibly long lines during peak vacation times: Arrive early to avoid the crunch. Also on West Fifty-seventh Street, between Fifth and Sixth Avenues, is a high-tech **McDonald's** that's eye catching—and convenient after a trek to F.A.O. Schwarz or Central Park. In the same neighborhood, **Mickey Mantle's,** 42 Central Park South (212-688-7777), is a big hit with baseball fans. The restaurant has sports memorabilia, ten television monitors, and a kid's menu.

The **Cowgirl Hall of Fame,** 519 Hudson Street (212-633-1133), features Tex-Mex food and rodeo relics. **Television City,** 74 West Fiftieth Street at Avenue of the Americas (212-333-3388), is conveniently located across from Radio City Music Hall with TV-themed decor and diner-style food.

Along with bagels and deli sandwiches, thin-crusted pizza is a true slice of ethnic New York food. The pizza pies at **Totonno's Restaurant,** 1544 Second Avenue, (212-327-2800), win praise for their aromatic, smoky flavor, a result of being cooked in coal-fired brick ovens. **Barney Greengrass,** 541 Amsterdam Avenue (212-742-4707), is acclaimed for its white fish salad, among other traditional deli selections. Groucho Marx and George Burns were known to be regulars.

One of the best vegetarian restaurants in the city, **Zen Palate,** has three locations, 663 Ninth Avenue (212-582-1669), 34 Union Square East (212-614-9396), and 2170 Broadway (212-501-7768) and will deliver food to your hotel room at no extra charge. **Caroline's Comedy Nation Restaurant,** 1626 Broadway (212-757-4100), serves up comedy skits with your ribs, chicken, seafood, and pasta.

Hamburger Harry's, West Forty-fifth Street and Broadway (212-840-2756), serves great burgers and has a children's menu. This location is also convenient for many popular NYC attractions. The **Harley Davidson Cafe,** Fifty-sixth Street and Sixth Avenue (212-245-6000; www.harley-davidsoncafe.com), literally has motorcycles and biking memorabilia hanging from the ceiling. The menu features sandwiches, burgers, salads, and pasta. The **Brooklyn Diner,** West Fifty-seventh Street between Seventh Avenue and Broadway (212-581-8900), with its shiny exterior, looks something like a traditional diner from the outside. The diner staples taste much better than standard diner fare, and the portions are large. You can get real chicken soup, sandwiches, burgers, pot roast, meat loaf and mashed potatoes, and chicken pot pie. The house special for dessert is a yummy Strawberry Blonde Cheesecake.

Serendipity 3, 225 East Sixtieth Street (212-838-3531), close to Bloomingdale's, is a favorite for ice cream concoctions. The place also has a funky gift/toy store. On Seventh Avenue the overstuffed sandwiches at the **Carnegie Deli,** at 854 (212-757-2245), and the **Stage Deli,** at 834 (212-245-7850), could feed an army. Both are good; the jury is still out on which has the best pastrami and corned beef.

The Olive Garden, Seventh Avenue and Forty-seventh Street (212-333-3254), may be a familiar restaurant, serving great Italian food at moderate prices, but its location and view of Times Square is worth seeing.

Consider a trip to Chinatown for local color and good, inexpensive food. One of the best, **Harmony Palace,** 98 Mott Street (212-226-6603), offers dim sum, appetizer-sized dumplings and other Chinese fare, on early weekend mornings. Dim sum is perfect for children's appetites and picky tastes, as the small portions offer a commitment-free way to sample various new foods.

Try **20 Mott Street,** the name of the restaurant as well as the address (212-964-0380). The restaurant has superb dim sum and daily specialties. Next door, stop in the arcade to play tic-tac-toe with a chicken (that's right, a chicken). Later, cross over Canal Street to Little Italy for a pastry at **Ferrara's,** 195 Grand Street (212-226-6150).

SIDE TRIPS

Most people find so much to do in Manhattan that they hardly consider leaving it for a day. But if you're so inclined—or are on your second or third trip to New York—head straight to the **International Wildlife Conservation Park,** formerly called the **Bronx Zoo,** the largest urban zoo in the United States and home to more than 4,000 animals. Explore 265 acres of green parklands and naturalistic habitats. The Bengali Express monorail travels over 2 miles of tracks through the forests and meadows of Wild Asia, where you'll see rhinos, elephants, and Siberian tigers roaming about. At the Children's Zoo, kids imitate what animals do: crawl through a prairie dog tunnel or climb a spider's web, for instance. JungleWorld is an indoor rain forest with tropical Asian plants and animals, and the zoo's newest exhibit, the Congo Gorilla Forest, the world's largest African forest re-creation. This huge

A day trip to the International Wildlife Conservation Park will be a day well spent.

exhibit boasts more than 300 animals, including one of the largest breeding groups of gorillas in North America. You can easily spend a complete day at the zoo. Although this zoo is open all year, the zoo shuttle, camel rides, and Skyfari aerial tramway close during winter. From late November through December, the zoo sparkles at night during Holiday Lights, a special event featuring ice sculptures, arts and crafts, and seasonal storytelling. Baby and adult strollers can be rented at the entrance. Call (212) 367-1010 for information. Liberty Lines runs express bus service between mid-Manhattan and the Bronxdale entrance to the zoo. Call (212) 652-8400 for schedules.

Don't leave New York without catching a glimpse of the magnificent Brooklyn Bridge, which you can see from Manhattan's Seaport area. You can cross over to Brooklyn Heights, a pleasant residential area, where the esplanade provides a great view of Manhattan. Brooklyn's **Coney Island** area, once the city's fun spot, has seen better days. Home to the **New York Aquarium,** as well as an amusement park and beach, the area is sadly run down, but the aquarium is modern and pleasant and has its own parking lot.

If it's sizzling hot and your family is in dire need of a beach, head to the Rockaways in the borough of Queens, where you'll find **Jacob Riis Park**

(IRT #2 subway to Flatbush Avenue, then bus Q35). Manhattan area beaches are not world famous, but this one, part of **Gateway National Park,** has a nice sandy stretch. Note that the western portion is almost exclusively gay. Call (718) 318-4300. If you have a car, head out to the **Hamptons,** on Long Island, a much more scenic option, although the traffic on weekends is horrendous. The Hampton Jitney (516-283-4600) has express motorcoach service from New York City. At the easternmost tip of the island, the town of **Montauk** has a beautiful, clean public beach, a scenic lighthouse, and two large oceanside state parks. Passenger ferries leave daily for Block Island (see the Block Island chapter) and Newport. Call the Montauk Chamber of Commerce at (516) 668-2428 for more information.

From New York you're also a day trip away from the sights in Mystic, Connecticut. (See the Mystic chapter.)

FOR MORE INFORMATION

New York Convention and Visitors Bureau, Inc., 810 Seventh Avenue (at 53rd Street), New York 10019; (212-484-1222 or 800-NYC-VISIT; www.nycvisit.com), have helpful literature, advice, and an information center that is open 365 days a year. For lodging availability during peak times, September 1 to December 31, call the bureau's Peak Season Hotel Hotline, (212-582-3352 or 800-846-ROOM). Volunteers (not professionals) at Big Apple Greeters (212-669-8273) are glad to tell visitors about some of the city's highlights as well as pass on access tips to the physically challenged.

For information on the accessibility of public transportation, obtain the free *MTA New York City Transit Accessible Travel Brochure* (call (718-330-1234). Two additional resources: the free *Access Guide for People with Disabilities,* available from the **Mayor's Office for People with Disabilities** (212-778-2830), and the *Access for All,* available from **Hospital Audiences Inc.** (212-575-7676). This offers details on access to the city's cultural institutions. Another helpful resource is the All Around Town listings in the front of the Yellow Pages phone directory, containing loads of basic information and phone numbers.

The Big Apple Parent's Paper (212-533-2277) and *New York Family* (914-381-7474) are publications that feature news and events of interest to families.

Emergency Numbers

Ambulance, fire, and police: 911

Poison Control Center: (212) 764–7667 or 340–4494

Twenty-four-hour pharmacy: Kaufman Pharmacy, Lexington Avenue and Fiftieth Street; (212) 755–2266

If your child has a middle-of-the-night ear infection, go to the twenty-four-hour emergency room at Manhattan Eye, Ear and Throat Hospital, 210 East Sixty-fourth Street; (212) 838–9200. For other emergencies head to one of the city's respected hospitals, which include Emergency Pavilion at New York Hospital Cornell Medical Center, 510 East Seventieth Street; (212) 746–5050.

Nova Scotia

N ova Scotia's beautiful, diverse landscape, which consists of the Atlantic coastal region and the interior woodlands, has long attracted tourists. This peninsula province is 350 miles from end to end, with a coastline that stretches for 4,625 miles. Visitors are never far from rugged shores dotted with sandy beaches, picturesque fishing villages, and scenic coves. The capital, **Halifax** (the official name is *Halifax Regional Municipality*, but *Halifax* will do), sits about midway along the Atlantic coast, making these areas an ideal base from which to explore the province. Perhaps your family will eventually wend its way east to Cape Breton Island to the spectacular Cabot Trail that winds around Cape Breton Highlands National Park. Or you may choose to follow one of the province's other ten scenic trailways that reflect its rich ethnic and geographic diversity. But don't rush off from Halifax: The area has some pleasures in store for families who linger.

GETTING THERE

Air Canada has daily flights to Nova Scotia, from New York, Boston, Toronto, Montréal, and Saint John's, Newfoundland; other carriers include Canadian Airlines, Northwest, and American. An affiliate offers connections within Atlantic Canada. **Limousine service** and **car** and motorhome rentals are available at Halifax International, Sydney, and Yarmouth airports; call (800) 565-0000 for information. Halifax Airport, Highway 102, is 24 miles from downtown. Airbus shuttle buses (902-468-4342) travel to major downtown hotels. **Share-A-Cab** (902-429-4444) services the airport from any part of Halifax, but the service suggests a three-hour notice.

Acadian Lines (902-454-9321) operates buses throughout the province. **Greyhound** from New York and Maine, and Voyageur from Quebec City and Montréal, connect in New Brunswick with SMT Bus Lines, which in turn connects with Acadian Lines. The Halifax bus terminal is at 6040 Almon Street (902-454-9321).

Nova Scotia

AT A GLANCE

▶ Explore the mix of rugged Atlantic coastline and interior woodlands

▶ Stroll the harborfront

▶ Visit the Maritime Museum of the Atlantic

▶ Nova Scotia information, (902) 424-4247 or (800) 341-6091—United States, (800) 565-0000—Canada; www.explore.gov.ns.ca/virtualns

VIA Rail travels throughout Canada. Amtrak passengers from Montréal or Toronto can connect with VIA Rail to reach the Halifax station, 1161 Hollis Street, in the south end (902-429-8421).

Car ferry service to Yarmouth, Nova Scotia, about 328 miles from Halifax, is a comfortable transportation option. Reserve the following in advance: *The Cat,* a high-speed ferry, from Bar Harbor, Maine (888-249-7245); Scotia Queen from Portland, Maine (800-341-7540—United States, 800-482-0955—Maine, 800-565-7900—Nova Scotia, New Brunswick, or Prince Edward Island). Other ferry service includes Newfoundland to North Sydney, Nova Scotia; Prince Edward Island to Caribou, Nova Scotia; and Saint John, New Brunswick, to Digby, Nova Scotia. Cruise ships dock at ocean terminals in the south end of Halifax.

Highways from all points in the United States and Canada join the Trans-Canada Highway from New Brunswick into Nova Scotia.

GETTING AROUND

Halifax is a compact city. You can walk to most of the major sights (although it is hilly walking from the harbor to the Citadel). Barrington is the city's main street. Metro Transit (902-421-6600) has buses that run regularly throughout the city and also offers the shopping trolley. A small fee gets you a ride to or from downtown's two shopping districts. Maps are available at any information center. Yarmouth-Halifax ferry operates daily from the foot of George Street, Halifax, to the harbor side of Dartmouth's City Hall. The inexpensive fifteen-minute trip offers a good view of the harbor.

WHAT TO SEE AND DO

Museums and Historic Sites

Combine museum visits with sight-seeing tours of different areas of Halifax. First, head to the **harborfront,** a lively place where your family can stroll through the shops of the nineteenth-century waterfront **Historic Properties** buildings, grab a bite to eat, see (or sail on) the *Bluenose II* schooner, and board the HMCS Sackville, a World War II convoy escort, now a Naval memorial with an interpretive center and multimedia presentation. The **Halcyon Playground,** near the Ferry Terminal, is designed like a tugboat and appeals to younger kids. There are miles of boardwalks, too.

While you're in the area, check out the **Maritime Museum of the Atlantic,** Lower Water Street (902–424–7490 or 424–7491). This pleasant, airy place houses some interesting objects, including relics from the *Titanic* (a number of the dead were brought to Halifax, where they were buried), and other vintage Cunard steamship memorabilia. The museum recently acquired one of the only known intact *Titanic* deck chairs. Downstairs is a permanent exhibit of photos and memorabilia devoted to the Halifax Explosion, which older school-age children and teens should find absorbing. Sit down to watch the short video that describes the 1917 disaster, which occurred when two ships—one carrying explosives—collided. The result was the biggest man-made explosion before the nuclear age. More than 1,900 people were killed immediately; 9,000 were injured, and almost the entire north end of Halifax was destroyed.

The museum also has a number of small boats, including one that belonged to Queen Victoria, and a full-size replica of a coastal schooner. The CSS *Acadia,* Canada's first hydrographic vessel, is permanently moored outside the museum.

Next door, at the small **Halifax Touch Tank Aquarium,** roll up your sleeves and carefully handle the marine animals in the pool. Young kids love this.

Board a Clydesdale-pulled antique replica draught wagon on **Alexander Keith's Magical History Tour,** named after the Nova Scotia brewery, for a free guided tour of the waterfront area. Call (902) 422–2069 for more information.

The next day, visit the star-shaped **Citadel Hill National Historic Park** (902–426–5080), which has dominated the city since 1759. This is Canada's most visited national historic park. At the foot of Citadel Hill, the Old Town Clock, a city landmark, was given to the city as a gift in 1803 by Prince Edward. Although the fort was never attacked by the French (or anyone else), it was considered the bastion of the British defense of North America. You can go inside the fortress, actually the fourth built on the site by British soldiers, and have a look around the barracks. Walk along the fortress walls for good views of the city and harbor.

A fifty-minute *Tides of History* audiovisual presentation on Halifax and its defenses may be a trifle too long for some kids, but their attention will be riveted by the college students who, playing members of the 78th Highlanders and Royal Artillery, reenact life within the fort. Activities (summer only) include artillery and infantry drills and firing the noonday cannon. Guided tours and food service are available.

Just behind the hill is **Nova Scotia Museum of Natural History,** 1747 Summer Street (902-424-7353). This facility, headquarters of the provincial museum system, presents the human and natural history of the province in an appealing way. Kids will especially enjoy the huge whale, which they can help measure; the stuffed black bear and moose, a colony of honeybees that enter their indoor hive via a tube connecting to the outside; and—everyone's favorites—lifelike dinosaurs. Artifacts belonging to the province's original inhabitants, the Micmac, are on display, including a 121-pound beaded costume. Changing exhibits frequently reveal the history and contributions of a particular ethnic group: A recent display, for instance, highlighted the Jewish heritage of Canada. Call ahead to find out about regularly scheduled activities.

The Discovery Centre, corner of Barrington and Sackville Streets (902-492-4422), offers changing interactive exhibits. Call to ask about the Science Workshops.

Parks and Beaches

Halifax is called "the City of Trees." How many cities can boast a formal English garden right in the middle of downtown? **Halifax Public Gardens,** across from the Citadel, is a wonderful place for a family stroll. Enjoy seventeen acres of formal Victorian gardens—the oldest in North America—including colorful and fragrant roses, hibiscus, magnolias, and formal floral displays. Sundays are especially festive, with afternoon musical performances on the bandstand. If you haven't brought a picnic, bring some bread crumbs to feed the ducks and pigeons.

Halifax Commons, just outside the city center, is Canada's oldest park. It boasts a large playground where your kids are sure to find lots of open spaces and playmates.

Point Pleasant Park, Point Pleasant Drive, at the south end of Halifax, has 186 acres with walking paths that lead along the Atlantic coast (where you can watch ships come in) and through forests. Motor vehicles are prohibited; park in the lots at the entrances. (A city bus comes here from Barrington Street.) The western entrance, at Tower Road and Point Pleasant Drive, features a large map indicating walkways and interesting

Summer brings BuskerFest to Halifax, where street performers from all over the world converge here to demonstrate their skills.

points, including the remains of several fortresses. Besides picnic facilities, this park features supervised saltwater bathing at Black Rock Beach, which also has canteen facilities. Because of the frequent "red tide," this beach is not always swimmable. (See Side Trips for nearby beaches.) Kids can play in the sand, however, and there are playgrounds nearby.

The heather at the southern tip of the park was brought to Halifax when the Scottish Highland Regiment shook out their mattresses and bedrolls after landing here—and heather seeds came falling out.

Have a look at the **Prince of Wales Martello Tower,** built in the late 1790s by Queen Victoria's father. This round, thick-walled structure, intended as protection against a French attack, was the first in North America of what was later known as a Martello tower. Exhibits portray the tower's history, and staff is on hand to answer questions.

Shopping

Many shops at **Historic Properties** and **Granville Mall** feature locally made products such as hand-knit blankets and sweaters, Nova Scotia tartan kilts, and pewter. Downtown **Barrington Street** has the more conventional shopping complexes of **Scotia Square, Barrington Place,** and **Maritime Mall.** At **Spring Garden Road,** another popular shopping area, **Clearwater Lobster** packs this local specialty for travel (at the airport, Atlantic Seafoods does this, too). **Jennifer's of Nova Scotia** features local crafts and maple syrup recipe books. The **Rose Bowl** deli across the street sells maple products, including syrup, butter, cream, and sugar. Don't miss the Farmer's Market on Saturdays at the historic **Brewery Center,** where arts, crafts, and foods are sold. An antiques, flea, and produce market takes place on Sundays at **Halifax Forum.**

Performing Arts

Unfortunately for tourists, the **Neptune Theater,** the city's leading professional company, and the **Symphony Nova Scotia** don't perform in summer. It's possible, however, that **Halifax Metro Centre** may host a musical performance during your visit. Call their recording: (902) 451-2602. The **Grafton Street Dinner Theatre** features music, comedy, drama, food—and fun for all. Call (902) 425-1961 to see what's on the entertainment menu. Summer theater is available in the town of Chester (see Side Trips).

SPECIAL EVENTS

Contact provincial or Halifax tourist information for more details on these exciting events.

Late June–early July. Nova Scotia International Tattoo, Halifax; military bands from around the world, gymnasts, dancers, choirs, and more. Greek Festival, Halifax; featuring music, dancing, and food. Multi-Cultural Festival; Dartmouth; the largest multicultural festival east of Montréal includes special children's programs.

July. Festival of Light, Halifax and Dartmouth waterfronts and harbors, includes fireworks and other festivities. duMaurier Atlantic Jazz festival, featuring the best of jazz, including Latin, blues, world beat, and fusion.

July–August. Tea with the Mayor, weekdays from 3:30 to 4:30 P.M. Casual tea, cookies, and chat with Halifax's mayor.

August. Halifax International Busker Festival features street performers from around the world who converge on downtown Halifax to juggle, clown, and ride unicycles.

September. Shearwater Air Show, Dartmouth, features daring stunts by air force planes. Atlantic Film Festival, which includes a section of children's films called "Screen Scene," held in various venues.

WHERE TO STAY

Check In Nova Scotia, the province's free reservation system, has a minireservation center in Halifax, but it's best to reserve as far ahead as possible. The phone numbers are the same as the provincial travel information numbers listed under For More Information. *The Greater Halifax Visitor's Guide* features a comprehensive chart of area lodgings. Here are a few choices for families.

Motel Halifax, 1990 Barrington Street (902-425-6700 or 800-828-7447—United States, 800-268-9411—Canada), is one of the luxurious Canadian Pacific hotels. You can't miss with its convenient location, indoor pool and parking, and lovely rooms and suites.

Delta Barrington, 1875 Barrington Street (902-429-7410 or 800-877-1133—United States, 800-268-1133—Canada), is also in a terrific location, only a block from the waterfront. Tastefully decorated rooms include triples and suites. A supervised Creative Children's Centre for ages two to twelve is open weekends. The property has a pool and health club, and the hotel is connected to two shopping malls.

Keddy's Halifax Hotel, on Chocolate Lake, St. Margaret's Bay Road (902-477-5611 or 800-561-7666), has 135 rooms, including suites, a recreation pool area, and lake swimming.

WHERE TO EAT

The Greater Halifax Visitor's Guide has a listing of restaurants, categorized by type of food. Here are some of the entries for families.

How could you resist a restaurant called **Alfredo, Weinstein and Ho?** Make everyone happy with inexpensive Italian, Jewish, and Chinese food at this delightfully named Grafton Avenue restaurant (902-421-1977).

The Waterfront Warehouse and Oyster Bar, 1549 Lower Water Street (902-425-7610) provides waterfront views of tugboats and serves seafood in a marine-themed atmosphere featuring a 50-foot oyster bar and lobster from the tank. The restaurant offers an outdoor patio in the summer and a giant fireplace in the winter.

SIDE TRIPS

Head southwest along the shore toward Yarmouth, following **The Lighthouse Route.** Some of the lighthouses along the way are still working and accessible by roads; others can only be reached by boats. Although it's 328 miles to Yarmouth, you need not venture that far. The charming fishing village of **Peggy's Cove** is about thirty minutes away. Set atop spectacular granite rocks, it's one of the most photographed spots in Canada. In summer a post office opens in the town's lighthouse. (Be prepared for summer crowds.) Another must-see: a monument to Canadian fishermen, carved into a 100-foot rock face over a ten-year period.

Continue south to **Queensland,** where there are three stretches of sandy beaches. Although it's not large, the Queensland Beach Provincial

Park is one of the South Shore's most popular. Arrive early to find a parking space. Farther on, the popular summer retreat of **Chester** sits on a peninsula at the head of Mahone Bay, overlooking some of the bay's 365 islands. A passenger ferry runs to the island of **Big Tanook,** where you can sample a local specialty—sauerkraut. Chester's large sailing regatta and professional Theatre Festival starts in mid-July. Cafes and restaurants are plentiful. Stroll to the old railway station, where local artists exhibit their work.

The **Fortress of Louisburg,** P.O. Box 1995, Louisburg (800-565-9464), founded in 1720 by Louis XV of France, is popular with kids. Open May to October, with summer celebrations from fireworks to parades and concerts, the historical reconstruction features costumed animators re-enacting scenes from eighteenth-century life. Nearby, Cape Breton Highlands National Park has more than twenty-seven great hiking trails, and the shores of Cheticamp are a whale-watchers delight.

In addition to the Lighthouse Route and Cabot Trail, Nova Scotia tourism can provide information about other distinctively different scenic provincial trailways to explore after leaving Halifax. These include Evangeline Trail, the land settled by the French in 1605; Glooscap Trail, with high Bay of Fundy tides, ancient fossils, and cliffs studded with semiprecious stones; and the Sunrise Trail area, where the Scottish influence is strong. This coastal trail skirts the Northumberland Strait, boasting the warmest waters north of the Carolinas and about one dozen beach parks.

The **Evangeline Express Excursion Train** travels every Sunday through the Bay of Fundy and other local areas of interest. For more information, call Nova Scotia tourism information at 800-341-6096—United States, 800-565-0000—Canada.

FOR MORE INFORMATION

For information on Nova Scotia, including the reservation service, call (902) 424-4247 or 800-565-0000—Canada/(800) 341-6096—United States/(800) 492-0643—Maine; www.explore.gov.ns.ca/virtualns. Ask about the Nova Scotia Host program, where your family can meet a compatible local family. Provincial Information Centres are located at Halifax Airport arrival area (902-426-1223) and in Red Store building, Historic Properties, Lower Water Street, Box 130, Halifax B3J 2M7 (902-424-4247). Tourism Halifax is in City Hall, corner of Duke and Barrington Streets (902-421-8736).

The *Greater Halifax Visitor's Guide* lists wheelchair accessibility for lodgings and restaurants. **Lewis Lake,** a provincial park 12 miles west of Halifax, offers disabled persons outdoor recreation, including wheelchair-accessible nature trails and lookouts, and two specially designed fishing piers. For additional information on Halifax, call Halifax Tourism Culture and Heritage at (902) 490-5946.

Emergency Numbers

Ambulance and medical emergencies: Izaak Walton Killam Hospital for Children, 5830 University Avenue; (902) 428-8050

Fire: 4103

Poison Control Centre: (902) 428-8161

Police: 4105

Shopper's Drug Mart, Fenwick Medical Center, 5595 Fenwick Street (902-421-1683), is open Monday through Saturday from 7:00 A.M. to 11:00 P.M.; Sunday and holidays from 9:00 A.M. to 11:00 P.M.

OTTAWA

When Queen Victoria selected Ottawa as Canada's capital in 1857, she made a shrewd—albeit unlikely—choice. Although it was then a small wilderness community called Bytown, Ottawa had a central location and was politically acceptable to both upper and lower Canada. Ottawa has come a long way since then. An attractive, down-to-earth, accessible city, it has great museums, natural beauty, and bountiful year-round recreation—much of it centering on the Rideau Canal, which divides the city in two. What's more, Ottawa is the only capital city in the world with an operating farm within its downtown. No matter what time of year your family comes, you'll find a variety of activities to keep everybody happy. Some are in Hull, just over the bridge, which is in the province of Quebec (and has a different area code).

Note: In Ottawa, where there's a 40 percent French population, everyone is bilingual, although English is the predominant language.

GETTING THERE

The MacDonald-Cartier International Airport, a twenty-minute ride south of the city (613-998-3151), is served by major carriers. Taxi and shuttle-bus services are available. Car rentals are at the airport and in town.

VIA Rail, Canada's national railway, runs several daily trains from Montréal and Toronto to Ottawa's VIA Rail Station, 200 Tremblay Road (613-244-8289; www.viarail.ca). Connections with Amtrak (800-USA-RAIL) can be made in Montréal or Toronto.

Voyageur Bus, 265 Catherine Street (613-238-5900), has service throughout Canada. Connections to the United States can be made via Montréal or Toronto through Greyhound.

Cars enter Ottawa by following the red maple leaf signs from Highway 417 and by highways 16 and 31.

Ottawa

AT A GLANCE

▶ Try the hands-on exhibits at the Canadian Museum of Civilization and the National Museum of Science and Technology

▶ Watch the changing of the guard at the Parliament building

▶ Learn about agriculture and animals at the Central Experimental Farm

▶ Hike and cross-country ski

▶ Ottawa Tourism and Convention Authority, (613) 237-5150 or (800) 465-1867; www.tourottawa.org

GETTING AROUND

OC Transpo is the city's excellent bus system. Call (613) 741-4390 for route information. All downtown routes meet at the Rideau Centre (Rideau Street between Nicholas and Sussex and the Mackenzie King Bridge). You may purchase tickets at OC Transpo offices, 112 Kent Street or 320 Queen Street (the Place de Ville building fronts on two streets; 613-523-8880). Two shopping centers, St. Laurent and Place d'Orleans, also have information on outlets on Saturday.

Along the Rideau Canal, which divides the city, are 150 kilometers of recreational pathways for cyclists, pedestrians, and rollerbladers. In the winter you'll see people skating to work on the canal, which is considered the world's longest skating rink. Recreational boaters arrive via the Rideau Canal or the Ottawa River.

An easy way to get around to major attractions is via Capital Trolley Tours (613-729-6888 or 800-823-6147), sight-seeing buses that allow you to get on and off at any of twenty sites, including Parliament Hill, Canadian Museum of Civilization, Aviation Museum, National Gallery of Canada, and Rideau Falls, plus several hotels.

WHAT TO SEE AND DO

Ottawa has a surprising number of museums. Although we've selected only those of special interest to families, see the complete museum listing in the *Visitor Guide* from Ottawa Tourism and Convention Authority.

Museums

Canadian Museum of Civilization, 100 Laurier Street, Hull (819–776-7000; www.civilization.ca). Although the name may not sound exciting, don't miss a visit to this architecturally splendid, large, and interesting attraction. Your kids will love this place as soon as they enter the Grand Hall and see the towering totem poles and six longhouses, tributes to Canada's Northwest Coast. At the stage area here, regularly scheduled performances by storytellers and performance artists are often geared to kids. The new **First People's Hall** honors Canada's East Coast aboriginal cultures. Like the Grand Hall, First People's Hall features native homes, actors sharing native legends, and many changing exhibits geared to children.

The adjoining **Canada Hall** presents Canada's past through life-size reconstructions, such as a sixteenth-century sailing vessel, with simulated sounds. The **Children's Museum** area is extremely popular with visitors as well as school groups, and recent renovations have tripled its size. Although it's geared for toddlers to about age eight, changing, hands-on exhibits may pique the interest of an older child. Upon entering the museum's permanent exhibit, **The Great Adventure,** children are issued a "passport" that can be stamped at exhibits showcasing different countries. At each destination, hands-on activities teach children about the native culture. Kids can learn traditional Japanese writing, help unload a cargo ship at the Port of Entry, or sample native foods from cooking demonstrations at Kid's Cafe.

An adjoining room full of art supplies is the site of various projects and programs. Get a schedule when you enter.

At the **Canadian Postal Museum,** moved to the Museum of Civilization, permanent exhibits focus on means of communication. Kids learn about animal communication, the first writing systems, and satellite communication at **Communication Studio,** a multimedia theater presentation. At **Write Like an Egyptian,** kids learn the writing style of ancient Egyptian scribes, while budding stamp collectors can view a complete catalogue of Canadian stamps at a CD-ROM station.

The Museum of Civilization hosts a variety of family programs throughout the year. **Kids in the Kitchen** cooking demonstrations are held monthly, while seasonal events include designing a paper bag Halloween costume or creating a holiday gingerbread house. Some activities require advance registration. Call (819) 776-7001 for a schedule and reservations.

The CINEPLUS theater (admission extra) projects either IMAX or OMNIMAX films, so plan to spend the day. Call (819) 776-7010 for show times.

Also of interest is the **Canadian Museum of Nature,** McLeod Street at Metcalfe (613-566-4700; www.nature.ca). The "castle" that houses

The Canadian Museum of Civilization, in Ottawa, is host to an assortment of kid-oriented exhibits and special programs.

this museum was briefly the governmental seat after the Parliament buildings burned down in 1916. On display are all the things that school-age kids like: huge dinosaurs, gems and minerals, birds, mammals, plants, and assorted creatures, plus a Discovery Den, with nature-related kid's activities and exhibits.

The **National Gallery of Canada,** 380 Sussex Drive (613-990-1985; www.national.gallery.ca), houses the world's most comprehensive collection of Canadian art and European, Asian, and American works. Chances are that won't impress the kids. What will is the physical appearance of this contemporary glass and granite building, which, as the museum puts it, "rises like a giant candelabrum." Inside, in the **Great Hall,** enjoy sweeping views of the city. The **Inuit gallery** is a kid favorite. An activities center, open on weekends, provides young children with art supplies and a treasure hunt guide for exploring the museum.

Most will find something of interest in the Contemporary galleries, flooded with light from the skylights overhead. There are two restaurants, on-site parking, and an excellent bookstore with kids' books. For a visual treat, drive or walk by at night, when this illuminated glass treasure house is a sight to behold.

If your kids are intrigued by vintage aircraft, they'll love the **National Aviation Museum,** Rockcliffe Airport (follow biplane signs on Rockcliffe Parkway; 613-993-2010; www.aviation.snst.ca). The collection is one of the world's largest. It spans aeronautical history and includes a reproduction of the *Silver Dart* (which Alexander Graham Bell helped to design) and the vintage Stearman biplane, which "passengers" are allowed to board. Family Sundays are held monthly; SkyStuff, weekday activities for children ages two to five are available. Call (613) 993-4264 for advance reservations and a schedule.

The **National Museum of Science and Technology,** 18678 St. Laurent Boulevard (613-991-3044), while not as sophisticated as some big-city counterparts, prides itself on being user friendly. A push of a button, turn of a dial, or pull of a lever activates such exhibits as printing presses and water pumps. **Energy** features forty-five interactive activities designed especially for kids, such as a cooperative energy balance game and giant pinwheel flowers that demonstrate wind as an energy source. Take a lopsided walk through the Crazy Kitchen where nothing is as it seems. Bring a picnic or get something from the cafeteria to eat in the shady adjacent parkland, where you can tour a real lighthouse, steam train, observatory, and rocket ship. When weather permits, evening astronomy programs are held at the museum and the **Helen Sawyer Hogg Observatory,** featuring Canada's largest refracting telescope; reservations are required. While you're there, discover the natural earth at **The Living Earth** exhibit, where kids can wiggle into a damp cave and stretch their necks as they wander through a rain forest and get showered by the spray of a tall waterfall. The **Simex Virtual Voyage** sends visitors on a virtual trip to Mars. Call (613) 991-3044 to find out about ongoing special activities and youth programs.

The **Royal Canadian Mounted Police Stables,** 8900 St. Laurent Boulevard North (613-993-3751), has guided tours of the premises; however, the real reason to visit is to catch the famous Musical Ride mounted drill team in training for the ceremonial equestrian show. Call ahead for the schedule, as the show is frequently on tour.

Historical Sites

Parliament Hill's Centre Block is home to the Senate and the House of Commons, where Canada's laws are created. When Parliament is in session (usually October through May), you can get tickets to sit in the public galleries and listen to debates in either of the two chambers. Older kids may find this interesting. Call (613) 239-5000 for information about the days and times.

On **Parliament Hill,** free **sound-and-light** shows (separate English and French performances) take place daily from early June to early September and four nights a week in May. Kids will like the carillon concerts held year-round on most weekdays from 12:30 to 12:45 P.M. On Tuesday and Thursday summer evenings, one-hour concerts are played on the bells in the Peace Tower, with special concerts on other occasions. Call (613) 239-5000 for information.

Changing the Guard is the best show in town—and it's free! It takes place daily at 10:00 A.M. from late June to late August (weather permitting) on the Hill. The guard is made up of two regiments: the Governor General's Foot Guards (with the red plumes) and Canadian Grenadier Guards (white plumes). The parade forms at Cartier Square Drill Hall (at Laurier Avenue, by the canal) at 9:30 A.M. and marches up Elgin Street to reach the Hill at 10:00 A.M.

Same-day reservations for free Parliament Hill Tours must be made in the Infotent, east of the Centre Block on Parliament Hill, from mid-May to early September. Tours, however, are available year-round. For more information, call (613) 992-4793.

Parks and Farms

Central Experimental Farm, Queen Elizabeth Driveway (613-991-3044), located on the edge of downtown Ottawa, is a 1,200-acre working farm that's delightful for a family excursion. Set up by the government in 1886 to improve techniques and offer farmers technical help, the complex attracts some half million visitors a year. Start with a free, fifteen-minute wagon ride, drawn by two Clydesdales (weekdays May to October; just east of the Agriculture Museum). In winter, sleigh rides are available. The dairy barn (where the museum and vintage farm machinery display is located) houses fifty cows of various breeds. The kids won't want to miss the calves in the southeast wing. Nearby are sheep, lambs, and piglets. Pack a picnic: There are lots of green spaces, including an arboretum along the canal with panoramic vistas. Take in a tropical plant show in the main greenhouse on Maple Drive or stop by the old observatory, which, though no longer in use, has a rotunda displaying instruments used to measure earthquakes and tides. The Ottawa Tourism and Convention Authority has a map of the farm that includes a self-guided walking tour.

Another kid-pleaser is **Dows Lake,** Queen Elizabeth Driveway (613-232-5278). There's lots going on in and around this man-made lake no matter when you visit. In the summer, rent pedal boats and canoes, cycle, stroll, or just relax. In May, come to see the colorful tulips—the pride and joy of this area. During the February Winterlude festival, centered on the Rideau Canal, skaters come to Dows Lake Pavilion (where skate rentals are available) to warm up, to use the bathrooms, or to have a bite to eat at one of three restaurants.

Gatineau Park, only minutes north of downtown Ottawa, is a huge recreational paradise, with forty lakes for water sports enthusiasts. The Gatineau Park Visitor Center, Meech Lake Road, Old Chelsea (819-827-2020), has maps and information year-round. **Lac Philippe**

Ottawa Outdoors

WHITE WATER RAFTING

- **Wilderness Tours:** one-day to weeklong packages (613–646-2291)
- **Esprit Rafting Adventures:** door-to-door transportation, various packages (819–683-3241)
- **River Run:** canoeing and kayaking also available (800–267-8504)
- **Owl Rafting:** family float trips offer a stable, comfortable ride (613–646-2263)

HORSEBACK RIDING

- **Captiva Farm:** reservations required, guides are optional (819–459-2769)
- **Pinto Valley Ranch** also offers pony rides and a petting zoo for children (613–623-3439)

FISHING/BOATING/ SWIMMING

- **Gatineau Park Lakes:** fishing with a license obtained via the Rideau Centre (613–238-3630); Lac la Peche, Lac Philippe, and the Group Campground offer canoe rental (819–827-2020); swimming available in Lac Meech, Lac la Peche, and Lac Philippe
- **Dow's Lake Marina:** paddle-boats and canoes for rent (613–232-5278)

- **Black Feather Wilderness Adventures:** canoe rentals available (613–722-4229)

BIKING

- **Dow's Lake Marina** (613–232-5278)
- **Rent-a-Bike** (613–241-4140)

HIKING

- **Gatineau Park** offers a large network of hiking trails (819–827-2020)
- **Stony Swamp Conservation Area** has 24 miles of trails (613–239-5000)
- **Riverfront Park** nature trails (613–592-4281)
- **The Rideau Trail** goes from Ottawa to Kingston (613–545-0823)

SKIING

- **Mount Cascades:** night skiing available, fifteen minutes away (819–827-0301)
- **Edelweiss Vorlage:** ski school, thirty minutes away (819–459-2328)
- **Mont St. Marie:** highest peak in the region; cross-country skiing, too (819–467-5200)

ICE SKATING

- **Rideau Canal:** rent skis at Dow's Lake (613–232-5278), or at the National Arts Center (613–996-5051)

(Highway 5 then Highway 366 west), forty-five minutes from Ottawa, is the most popular summer area. It offers two beaches with lifeguards (fee), camping sites, picnic facilities, hiking trails, and boat rentals. The site has a snack bar and a swimming pier for visitors of impaired mobility. The Lac Philippe Visitor Center is open weekends in the summer.

In all, the park has 115 miles of hiking and cross-country skiing trails, rolling hills, and scenic lookouts. If you have time, visit the 568-acre Mackenzie King Estate, summer retreat of Canada's tenth prime minister. Take a stroll through the restored cottages and along walking trails and formal gardens that feature interesting ruins collected by King.

Special Tours

Paul's Boat Lines offers ninety-minute cruises of Ottawa's attractions on the Rideau Canal from the Conference Center. Call the office at (613) 225-6781, or summer dock at (613) 235-8409.

The **Ottawa River Cruises** (613-562-4888) features ninety-minute sight-seeing cruises with taped narration on the Ottawa River. Come aboard the **Hull-Chelsea-Wakefield** steam train (819-778-7246 or 800-871-7246) for a half-day trip (36-mile round trip) ride to Wakefield. The train stops here for a two-hour lunch break (bring a picnic) and includes live entertainment. Extra tours are scheduled during the Canadian Tulip Festival and during fall foliage.

Performing Arts

National Arts Centre, 51 Elgin Street, showcases a variety of performing arts from pop to classical music, theater, dance, and other entertainment. Call the box office at (613) 996-5051, or TicketMaster at (613) 755-1166. For specific entertainment information, check the *Ottawa Citizen,* the official daily tourism newspaper, *WHERE Ottawa-Hull* magazine's monthly events listing, and the *Ottawa Sun* English-language newspaper, Sunday through Friday. Alternatively, a free calendar of events is available from NAC communications department at (613) 996-5051.

Landsdowne Park, Bank Street at the Rideau Canal, hosts programs throughout the year that include stage shows, concerts, craft exhibitions, and other family fare. The Ottawa 67's hockey team plays here. (See Special Events.) *The Capital Calendar,* available from the Ottawa Tourism and Convention Bureau, has listings, or call (613) 564-1485.

Shopping

The street stalls of the **By Ward Market,** Lower Town, have been selling seasonal produce, ranging from maple syrup to flowers to honey, since 1840. This lively market successfully blends the old with the new: specialty food shops (some more than a hundred years old), art galleries, cafes, restaurants, and, in the old Market building, arts and crafts stalls. For more conventional shopping, the downtown **Rideau Centre** is the city's main shopping mall.

SPECIAL EVENTS

Sports

A twenty-minute drive from downtown Ottawa, the Corel Centre in Kanata is home to the **Ottawa Senators** of the National Hockey League (613-599-0300). Call TicketMaster (613-755-1166).

The farm team for the Montréal Expos, the **Ottawa Lynx Baseball team** (613-749-9947), plays at Jetform Park, 300 Coventry Road, from April to September.

Fairs and Festivals

Be sure to get a calendar of events from the Ottawa Tourism and Convention Authority; there's lots going on. Here are some highlights.

February. Winterlude: Watch the family celebration at various sites on the Rideau Canal; includes shows, skating, ice sculptures, kids' snow playground, entertainers, food, and fireworks.

May. Canadian Tulip Festival, with entertainment, crafts, food.

Late June. National Capital Air Show featuring Canada's aerobatics pilots, the Snowbirds. Children's Festival featuring dance, music, mimes, magic.

July. Canada Day (July 1) celebrates the country's birth. Ottawa International Jazz Festival includes Children's Day.

August. The Central Canada Exhibition features midway and exhibits. Hull's International Cycling Festival with family events.

Labor Day Weekend. Gatineau Hot Air Balloon Festival.

November. Chrysanthemum Show, Central Experiment Farm in the main greenhouse.

December. Christmas Lights Across Canada features more than fifty sites throughout the capital ablaze with tiny lights.

WHERE TO STAY

Ottawa has a wide choice of accommodations in every price range. The **Visitor Information Center,** 65 Elgin Street (613) 233-3035, offers a free summer booking service with participating hotels, motels, or bed and breakfasts. The visitor guide has a handy grid chart of hotels and

B&Bs that include locations and features. Yes, you can save money by staying on the outskirts of town. But the following lodgings in central Ottawa frequently have summer packages for families, so check with them first.

Chateau Laurier, 1 Rideau Street (613-241-1414 or 800-268-9411), is in a convenient location, overlooking the canal and next to Parliament Hill. This elegant grande dame has hosted an endless assortment of notables, including Queen Elizabeth. The vintage indoor pool is delightful. Although the rates can be on the steep side, check for summer family packages, which may include Children's Play Centre activities.

Delta Ottawa, 361 Queen (613-238-6000 or 800-268-1133), part of the family-friendly Delta hotel chain, has a large indoor pool with a two-story waterslide and a children's creative center with toys, art supplies, and video games. Kids under six eat free.

Minto Place Suite Hotel, 433 Laurier Avenue, West (613-782-2350 or 800-267-3377), offers various-size suites with fully equipped kitchens. Located close to Parliament, the high-rise hotel has an indoor pool, restaurants, shops, and indoor parking. There's also often a summer Kids' Club, with supervised activities and outings for ages four to fourteen; ask if it's in operation when you call.

WHERE TO EAT

The *Visitor Guide* groups restaurants by specialty and includes price ranges and other features. For a special treat, take your kids to **The Tea Party,** 119 York Street, near Byward Market (613-562-0352), for English afternoon tea, complete with scones and cream. The atmosphere is charming, and the shelves of teapots and collectibles are all for sale. In addition, both **Chinatown** (Somer Street West), and **Little Italy** (Preston Street) offer a variety of family dining choices.

SIDE TRIPS

Following the Ottawa River west of the capital region, you'll find scenic farm country, nature trails, beaches, and riverside parks. **Pinto Valley Ranch,** near Fitzroy Harbour (613-623-3439), offers horseback riding, wagon rides, nature trails, pony rides, and a petting zoo. In Lanark County, **Fulton's Pancake House and Sugarbush,** near Pakenham (613-256-3867), has cross-country skiing, sleigh rides, maple sugaring, a playground, nature trails, and guided tours; it's open winter weekends and daily in the spring. **Storyland,** 50 miles west of Ottawa, just west of Renfrew (613-432-2222), is a theme park, with minigolf, pedal boats, nature trails, a puppet theater, a petting zoo, and more. **Logos Land**

Resort, farther west near Cobden (613-646-2313 or 800-267-5885—Canada), is an amusement park with water slides, horseback riding, minigolf, and pedal boats. In the winter, skiers head to **Mont Cascades,** twenty minutes north of town. Mount Cascades is also fun to visit in the summertime, as it is a testing site for new waterslide ride prototypes.

FOR MORE INFORMATION

Ottawa Tourism and Convention Authority, Visitor Information Centre, National Arts Centre, 65 Elgin Street, offers visitors free half-hour underground parking. Call (613) 237-5150; automated line: (613) 692-7000; (800) 465-1867. Canada's Capital Information Centre is opposite the Parliament Buildings at 14 Metcalfe Street. Call (613) 239-5000 or (800) 465-1867—Canada/United States. For a detailed listing of events in Ottawa, see www.tourottawa.org. For information on the entire province of Ontario, call 800-ONTARIO.

Special Needs
Door-to-door wheelchair-accessible service is available to qualified disabled visitors in Ottawa-Carleton. Call Para Transpo at (613) 244-4636 before arrival. All national museums and attractions in Ottawa and Hull are universally accessible. Wheelchair-accessible codes are listed in the *Visitor Guide.*

Emergency Numbers
Ambulance, fire, and police: 911

Ontario Provincial Police: (800) 267-2677

Poison Control: (613) 737-1100

Twenty-four-hour emergency service: Children's Hospital, 401 Smyth Road (located between Ottawa General Hospital and National Defense Medical Center); (613) 737-7600

Twenty-four-hour pharmacy: Shoppers Drug Mart, 1460 Merivale Road: (613) 224-7270. A list of pharmacies open until midnight appears in the Sunday edition of the *Ottawa Citizen.*

BRANDYWINE VALLEY AREA

For more than 300 years—from the time of William Penn—people have sought refuge and renewal in the Brandywine Valley. This bucolic landscape on either side of the Brandywine River in Pennsylvania and Delaware offers the weekend sojourner an American sampler. Here, where southeastern Pennsylvania meets northern Delaware, you find extravagant country estates and simple farmhouses, fine art and nineteenth-century factories, Revolutionary War history, Colonial crafts fairs, and pastoral backcountry roads.

GETTING THERE

Philadelphia International Airport (610-917-6937), the one closest to Brandywine Valley, serves most major airlines and has car rental agencies.

By car from the north, take Route 202 into the area. From the south I-95 north leads to Route 202. To visit by train take **Amtrak** (302-429-6530 or 800-USA-RAIL) to the Wilmington, Delaware, station at the intersection of Martin Luther King Jr. Boulevard and French Street. The Wilmington station has car rental agencies.

GETTING AROUND

The best way to travel and tour the Brandywine area is by car. The Delaware Administration for Regional Transit (DART) provides transit service within northern New Castle County and the Greater Wilmington area. Call the DARTline at (302) 655-3381.

WHAT TO SEE AND DO

Parks and Green Spaces
Brandywine Battlefield Park, on Park Drive between the Augustine and Market Street bridges (610-459-3342), is a historic site. On September

Brandywine Valley Area

AT A GLANCE

► Learn about Revolutionary War history

► Stroll through Longwood Gardens, over 1,000 acres of flowers, trees, and shrubs

► Wander through Winterthur's outstanding rooms of American antiques and hundreds of acres of gardens

► Enjoy three generations of Wyeth art at the Brandywine River Museum

► Discover the 15,000-acre Bombay Hook National Wildlife Refuge

► Brandywine Valley Tourist Information Center, (610) 388-2900 or (800) 228-9933; Chester Country Tourist Bureau, (610) 334-6365; www.brandywinevalley.com

11, 1777, when the morning mist rose over these Pennsylvania meadows and apple orchards, one of the most significant battles of the Revolutionary War began. By day's end 25,000 British and Revolutionary soldiers lay dead in the fields. Despite General George Washington's defeat by British General William Howe, the nascent Revolutionary forces scored an important psychological victory: Washington prevented Howe from capturing the iron forges that supplied ammunition and muskets for the soldiers, and Washington proved his forces were capable of sustaining a difficult attack by the skilled British. This helped Washington obtain official support from the French the following spring. From late June through mid-August, kids ages six to thirteen can participate in eighteenth-century drills, crafts, and cooking at **Summer History Camp,** the park's weekly programs.

September is an especially good time to visit. During **Brandywine Battlefield Days** the park stages a reenactment of this battle, complete with cannon, cavalry, a horse unit, 300 soldiers in period dress, and camp followers. At night enjoy the troops' encampment, featuring demonstrations of eighteenth-century tenting, cooking, and wound dressing.

For more Revolutionary spirit during fall, board the shuttle bus for the quick ride to Chadds Ford for a Colonial crafts festival, called **Chadds Ford Days.** Stroll around the grounds and watch as blacksmiths, broom makers, weavers, potters, quilters, toy makers, and other costumed crafts-people demonstrate these essential eighteenth-century skills.

Museums

Nearby **Winterthur,** 6 miles northwest of Wilmington, Delaware (302–888–4600 or 800–448–3883), also features hundreds of acres of gardens and woodlands. From mid-April through October sign up for the **tram tour,** which is a great way to see the blooms, beeches, maples, and oaks, and save your feet.

The estate belonged to Pierre du Pont's cousin Henry Francis du Pont. Henry's passion was American furniture, and the furnishings at Winterthur will dazzle you and older kids, especially preteens in love with historical mansions. The 196 rooms of this magnificent country estate hold more than 60,000 antiques. From the William and Mary carved wardrobes to the eighteenth-century Pennsylvania blanket chests to the fine examples of Chippendale styling, Winterthur houses an astonishing collection of furniture, textiles, and other objects made or used in America between 1650 and 1850.

The galleries opened in October 1992 with a permanent exhibit, Perspectives on Decorative Arts in Early America. This is a good place to begin your tour with kids. They can choose one of six perspectives from which to look at objects. For example, Change Over Time shows how fashions changed in certain periods. Change Over Place shows how design and craftsmanship differed from one city to another. The Henry S. McNeil Gallery, intrigues future furniture builders with its tools, exhibits on the evolution of design styles, and lessons about furniture study. There is also a gallery for changing exhibits.

You can't see all of Winterthur in one visit. A popular overall tour is the **Winterthur Experience,** which includes a forty-five-minute tour of about twenty rooms, plus a short tour of the gardens. Special tours focus on specific topics such as textiles, craftsmanship, folk art, and Queen Anne furniture. It's best to reserve these ahead of time.

Highlights of the museum include the elegant Port Royal parlor, with its matched Chippendale highboys and lavender-and-yellow color scheme; the Chinese parlor, noted for its vivid green Oriental wallpaper; the Baltimore drawing room, with its woodwork salvaged from a Baltimore mansion; and the Montmorenci stairway, a graceful curved staircase rescued from a North Carolina home built in 1822. Winterthur's **Terrific Tuesdays!** programs in July and August allow children ages four to eight to explore a Touch-it room, listen to stories, and participate in special kid-friendly gallery tours.

The Brandywine River Museum, U.S. Route 1, Chadds Ford (610–388–2700; www.brandyrivermuseum.org), on the banks of the Brandywine

Longwood Gardens

Longwood Gardens is at the junction of U.S. Route 1 and Route 52 near Kennett Square, Pennsylvania (610–388–6741; www.longwoodgardens.org). The gardens transport you from the rustic, rugged history of the Revolution to the tranquil, mannered society of the du Ponts, Brandywine's nineteenth- and twentieth-century industrial heroes. The former summer estate of Pierre du Pont, the onetime board chairman of General Motors, Longwood features 1,050 acres of outdoor gardens, woodlands, and meadows, plus twenty indoor conservatories, several ponds, three acres of fountains, even an open-air water theater.

Walk among rows of trees, sit on a stone whispering bench, or stroll through conservatories bursting with orchids, roses, and blooming cacti. In summer watch a dazzling dance of colored fountains choreographed to classical music, capped by fireworks. Touring Longwood can take all day, but allow at least three hours. After an introductory slide show at the visitor center, start your walking tour of the outdoor gardens under the towering beeches and ginkgoes planted by the original Quaker settlers in 1730. Walking tour highlights, depending upon the season, include tulips and rose gardens or fall gardens bright with red, yellow, and gold chrysanthemums.

Throughout the gardens, especially along the woodland walk, enjoy the sunlight streaming through the sugar maples, beeches, and poplars.

For an *Alice in Wonderland* maze of outlandish shapes, tour the topiary gardens. Surrounded by a sundial that took du Pont and his engineers five years to build, the carefully clipped yews assume unlikely geometric and animal shapes. The topiary garden even has a rabbit—reputedly created in tribute to Bunny du Pont, a relative of Pierre.

Be sure to allow time for a tour of the conservatories. These nurseries, with Palladian windows, house everything from bonsai, cacti, and palms to medicinal plants and rare orchids. The East Conservatory, where concerts are held, contains a 10,010-pipe organ. The Main Conservatory, an elegant pillared structure, provided shelter for du Pont's garden parties. Pink bougainvillea drape the archways around the original dance floor.

Afterward enjoy the water displays mid-June through August. Legend has it that, as a child du Pont would open the bathroom faucets to watch the water run—despite the reprimands of his parents.

At Longwood du Pont gave free rein to his water fantasies. Start with the Italian water garden, lined

(continued)

Longwood Gardens *(continued)*

with linden trees, and based on the fountains of an Italian villa du Pont loved. Four large fountains delicately frame a tranquil scene. Du Pont devilishly inaugurated the cascading staircase fountain: He positioned his nieces and nephews on the marble stairs, dressed in their Sunday best, then drenched them with water.

Check the schedule of events, as Longwood often features such family activities as Fabulous Fun Days for Children. Enliven a dreary winter day with a plant hunt amid acres of blooming plants in an indoor conservatory.

The Idea Garden has several just-for-kids spaces. Kids like the A-to-Z garden of edible plants, the living playhouse that has sunflower walls and a morning glory roof, and the arbor with hard-shelled fruits shaped like birdhouses, bottles, and serpents. On Wednesday mornings and weekend afternoons, the garden clubhouse has scavenger hunts and garden-themed arts and crafts.

River is housed in a converted nineteenth-century gristmill. The pastoral setting and unpretentious galleries provide a low-key way for kids to enjoy art. This is an especially good place to introduce children to American illustrators.

In the museum the American countryside comes to life. Those who have been captivated by three generations of Wyeth paintings—by patriarch N.C. Wyeth, son Andrew Wyeth, and grandson Jamie Wyeth—will especially enjoy these special exhibits.

View Andrew Wyeth's paintings: the wistful *Christina's World,* the weathered barns of *Night Sleeper,* the country boy by the roadside in *Roasted Chestnuts.* Enjoy Jamie Wyeth's whimsical *Portrait of Den Den,* a likeness of his pig. You also can see such illustrations as N.C. Wyeth's drawings for *Kidnapped* and *Treasure Island,* Howard Pyle's Brandywine settings, William Smedley's New York scenes, and Harrison Cady's lion drawings.

After your tour take a Wordsworthian turn through the grounds to experience firsthand the countryside you've viewed in the museum. Follow the trail along the banks of the winding Brandywine River, where lush birches and maples grow near fields of wildflowers. Pack a picnic lunch or buy one from the museum's cafe, where you may dine overlooking the Brandywine. In fall the museum's cobbled courtyard comes alive with a crafts festival and harvest market each weekend from mid-September to mid-October.

The Hagley Museum and Library is off State Route 141, in Wilmington (302-658-2400). The du Pont fortune that nourished Longwood and Winterthur began at the Hagley in Greenville, Delaware, 3 miles north of Wilmington. The Hagley is strung along the banks of the Brandywine River on 230 acres. Here nineteenth-century industrial history is set against a sweep of centuries-old trees, including such unusual ones as blue Atlas cedars transplanted from Africa and Chinese empress trees from the Orient. After all, in 1799, when E. I. du Pont emigrated to America, he listed his occupation as "botaniste." The careful cultivation of these grounds was his lifelong interest.

To the rustle of the river and the wind, this mostly outdoor museum tells the story of nineteenth-century America's booming need for explosives and the birth of the Du Pont Company. The new nation demanded black powder not only to fight the War of 1812 but to blast its way west —clearing farmland, developing mines, and building railroads. Here along the Brandywine River, Eleuthère Irénée du Pont built gunpowder mills in 1802 to supply the United States Army.

With prosperity came the mansion and the workers' village, blacksmith's shop, machine shop, and schoolhouse. All are restored and open to the public. This industrial park displays the stark contrasts of wealth and poverty that characterized nineteenth-century industrial life.

Start with the exhibits in the **Henry Clay Mill.** Once a cotton-spinning mill, it was converted by the Du Pont Company to barrel manufacturing and is now a museum. The exhibits offer an overview of eighteenth- and nineteenth-century Brandywine Valley industry and include explanations of tanning, water turbines, and an interesting model of Oliver Evans's 1819 automatic flour mill. This Rube Goldberg-looking device of conveyors, descenders, and elevators greatly increased a mill's efficiency.

At the mill purchase a ticket for the five-minute jitney ride to **Eleutherian Mills,** du Pont's first property. With borrowed money E. I. du Pont began the family's American fortune. The house, completed in 1803 and later enlarged, was home to du Ponts for nearly one hundred years. A tour reveals the tasteful antiques of the last occupant, E. I. du Pont's great-granddaughter, Louisa Evelina du Pont Crowninshield, who received the house as a wedding gift from her father in 1923.

But the drawings lining the ground floor hallway and the view from the veranda reveal the most. Instead of the terraced garden that now sweeps down the hill, the pictures depict rows of billowing smokestacks. E. I. du Pont built this home in the European tradition of close proximity to the factory. This pastoral landscape once bustled with workers, smelled rancidly of sulfur, and rang with frequent blasts from the mills just below.

Before heading to the heart of the museum—the **Hagley Yard**—tour the original office and visit the barn, with its cooper shop, cars, carriages,

Great Family Adventures

- **Float in a hot air balloon.**
Flights take you over farm-
lands and estates of the
Brandywine Valley. Contact US
Hot Air Balloon Team, St.
Peters, Pennsylvania
(800-763-5987), or Lollipop
Balloon, 109 Ashland Drive,
Downingtown, Pennsylvania
(610-827-1610).

- **Canoe the Brandywine River.**
Northbrook Canoe Company,
1810 Beagle Road, West
Chester (610-793-2279)
offers a variety of trips as does
the Wilderness Canoe Com-
pany, Box 7125, Talleyville,

Wilmington, Delaware (302-
654-2227).

- **Ride scenic railroads.** The
Brandywine Scenic Railway,
P.O. Box 403, Pocopson,
Pennsylvania (610-793-4433),
offers one-hour and ninety-
minute trips through farm-
lands and woods, as well as
combination canoe and rail
excursions. Take the train one
way and paddle back. The
Wilmington & Western Railroad, 2201 Newport Gap Pike
(302-998-1930) has steam
and diesel journeys through
Wilmington's Red Clay Valley.

and a Conestoga wagon. Reboard the jitney to visit the engine house where, upon request, volunteers demonstrate the 1870 slide-valve box-bed steam engine used to power the pack house where the finished powder was packaged. Take the quarter-mile walk along the tree-lined riverbank to the 16-foot wooden waterwheel, which was used until the 1840s, when the family switched to water turbines.

At the **Millwright Shop** in Hagley Yard, an interpreter explains the manufacture of black powder. Displays show how saltpeter imported from India and sulfur from Sicily were heated, purified, and blended with local charcoal to create the volatile substance. Stamping mills were originally used to mix these materials, but by 1822 more efficient rolling mills replaced them. A rolling mill ground the mixture between its two 8-ton cast-iron wheels for three to eight hours, depending on the consistency required.

The rolling mills are the paired, granite curiosities lining the river banks. Several stand tall, and some are just foundations covered by plants. With 3-foot-thick walls, a thin roof, and a gaping opening, these buildings were designed to channel the force of any explosion toward the water. Just one rolling mill, originally built in 1839 and rebuilt in 1886, survives intact. The others sacrificed their iron wheels for World War II.

Still powered by a water turbine, this one mill operates at selected intervals. A guide explains how Du Pont used the millrace, a man-made

Young visitors admire the magical waterworks at Longwood Gardens, the 1,050-acre horticultural showplace near Kennett Square, Pennsylvania.

canal, to harness the natural power of the 17-foot drop in water level. Then the guide opens the sluice gate to set the force in motion.

But the rolling mill was just one step in the production process. Before the powder could be sold, the mixture still needed to be compressed in the pressing house, broken into chunks and ground in the graining mill, polished in the glazing mill, dried in the dry house, and screened and packed in the pack house.

Take time to stroll along the millrace and to follow the river path to the creek banks. With its contrast of stone, water, and rows of trees, this area is among the nicest spots at the Hagley. Stop by the machine shop as well. Inside, hear the slap and leathery hum of belts that drive nineteenth-century lathes, planers, and presses used in repairs.

Blacksmith's Hill and other areas hold periodic demonstrations, including living history interpretations. Check the schedule. Spring and summer are beautiful at the Hagley, but autumn is a special gift with the area's brilliant foliage.

Delaware Art Museum, 2301 Kentmere Parkway, Wilmington; (302) 571-9590. This respected museum is known both for the works of Howard Pyle and his disciples and for its pre-Raphaelite collection, the largest collection on permanent view in the United States. As an intriguing aid in your tour, pick up *Take Apart Art,* a booklet with fill-in blanks that helps kids and parents talk about such components of art as color, line, shape, and texture. The booklet makes the illustrations and paintings more accessible to kids. Pyle, born in Wilmington in 1853, is an important American illustrator credited with training such soon-to-be-famous students as N. C. Wyeth and Maxfield Parrish, whose works are also here. Most kids respond to the techniques, colors, and subject matter of these noted American illustrators.

Take younger children to the Pegafoamasaurus, otherwise known as the **Children's Participatory Gallery.** Kids create their own artwork from foam pieces of various shapes and colors. January features the annual Children's Event, a festive affair that in the past has included tea parties and teddy bear picnics. Summer offers "Jazz-On-Tap" in the early evenings.

The **Delaware Museum of Natural History,** on Kennett Pike, Route 2 (302–658–9111), is 5 miles northwest of Wilmington. Must-sees here include the 500-pound clam shell; the world's largest bird's egg; and the re-created natural habitats, such as an African watering hole and the Great Barrier Reef. For some hands-on exploration, take younger children to the Discovery Room, open to the public weekday afternoons and weekends.

Ask about the museum's special event Children's Weeks in spring and winter, usually coinciding with holiday school breaks.

Rockwood, 610 Shipley Road, Wilmington (302–571–7776), is an 1851 Gothic-style country estate, on seventy acres. The period furnishings here will probably appeal only to older children with an interest in antiques, but the landscaped grounds offer a pleasing place for a family romp, especially during the mid-July Old Fashioned Ice Cream Festival when Victorian bicyclists, jugglers, clowns, and interpreters in period dress take over.

The American Christmas Museum, Route 1, Chadds Ford (between Longwood Gardens and Brandywine River Museum); (610) 388–0600. Closed mid-January to mid-March.

Phillips Mushroom Museum, Kennett Square on Route 1 south of Longwood Gardens (610–388–6082), is of interest to mushroom lovers.

SPECIAL EVENTS

May. Winterthur Point-to-Point Races, an equestrian event with tailgate picnics and a parade.

July. Rockwood Museum sponsors its annual Ice Cream Festival on the first weekend following the Fourth of July. The **Philadelphia Eagles** host their summer camp in the Brandywine Area from mid-July through August at West Chester University's football stadium.

September. **Revolutionary Times at Brandywine Battlefield Park** features a battle reenactment.

October. **Chadds Ford Pumpkin Carve,** at the Chadds Ford Historical Society Fairgrounds, features professional carvers showing their skill at carving jack-o'-lanterns, plus food and drink for the public.

November–December. **A Brandywine Christmas** is an areawide celebration with concerts, along with decorated house and museum tours.

December. **Old-Fashioned Christmas in West Chester, Chester County Historical Society,** is a fun-filled CCHS open house with music, entertainment and family activities, plus a Holiday Treasures hunt. **Patchwork Puppet Theater, Chester County Historical Society,** encourages audience participation from all ages with adapted stories of Rapunzel and Jack and the Beanstalk.

WHERE TO STAY

A nice way to experience the bucolic Brandywine Valley is to stay at a farmhouse or country inn. Two reservation services can help you find family-friendly properties. Call **Association of Bed and Breakfasts,** P.O. Box 562, Valley Forge (610-783-7838 or 800-344-0123), and **A Bed and Breakfast Connection/Bed and Breakfast of Philadelphia,** Box 21, Devon (610-995-9524 or 800-448-3619).

Wilmington offers a range of accommodations, from the posh **Hotel du Pont,** Eleventh and Market Streets (302-594-3100 or 800-441-9019), to the **Days Inn,** 1102 West Street (302-429-7600 or 800-325-2525). The **Best Western Brandywine Valley Inn,** 1807 Concord Pike, Wilmington (302-656-9436 or 800-537-7772), offers rooms as well as suites with kitchenettes. The Best Western frequently offers lodging packages that include admission to attractions, as does the **Holiday Inn,** 4000 Concord Pike, Wilmington (302-478-2222 or 800-HOLIDAY). The Harpstin Inn Great Valley, Routes 202 and 301, Frazer (800-HAMPTON), offers an outdoor pool and complimentary breakfast.

Summerfield Suites Malvern-Great Valley, 20 Morehall Road (610-296-4343 or 800-833-4353), offers one- or two-bedroom suites with kitchen facilities and a daily continental breakfast plus breakfast buffet. There are also children's videos to rent (the two-bedroom units have three televisions plus a VCR) and a twenty-four-hour convenience store on-site. Ask about special weekend rates.

The **Fairville Inn,** Route 52 south of Longwood Gardens and Chadds Ford, Mendenhall (610-388-5900), just fifteen minutes away from the business district, has rooms and suites with country decor and accepts well-behaved children age ten and older.

Farms and Country Getaways

Get into the country spirit by staying at a farmhouse. Several properties welcome families check out www.pafarmstay.com for more information.

- **Lenape Springs Farm,** Pocopson (800-793-2234), located on thirty-two acres along the Brandywine Creek, has an 1850 three-story farmhouse. Kids like seeing the horses and cows in the pasture and parents like the hot tub. The carriage house has two rooms that share a bath.

- **Meadow Spring Farm,** 201 East Street Road Route 926, Kennett Square (610-444-3903), has acres of land and an 1836 farmhouse filled with antiques and collectibles. Ask to see the antique dollhouse.

- **East Wind Farm,** P.O. Box 355, Oxford (610-932-4772) is a working horse farm. Guests stay in the 1837 farmhouse.

- **Sadonjaree Farm,** 505 Broad Run Road, West Chester (610-793-1838), features a 1755 farmhouse with two bedrooms and a connecting bath.

- **Sensenig Bed and Breakfast,** 41 Black Rock Road, Quarryville (717-786-3128), is a small farm operated by Mennonites. There are two bedrooms and two private baths. Guests are welcome to attend a Mennonite service.

- **Elver Valley Bed & Breakfast,** 432 Sawmill Road, Cochranville (717-529-2803; www.pafarmstay.com/elvervalley), offers guest rooms in the farmhouse plus a cabin that sleeps twelve.

- **Sweetwater Farm,** 50 Sweetwater Road, Glen Mills (610-459-4711), is an eighteenth-century fieldstone farmhouse on fifty acres. Guestrooms have canopied beds, fireplaces, and private baths. The property has a swimming pool.

WHERE TO EAT

The Chadds Ford Inn, Routes 1 and 100, Chadds Ford, Pennsylvania (610-388-2613), is just up the street from the Brandywine River Museum. Established in 1763 for travelers fording the Brandywine River, the restaurant offers Continental and American fare and is a good choice for families with older children and teens.

Buckley's Tavern, 5812 Kennett Pike, Centreville (302-656-9776), is housed in a 160-year-old building in the historic town of Centreville, near Winterthur, Longwood, and the Brandywine River Museum. The tavern has everything from burgers for the kids to grilled salmon for their parents.

Two diners offer moderately priced American staples. **Downingtown Diner,** 81 West Lancaster Avenue, Downingtown (610-873-9032), is where scenes from the 1950s science fiction movie *The Blob* were filmed. Also try **Hank's Place,** Routes 1 and 100, Chadds Ford (610-388-7061), which caters to locals and tourists.

Dinardo's Restaurant, 405 North Lincoln Street, Wilmington (302-652-9503), is known for hard-shelled crabs, lobster tails, and fisherman stew. **Arthur's Family Restaurant,** 215 North Dupont Highway, New Castle (302-322-3279), offers good seafood and homemade pastries.

SIDE TRIPS

Easy side trips include Philadelphia and Valley Forge (see the chapter on Philadelphia) and the Amish areas near Lancaster and Hersheypark (see the chapter on Hershey and the Pennsylvania Dutch Region).

Bird lovers and nature lovers should visit the **Bombay Hook National Wildlife Refuge,** R.D. 1, Box 147, Smyrna, Delaware (302-653-9345). The refuge includes 15,122 acres, three-quarters of which are tidal salt marsh. In fall and spring thousands of migratory birds fill the skies over the refuge. In October and November look up to see peak populations of snow geese, Canada geese, and ducks. Shorebirds arrive in quantity in May and June. Obtain a map for a driving tour—kids enjoy the comfort—and a trail guide. Some trails are easily conquered by young kids.

FOR MORE INFORMATION

For more information, visit the Brandywine Valley Tourist Information Center at Longwood Gardens, Kennett Square, Pennsylvania; (610-388-2900 or 800-228-9933). For information about Delaware attractions, contact the Greater Wilmington Convention and Visitor's Bureau (302-652-4088 or 800-422-1181; www.brandywinevalley.com).

Emergency Numbers

Ambulance, fire, and police: 911

Medical attention in Pennsylvania: Southern Chester County Medical Center, 1015 West Baltimore Pike, West Grove, Pennsylvania; (610) 869-1000.

Medical Attention in Delaware: Christiana Hospital, 4755 Ogletown/ Stanton Road (off Kirkwood Highway), Newark, Delaware; non-emergency (302) 733-1000.

Poison Control in Delaware: (800) 722-7112

Poison Control in Pennsylvania: (610) 386-2100

Pharmacy in Delaware: Brandywine Drug Center, 4605 North Market, Wilmington (302-762-6940), open Monday to Saturday from 9:00 A.M. to 8:00 P.M. and Sunday from 9:00 A.M. to 4:00 P.M.; Eckerd Drugs, 2003 Concord Pike, Wilmington (302-655-8866), open daily from 8:00 A.M. to 10:00 P.M.

Twenty-four-hour pharmacy in Pennsylvania: CVS Pharmacy, 246 Concord Road, Aston; (610) 497-2225

GETTYSBURG

Take your family back to July 1863 when Confederate General Robert E. Lee's army met the greater forces of the Northern army in a historic battle and turning point of the Civil War. The **Gettysburg National Military Park,** encompassing some 1,000 monuments and cannons, commemorates this important national event. Add a bonus to your visit by timing it to coincide with one of Gettysburg's popular festivals, such as the apple festival in May or the bluegrass music festival in May and September. A special time to visit is during the Gettysburg Civil War Heritage Days, the end of June through July 4th, when battle reenactments and special events will add excitement to your visit. Besides visiting the battlefield, take time to enjoy driving and picnicking in the rolling countryside, dotted with apple orchards.

GETTING THERE

It's best to drive to Gettysburg. Several roads lead to the battlefield park, including U.S. 30 and 15, as well as state routes 134 and 116.

GETTING AROUND

There is no public transportation in Gettysburg. During the summer season a trolley runs every half hour; however, a car is a necessity.

WHAT TO SEE AND DO

Civil War History

Gettysburg National Military Park (Visitor's Center: Route 134, Gettysburg; 717-334-1124) is the site of one of the most significant, and bloodiest, battles of the Civil War. A visit here makes textbook history come alive, especially if you get your kids involved. Children ages five to thirteen can earn a Gettysburg **Junior Ranger** badge by completing activities in a free booklet available at the Visitor's Center. At the **Visitor's Center,** brush up on your history by reviewing the 750-square-foot electric map that illustrates the famous battle and is accompanied by a

Gettysburg

AT A GLANCE

▶ Tour the site of the Civil War's turning point

▶ Gettysburg National Military Park makes the war real for everyone

▶ Explore a dozen other museums in the area

▶ Take historic walking and driving tours

▶ Enjoy Civil War Heritage Days, held in July and August

▶ Gettysburg Travel Council, (717) 334-6274; Gettysburg

▶ National Military Park Visitor's Bureau, (717) 334-1124

taped narration. Books and souvenirs are also available, some aimed at children.

From here there are three options for a comprehensive tour of the 25-square-mile battlefield. Obtain a Park Service tour pamphlet, and try a self-guided drive that takes you past the designated landmarks. Another option is to rent a narrated tape produced by a private company. The **CCInc. Auto Tape Tours** add voice, music, and sound effects to enliven your self-guided driving tour. The rental tapes are available from the **National Civil War Wax Museum,** 297 Steinwehr Avenue (717-334-6245), or the tape can be ordered for about $13, including postage, by writing to CCInc., P.O. Box 631, Goldens Bridge, New York 10526.

The best way, we think, is to hire a National Park guide to accompany you in your car (717-334-1124). A real guide makes dramatic history of what might be dubbed "boring stones and markers" by some kids. Guides add the vivid narrative and background necessary to turn these grassy slopes into important history. The guides will also tailor a tour to meet your family's interests. Ask where your state's or a distant relative's unit was positioned, and the guide will take you to the spot and tell you a more specific story.

Some guides cater to children, commanding them to disembark from their vehicle and assume the positions of an artillery crew in order to explain how a cannon was fired. Another kid-favorite place that a guide can easily lead you to is the monument for **Sally the War Dog,** who saw her share of battle.

The best time to visit the outdoor park is when the weather is warm.

Your kids will feel freer to roam outside, and from mid-June to mid-August the National Park Service presents a living history program, in which costumed interpreters act out Civil War roles. A nineteenth-century civilian carefully explains what it was like for him when the battle rolled into his hometown, and a soldier sitting next to him relates a different story of woe and worry.

The Cyclorama Center, also on the grounds of the national park, presents the *Gettysburg Cyclorama,* Paul Philippoteaux's painting of Pickett's charge, which is accompanied by an entertaining sound-and-light presentation. The center also displays exhibits and a ten-minute film.

Be sure to climb the **National Tower,** an observation tower, across from the National Park Visitor's Center, but not officially part of the park. The 307-foot tower affords a panoramic view of the battlefield. There's also a twelve-minute tape that details the battle.

If your kids aren't scared of graveyards, don't miss the **Gettysburg National Cemetery,** which encompasses twenty-one acres and contains nearly 4,000 graves of Civil War soldiers. It was at the dedication of this cemetery on November 19, 1863, that President Abraham Lincoln delivered his two-minute speech. Since then Lincoln's Gettysburg Address has been immortalized as inspired rhetoric and a moving speech about the sacrifices of war.

Additional Attractions

Adjacent to Gettysburg Park is the **Eisenhower National Historic Site** (717-334-1124). A tour of this site may interest older children who have some knowledge of former president Eisenhower. A one-hour narrated tour takes visitors through the decorated rooms of the retirement home of Dwight and Mamie Eisenhower. Tours of the home are conducted from the Visitor's Center only. Be sure to get your tickets first thing, as there is a limited number of tours per day.

The following museums are not part of the National Park Service but are privately run; they expound on aspects of the famous battle and surrounding history. Some families like these; others find them not worth the trouble. If you plan to visit a number of these attractions, look into a package plan, which includes a two-hour bus tour and admission costs to either four or eight of the participating attractions. Package plans are available from the Gettysburg Tour Center (717-334-6296).

Jennie Wade House & Olde Town, Baltimore Pike (717-334-4100), strikes a chord with children who can easily identify with the story of Jennie Wade, the only civilian killed in the battle of Gettysburg. Across the street in Olde Town, you'll find a gathering of old-fashioned crafts and merchant shops.

Adults and children alike can learn what Civil War life was like at Gettysburg National Military Park.

The National Civil War Wax Museum, Steinwehr Avenue (717–334–6245), is another favorite for kids. They can watch and listen to a full presentation, where two hundred life-size wax figures re-create the Battle of Gettysburg and Lincoln's Gettysburg Address.

Battle Theatre, Steinwehr Avenue (717–334–6100), presents a general overview of the battle as well as a multimedia reenactment on a 50-foot diorama screen. Visit **General Lee's Headquarters and Museum,** Route 30 West, 8 blocks west of Lincoln Square. In this old stone building, now displaying Civil War relics, General Lee and his advisors planned for the Battle of Gettysburg. **The Lincoln Room Museum,** Wills House, Lincoln Square (717–334–8188), is the former home of David Wills, where Lincoln revised his famous Gettysburg Address in November 1863.

Lincoln Train Museum, Steinwehr Avenue (717–334–5678), interests young children and train enthusiasts. Visitors take an imaginary ride from Washington to Gettysburg and eavesdrop on reporters and other distinguished guests. There are model trains to see as well. The **Hall of Presidents and First Ladies** (717–334–5717) offers more wax figures, this time presidents and first ladies, relating their visions of America. The kids might like the first ladies' inaugural dresses. **The Confederate States Armory & Museum,** 529 Baltimore Street (717–337–2340), displays rare and original Confederate edged weapons and small arms. The **Soldier's National Museum,** Baltimore Pike (717–331–4890), displays

Gettysburg National Military Park Trails and Tours

Walking along one of the several marked trails in the Gettysburg National Military Park not only gives you a different perspective on the battle but also enables your kids to see the monuments and cannons up close. Trails vary in length from about 1 to 9 miles. Bring along a picnic lunch and break for food at one of the various picnicking sites. Maps of the trails and picnic areas can be obtained at the Visitor's Center.

- **High Water Mark Trail.** This popular mile-long path begins at the Cyclorama Center and takes you by regimental monuments, Union soldier territory, and General Meade's headquarters. Boy Scouts should ask about hiking on the Johnny Reb and the Billy Yank Trails, which, when completed, can lead to a Gettysburg Merit Badge.
- **Bicycling or horseback riding.** Biking trails wind through parts of the park, and an 8-mile horseback bridle trail meanders through the second- and third-day battle areas. Bicycle and horse rentals are available at the **Artillery Ridge Campground,** 610 Taneytown Road (717-334-1288), from April 1 through October 30.
- **Battlefield Bicycle Tours** (717-691-0236 or 800-830-5775), offers 8-mile, two-hour guided bicycle tours through the park on weekends from April to October.
- **Ghost tour. Ghosts of Gettysburg Candlelight Walking Tours,** 271 Baltimore Street (717-337-0445), takes you past haunted sights on a 1-mile walk.

dioramas and exhibits of the Civil War from 1861 as well as the Charley Weaver Collection, miniature carved figures from ten major battles of the Civil War.

Gettysburg Land of Little Horses, off Route 30 West; follow signs (717-334-7259), offers a good rainy-day activity. Watch these 3-foot-tall horses race, jump, and perform in the indoor arena. Call in advance for performance times.

More Tours

Downtown Historic District Tour of the more than one hundred recently restored buildings will give visitors a feel of the town that gave the battlefield its name. The walking starts at the Gettysburg Travel Council Office and includes the Wills House, where President Lincoln composed his Gettysburg Address, and Samuel Gettys' Tavern, originally owned by James Gettys, the town's founder. Tour brochures are available at the Gettysburg Travel Council (717-334-6274).

The Adams County Scenic Valley Tour is a self-paced driving tour covering 36 miles south, west, and north of Gettysburg. The estimated driving time is two hours. Tour brochures are available at the Gettysburg Travel Council (717-334-6274), and posted signs mark the route. Highlights of the tour, which covers some of the famous orchards in Pennsylvania, include the Civil War site "Cashtown Pass," the 1790 Lower Marsh Creek Presbyterian Church, and Biglerville, the "Apple Capital."

The **Historic Conewago Tour** is a 40-mile driving tour, about two hours, which weaves around the Conewago Creek on the eastern side of the county. Tour highlights include the East Cavalry Battlefield, the historic towns of New Oxford and East Berlin, and country farms, churches, and the Adams County countryside. Tour brochures are available at the Gettysburg Travel Council (717-334-6274).

Gettysburg Battlefield Bus Tours (717-334-6296) presents various battlefield tours, including a sunset tour on a double-decker bus. Tours are conducted by a cast of actors who use sound effects to act out the drama of the battlefield.

SPECIAL EVENTS

Antiques Shows
There are several large antiques shows in and around the Gettysburg area. For more information call the Gettysburg Travel Council at (717) 334-6274.

Festivals
May. Gettysburg Spring Bluegrass Festival the first full weekend in May. Join in the Apple Blossom Festival for a fuller appreciation of Adams County's outstanding apple orchards and enjoy magic shows, apple-bobbing contests, music, and dancing. Gettysburg Square-Dance Round-up is the real thing, featuring nationally recognized square-dance callers. Memorial Day Parade.

June/July. Civil War Heritage Days is a nine-day event including a historically accurate reenactment of the Battle of Gettysburg. A Living History Camp has costumed soldiers who demonstrate Civil War tactics and infantry drills.

In conjunction with the Civil War Heritage Days, a Civil War Book Fair is held on the first weekend in July. Book dealers sell new, used, and out-of-print Civil War–related documents.

September. East Berlin Colonial Days, an eighteenth-century crafts and cultural fair. Gettysburg Fall Bluegrass Festival.

October. National Apple Harvest Festival, Biglerville, Pennsylvania. Two weekends of country music, crafts, rides, and, of course, apples. The festival is organized with kids in mind.

November. Anniversary of Lincoln's Gettysburg Address and Remembrance Day.

December. Yuletide Festival, a three-day festival of Christmas music, crafts, and food. Ask about special children's events.

WHERE TO STAY

Colonial Motel, 157 Carlisle Street (717-334-3126 or 800-336-3126), just north of Center Square, is centrally located and offers family rates. Kids stay free at the **Criterion Motor Lodge,** 337 Carlisle Street (717-334-6268). Other family-friendly hotels where children stay for free are the **Quality Inn-Gettysburg Motor Lodge,** 380 Steinwehr Avenue (717-334-1103 or 800-221-2222), and the **Howard Johnson Lodge,** 301 Steinwehr Avenue (717-334-1188 or 800-654-2000). Teens and kids stay free at the **Holiday Inn Battlefield,** Routes 97 and 15 (717-334-6211), which also offers discount meals. Be sure to ask your hotel about special battlefield tour arrangements.

The Gettysburg region is well stocked with country inns and bed and breakfasts; however, most prefer children ages twelve and older. An exception is the **Keystone Inn,** 231 Hanover Street (717-337-3888), which welcomes children older than infants. The **Doubleday Inn,** 104 Doubleday Avenue (717-334-9119), located on the battlefield, is decorated with war artifacts and period furniture and offers free Civil War lectures. Children over the age of ten are welcome here.

The following inns prefer children twelve and older: The **Old Appleford Inn,** 218 Carlisle Street (717-337-1711), a historic Victorian Inn that dates to 1867, and the **Baladerry Inn,** 40 Hospital Road (717-337-1342), was the site of a Civil War hospital. The **Homestead Guest Home,** 785 Baltimore Street (717-334-2037), is the Historic Dormitory of Civil War Soldier's Orphanage, and it offers family rates.

Campgrounds are another option. Try the **Drummer Boy Campground,** 1300 Hanover Road, Gettysburg (800-336-DBOY), or call the Travel Council (717-334-6274) for a longer listing.

The **Gettysburg Hotel,** 1 Lincoln Square (717-337-2000), in the heart of Gettysburg historical district, has family efficiency suites during the summer season.

For a full listing of area accommodations, call the Gettysburg Travel Council at (717-334-6274).

Where to Eat

Dobbin House Tavern, 89 Steinwehr Avenue (717-334-2100), a 1776 tavern, includes a country store, a bakery, and an underground railroad hideout that guests can tour. The **Herr Tavern Publick House,** 900 Chambersburg Road (717-334-4332), was standing as the Confederate troops attacked in 1863. The **Farnsworth House Inn,** 410 Baltimore Street (717-334-8838), is open for dinner only and has children's menus. Among its Civil War-era food offerings are peanut soup, spoon bread, and pumpkin fritters. **General Pickett's Buffets,** 571 Steinwehr Avenue (717-334-7580), a good spot for lunch, has all-you-can-eat buffets and children's menus. **Hickory Bridge Farm,** west of Gettysburg in the Orrtanna orchard area (717-642-5261), features farm-style dinners.

Side Trips

Hersheypark, a little over 50 miles from Gettysburg, has a full day's chocolatey adventure for every sweet tooth in your family, including roller coasters and live entertainment. (See the chapter on Hershey for more information.)

For More Information

The local newspaper, the *Gettysburg Times,* published Monday through Saturday mornings, is a good source of information about local events.

Visitor Information Centers

Gettysburg Travel Council, 35 Carlisle Street (717-334-6274), has free tour brochures and maps available to the public.

Gettysburg National Military Park Visitor's Center: (717) 334-1124.

Emergency Numbers

Ambulance, fire, and police: 911

Gettysburg Hospital, 147 Getty Street; (717) 334-2121

Poison Hotline: (800) 521-6110

Rite Aid Pharmacy, 236 West Street (717-334-6447), is open Monday through Saturday from 9:00 A.M. to 9:00 P.M., Sunday from 10:00 A.M. to 4:00 P.M.

Twenty-four-hour emergencies: (717) 337-HELP

HERSHEY AND THE PENNSYLVANIA DUTCH REGION

On a visit to Hershey, you can combine the thrills of a theme park with the sweet excesses of chocolate and the simple lifestyle and scenic back roads of the Pennsylvania Dutch countryside. Easy day trips take you into Adamstown, the antiques capital of the state, to browse for treasures or to Reading, the self-proclaimed "Outlet Capital of the World," to search for bargains on clothing and housewares.

GETTING THERE

Twelve airlines offer more than ninety nonstop departures to Harrisburg International Airport. Amtrak trains and Greyhound/Trailways buses arrive at the Harrisburg Transportation Center, 411 Market Street (717-232-4251 or 800-872-7245). If you're staying at the Hotel Hershey or the Hershey Lodge, there's a complimentary shuttle from the airport and from the Amtrak and Greyhound/Trailways stations in Harrisburg.

Hershey is easy to reach by car, since many highways lead into town. From the north and east, take I-81 and I-78. From the south take I-83, and from the east and west take the Pennsylvania Turnpike (I-76).

GETTING AROUND

It's easiest to get around by car. During the summer months Hershey provides a free shuttle service throughout the park, Hotel Hershey, the Hershey Lodge, Campground, and ZooAmerica.

Hershey and the Pennsylvania Dutch Region

AT A GLANCE

▶ Get thrilled on roller coasters and doused on water rides at Hersheypark

▶ Explore ZooAmerica, with its 200 North American birds and animals.

▶ Tour Amish and Mennonite communities

▶ Browse through crafts and antiques stores

▶ Shop at the outlet stores of Reading

▶ Hershey information, (717) 534–3090 or (800) HERSHEY; Pennsylvania Dutch Convention and Visitors Bureau, (717) 299–8091; www.800padutch.com; Reading and Berks County, (610) 375–4085 or (800) 443–6610; www. readingberkspa.com

WHAT TO SEE AND DO

Hershey

The main draw here is **Hersheypark,** 100 West Hersheypark Drive (800-HERSHEY). With more than fifty attractions on eighty-seven acres, the park offers a sweet day's outing for kids of all ages. The daring will want to ride the six roller coasters, including the **Great Bear,** the first steel inverted looping coaster in Pennsylvania; the **SooperDooperLooper;** the **Sidewinder,** which twists and turns upside down; the **Wildcat,** a wooden roller coaster; the **Comet;** and the **Trailblazer.** Beat the heat with Canyon River Rapids white-water rafting ride, the **Coal Cracker Flume Ride,** and **Tidal Force.** For a slower pace go to **Carousel Circle** to sit astride one of the sixty-six hand-carved wooden horses that adorn this 1919 carousel. Preschoolers like this attraction as well as the **Tiny Timbers** ride.

Especially if you have young kids, book the **Breakfast in the Park package** (See Where to Stay). This special deal lets your kids cuddle with such Hershey characters as Mr. Hershey Bar and Ms. Reese's Peanut Butter Cup before the park's official morning opening. Another bonus: This package gets you beyond the turnstiles before the crowds, so your children have first crack at the kiddie rides.

Take a spin on Great Bear, Hersheypark's steel inverted looping roller coaster.

For a respite from lines and rides, sit and enjoy the live entertainment, which often includes a barbershop quartet, dolphin shows, a Dixieland music band, and strolling performers.

The park is open from May to September. Part of the park reopens in mid-November through December for **Christmas Candylane,** a wonderland of 300,000 lights that puts holiday stars in your child's eyes. At **Dinner with Dickens** you dine with Scrooge and Tiny Tim, who recite key parts from the Dickens classic.

Midway America is a themed area featuring classic boardwalk rides such as a Ferris wheel and arcade midway attractions.

Considered the most popular attraction at Hersheypark, besides the rides, is **ZooAmerica,** an eleven-acre North American Wildlife Park. Open year-round, the park represents five North American ecosystems, including the Southern Florida Everglades, Cactus community from Arizona's Sonoran Desert, and Big Sky Country from the Rocky Mountain region. You'll most likely spot bison, white-tail deer, alligators, and eagles from among the 200 animals.

Not to be missed is the **Chocolate World Visitors Center,** Park Boulevard (717–534–4900). On this twelve-minute tour, trace the creation of a candy bar from the harvesting of a cocoa bean to the wrapping in tinfoil. Follow up with lunch at the Hershey Cafe inside an enclosed tropical garden. Of course if it's past lunchtime, go straight to the Chocolate Fantasy dessert counter for a milk shake, hot fudge sundae, or delectable cookies.

The Hershey Museum, 170 West Hersheypark Drive (717-534-3439), gives you the scoop on the man behind this chocolatey world. Trace the history of Milton Hershey from his beginnings as a farm boy to the sweet success of his dreams, and explore the Hershey collection of Pennsylvania German and Native American objects, including furnishings and folk art.

Founders Hall, south of Hersheypark, is the center of the Milton Hershey School. Founded in 1909 by Milton and Catherine Hershey as a school for orphaned and abandoned boys, it's now a coed facility for disadvantaged children. Pick up a brochure and take a self-guided tour of the school beginning with a twenty-minute video, *The Vision,* on the Hersheys' mission to provide top-notch education to disadvantaged children.

Hershey Trolley Works Tours (717-533-3000) escorts visitors on a forty-five-minute tour through "the sweetest place on earth," where even the streetlights look like chocolate kisses. Costumed players are on board to entertain with historic anecdotes as you ride by the gardens, Hershey's childhood home, and the chocolate factory. A separate ticket is necessary for these tours, which depart from Chocolate World mid-May through Labor Day and again in November through December. During Christmas Candylane the trolley has special rides with Santa.

Hershey Gardens, Hotel Road (717-534-3492), covers twenty-three landscaped acres, including a Japanese garden and an area of dwarf conifers. Spring brings forsythia, magnolias, and 25,000 tulips. Take time to smell the award-winning roses, at their best in June.

Pennsylvania Dutch Country

Lancaster County, about thirty-five minutes from Hershey, is the heart of the Pennsylvania Amish and Mennonite locales. In addition to its religious past, the region made history as a station for both the underground and the above-ground railroad. Also, be sure to explore the region's famous covered bridges.

To decide which tourist attractions will interest your family, start at the **Pennsylvania Dutch Convention and Visitor's Bureau,** 501 Greenfield Road, Lancaster (717-299-8091). Here you will find information on attractions, accommodations, and restaurants. You'll also want to take in the introductory film *People, Places, Passions* on the region's cultural history. The multiimage slide presentation is given daily from April to November. Call in advance for film times.

The town of Lancaster is rich with history and home to Franklin and Marshall College, the country's fourteenth oldest. A 1.5-mile **Historic**

Amish and Mennonite Life

- **Amish Country Homestead,** Route 340 (317-768-8400). Tour the home of fictional Old Order Amish characters Daniel and Lizzie Fisher. The location was the site for the filming of *Jacob's Choice,* and you'll find propane-powered lamps as well as authentic Amish clothes hanging in the bedrooms. Experience a world without television, telephones, or Nintendo.
- **Amish Farm and House,** 2395 Lincoln Highway East, south of Smoketown (717-394-6185). Includes a blacksmith shop with crafts.
- **The Amish Village,** State Route 896, between Smoketown and Strasburg (717-687-8511). Features a guided tour of an 1840 farmhouse and a self-guided tour of a working smokehouse, windmill, waterwheel, and schoolhouse.
- **The People's Place and Quilt Museum,** P.O. Box 419, on State Route 340, west of Route 30 in Intercourse (717-768-7171). The twenty-five-minute *Who Are the Amish?* film is informative. For older kids try the hour-and-forty-five-minute *Hazel's People,* a fictional documentary on the Mennonites. You'll also find arts and crafts, a bookstore, and Amish World, an exhibit area that gives kids an up-close view of the clothes, books, and objects of daily Amish life.
- **Mennonite Information Center,** 2209 Millstream Road, between Smoketown and Strasburg (717-299-0954). As a quick introduction to the region's religion and culture, watch the twenty-two-minute movie *Postcards from a Heritage of Faith.* An exceptional way to learn about these hardworking people is with a two-hour or longer Farm Country Tour. With prior reservations a Mennonite guide will hop in your car and narrate the region's rich history, answering any questions you may have.

Lancaster Walking Tour stops at the town's major community structures. Guides well stocked with historic tidbits leave daily from the **Lancaster Information Center,** 100 South Queen Street (717-392-1776), April through October, and by prior reservation from November through March.

If visiting on a Tuesday, Friday, or Saturday, stop by the **Central Market** on Penn's Square. It's open from 6:00 A.M. to 2:00 P.M. Laying claim to be the nation's oldest continually operating farmer's market, it offers truly farm-fresh vegetables, meats, and cheeses. This is a good place to

Amish Crafts

- **Old Country Store,** 3510 Old Philadelphia Pike (717–768-7101). This shop features the work of more than 450 local craftspeople, including a fine collection of quilts.
- **The Quilt Museum,** upstairs in the Old Country Store. Displays some of the finest Amish handiwork.
- **Old Candle Barn,** Main Street (717–768-3231). Watch candles being dipped.
- **Lapp's Coach** 3572 West Newport Road (717–768-8712). See buggies being restored. Abner Lapp also fashions fine hobbyhorses and beautiful little red wagons. (Be forewarned: Your children are going to want you to purchase at least one.)

buy those famous Pennsylvania baked goods from whoopie pies (cakes with filling) to shoo-fly pies (has gooey-but-good molasses and brown sugar). On the Square as well is the **Heritage Center of Lancaster County,** 13 West King Street (717-299-6440). It showcases such Pennsylvania Dutch arts and items as grandfather clocks and quilts. The **Landis Valley Museum,** 2451 Kissel Hill Drive, Lancaster (717-569-0401), depicts Pennsylvania German life. Families enjoy the crafts demonstrations and the Harvest Days festival in October.

In northern Lancaster County the **Ephrata Cloister,** 632 West Main Street, Ephrata (717-733-6600), is the restored cloister established in 1732 by Conrad Beissel. Imagine yourself a part of this religious commune on a guided tour of the twenty historic buildings.

If you're interested in the history of this charming old Moravian village, stop by the Lititz Historical Foundation at the **Johannes Mueller House,** 137-39 East Main Street (717-626-7958), for a brochure and a walking tour. It's open from Memorial Day to October 31.

At the **Strasburg Railroad,** State Route 741 East, just east of Strasburg (717-687-7522), come aboard for a steam train ride on one of the oldest operating train lines in the country. It's open daily from May through October and some weekends in the off-season. There are also special holiday theme rides.

But don't just go along for the ride; learn about the history of the railroad at the nearby **Railroad Museum of Pennsylvania,** State Route 741 East; (717-687-8628). Here train lovers find train cars from sleepers to diners. There's also a railroading film shown in the station.

If toy trains are more your speed, take a quick look at the **Toy Train Museum,** 300 Paradise Lane off State Route 741 (717-687-8976). Kids are enthralled by five toy train displays and a video presentation. The museum is open daily May through October and on limited weekends in the off-season.

SPECIAL EVENTS

Performing Arts

Hersheypark Arena and Stadium hosts the Ice Capades, Disney on Ice, Sesame Street Live, and the circus, plus musicians and comedians. Call the Arena Box Office at (717) 534-3911 for information.

Hershey Theatre hosts touring Broadway shows, dance performances, classical music recitals, and vintage films. Call (717) 534-3411 for general information and (717) 534-3405 for tickets.

The Sight and Sound Millennium Theater, Route 896, Strasburg (717-687-7800), offers a variety of productions.

Sports

Hersheypark Arena hosts the Hershey Bears hockey team most Wednesday and Saturday nights from October through March. For tickets and game schedules, call (717) 534-3911.

Festivals

January. At Winter Fantasy at Chocolate World kids learn to ski indoors on a 32-foot-long skiing deck.

February. At Chocolate Lover's Extravaganza, Hotel Hershey, sample chocolate, learn to create chocolate desserts, and play chocolate games with your valentine. Pennsylvania Dutch Food Festival, Lancaster.

March. Great American Chocolate Week featuring kids games, live entertainment, and scrumptious desserts. Murder Mystery Weekend, Hotel Hershey. Annual Quilters' Heritage Celebration, Lancaster. Berks Jazz Fest, VF Factory Outlet, Reading.

April. Family Easter in the Country, Hotel Hershey and the Hershey Lodge. Easter Bunny Express, Blue Mountain & Reading Railroad (717-562-2102 or 717-562-4083).

May. Hersheypark opens for the season with live entertainment.

June/July. The Kutztown Folk Festival celebrates the Pennsylvania Dutch way of life with old-time art, hand-woven coverlet displays, and food.

July. All American Ragtime Festival and Contest, Strasburg. Scenic River Days, Reading, with music, arts, and children's events.

July–October. Pennsylvania Renaissance Faire, Cornwall.

October. Antique Auto Show, Hershey. Balloon Classic, Hershey. Take a hot air balloon ride or stay on ground for arts, crafts, and entertainment. Oktoberfest, Blue Mountain & Reading Railroad (717-562-2102 or 717-562-4083).

December. Christmas Candylane in Hersheypark.

WHERE TO STAY

Hershey

Hotel Hershey, Hotel Road, Hershey (717-533-2171 or 800-533-3131). If you're looking to travel in style, Hotel Hershey, a four-diamond resort, offers several family packages including admission and shuttle service to the park and ZooAmerica. A Breakfast in the Park package allows little ones to breakfast with the Hershey cast of characters and enter the park before the crowds.

Although Hersheypark is closed from late September to early May, Hotel Hershey is open and features a host of themed weekends. Besides the monthlong Christmas Candylane for the holidays, just after New Year's the Teddy Bear Jubilee—have your children dress up their favorite fuzzy for the parade—is a "beary" good pageant. Kids are Special Weekend in mid-February jam-packs two days of fun with cupcake decorating, T-shirt designing, pony races, and storytelling. In April try a Family Easter in the Country featuring a springtime trolley ride, a country fair, and, of course, the Easter Bunny.

Spring through Labor Day there is a Kids' Kiss Kamp on Saturday mornings from 9:30 to 11:00 A.M., with lots of crafts, sing-alongs, and games For a complete listing of packages and reservations, call (800) 533-3131.

Hershey Lodge, West Chocolate Avenue and University Drive, Hershey (800-533-3131), is more casual than the hotel but features such family-friendly amenities as indoor and outdoor pools, tennis courts, a nine-hole pitch-and-putt golf course, and nightly movies in the Lodge Cinema. Family packages are available, including admission and transportation to Hersheypark and ZooAmerica. Go on a chocolate egg hunt on Easter or breakfast with Santa on Christmas.

Hershey Highmeadow Campground, Hershey (717-566-0902), has 296 campsites on fifty-five acres. Roughing it is easy when there's a country store, playgrounds, a game room, picnic tables, grills, and two outdoor swimming pools. Bring an RV, a tent, or stay in a cabin that comes with laundry service.

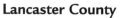

Lancaster County

The Village Inn of Bird-in-Hand, 2695 Old Philadelphia Pike, Bird-in-Hand (717-293-8369), is a nineteenth-century Victorian inn just east of Lancaster.

At the **Historic Smithton Inn,** 900 West Main Street, Ephrata (717-733-6094), you'll sleep soundly under Pennsylvania Dutch quilts in beds handcrafted by co-owner Allen Smith. Then wake up to homemade waffles at this cozy bed and breakfast in the heart of Pennsylvania Dutch country. Kids are welcome, especially in the self-contained two-level South Wing suite that includes a kitchenette, a living area, a pull-out couch, and an upstairs bedroom with a sleeping nook for wee ones.

The **Swiss Woods Bed & Breakfast,** 500 Blantz Road, Lititz; (717-627-3358 or 800-594-8018), is tucked in the woods about 15 miles north of Lancaster. Guests stay in chalet-style rooms. Outdoor enthusiasts and families are welcome to hike in the surrounding countryside.

As one of American Historic Inns' top 10, the **King's Cottage,** 1049 East King Street (717-397-1017), is a Spanish-style mansion built in 1913. It is elegantly decorated with nineteenth-century antiques and has a marble fireplace in the library, stained-glass windows, and a sweeping staircase. Meals include a full gourmet breakfast, served in the dining room, and an afternoon tea. The innkeepers will gladly arrange private dinners with Amish families, as well as sight-seeing tours. Older children welcome.

Green Acres Farm Bed and Breakfast, 1382 Pinkerton Road, Mount Joy (717-653-4028), is a 150-year-old farmhouse with twelve guest rooms. **Old Fogie Farm,** 106 Stackstown Road, Marietta (717-426-3992), has B&B rooms as well as two self-contained apartments for families. **Vogt Farm,** 1225 Colebrook Road, Marietta (717-653-4810 or 800-854-0399; www.patravel.org/members/vogtfarms), has three air-conditioned rooms for families

Call the **Lancaster County Bed and Breakfast Inns Association** for family-friendly inns (717-464-5588 or 800-848-2994; www.padutchinns.com). For more lodging information and seasonal package deals, request a map and visitors' guide from the Pennsylvania Dutch Convention and Visitors Bureau (800-PA-DUTCH).

Reading

The Inn at Reading, 1040 Park Road, Wyomissing (610- 372-7811 or 800-345-4023), and the **Sheraton Berkshire,** Route 422 West, Paper

Mill Road Exit, Reading (610-376-3811), both offer special weekend rates in the off-seasons.

The Reading and Berks County Visitors Bureau (610-375-4085) has a *Bed and Breakfast Guide.* Be sure to ask if children are welcome, if the guest rooms are comfortable, and whether the bathrooms are shared or private.

WHERE TO EAT

Lancaster County

Fill up on homemade breads, mashed potatoes, and fresh pies at the region's family-style and buffet restaurants. One of the best is **The Amish Barn Restaurant,** Route 340 between Bird-in-Hand and Intercourse (717-768-8886). Enjoy the apple dumplings and other Pennsylvania Dutch specialties.

Reading

Visit one of Reading's oldest neighborhoods for outstanding wild mushroom dishes at **Joe's Restaurant,** 450 South Seventh Street (610-373-6794). If the kids say "yuck" to mushrooms, then try **The Peanut Bar,** 332 Penn Street (610-376-8500); tykes can toss their peanut shells onto the floor while waiting for their burgers.

SIDE TRIPS

Outlet Shopping in Reading

Reading, about an hour away from Hershey, bills itself as "the outlet capital of the world." Here a bargain hunter has to smile while tracking the red-brick paths around the minimalls. Refurbished former factory mills now harbor more than 200 stores that promise 20 to 70 percent off retail prices.

Begin the adventure at the **VF Outlet Village,** Penn Avenue and Park Road, West Reading (610-378-0408 or 800-772-8336). Start here because you may not wend your way out of this huge complex—900,000 square feet and nine factory buildings, until nightfall. Stay here if your nerves can take only one outlet complex per trip. In a slightly prettier part of town than Reading's urban milltown heart, the VF stores offer easy parking, clear signs, a McDonald's for burger lovers, and more floor space for goods. VF also has such kid-friendly names as Health-tex, Lee, and Wrangler.

If you can still stand, stop by the **Reading Station Center,** Sixth and Spring Streets, Reading (610-478-7000 or 800-5-OUTLET).

At **Hiesters Lane,** 755 Hiesters Lane, Reading (610-921-8130), two family favorites are Kids Depot for clothing and Baby Depot for strollers and furniture.

Antiquing in Adamstown

If Reading is the outlet capital, then Adamstown, in the east of Pennsylvania's Dutch Country, is the state's antiques capital. You will find 1,000 antiques dealers within a 2-mile strip along U.S. 272 and U.S. 222. Head here to find antiques and collectibles ranging from scanty 1920s satin camisoles to nineteenth-century pocket watches, oak rolltop desks, and even 1950s Hopalong Cassidy mugs.

Bring along some quiet entertainment for the kids while you browse through the bargains, often 10 to 30 percent lower than in the city. Begin at **Ed Stoudt's Black Angus Restaurant and Antiques Mall,** U.S. 272, a mile north of Pennsylvania Turnpike, exit 21 (717-484-4385). Among the 200 neatly displayed dealers' stalls. you'll find jewelry, linens, china, and furniture—all this within a pink fantasy Bavarian building filled with a wafting aroma of sauerkraut and lager from the adjoining cafeteria. **Renninger's** (717-267-2177), almost next door, is a single-story sprawl of gray cinder blocks packed with 400 booths. The kids can snack on pretzels and popcorn while you browse through cluttered aisles filled with quirky collectibles: dinner plates with Richard Nixon smiling demonically or Howdy Doody dolls. **Adams Antiques and Collectibles,** just down the strip (717-267-8444), features an array of 150 shops. Besides such small dealer staples as 1930s music scores and old tins, browse through Adams for 1950s furniture and a good selection of oak.

Take in some Civil War history at **Gettysburg,** a forty-five-minute drive from Hershey. (See the chapter on Gettysburg.)

FOR MORE INFORMATION

For **Hershey** information and reservations, call (717) 534-3090 or (800) HERSHEY. Request a *Vacation Guide,* which describes the various family packages available, park schedules, and event information. Harrisburg-Hershey-Carlisle Tourism and Convention Bureau, 114 Walnut Street, Harrisburg (717-232-1377 or 800-995-0969), offers a free visitor's guide.

The **Pennsylvania Dutch Convention and Visitors Bureau,** 501 Greenfield Road, Lancaster (717-299-8901 or 800-PA-DUTCH), publishes a comprehensive map and visitor's guide with information on attractions, events, accommodations, and dining. Stop by the downtown Visitors Information Center, South Queen and Vine Streets, Lancaster.

The **Reading and Berks County Visitors Information Association,** 352 Penn Street, Reading (610-375-4085 or 800-443-6610) publishes a visitor's guide listing the area's outlet shops, restaurants, and hotels.

Emergency Numbers

Ambulance, fire, and police: 911

Medical emergencies: In Hershey contact the Hershey Medical Center, 500 University Drive; (717) 531–8521. The facility also operates a twenty-four-hour pharmacy. In Lancaster contact the Lancaster General Hospital, 555 North Duke Street, Lancaster; (717) 290–5511. In Reading call the St. Joseph's Hospital, Twelfth and Walnut Streets, Reading; (610) 378–2000.

PHILADELPHIA

Philadelphia, the site of America's first capital, is rich in history. Your kids will enjoy seeing all the things they've read about, from the Liberty Bell to Independence Hall. After exploring the birth of American democracy, families can discover their personal heritage at the city's ethnic museums. There is more fun at the waterfront, which, in warm weather, hosts several cultural festivals that feature music, food, dance, and entertainment.

GETTING THERE

Philadelphia International Airport (215-937-6800 or 800-PHL-GATE; www.phl.org), 8 miles south of central Philadelphia (or Center City, as it's known here), services all major domestic airlines and several international lines. The Southeastern Pennsylvania Transportation Authority (SEPTA) railway system is a good way to get downtown from the airport.

Amtrak train lines (800-USA-RAIL) run out of Amtrak's Thirtieth Street Station (215-824-1600), just across the Schuylkill River from downtown. Philadelphia is a regular stop on the northeast corridor line for the high-speed Metroliner that runs between New York and Washington. Train lines also connect the city to Atlantic City and Harrisburg. For more luxurious accommodations try the American-European Express (800-677-4233), a deluxe overnight train servicing Chicago, Indianapolis, and several eastern locations.

The bus that connects Philadelphia with New England, Chicago, St. Louis, and the rest of the country is another option. Intercity buses stop at the Greyhound Terminal, Tenth and Filbert Streets (800-231-2222; www.greyhound.com). Bus travel is a cheap alternative for short trips.

GETTING AROUND

You can tour the city by bus or subway. For specific information call SEPTA at (215) 580-7800. Dial-A-Schedule (215-574-7777) will mail you a schedule in advance.

Philadelphia

AT A GLANCE

▶ See the Liberty Bell, Independence Hall, and the rest of Independence National Historical Park

▶ Tour first-rate museums

▶ Explore the waterfront

▶ Visitor's Center of Philadelphia, (215) 636–1666 or (800) 537–7676; www.gophila.com

The commuter rail system circulates throughout Center City and connects downtown with the airport, the Amtrak station, and the suburbs. The Port Authority Transit Corporation (PATCO) is an inexpensive way to travel to southern New Jersey. For more information call (215) 922–4600 or (609) 772–6900 in New Jersey.

SEPTA offers a day pass to all buses and trains, including a one-way trip on the airport line. Passes can be obtained at the visitor's center on Sixteenth Street and John F. Kennedy Boulevard (215-636-1666 or 800-537-7676).

For information on parking within the city, call the Philadelphia Parking Authority at (215) 563-7670 or (215) 977-7275.

WHAT TO SEE AND DO

Historic Sites

Independence National Historical Park, with forty buildings on thirty-seven acres, is a must-see in Philadelphia. By 2000, the Liberty Park area will be expanded and will have a new visitor's center. Stop off first at the **Visitor's Center,** Third and Chestnut Streets (215-597-8974 voice, 215-597-1785 TDD), to get a map and to watch the short film *Independence.* Then choose the historic sites that interest you most. The Declaration of Independence was adopted and the Constitutional Convention was held at **Independence Hall,** which offers daily tours. The **Liberty Bell Pavilion,** on Chestnut Street between Fifth and Sixth Streets, hosts talks on the nation's symbol of independence. **Carpenters' Hall,** at 320 Chestnut Street (215-597-8974), is the site of the first Continental Congress. Other attractions include an **Army-Navy Museum,** Chestnut Street between Third and Fourth, which details the development of these military branches; **Congress Hall,** Sixth and Chestnut Streets, where the

U.S. Congress met from 1790 to 1800; and **Declaration House,** Seventh and Market Streets, where Thomas Jefferson drafted the Declaration of Independence in rented rooms.

Other sites of interest on the historic square mile include **Franklin Court,** Market Street between Third and Fourth (215-597-2761), with its museum, theater, and printing and binding exhibit, all dedicated to Benjamin Franklin; and the **Old City Hall,** Fifth and Chestnut Streets, where the U.S. Supreme Court met from 1791 to 1800.

It won't take long to tour the **Betsy Ross House,** 239 Arch Street (215-627-5343), the restored Colonial home of the woman credited with the creation of the first American flag. The **Edgar Allan Poe National Historic Site,** 532 North Seventh Street (215-597-8780), is for Poe buffs. Here the author probably wrote "The Tell-Tale Heart" and "The Black Cat." Attractions include a reading room and slide show.

Art Museums

When you tire of history, enjoy the city's art. Turn this into a treasure hunt by asking your kids to find the great works in these galleries.

The **Philadelphia Museum of Art,** Twenty-sixth Street and Benjamin Franklin Parkway (215-763-8100), is the nation's third-largest art museum, with works varying from paintings to furniture to period rooms. Some of the many highlights include works by Renaissance masters and by a nineteenth-century Philadelphia artist Thomas Eakins. Kids also like to browse in the collection of arms and armor. The museum hosts special programs for kids one Sunday each month. Call for more information. Among the delights at the **Rodin Museum,** Twenty-second Street and Benjamin Franklin Parkway (215-787-5476), is the *Thinker* and a cast of the *Burghers of Calais.* This museum boasts the largest collection outside Paris of the famous sculptor's works.

The **Institute of Contemporary Art,** Thirty-sixth and Sansom Streets (215-898-7108), presents temporary exhibitions in all mediums, including performance art. **The Pennsylvania Academy of the Fine Arts,** 118 North Broad Street (215-972-7600), displays a wide variety of both older and contemporary artwork.

More Family-Friendly Attractions

Take a self-guided tour of the **U.S. Mint,** Fifth and Arch Streets (215-597-7350). You will get an inside view of the money-making process. Watch as molten metal is cooled and rolled into thin sheets, blank coins are punched out, and coin designs are impressed. In summer the museum is open on Saturday and during the week.

The **Academy of Natural Sciences,** Nineteenth and Benjamin Franklin Parkway (215-299-1002), is for dinosaur lovers. Here the kids

The Liberty Bell is just one of the many historical attractions in Philadelphia kids can see firsthand.

and you get to finger replicas of bones and eggs. In the newly renovated Dinosaur Hall, budding paleontologists can dig for fossils at a re-created dig site. Visitors can view six fossil dinosaur skeletons, including *Gigantosaurus,* thought to be the largest carnivore. Check out the temporary shows, which are often designed for children.

The **Franklin Institute Science Museum and Mandell Center,** Twentieth Street and Benjamin Franklin Parkway (215-448-1208; www. fi.edu), has a host of hands-on science fun and merits a full day. Benjamin Franklin would be proud of the scientific achievements and exhibits displayed here, including a heart you can walk through, a 350-ton locomotive, a rooftop observatory, and an astronomy exhibit. The Mandell Center houses traveling exhibits, along with an Omniverse movie theater. It also houses a permanent Internet exhibit, offering a user-friendly introduction to the World Wide Web. The **Fels Planetarium** features fun-filled lessons in astronomy as well as less scientific laser shows. Celebrating Franklin, a new permanent exhibit opening in 1999, explores the history of the institute's namesake. The **Ben Franklin National Memorial,** the only national memorial outside Washington, D.C., is also located at the Franklin Institute. Among the Franklin artifacts on display is the electro-static machine he used to generate electricity for his experiments. The institute has holiday and spring break programming for families and children; call for more information.

Science Park, presented by First Union National Bank in collaboration

Parks, Zoos, and Green Spaces

The Philadelphia Zoo, 3400 West Girard Avenue (215–243–1100), established in 1874, was the nation's first. It now encompasses more than forty acres. Be sure to visit the Carnivore Kingdom, where animals wander around in simulated natural habitats; the Reptile House, for slithery snakes and slow-moving tortoises; and the Jungle Bird Walk, where you stroll through an aviary where birds fly free. The new Primate Reserve features interactive activities in a no-barrier environment—monkeys swing from the trees above visitors' heads. Kids can try on a gorilla-size T-shirt and compare their handprint to that of a gorilla. Visitors can also try on the equipment used to track animals in the wild. In addition, the zoo has a new animal hospital that is open for tours (call for more information). The Children's Zoo is great for little kids who love riding the camels, petting and feeding the goats, and exploring the Treehouse, with exhibits to climb through and touch.

The zoo is located in **Fairmount Park** (215–685–0000). This park, covering nearly 9,000 acres at the north end of the Benjamin Franklin Parkway, is the world's largest landscaped city park. Besides the zoo other highlights include the **Japanese House and Gardens** at North Horticultural Drive off Belmont Avenue (215–685–0104), a replica of a seventeenth-century home; and **Strawberry Mansion** at Strawberry Mansion Drive (215–228–8364), a Federal and Greek Revival mansion that houses some fine period furnishings and an antique toy exhibit. At **Boathouse Row** (215–686–2176) enjoy seeing for yourself this frequently painted and photographed image of Philadelphia. The kids might enjoy catching one of the rowing clubs at practice. Also, be sure to take a break from the city to hike or bike miles of trails. The Visitors Center (215–636–1666) offers a shuttle that takes visitors through Fairmont Park. The shuttle departs from downtown and riders can get on and off at any site for one price.

Smith Memorial Playground, Reservoir Drive by Thirty-third Street, (215–765–4325), is fun for children of all ages and features an outdoor swimming pool and sliding board.

with the Please Touch Museum, is a 38,000-square-foot urban garden, just the place to romp between museums, and for that reason, is located between the Franklin Museum and the Please Touch Museum. The family fun here includes testing your balance on a high-wire tandem bicycle, playing tunes on a step-on organ, and climbing on a 12-foot tire.

Waterfront Attractions

Take a walk down to **Penn's Landing** along the Delaware River to visit the historic ships in port. Among them are the cruiser *Olympia* and the World War II submarine U.S.S. *Becuna,* at Christopher Columbus Boulevard and Spruce Street (215–922–1898). In the Basin check to see if *Gazela of Philadelphia* is in dock; this masted sailboat is more than one hundred years old. Call the Basin at (215) 923–9030 for visiting hours.

The Family Entertainment Center is scheduled to open in the spring of 2001 at Penn's Landing. The center will include an IMAX theater, two year-round ice rinks, shopping, and interactive changing exhibits focusing on different periods in American history.

For a glimpse of the art of wooden boatbuilding, visit the Philadelphia Maritime Museum's floating **Workshop on the Water,** at the Boat Basin (215–925–5439). The **Independence Seaport Museum,** Penn's Landing, Columbus Boulevard and Walnut Street (215–925–5439), focuses on the maritime history of the Delaware Valley. Interactive exhibits let you unload a container ship, experience a general quarters drill aboard a naval destroyer, and try welding and riveting a ship's hull. Also on view is a 1910 Atlantic City Catboat, one of only forty ever manufactured. Purchase an all-inclusive ticket for admission to the Seaport Museum, tours of the ships in port, and a ferry ride to the aquarium across the river in Camden, New Jersey (see Side Trips).

Just for kids, the **Please Touch Museum,** 210 North Twenty-first Street (215-963-0667; www.liberty.org/~pleastch), offers interactive exhibitions for ages seven and under. The museum features eight major exhibit areas including a permanent farm exhibit that lets children ride a tractor, milk a cow, and play with scarecrows in a cornfield. A new permanent exhibit opening in the summer of 1999 will bring to life character's from *Alice's Adventures in Wonderland* in an interactive setting. The museum's theater offers children's performances free with admission to the museum (call for more information).

At **RiverRink,** open November through March, Penn's Landing Delaware Avenue and Chestnut Street (215-925-7465), glide hand in hand with your children or practice figure eights and double axels at this hockey-size outdoor ice rink. Check the schedule for special performances.

Ethnic Philadelphia

The City of Brotherly Love offers a good place for you and your kids to explore your ethnic heritage. Begin at the **Balch Institute of Ethnic Studies,** 18 South Seventh Street (215-925-8090). A permanent exhibit on the history of immigration in Pennsylvania provides a historical background, while rotating exhibits focus on various ethnic group heritages.

The **African American Museum in Philadelphia,** Seventh and Arch Streets (215-574-0380), traces the history of African-American culture, displays African-American artwork, and talks about people who have made contributions to sports, theater, music, and the sciences. There's also a moving depiction of slavery in the United States. The **National Museum of American Jewish History,** at 55 North Fifth Street (215-923-3811; www.nmajh.org), explores the evolution of Jewish identity in America. Other ethnic museums include the **American Swedish Historical Museum,** 1900 Pattison Avenue (215-389-1776), and the **Polish American Cultural Center Museum,** 308 Walnut Street (215-922-1700).

To learn about an interesting group that has no one ethnic identity, visit the **Mummers Museum** at Second Street and Washington Avenue (215-336-3050). You'll find out there's more to them than the New Year's parade.

Performing Arts and Entertainment

The redevelopment of Broad Street in Center City added or reinvigorated sixteen performance, visual, and educational facilities to what's called **Avenue of the Arts** (check out the Web site www.AvenueoftheArts.com for more information). Kids like the "street concerts" played on the thirty-nine bronze bells on Broad Street between Chestnut and Carpenter Streets. Check out the **Annenberg Center,** 3680 Walnut Street (215-898-6791), for international productions and a children's theater series. **The Freedom Theatre,** 1346 North Broad Street (215- 765-2793), established in 1966, has been rated one of the top six theaters in the country. It's located in the historic Heritage House. Other options are the **Merriam Theater,** 250 Broad Street (215-875-4800), the **Philadelphia Theatre Company,** 1714 Delancey Street (215-735-0631), and **Society Hill Playhouse,** 507 South Eighth Street (215-923-0210), for off Broadway plays.

If music is more your style, you can listen to the **Philadelphia Orchestra.** Call (215) 893-1999 for performance information, including children's productions. For the city's Bach Festival, call (215) 247-BACH; for the Mozart Orchestra, call (610) 284-0174. The **Curtis Institute of**

Music, 1726 Locust Street (215-893-7902), presents free student performances.

The **Pennsylvania Ballet** performs at the Academy of Music, Broad and Locust Streets (215-551-7000), along with the Opera Company of Philadelphia (215-928-2110).

Sports

Philly is a town for sports lovers as well. In summer check out the **Phillies** baseball team at Veterans Stadium, Broad Street and Pattison Avenue. For tickets and information, call (215) 463-1000. In autumn the **Eagles** football team takes over Veterans Stadium. Call (215) 463-5500 for tickets and information. The **76ers** basketball team plays at the First Union Center, Broad Street and Pattison Avenue, Philadelphia. For tickets and information, call (215) 339-7676. Hockey fans can watch the **Flyers** in season at the First Union Center. Tickets and information are available at (215) 465-4500.

More Useful Numbers

For general entertainment and sports tickets, there are a few ticket sales bureaus: Central City Ticket Office, 1312 Sansom Street (215-735-1350 or 735-1351); TicketMaster (215-336-2000; www.ticketmaster.com); Upstages, 1412 Chestnut Street (215-567-0670); and Plays and Players Theater, 1714 Delancy Place (215-569-9786).

Special Tours

Conduct your own walking tour of **African-American history** in Philadelphia with the *Share the Heritage Guide* published by the Philadelphia Convention and Visitors Bureau (215-636-1666). Highlights include the Mother Bethel African Methodist Episcopal Church, founded in 1794 and considered to be the oldest piece of property continually owned by blacks in the country, and Heritage House, the oldest black cultural center. This helpful guide includes information on restaurants, shopping, and nightlife as well.

A guided walking tour of **historic Philadelphia** begins at the Commodore Barry Statue, Sixth and Walnut Streets. Call (215) 592-1971 for more information. If you prefer to go at your own pace, try **Audio Walk & Tour,** Sixth and Sansom Streets (215-925-1234), for a self-guided cassette tour. **Candlelight Tours** (215-735-3123) offers a candlelight stroll with costumed guides on selected evenings.

If you're looking to get off your feet, old trolley tours of the historic district leave from the Visitor's Center at John F. Kennedy Boulevard and Sixteenth Street (215-333-0320).

Horse and Buggy. The even more old-fashioned enjoy horse-drawn carriage rides available at Fifth and Market Streets and South Street at Headhouse Square.

SPECIAL EVENTS

Festivals

The Visitor's Center (215-636-1666 or 800-537-7676; www.libertynet. org/phila-visitor) has a list of events.

January. Start off the new year with the Mummers Parade on New Year's Day. This world-famous event features 30,000 mummers. Later in the month enjoy Valley Forge Day and the Chinese New Year Celebration.

February. Presidential Jazz Weekend offers three days jam-packed with jazz for the whole family.

March. The Philadelphia Flower Show, the largest flower show on the East Coast. In March or April The Book and the Cook, a celebration of cookbook authors and fine food, is featured at many area restaurants.

Summer/Fall. Penn's Landing Summer Season sponsors more than sixty free concerts on the waterfront. Mann Music Center Summer Concerts are staged in Fairmount Park.

May. USAir sponsors a Jam on the River, a festival of food and music on Memorial Day weekend. Other festivals include Africamericas Festival, Italian Market Festival, and International Choral Music Festival. Philadelphia International Theatre Festival for Children at the Annenberg Center features juggling workshops and an international atmosphere.

June. The Odunde Festival of the African New Year, Twenty-third and South Streets, features live performances. Rittenhouse Square Fine Arts Annual Festival and Mellon Jazz Festival also are highlights.

July. Welcome America! (www.americasbirthday.com) Philadelphia International Film Festival (Philafilm).

August. Polish Festival at Penn's Landing, Great Gospel Picnic Weekend in Fairmount Park, and African American Extravaganza.

September. South Street Seven Arts Festival. Annual Pepsi Penn's Landing Jazz Fest.

October. Freedom Fest sponsored by the Freedom Theatre.

November. Thanksgiving Day Parade.

December. Attend the Presence of Kwanzaa, and ring in the new year with Neighbors in the New Year and fireworks on the waterfront.

WHERE TO STAY

Hotels

Philadelphia has a wide range of accommodations. Some upscale choices include the **Rittenhouse,** 210 West Rittenhouse Square (215-546-9000). Situated on historic Rittenhouse Square, it offers large rooms and luxurious bathrooms. **The Four Seasons,** One Logan Square (215-963-1500 or 800-332-3442), is a full-service luxury hotel, including complimentary town-car service within the city. **The Ritz-Carlton** (215-563-1600) at Liberty Place in the business district features luxury accommodations, including a fitness center and three restaurants. **Philadelphia Mariott,** 1201 Market Street (215-625-2900 or 800-320-5744), is a short walk to most museums.

Less expensive choices, especially with weekend packages, include the **Sheraton Society Hill** at 1 Dock Street (215-238-6000) near Independence National Historical Park. The **Holiday Inn Independence Mall** at Fourth and Arch Streets (215-923-8660) is close to the Liberty Bell. The **Crown Plaza,** Eighteenth and Market Streets (215-561-7500), is centrally situated. The **Comfort Inn at Penn's Landing,** 100 North Delaware Avenue (215-627-7900), is on the waterfront and has relatively inexpensive weekend rates.

Near the airport are two all-suite choices. **Embassy Suites,** 9000 Bartram Avenue (215-364-4500), has five floors of suites and weekend packages. **Westin Suite Hotel,** 401 Island Avenue (215- 365-6600), also near the airport, offers suite space.

Bed-and-Breakfast Accommodations

Bed and Breakfasts offer an especially nice alternative for families in Philadelphia because many are located in historic districts.

A B&B registry to check out is **Bed and Breakfast Connections,** P.O. Box 21, Devon (215-687-3565 or 800-448-3619; www.bnbphiladelphia. com). Family accommodations located in historic districts include **The Bed and Breakfast Man,** 218 Fitzwater Street (215-829-8951), a short distance from most historic and entertainment attractions.

All About Town Bed and Breakfast, P.O. Box 562, Valley Forge (215-783-7838 or 800-344-0123), has listings for the Valley Forge region, in town, and in other suburbs.

WHERE TO EAT

You've got to have an authentic hoagie or steak sandwich while staying in Philadelphia. Two good suppliers are **Jim's Steaks,** 400 South Street (215-928-1911), and **Pat's King of the Steaks,** 1237 East Passyunk

Avenue (215-468-1546). **Tacconelli's,** Somerset Street and Aramingo Avenue (215-425-4983), has some of the best pizza in town.

A fun place to stop for a quick bite, coffee, or dessert is **Reading Terminal Market,** Twelfth and Arch Streets, just off Market Street. Here you can put together a lunch, mixing fresh produce, deli meats, and cheeses available from a bustling array of individual food service booths. Or get some chicken pot pie from the Amish vendors who come to the market on Wednesday and Saturday.

Philadelphia's **Hard Rock Cafe,** 1113-31 Market Street (215-238-1000), is always a popular choice with kids. Also try **Dave & Busters,** 325 North Columbus Boulevard, Pier 19 North (215-413-1915), for an evening of food and family entertainment.

When your stomach is growling in Independence Park, the **Food Court at Liberty Place** is not far away on the second floor of Liberty Place between Chestnut and Market Streets in Center City. It's well stocked with fast-food spots.

If you're in the mood for Chinese food, Chinatown's the place, with a lineup of restaurants stretching from Ninth to Eleventh Streets. Good picks are the **Imperial Inn,** 142 North Tenth Street (215-627-5588), and the **Harmony Vegetarian Restaurant,** 135 North Ninth Street (215-627-4520).

For fine dining with older kids and teens, **Le Bec-Fin,** 1523 Walnut Street, in Center City (215-567-1000), has excellent French cuisine. In the Historic District try **The Dickens Inn,** 421 South Second Street (215-928-9307). Housed in a Federal-style town house, the restaurant is decorated with Dickens paraphernalia. For Italian cuisine and a waterfront view, go to **Ristorante Panorama** on Front and Market Streets (215-922-7600).

SIDE TRIPS

Explore the wonders of the water at the **New Jersey State Aquarium,** Riverside Drive and Delaware River, Camden, New Jersey (609-365-3300; www.njaquarium.org). Take the Riverbus Ferry (218-925-5465—RiverLink), from Penn's Landing to the Camden Waterfront, right next to the aquarium. If you prefer to be on land, take the PATCO train line, which connects downtown Philadelphia to the aquarium by way of the scenic Ben Franklin Bridge. The aquarium features a huge open-ocean tank, with fish species ranging from sharks to minnows.

Ocean Base Atlantic features 1,000 tropical fish, plus such "awesome" real artifacts as a 7-foot shark jaw, complete with 275 fossilized teeth. The Touch-a-Shark Tank allows visitors to stroke the backs of small sharks and stingrays. Interactive computers make learning about

Sesame Place

This ten-acre theme park for kids ages two to thirteen blends physical play with water activities and is peopled with Elmo, Twiddlebugs, and other much-loved characters from the popular television show. This is a great place for young kids and a wonderful introduction to the fun of theme parks. Highlights include:

- **Breakfast with Big Bird.** Arrive early and you can eat breakfast with Big Bird and get into the park ahead of the crowds. Reserve early.

- **Twiddlebug Land.** Surrounded by giant tinker toys, playing cards, and postcards, even adults feel as tiny as bugs. Sky Splash is the area's water highlight.

- **Vapor Trail.** This family coaster is just the right size for first thrills.

- **Rubber Duckie Pond.** Toddlers can splash in the pond, and parents and kids can float in an eight-foot-wide raft through 50,000 gallons of water and enjoy the many other water rides and attractions.

- **Sesame Neighborhood.** This outdoor full-size re-creation of the Sesame Street neighborhood features Bert and Ernie's house, Mr. MacIntosh's fruit stand, Engine House Number 1, and Oscar the Grouch's garage.

Sesame Place, Oxford Valley Road, Langhorne (215-757-1100).

this sea life hands-on fun. Other fishy finds include a 3,000-gallon Rainbow Seas Caribbean reef tank, a trout stream, and a 170,000-gallon Seal Pool with nine seals.

Another treat in Camden is the **Blockbuster-Sony Music Entertainment Centre,** right across the Delaware River from Penn's Landing. Big-name concerts take place outdoors May through October at this 25,000-seat amphitheater. In winter walls create a climate-controlled theater.

The **Valley Forge National Historic Park,** Route 23 and North Gulph Road, Valley Forge (215-783-1077), is thirty minutes outside the city and worth the trip. In 1993 the area celebrated its one-hundredth anniversary, and there's always something to celebrate at this Revolutionary War site where George Washington and 12,000 soldiers waited out the British for six months. Take a self-guided tour of the reconstructed huts, headquarters, and fortifications of the encampments. Other attractions in the area include the 1770 **Isaac Potts**

House; the **Washington Memorial Chapel,** a 1903 Gothic chapel that offers Sunday concerts; and the **Valley Forge Historical Society Museum** (215-783-0535).

Bucks County, about an hour by car from Philadelphia, is well stocked with historic estates, antiques stores, and country inns. Call **Bucks County Tourist Commission,** 152 Swamp Road, Doylestown (215-345-4552), for more information.

The **Pearl S. Buck House** at Green Hills, 520 Dublin Road, Perkasie (215-249-0100), also in Bucks County, is a good place for a picnic. Relax at this sixty-acre farm, a National Historic Landmark and home of the Nobel and Pulitzer prize winner.

The **Pennsylvania Renaissance Faire,** on the grounds of Mount Hope Estate and Winery in Cornwall (717-665-7021), simulates a 1599 English country "faire" for fifteen weekends throughout the summer and fall beginning in late June or July. Activities on this thirty-acre spread include crafts, sporting events, music, and food. Many, including a petting zoo and marionette shows, are expressly for children. The Faire runs Saturday through Monday during early September, and weekends only from then until October. Summer hours are 11:30 A.M. to 7:00 P.M.; fall hours are 10:30 A.M. to 6:00 P.M.

The **Brandywine Valley,** about an hour's drive from Philadelphia, mixes scenery and history. (See the chapter on the Brandywine Valley.)

FOR MORE INFORMATION

The **Visitor's Center of Philadelphia,** Sixteenth Street and John F. Kennedy Boulevard, Philadelphia: (215) 636-1666 or (800) 537-7676; www.gophila.com

Twenty-four hour event hotline: (215) 337-7777, ext. 2540

The Philadelphia Convention and Visitors Bureau, 1515 Market Street, Philadelphia: (215) 636-3300

International Visitors Center: (215) 823-7261

Philly Fun Line: (215) 568-7255

Travelers Aid Society: (215) 546-0571 or 386-0845, for travel problems, lost luggage, etc.

The Philadelphia *Inquirer* puts out a Weekend section of entertainment events on Fridays. The *Daily News,* a paper with heavier local coverage, also lists events.

Persons with disabilities can get referrals and information from the **Mayor's Office for the Handicapped,** Room 143, City Hall, Philadelphia; (215) 686-2798.

Emergency Numbers

Ambulance, fire, and police: 911

Children's Hospital of Philadelphia: (215) 590-1000

Health Hotline: (800) 692-7254

Philadelphia Police: (215) 231-3131

Poison Control Center: (215) 386-2100

Twenty-four-hour pharmacy: CVS, 6501 Harbison Avenue; (215) 333-4300

MONTRÉAL

M ontréal, an island city on the St. Lawrence River, is exciting and dynamic, with a distinctively Continental flavor. French is the official language, although you'll find English widely spoken, especially in the western half of the city. If your kids have never been to Europe, a visit here will definitely make an impression; they'll certainly notice the cultural differences and may even pick up some French. Indeed, in Montréal there is so much to see and do that your family will pronounce it "magnifique!"

GETTING THERE

Montréal International Airport in Dorval (514-842-2281) services approximately forty major American and Canadian airlines. The airport, twenty to thirty minutes from downtown, can be reached by taxi or regular bus lines. Call Autobus Connaisseur (514-934-1222) for information. Car rentals are available at the airport.

Mirgbel Airport (514-476-5355) about 35 miles north of the city, serves charter flights. For airport information, check www.admtl.com.

Voyageur, which provides bus service from other Canadian cities, has a terminal at 505 boulevard de Maisonneuve East (514-842-2281), situated above Berri/UQAM Metro station. Other bus service: **Greyhound/Trailways** (800-231-2222) from New York and **Vermont Transit** (508-343-3064 or 508-537-6669) from Boston.

Train service from the United States is provided by **Amtrak** (800-426-8725) and from Canadian destinations by **VIA Rail** (514-871-1331 or 800-361-5390—Québec, 800-561-8630—Canada). Both arrive and depart from Central Station, 935 de La Gauchetière Street West (under the Queen Elizabeth Hotel), at Bonaventure Metro station. VIA Rail Canada Inc., Central Station, 895 de La Gauchetière Street West (514-989-2626; www.viarail.ca), has departures to Montréal from Québec City, Ottawa, Toronto, Windsor, and other cities.

From the United States take I-87, which becomes Autoroute 15.

The major artery leading to Montréal from Toronto and Ottawa is Highway 401; from Québec you can take Highway 20 or 40. Most U.S.

Montréal

AT A GLANCE

▶ Discover a delightfully European city in North America

▶ Enjoy beautiful parks

▶ Explore Île Notre-Dame and Île Sainte-Hélène

▶ Squirm at the thousands of insects at the Insectarium

▶ Tourisme Montréal Convention and Visitors Bureau, (514) 844–5400 or (800) 363–7777; www.tourisme-montreal.org

interstates connect with Highway 10, which runs through the Eastern Townships area.

GETTING AROUND

Montréal has a quiet, clean, and efficient Metro subway—an experience not to be missed. Save money by buying a strip of six tickets or one of three types of day passes. Four color-coded interconnecting lines service sixty-five station stops. In addition, there are more than 150 bus routes. Call (514) 288–6287 for transportation information. The Metro connects a huge underground city network of shops, restaurants, banks, hotels, theaters, and railway and bus terminals.

The city is divided into east-west streets by boulevard St. Laurent (The Main), which runs north-south. Montréal is a compact city and highly walkable. Old Montréal *(Vieux Montréal),* where you'll find the Old Port *(Vieux-Port),* is a great place to stroll. In summer water shuttles operate between the Old Port and the city's two islands, Île Notre-Dame and Île Sainte-Hélène (see Parks section) as well as to Cité du Havre Park, where there are outdoor children's activities, picnic tables, and bicycle paths.

WHAT TO SEE AND DO

Parks, Green Spaces, and Play Areas

Montréal is the most fun for families in late spring and summer, when the weather lets visitors enjoy the wonderful gardens, parks, and street life. The city's biggest draw, **Old Montréal (Vieux Montréal),** a historic area, features narrow lanes and cobblestoned streets.

For children, much of the spirit of the city is found outdoors. Lingering in sidewalk cafes—a good place for your kids to sample real frites (French fries)—is a time-honored tradition, and the people watching is prime. The jugglers, violinists, mimes, and other street performers frequently found in Old Montréal, especially near **Place Jacques Cartier,** a lively square, fascinate kids, especially little ones. From here you can catch *Le Bateau Mouche,* Jacques Cartier Pier (514-849-9952 or 800-361-9952; www. Bateaumouche.com), a sight-seeing riverboat, for a ninety-minute narrated cruise. The wind-blown mix of scenic islands and city skyscrapers offers a pleasing respite in a day of busy sight-seeing.

The **Old Port** (514-496-7678 or 800-971-7678; www.svpm.ca), a renovated harbor area and federal park, is great for families. Along with an **IMAX Theater,** quai King Edward (514-349-4629; www.svpm. ca/imax), showing films on a giant screen, a

Basilica of Notre-Dame-de-Montréal

One of the largest churches in North America, the **Basilica of Notre-Dame-de-Montréal,** 116 Notre Dame Street West (514-849-1070), has an elaborate interior featuring intricate carvings and exceptional stained-glass windows. Although children won't want to spend a long time here, they will probably be awed by a quick walk-through.

flea market, *le Marche Bonsecours,* 350 Saint Paul Street East (514-872-7730), and a **children's theater,** this lively area sports cafes, a playground, an observation deck atop the **Clock Tower,** and a **life-size labyrinth.** At the **S.O.S Labyrinthe,** King Edward Pier (514-496-7678), visitors wander through twisting paths and conquer challenges such as a net ladder, a secret passage, and a tunnel. Guides assist those who need help and the course changes weekly.

The **Lockkeepers Hut** (514-496-4629) at the entrance to the Lachine Canal is a tourist information and interpretation center dispensing facts on the locks.

Bicycles are for rent, as are quadracycles, four-wheeled vehicles whose seats make it easy to take young kids along. The path adjacent to the **Lachine Canal** provides scenic views and easy pedaling. **Velo Aventure,** quai King Edward (514-847-0666), rents bikes as well as inline skates.

Île Sainte-Hélène

For more outdoor fun, spend most of the day on **Île Sainte-Hélène,** an island in the St. Lawrence River. There are swimming pools, picnic tables, and **La Ronde,** Parc des Isles (514-872-6222 or 800-361-8020) an

Steeped in history, the Old Port section of Montréal offers an exciting array of cultural, historic, and scientific attractions.

amusement park noted for the world's highest wooden double-track roller coaster, a thriller that delivers a scream-worthy, swaying, clackety-clack ride. For younger children the park has kiddie rides. In June La Ronde hosts the international fireworks competition. On each Saturday night different countries light the skies with blasts and bursts timed to musical compositions.

At **the Old Fort and David M. Stewart Museum (Le Vieux Fort et Musee David M. Steward)**, Parc Helene-de-Champlain (514–861–6701; www.mlink.net/~stewart/), tour barracks, the armory, the blockhouse, and the powder magazine. Among the museum's military artifacts of interest to kids is a cannon dating to 1760. In summer the eighteenth-century military drills performed by costumed interpreters add excitement. Summer also brings theme weekends, including a family day.

Olympic Park and the Botanical Gardens

There's much to do in Olympic Park, 4141 Pierre-de-Coubertin (514–252-8687; www.rio.gouv.qc.ca), 114 acres in the eastern part of the city and the site of the 1976 Summer Olympics. Start with a tram ride up one of the world's largest inclined towers, the 623-foot-high **Olympic Tower** (514-252-8687), for panoramic views of the city. **Olympic Stadium** is open to the public, as are the complex's **swimming pools.**

The Montréal Biodome, 4777 Pierre-de-Coubertin (514–868–3000), in Olympic Park, is an environmental museum. It's not a zoo, although four reconstructed ecosytems are inhabited by birds, mammals, and fish. The Polar World, Tropical Forest, Laurentian Forest and Saint-Laurent habitats include waterfalls, towering trees, and an interactive discovery room for kids. The steamy tropical forest, with its swimming rats, bats, and lush greenery, is a kid-pleaser.

From the Olympic Park it's easy to take a shuttle to the not-to-be-missed **Botanical Gardens (*Jardin Botanique*)**, 4101 Sherbrooke Street East (514–872-1400; www.ville.montreal.qc.ca/jardin and www.montreal.qc.ca/insectarium). With thirty gardens and ten greenhouses on 180 acres, it's too much for some kids to see in a day. Pick and choose the special places that please your family. Favorites of ours include the **Chinese Garden,** with its miniature trees and 30-foot waterfall; the **Japanese Garden,** with its koi ponds, bridges, and bonsai; the **Wizard of Oz Greenhouse,** featuring roses and lilacs in season; the **Butterfly Aviary,** with thousands of fluttering critters; and the **Insectarium,** with its living and mounted insects. The "dead" locusts, maggots, beetles, and other bugs aren't as interesting as the live scorpions, tarantulas, cockroaches,

Bicycling

Cycling, a passion in Montréal, which has more than one hundred miles of trails, peaks during May's **Tour de Ile de Montréal.** The nice part is that this bicycling marathon attracting 45,000 pedalers is more display than competition; the emphasis is on participating. If you're in town, treat your kids to the sight of waves of two-wheeled enthusiasts departing at fifteen-minute intervals for the 65-kilometer (40-mile) island tour. If your children like bicycling, they can sign up for the May **Tour des Enfants,** a 25-kilometer (15-mile) route just for children ages six to twelve. More than 10,000 youngsters join the fun each year.

and crickets. Ask about summer's Insect Festival, when the treats include real bug lollipops.

Ice Skating

Ice skating is a nice break from museum tours. At downtown's **L'Amphithéâtre Bell,** 1000 de la Gauchetière Street West (514-395-0555), an indoor rink, you can glide along the ice year-round. Skate rentals are available.

Other Parks

Other superb parks located throughout the city include the following.

MacDonald Campus of McGill University, 21-111 Lakeshore Road, Sainte-Anne-de Bellevue (Route 40). Located on Montréal's southwest tip, this vast area features three attractions with family appeal. **The Morgan Arboretum** (514-398-7812) has nature and wooded trails and cross-country skiing. **The Ecomuseum** (514-457-9449), devoted to the St. Lawrence Valley, features sixteen exhibits in outdoor settings that include turtles, bears, and a walk through a waterfowl aviary. **The Farm** (514-398-7701) welcomes families to view its animals and use the picnic and play area.

Mont Royal Park, the lush green stretch of land that sweeps up the highest peak of Mont Royal (from which the city took its name), is the finest in town. The 83-foot-tall cross at the top of the mountain, lit at night and visible for miles, was installed in 1924 and paid for mostly with children's donations. It commemorates the cross that Maisonneuve, founder of Montréal, carried to the mountaintop in 1643 after the colony was spared from a flood.

Approach this must-see park from Camillien-Houde Parkway from the east or from Remembrance Road from the west. Frederick Olmsted, who also planned New York's Central Park, designed this oasis. Picnic, stroll, bike, jog, and enjoy spectacular vistas of downtown and the Appalachian Mountains from Mountain Chalet and Parkway lookouts. Winters bring cross-country skiing, skating, and sledding.

The Centre de la Montagne (514-844-4928), a nature appreciation center, offers interpretive programs and information. The kids will enjoy

Trains and Space Rockets

Two museums just outside the city are worth the trip. The **Canadian Railway Museum,** 122-A Saint-Pierre West, Saint-Constant (514-283-4602), about 15 miles southwest of the city delights train aficionados with its collection of steam locomotives and railway and tram cars. On Sundays there are train rides.

The **Cosmodome,** 2150 Autoroute des Laurentians, Laval (514-978-3600), about 10 miles northwest of the city, delivers an out-of-this world experience. At the **Cosmodome's Space Science Center,** an interactive museum, kids can walk through a space shuttle, look at a moon rock, and learn with interactive exhibits. The **Cosmodome's Space Camp,** Space Camp Canada (514-978-3615 or 800-565-CAMP; www.sim.qc.ca/cosmodome/), offers overnight and extended programs to parents, children, and school groups. The Space Camp also lets day visitors (ages nine and older) signup for half-day programs (reserve in advance) to sample simulators that emulate "weightlessness" and to try the bouncy jumps of a moonwalk.

seeing the only Mounted Police in Montréal patrolling the park. Their horse stables are open to visitors from 9:00 A.M. to 5:00 P.M.

Île Notre-Dame now serves as a recreational haven with a beach, boat rentals, winter ice skating, a lovely floral park, and a world-class casino.

Lafontaine Park is centrally located (bordered by Sherbrooke, Rachel, Papineau, and Park Lafontaine Streets). Stroll through this park and see a slice of Montréal life, including street musicians and, on weekends, families out to have fun. There are wading pools, pedal boats, tennis courts, and a puppet theater. In winter cross-country skiing and illuminated skating rinks make this a popular retreat. Call (514) 872-6211 for more information.

Museums

This sophisticated city has a rich assortment of fine museums. Unless your kids are avid museum-goers, however, they may find some too sophisticated or esoteric. The following though, are surely worth a visit.

Enjoy the **Planétarium de Montréal,** 1000 Saint-Jacques Street West (514-872-4530; www.planetarium.montreal.qc.ca). A lecturer provides live commentary for original star shows presented under the theater dome. Shows alternate in English and French.

The **International Museum of Humour**, 2111 St.-Laurent Street (414-845-4000), opened its doors on April Fool's Day 1993. You won't find a museum like this anywhere else. The fun exhibits here create laughs and treasured memories of days past. Although the museum's exhibits rotate because there is no permanent gallery exhibit, favorite exhibits feature clips of Charlie Chaplin, American sitcoms, cartoons, and the Humour Hall of Fame, where your kids can watch Mickey Mouse cartoons and relax in huge, cushy chairs.

Montréal Museum of Fine Arts, 1379-1380 Sherbrooke Street West (514-285-1600). Head to Canada's oldest art museum on Sunday, when family activities, such as films and workshops, are included with the admission. The impressive collections of paintings, furniture, sculpture, and other art include works by Renoir, Monet, Picasso, and Rodin.

Also check out **Redpath Museum**, 859 Sherbrooke Street West (514-398-4086). Kids are captivated by the old fossils, rocks, crystals, and gems and by the fascinating antiquities of ancient Egypt.

McCord Museum of Canadian History (Musée McCord), 609 Sherbrooke Street West (514-398-7100), focuses on Canadian history. Simply Montréal, a permanent exhibit, details the city's past through photographs and artifacts. Parts that appeal most to kids are the collection of old toys and sports equipment and the array of fancy gowns worn by the famous. Items in the other collections rotate, but the beadwork, jewelry, and clothing generally displayed in the First Nations gallery are interesting.

In 2000 the **Centre for Science and Technology** (formerly the site of Expotec), Saint Laurent Boulvard and de la Commune Street, will open as an interactive science museum.

Museums in Old Montréal include the Chateau Ramezay Museum, 280 Notre-Dame Street East (514-861-3708) which depicts life in the region in the eighteenth century. Despite the English-speaking guide and artifacts, such as beaver hats and old kitchen implements, kids are likely to be quickly bored.

Special Tours

Call **Lachine Rapid Tours** (514-284-9607) and shoot the only rapids on the St. Lawrence River in a jet boat. It's definitely not for kids under six or the faint of heart: You wear slickers and get wet. The trip lasts about ninety minutes. You can also white water raft down the St. Lawrence River with **Rafting Montréal**, 8912 LaSalle Boulevard (514-767-2230; www.raftingmontreal.com). Special familytrips are offered.

More sedate excursions include the **Montréal Harbor Cruises**, departing from the south end of Berri Street at the Clock Tower Basin in Old Port (514-842-3871 or 800-667-3131).

Ski Resorts

Gray Rocks, P.O. Box 1000, St. Jovite, Québec, J0T 2H0 (819–425–2771 or 800–567–6767), about 75 miles northwest of Montréal, is sprawled on 2,000 acres in Mont Tremblant. Before or after a city tour, this mid-price resort offers a friendly respite for families. In winter Gray Rocks features ski programs for kids along with other outdoor activities. Because the skiing here is fairly easy, it's best for grade-schoolers and novice skiers. In summer there are supervised children's programs for ages three to twelve. Warm-weather fun includes boating on the lake plus perfecting your tennis game at the intensive camp.

Near Gray Rocks is **Tremblant,** 3005 Prencipal, Mont-Tremblant, Québec (800–461–8711). Tremblat, a major eastern ski area, is a great place for families. The pedestrian village, part of the ski area's $350 million renovations, adds charm, an off-the-slopes focus, and a variety of eateries. The lack of cars makes this area particularly family friendly. The kids' ski and snowboard programs are good, and there's child care for nonskiing tots. Teens can socialize at Bizztrado, a supervised juice bar.

Slopeside hotel rooms and condominiums are available for rent.

Shopping

Because of Montréal's extreme temperatures—frigid winters and hot summers—many of the city's shops and services are part of a vast **Underground City** network. It's connected throughout by the Metro, so you can enter from any stop or from the **Place Montréal Trust,** which houses delightfully diverse shops.

Performing Arts and Spectator Sports

Montréal offers a wide variety of cultural activities, including some of special interest to kids. The **Théâtre Biscuit** (514–845–7306) is the only permanent puppet theater in the city and has weekend performances. All of the plays at **Maison-Théâtre** (Salle Tritorium) are geared to children; call (514) 288–7211.

If you're in town when the **Cirque du Soleil** is performing, be sure to see this incredibly original theatrical performance. This is not a conventional circus (there are no animals), but it is a truly unique experience. Performances are generally from late April to June. Call (514) 722–3692.

The **Centaur Theatre,** 453 Saint-Francois-Xavier Street (514–288–3161) presents dramas, classics, and musicals in English.

Montréal **Expos** play home games during baseball season (April to October) at the stadium in Olympic Park. For more information, call (514) 790-1245; or check out the team's Web site at www.montrealexpos. com. The **Canadiens** of the National Hockey League play at the Molson Centre, 1260 de la Gauchetière Street West (514-932-CLUB). The **Alouettes,** a professional football team, play at Olympic Stadium (514-254-2400).

SPECIAL EVENTS

Fairs and Festivals

They don't call Montréal "Festival City" for nothing. It seems that no matter when you come, there's something special going on. Tourisme Montréal (514-844-5400) has a complete calendar of events.

End of January–mid-February. Winter Festival (La Fête de Neige) has snow games, dog sledding, sleigh rides, ice skating, and more.

May–June. International Music Competition.

June–July. International Fireworks Competition, weekends.

July. International Jazz Festival features more than ninety indoor and 200 outdoor shows and events. Just For Laughs, the world's largest comedy festival, includes outdoor performances. Player's International Tennis Tournament.

August–early September. World Film Festival.

WHERE TO STAY

The *Tourist Guide* from Tourisme Montréal has listings that classify some (but not all) lodgings by type and quality and include details on accessibility for persons with reduced mobility: **Infotouriste Centre** is a free service for all major hotels in Greater Montréal. Also contact **Hospitalité Canada:** (514-393-9049 or 800-665-1528).

For information on local bed and breakfasts, contact the **Bed and Breakfast Downtown Network,** 3977 Laval Avenue (514-289-9749 or 800-267-5180) or **Relais Montréal Hospitalite,** 3977 Lavel Avenue (514-287-9635 or 800-363-9635).

There are so many hotels in Montréal in so many price ranges that deciding on one can be an arduous task. You'll find many familiar, reliable names such as Best Western, Holiday Inn, Hilton, Le Meridien, Intercontinental, Journey's End, and Ritz Carlton Travel Lodge. This small selection—all conveniently located downtown—indicates the variety available for families:

Delta Montréal, 450 Sherbrooke Street West (514-286-1986 or 800-877-1133), offers both rooms and suites, two pools, and a game room. The supervised Children's Creative and Activity Center is open weekends year-round for ages two to twelve (small fee) who may stay for up to three hours.

Hotel Novotel, 1180 Rue de la Montagne (514-861-6000 or 800-221-4542), lets kids up to sixteen stay free and enjoy a free breakfast when sharing with parents (maximum two kids). There's indoor parking.

The **Holiday Inn Montréal Midtown,** 420 Sherbrooke Street West (514-842-6111 or 800-465-4329—United States, 800-387-3042—Canada), is conveniently located, has an indoor pool, and lets two kids eighteen and under stay free with parents. Kids twelve and under eat free.

The **Montréal Bonaventure Hilton,** 1 Bonaventure Place (514-878-2332 or 800-445-8667—United States, 800-267-2575—Canada), is another good choice. The hotel is convenient to the Underground City, kids under eighteen stay free, and the property has an indoor pool.

Expensive options include **Westin Mont-Royal,** 1050 Sherbrooke Street West (514-284-1110 or 800-228-3000), formerly the Four Seasons. The rooms are large, and the hotel sports an indoor pool and a health club. **Ritz-Carlton Kempinski Montréal,** 1228 Sherbrooke Street West (514-842-4212 or 800-426-3135—United States, 800-363-0366—Canada), is another upscale property.

WHERE TO EAT

The *Montréal Restaurant Guide* from Tourisme Montréal contains tips on a number of fine dining experiences, including elegant restaurants for special nights out. But, honestly, you don't have to spend a fortune to eat well in this city. In summer, residents and tourists take to the streets to eat at outdoor cafes and bistros. Your kids will want to try *poutine,* a mixture of cheese, gravy, and *frites* (French fries) served at establishments around town, including McDonald's. Do give Montréal's ethnic restaurants a try. The Jewish area north of downtown, for instance, has superb bakeries and great delis. Montréal's bagels are said to rival, even surpass, New York's—taste for yourself. Those from the brick oven at **La Maison de Óriginal Fairmount Bagel,** 74 West Fairmount Street (514-272-0667), are reputedly the best in town.

SIDE TRIPS

Where do Montréal families go for a nearby getaway? The **Laurentian Mountains** and **Eastern Townships** are each about two hours' drive from the city and present a wealth of recreational opportunities, from skiing and skating in winter to summer activities. A one-hour drive east on Highway 3 is the **Granby Zoo** (514-372-9113), where the kids can take an elephant ride and delight in seeing more than 750 animals, including wildlife species from all continents.

South of the city in Hemmingford, **Safari Park** (514-247-2727 or 800-465-8724; www.parcsafari.com), combines a drive-through animal reserve, petting area, deer trail, water play area, and amusement park.

Québec City, the provincial capital, is about two and a half hours east; **Ottawa,** about two hours to the west. (See chapters on Ottawa and Québec City.)

FOR MORE INFORMATION

To request Montréal information by mail, write to Tourisme Montréal, 1555 Pell Street, Suite 600, Montréal H3A 1X6, or call (514) 844-5400 or (800) 363-7777; www.tourisme-montreal.org. In person visit Info-touriste, 1001 Square-Dorchester, for tourist information, services, and brochures on Montréal and Québec province. Tourism Québec also operates several seasonal bureaus at major highways throughout the province. For information or accessibility call (514) 252-3104 or visit the Web site at www.craph.org/keroul/.

Canadian National Institute for the Blind (514-284-2040) supplies volunteer escorts, if needed. Reserve in advance.

Emergency Numbers

Ambulance, fire, and police: 911

Sainte-Justine Hospital, 3175 Côte-Sainte-Catherine Road; (514) 345-4931

Montréal Children's Hospital, 2300 Tupper Street; (514) 934-4400

Poison Hotline: (800) 463-5060

Twenty-four-hour pharmacy: Pharmaphix at 901 Sainte-Catherine Street East (514-842-4915) and 5122 Côte-des-Neiges Road (514-738-8464)

QUÉBEC CITY

Perched atop the rocky Cap Diamant (Cape Diamond) and overlooking the St. Lawrence River, Québec City offers families a distinctly different vacation experience. This provincial capital is the only fortified city in North America. Indeed, from the seventeenth through the nineteenth centuries, Québec was vital in the ultimate defense of all of northeastern America. The historic district, Old Québec (Vieux Québec), has been proclaimed a "world heritage treasure" by UNESCO. Wherever you venture in this district, you'll be immersed in history. The French influence dominates in culture, cuisine, and language: At least 95 percent of the population is French-speaking. It helps to speak the language, although it's possible to get by without it. Just minutes from the city, your family will find unlimited outdoor activities in stunning natural settings.

GETTING THERE

Jean Lesage International Airport in Sainte-Foy, 12 miles outside town, is served by Air Canada and affiliates and by Northwest Airlink. Daily shuttles from the airport to major city hotels are run by Autobus La Québecoise (418–872–5525). Car rentals are available at the airport.

VIA Rail Canada arrives and departs from Gare du Palais and Sainte-Foy station. For information and reservations call (418) 692–3940. It's possible to connect with Amtrak trains in Montréal or Toronto.

Orleans Express bus lines, whose main station is at Gare du Palais, 320, Abraham-Martin (418–525–3000), serves this area. You can make connections with Greyhound in Montréal . A number of highways connect to Québec City, which is approximately six hours from Boston and eight and a quarter hours from New York City.

GETTING AROUND

STCUQ (*Societé de transport de la Communauté Urbaine de Québec*) buses run regularly. Call (418) 627-2511 for routes and schedules. During ski season the daily winter shuttle leaves from fifteen downtown hotels

Québec City

AT A GLANCE

▶ Explore the only fortified city in North America

▶ Visit numerous museums and historical sites in Old Québec

▶ Play at thirty-six green spaces within the city

▶ Ski at nearby parks and resorts

▶ Québec information, (800) 363-7777; www.tourisme. gouva.qc.ca

to Mont Sainte-Anne and Stoneham (418-525-5191).

A ferry leaves opposite Place Royale to Lévis on the south shore. The scenic ten- to fifteen-minute ride affords panoramic views of Old Québec from the St. Lawrence River. Call (418) 644-3704.

WHAT TO SEE AND DO

Museums and Historical Sites

Wherever you go in and outside the walls of Old Québec, you'll be near a monument, museum, or historical site. If your kids are school age, prepare them with a brief historical summary; it will make their visit much more meaningful. The city's history in a nutshell: Québec served as the base for early French explorers and missionaries in North America. In 1608 Samuel de Champlain built its first dwelling; the town ultimately grew into a fortified city. In 1759 British troops defeated the French, and, in 1763, Canada was ceded to Great Britain. The British, in turn, threatened by the patriot army during the American Revolution, rebuilt many of the French fortifications and constructed structures of their own. The last battle was fought in Québec City in 1776, when the British repulsed an American patriot army invasion led by Benedict Arnold.

There's lots to see in Old Québec, but be selective. Balance museum and historical sites with parks and cafe stops. You can take a tour of Old Québec, but it's more fun to explore it yourself. Make sure you have a good map (available from the Convention and Visitors Bureau), cluster the sights you want to see, and take your time. Here are some highlights.

If you visit Québec during February, be sure to participate in the Winter Festival happenings.

The Citadel and Parc des Champs-de-Bataille

At the **Promenade des Gouverneurs,** a stairway and scenic boardwalk with river views lead uphill to the star-shaped **Citadel,** 1 Côte de la Citadelle, dramatically set atop Cap Diamant, the eastern flank of Québec's fortifications. The entrance is on rue St. Louis (418-694-2815). The facility comprises twenty-five buildings, including the officers' mess and Governor General's residence. Guided tours are available. Some kids may enjoy the **Royal 22e Regiment Museum,** an old military prison, with a collection of uniforms, documents, firearms, and other memorabilia from the seventeenth century to the present. The regiment still guards the citadel. A must-see: the Changing of the Guard, held at 10:00 A.M. daily from mid-June to Labor Day (weather permitting); it lasts forty minutes. The noon and 9:30 P.M. cannon is another military tradition, as is the Beating of Retreat, four nights a week in July and August.

Next to the citadel is the **Parc des Champs-de-Bataille** (Battlefields Park), located between Grande Allée and Champlain Boulevard (418-649-6187). The park is the site of the Plains of Abraham, where the 1759 battle between British and French forces took place. Besides viewing the numerous military artifacts and monuments, come here for the 250 acres of gardens and woodlands. Picnic and hike, or, in winter, cross-country ski and skate.

A summer shuttle takes passengers to a number of the park's main sites including the **Musée du Québec** (418-643-2150; www.mdq.org) which spans generations of Québec art. The museum includes a pavillion

Parks and Green Spaces

In addition to thirty-six green spaces within the city, the Greater Québec Area, with its St. Lawrence River location, has a number of parks and wildlife reserves where families can enjoy the great outdoors. Going east along the Côte de Beaupré, you'll find these attractions.

- **Cap-Tourmente National Wildlife Area,** Saint-Joachim (418–827–4591 from April to October and 418–837–3776 from November to April). About thirty-five minutes east of Québec, this striking preserve on the St. Lawrence River's north shore was created especially to protect the natural habitat of the greater snow goose. During migration periods the area attracts some 300,000 geese. The preserve is made up of four separate environments: marsh, plain, cliff, and mountain. Footpaths reveal a wide variety of plants, trees, nesting and migratory birds, and mammals. Some trails lead to the summit of Cap-Tourmente, or you can opt for the views from an observation tower. The welcome and interpretation centers have exhibitions and films. In season, naturalists offer activities and guided tours.

- **North of the city: Parc de la Jacques-Cartier,** Route 175 north (418–848–3169 during the summer, 418–622–5151 the rest of the year). Summer canoeing, rock climbing, mountain biking, and hiking are the big attractions at this beautiful provincial park on the Jacques Cartier River. You can rent equipment. During mid-May to October, activities include canoe excursions, outings, and a moose and wolf observation safari in September and October.

- **West of the city: Lac-Saint-Joseph,** in Sainte-Catherine-de-la-Jacques-Cartier, has a beach that is popular with local families. It adjoins the Station forestière de Duchesnay (Forest Educational Centre), which is open to the public for nature walks. Call (418) 334–2900.

- **Parc De La Chute–Montmorency,** Route 40 to Beauport (418–663–2877). Visit eastern Canada's highest waterfall. A cable car ride drops visitors off at the top of the falls, where a footbridge provides astonishing views of the 272-foot-tall waterfall.

that once housed the former Québec prison. Here, visitors can explore what life in a nineteenth-century prison was like. Two museums that will be of more interest to kids, however, are listed in the following section.

Museums and Parliament

Take the Promenade des Gouverneurs downhill to Terrasse Dufferin promenade. At the bottom of this popular promenade rises the huge, baroque **Château Frontenac** (418-692-3861), built in 1893 by Canadian Pacific Company and now a luxury hotel. If you're not staying here, stop in for a peek at its grand hall and ride down the hillside at a 45° angle on the funicular located near the Terasse. Nearby, the Place d'Armes has fountains and horse-drawn buggies *(calèches)*. While not inexpensive, the rides provide a picturesque mode of transportation.

Next to the Place d'Armes, you may want to stop in for a look at the interior of the ornately decorated **Notre Dame Basilicá,** 16 rue Buade (418-692-2533). Nearby are two museums of interest to families.

Musée du fort, 10 rue Sainte-Anne (418-692-2175), is a good place to introduce the kids to the city's history. There's a model of the city as it looked in 1750.

Stop in at the wax museum, the **Musée historique de cire-Grivin,** 22 rue Sainte-Anne (418-692-2289). Kids (and adults) may not recognize many of the eighty figures represented here, such as Montcalm and René Levesque, but most kids like wax museums. Christopher Columbus and his shipmates are included.

Québec Expérience, 8 Rue Du Tresor (418-694-4000), a 3D multimedia show, is another good choice for introducing kids to the Old Capital's history. The show includes multiple screens and "holovideos," which summarize 400 years of history lessons in under thirty minutes.

Many sidewalk cafes and restaurants line rue Sainte-Anne, where these museums are located. In summer musicians and street entertainers make this a lively place to linger.

From here it would be convenient to walk east down the *casse cou* (breakneck) stairways—not really that bad—or to the funicular, to go down to the Lower City, the oldest part of Québec.

Musée de la Civilisation, 85 rue Dalhousie at St.-Antoine (418-643-2158; www.mcq.org), features four permanent exhibits and at least five thematic rotating exhibits. Memoires, a permanent show, traces Québec City's history and includes many examples of daily life in the nineteenth-century fur-trading colony. Past temporary shows have examined the history of hockey and the circus.

If you're interested in seeing **Parliament Hill,** however, head southwest to avenue Dufferin and the tree-lined Grande Allée Est, considered the Champs Elysées of Québec. Stop for a bite at one of the many restaurants along the way. You can take a guided tour of Parliament, including the National Assembly Chamber, where Québec's elected representatives meet, although the experience may be lost on the very young. Call (418) 643-7239.

Lower City

In **Place Royale,** (418-643-6631), one of the oldest districts on the continent, stroll through narrow streets and past historic homes, boutiques, and workshops. The parks of Place Royale host a number of events with family appeal, including plays and variety shows. Stop by the Information Centre, 215 rue du Marché-Finlay, for schedules of activities. In the Quartier Petit Champlain, the quaint, narrow streets sport musicians, clowns, and jugglers. **Explore,** 63 rue Dalhousie (418-692-2175), is a sound-and-light show that retells the discovery of America and the voyages of early French explorers up the St. Lawrence River. The lively Old Port includes a farmer's produce market and a cinema.

Attractions

Aquarium du Québec, 1675 avenue des Hôtels, Sainte-Foy, Québec (418-659-5266). Located in a wooded area southwest of Old Québec, with nice views of the St. Lawrence River, the aquarium is home to some 2,000 sea creatures. The ever-popular seals perform twice daily. You might combine a trip here with another Sainte-Foy attraction: **Musée de géologie,** Pavillon Adrien-Pouillot (fourth floor), avenue de la Médecine (418-656-2131, ext. 8127). Most kids like fossils and minerals, and you'll find hundreds of them here from all around the world.

Paec récréatif des Galeries de la Capitale, 5401 boulevard des Galeries (418-627-5800). This enormous recreation center, part of a shopping mall, sports a Ferris wheel and roller coaster among its rides, and, for more fun, there's a skating rink and minigolf, also the Imax Maison de l'image (418-627-IMAX).

Jardin Zoologique du Québec, 9141 avenue du Zoo, Charlesbourg, Québec (418-622-0312). Along with the usual bears, chimps, and wild cats, kids enjoy the sealion show and the farm. A river linked by waterfalls crosses through the zoo, and, in winter, the surrounding trails are open for cross-country skiing and snowshoeing.

Village des Sports, 1860 boulevard Valcartier, Saint-Gabriel-de-Valcartier, Québec (418-844-3725—Canada). Bring your bathing suits: This place boasts a huge wave pool, water games, water slides, and acrobatic diving shows. When you dry off, choose from roller-skating trails,

Maxi-Golf, and a racing-car circuit. Winters, this enormous recreation center north of the city has sledding on inner tubes or carpets, skating paths with music, and cross-country skiing.

For a sea kayak adventure on the St. Lawrence River, visit **Chaudiere-Appalaches,** where guided tours (experience not necessary) offer trips lasting from a few hours to a few days. Call Explore Kayak de Mer (418-831-4411), or see www.chaudapp.qc.ca for more information.

A true taste of Canada can be enjoyed at one of the many **maple sugar cabins** located just outside Québec City. Try sampling products such as maple syrup, butter, taffy, and jelly at a favorite tourist spot. **Erabliere le Chemin du Roy,** Highway 138, Saint-Augustin-de-Desmaures (418-878-5085).

Special Tours

Try a scenic boat ride with **Québec City Cruises,** Quai Chouinard at 10 rue Dalhousie. From mid-June through Labor Day, choose from one-hour harbor tours, ninety-minute excursions to **Île d'Orléans** (418) 692-1159. (See Side Trips.)

Performing Arts

Among the city's cultural attractions are the **Québec Symphony Orchestra,** which performs at the Grand Théâtre de Québec; the **Trident** theater troupe; the **Danse-Partout Dance** company; and the **Québec Opera,** with spring and fall productions. In addition, the Greater Québec area has excellent summer theater performances. Listings of area cultural events are published every Wednesday in English in the Québec *Chronicle Telegraph.*

Shopping

In Québec's Lower City stroll and browse along rue Saint-Paul's antiques shops, boutiques, and art galleries. Across from the Château Frontenac, sketches and watercolors are sold on the narrow rue du Tresor. At **La Cabane,** 94 Petit Champlain in Old Québec (418-692-1543) sample (and buy) maple sugar products.

New France

Old Québec's New France celebrations take place in August, highlighting the founding of the first French-speaking city in North America. Period costumes and reenactments abound. Visitors are invited to don costumes and join in the festivities. In the Sanguenay–Lac-Saint-Jean region, the town of **Mistassini** is the blueberry capital of the world and celebrates this title during Augusts's **Le Festival de bleuet.** Enjoy picking your own crop and learning about the multitude of uses for this fruit. Call (418) 276-1241 for additional information.

Ski Areas

The ski season can last almost six months in Greater Québec. Two of the province's best downhill-ski areas are within a half-hour's drive of the city.

- **Mont-Sainte-Anne,** Route 360, Beaupré (418-827-4561). Thirty minutes east of downtown Québec, Mont-Sainte-Anne, a popular winter downhill-ski area, is the largest in Québec. Day care and a kinderski program are available for ages two to six.

  In summer the park becomes a recreational mecca, with golf, mountain biking, picnicking, and cable-car rides to the mountain summit of Mont Sainte-Anne. Ski area reserva-

  tions: (418) 827-4561.
- **Stoneham,** 1429 avenue du Hibou, Stoneham, Québec (418-848-2411 or 800-463-6888—Canada). Twenty-five minutes north of town, Stoneham offers a network of twenty-five runs on four mountains. The nursery takes kids two years and up, and teens meet at the Coketail Bar. Lodging includes 600 hotel or condo rooms, either slopeside or at the mountain base.

On your way back into the United States, you might want to do some shopping at the duty-free shops at **BHTE,** at junction 55 and 91, Rock Island (819-876-5249), or **IGL,** at junction 15 and 87, Saint-Bernard de Lacolle (514-246-2496).

SPECIAL EVENTS

Fairs and Festivals

The Greater Québec area abounds in year-round fairs and festivals. *The Greater Québec Area Tourist Guide* has an exhaustive listing of events. Some highlights include the following.

February. Winter Carnival, the world's largest, features dogsled races, parades, ice sculpture contests, and numerous other activities and events over three weekends. www.carnaval.qc.ca.

July. Québec International Summer Festival, French-speaking cultural events held in the streets and parks of Old Québec (888-992-5200; www.festival-ele.quebec.qc.ca).

August. Expo Québec, Parc de l'Exposition, is a huge agricultural exhibition with a fair, rides, and entertainment. New France celebrations.

September. Festival of Colors includes sports, outdoor activities, and cultural events to herald the start of the fall and winter season, Mont Sainte-Anne.

WHERE TO STAY

The Greater Québec Area Tourist Guide features listings of hotels. If you're on a budget, consider one of the convenient lodgings outside the city. In Mont-Sainte-Anne area, call (800) 463-1568. Here's a family-friendly selection that includes a variety of locations and price ranges.

Downtown
Hotel Classique, 640 St.-Jean Street (418–529–0227 or 800–463–5753—Canada), offers large rooms with kitchenettes, indoor pool, and parking.

Old City (outside walls)
Ramada Québec, 395 rue de la Coutonne (418–647–2611 or 800–267–2002), is within walking distance of Old Québec's walled city. The eighteen-story high rise features 232 rooms, with seven suites. The kids will love the pool—the largest in town.

    Hilton International Québec, 3 place Québec (418–647–2411 or 800–445–8867), connected to the Place Québec shopping complex across from the city walls and near Parliment, has undergone recent renovations. Features include an airport shuttle, dry cleaning, baby-sitting, jogging track, business center, and car rental.

    Nearby, the **Radisson Gouverneurs,** 690 boulevard René-Levesque East (418–647–1717 or 800–333–3333), features a rooftop pool in the summertime and proximity to Winter Carnival activities during the winter. The hotel is also part of Place Québec and is connected to the Québec City convention center.

Old City (inside walls)
L'Hôtel du Vieux Québec, 1190 rue Saint-Jean (418–692–1850), is housed in a historic building. It features twenty-seven comfortable rooms feature kitchenettes.

    Hotel Manoir Victoria, 44 Côte du Palais (418–692–1030 or 800–463–6283). In the heart of the Old City, this property has an indoor pool and babysitting services.

Côte-de-Beaupré
A standout is the **Chalets Montmorency et Motels,** 1768 avenue Royale Saint-Ferreol-les-Neiges (418–826–2600 or 800–463–2612). In a

quiet setting near Mont-Sainte-Anne, this Swiss-style apartment lodge features spacious one- to four-bedroom suites, an indoor pool, and golf packages.

WHERE TO EAT

A dining guide is available from the Tourism and Convention Bureau. The local cuisine has lots for kids to like: try croque monsieur, an open ham sandwich covered with melted cheese, and crêpes. Depending on the filling this serves as either a main course or a dessert. For inexpensive crêpes try **Casse Crêpe Breton,** 1136 rue St. Jean (418-692-0438), where you can also get sandwiches, salads, soups, and a hearty breakfast.

Fondue is fun: Dip right in at **Au Café Suisse,** 32 rue Sainte-Anne (418-694-1320), where seafood, steaks, and raclette are also on the menu. Two-hour free parking at city hall is included. The location is good, too, right near the Musée du fort and the Musée historique de cire-Grivin.

Kids love the pink pig statue outside of **Le Cochon Dingue,** 46 boulevard Champlain, across from the Lévis ferry (418-523-2013). The house specialty: steaks and fries, along with desserts such as strawberry squares and maple syrup pie. For a big-splurge meal with a twist, head to **L'Astral,** at Loews Le Concorde, 1225 Place Montcalm (418-647-2222). The restaurant slowly revolves to reveal fabulous vistas below.

The buffet at **Cafe de la Terrasse,** in the Chateau Frontenac Hotel, 1 Rue des Carrieres (418-692-3861), has a good selection. The hotel's boardwalk overloooks the St. Lawrence River.

SIDE TRIPS

Île d'Orléans, (418-828-9411: tourist information office) about 6 miles downstream from downtown and accessible by car, is a pleasant excursion for those who like simple charms. This sparsely populated island (about 7,000 people) offers historic homes, churches, mills, and chapels. In season, roadside stands have fresh produce, and some producers allow the public to pick their own strawberries, apples, and corn. In the village of Saint-Laurent, where shipbuilding was once the largest industry, there's a maritime museum and riverfront views. An arts and crafts center sells handmade traditional handicrafts, such as pottery, wood carvings, knitted garments, and porcelain jewelry. During July and August weekends, local artists offer demonstrations.

From the Île d'Orléans head east to Route 138 to the lower section or **Chute Montmorency,** in Beauport-Boischatel (bus 50 or 53). The upper section is accessible via Route 360. This is a breathtaking waterfall, one and a half times as high as Niagara Falls. The site, divided into upper and lower sections, features lookout points, trails, picnic tables, and a tourist information center, which is open from mid-May to late October. Upstream, Manoir Montmorency, now host restaurants, boutiques, and an interpretive center surrounded by lovely gardens. In winter an unusual phenomenon occurs. The crystallized water vapor forms an enormous ice cone that locals call *pain de sucre,* or sugar loaf.

Continue east about 13 miles to **Sainte-Anne-de-Beaupré Basilica.** It's long been believed that Sainte-Anne, mother of the Virgin Mary, has saved shipwreck victims off Cap-Tourmente. Many still believe she works miracles. Every year, more than 1.5 million pilgrims come to pray to this saint.

Farther east, near **Mont-Sainte-Anne,** the Grand Canyon des chutes Sainte-Anne is a waterfall with breathtaking chasms and streams. Shuttle service in open sight-seeing cars is included in the admission fee (open May to October). There's also a cafeteria and picnic area. Call (418) 827-4057.

FOR MORE INFORMATION

For booklets and maps of the area: **Maison du Tourisme de Québec,** 12 rue Sainte-Anne (across from Château Frontenac), is open seven days a week; or write to Tourisme Québec, Case postale 979, Québec, Canada H3C 2W3; www.tourisme.gouv.qc.ca. In the summer in Old Québec's historic area, motorized tourist information agents ride green mopeds with a "?" sign. Information on Québec's nineteen tourist regions is available by calling (800) 363-7777 from Québec, Canada, and the United States or visit www.quebec-region.cuq.qc.ca.

Emergency Numbers

Fire and police in Québec: 911

Pharmacie Brunet, Les Galeries Charlesbourg, 4266, 1ère (Première) Avenue, Charlesbourg, is open until midnight seven days a week, opening at 8:00 A.M. Monday through Saturday and 10:00 A.M. on Sunday: (418) 623-1571.

Poison Control: (418) 656-8090 or (800) 463-5060

Twenty-four-hour emergency room: L'Hôtel Dieu, 11, Côte du Palais, Old Québec, (418) 691-5151. A hospital specializing in children's health: CHUL (Laval University Hospital Center), 2705 boulevard Laurier, Sainte-Foy (a western suburb); (418) 656-4141

BLOCK ISLAND

Seven-mile-long Block Island is for beach lovers. While not perfect—it can be crowded and noisy near the Old Harbor—the island still has all the ingredients necessary for an old-fashioned beach vacation. These include great stretches of sand, windswept dunes, and such picturesque touches as two lighthouses and 200-foot-high bluffs. Other bonuses include nature trails, birds, and white-tailed deer. Many of the Victorian-era grand hotels, turreted homes, and cottages have been renovated and turned into bed-and-breakfast accommodations. Their silhouettes lend an old-world graciousness to the streets. Stroll or bike along the roads in-season, and smell the honeysuckle, bayberries, and blackberries. Devotees swear Block Island is less expensive and less pretentious than other New England beach areas.

GETTING THERE

Block Island, located in Block Island Sound, about 9 miles south of the Rhode Island mainland and 13 miles east of Montauk, New York, on Long Island, is most easily reached by ferry. If the waves are friendly, this is a fun trip and an exciting start, especially for young children who may not have spent much time on a boat. Bring some bread to throw to the seagulls who hover nearby. Then listen to your kids' giggles as the gulls dive for the treats.

Ferries run fairly frequently from mid-June to mid-September, less frequently in the off-season. Only ferries from Galilee State Pier, Point Judith, Rhode Island, to the Old Harbor area, the quickest run, operate year-round. The first rule about ferries, though, is to make reservations well in advance, especially if you want to bring your car. Interstate Navigation (401-783-4613), which takes both cars and people, operates the run from Point Judith to Block Island.

Nelseco Navigation (860-442-7891) operates a summertime ferry from New London, Connecticut. Viking Ferry Lines (516-668-5700 or 800-MONTAUK) on Block Island provides the quickest ride (beach-goers and bikes only) from Montauk: one hour and fifteen minutes. In summer

Block Island

AT A GLANCE

▶ Enjoy a small-island vacation

▶ Swim, boat, and beachcomb

▶ Explore miles of nature trails and bike paths

▶ Block Island Tourism Council, (401) 466–5200 or (800) 383–BIRI; www.blockisland.com

a ferry also makes the two-hour trip from Newport. For general ferry information, call (401) 783–4613.

Those with their own boats are welcome to dock at public harbors and private marinas. Since New Harbor has more public moorings than Old Harbor, it has become the place for private boats. Call the dockmaster at (401) 466–3235 or harbormaster at (401) 466–3204 for more information.

You also can arrive by plane, landing at Block Island State Airport (401–466–5511). Commercial airlines access the island via New England Airlines, Westerly State Airport, Westerly, Rhode Island (401–596–2460 or 800–243–2460). Action Air, Groton/New London Airport (203–448–1646 or 800–243–8623) provides air flights from Groton, Connecticut. Resort Airlines (800–683–9330) also flies to Block Island.

GETTING AROUND

The best way to explore this 10-square-mile island is by bicycle or on foot. If your accommodations are near the harbor, you'll have no need for a car at all since the Old and New Harbors are less than a mile apart and within walking distance to the beaches. While you might be tempted to book your car aboard the ferry, don't. Instead, park in the long-term lots, and start your vacation free from automobile hassles and open to the slower holiday pace of strolling or pedaling.

If you must have a car, rentals are available from Block Island Bike & Car Rental (401–466–2297) and Old Harbor Bike Shop (401–466–2029).

You will probably want to rent bicycles, which come in all shapes and sizes for different island uses. Mountain bikes or beach cruisers with thick treads are best equipped to handle the dirt roads. The *Travel Planner* brochure available through the Block Island Chamber of Commerce (401–466–2982) has a full listing of several rental shops on the island.

Special Tours

For an overview of the island and the low-down on its lore, legends, and local happenings, take a guided tour of the island from **O.J.'s Taxi,** (401–782–5826 or 401–466–2872). This is a particularly good trip if you have little tots too young to bike, or if you don't enjoy pedaling in the sun. A seasoned islander himself, O.J. gives you the inside scoop from the Indian skirmish at Mohegan Bluffs to the island's present-day fight against commercialization. He'll even tell you how Cow Cove got its name when white settlers made their cows swim ashore to test the depth of the water.

Other historic tours are available through the Chamber of Commerce. Call them at (401) 466–2982 for more information.

Mopeds are also available but are restricted to paved roads only. For bicycles, check ahead to be sure the shop has the right size equipment (as well as helmets) for your child. Ask if you can reserve bikes and mopeds ahead of time. Another shop you might call is the Moped Man (401–466–5444).

WHAT TO SEE AND DO

Since the island is so small, most locations are pinpointed by street names alone, not addresses.

Beaches
The island's best beaches are on the east side, running from Old Harbor up to Jerry's Point, in a strip called **Crescent Beach. Fred Benson Town Beach** (formerly State Beach) (401–466–2611) is a bustling place, equipped with public bathrooms, lifeguards, and refreshments. It's also one of the most crowded beaches. If you're looking to browse through the shops in town, but your older kids and teens can't get enough of the sand, drop them off at **Ballards Beach,** adjacent to Ballard's Inn at the Old Harbor, a half-mile long, often crowded strip that draws many boaters and twentysomethings. But the beach does have lifeguards and a food court, plus Ballard's.

Quieter choices include **Mansion Beach,** which is just north of the Great Salt Pond. The gradual slope provides a shallow place for kids to splash and wade. Your family will enjoy the waves, the sandy bottom, and searching for "points," small arrowheads left by the Manissean Indians.

Nature Exploration and Bicycle Trips
With 25 percent of Block Island's land designated as protected open space, getting off the beaten path is fun, and easy. One way to become acquainted with the island's wildlife is to book a ninety-minute hike with **The Nature Conservancy,** Ocean Avenue (401–466–2129). These guided nature walks are available mid-June through Labor Day. The *Block Island Times* lists some of the departures, but feel free to call and schedule your own tour, a special treat because guides are glad to tailor your walk and their commentary to any age group. The Nature Conservancy sponsors children's

nature walks. Bring along binoculars to help you spot some of the hundreds of bird and insect species. In autumn some 150 species of migratory birds stop for their own island vacation on their way south.

Sponsored by The Nature Conservancy, the **Greenway Trail** offers great walking terrain that meanders through the Enchanted Forest, a wooded area of pine, spruce, and maple trees, past fields of wildflowers, to Black Rock Beach. Directions: From Old Harbor take Old Town Road and turn left onto Center Road. Follow to the parking lot across from the airport at Nathan Mott Park.

Sandy Point, at the northernmost point of the island, serves as a large gull rookery. While strolling past dunes and swamp grasses, look for black-backed and herring gulls.

After you are oriented, explore on your own. Bicycles come in handy here. Trip number one should be to the **Clayhead Nature Trail,** on the northeast side of the island off Corn Neck Road. Here you'll find 11 miles of grass trails winding through a 192-acre preserve. Start along the waterside cliffs and work your way north to **Settler's Rock** on the edge of Sachem Pond. This is where sixteen men from Boston, in search of religious freedom, landed in 1661. Read their names engraved on a plaque and try to imagine their first thoughts as they gazed out over Sachem Pond. Just off the Clayhead Trail, you'll find **Lapham's Bluestone** bird sanctuary, a.k.a. "The Maze." This puzzle of trails cuts through thick trees and brush and leads to unexpected ocean vistas.

Visiting **Rodman's Hollow,** on the southwestern part of the island, offers another good bike trip. Once you've arrived you'll want to explore this ancient formation on foot. Created by a prehistoric glacier, the ravine is actually below sea level. A pond never formed here, however, since the sandy soil wouldn't hold water. One of the island's five wildlife refuges, the Hollow is a good place for bird-watching.

After exploring here take one of the winding paths down to **Mohegan Bluffs** on the island's southern shore. The bluffs are named after fifty Mohegan Indians who invaded the island only to be tossed from these heights by the island's native Manissean tribe. From the bluffs, some of which are 200 feet high, it's a long fall to the rocks below! The view here of the ocean to the south and off the island's rocky southern shoreline is exceptional. On a clear day you can see all the way to Montauk Point in New York.

Beaches

- **Fred Benson Town Beach** (formerly State Beach)
- **Ballards Beach**
- **Mansion Beach**
- **Andy's Way,** on the Great Salt Pond off Corn Neck Road, New Harbor. A great beach for beach-combing, bird-watching, fishing, and finding horseshoe and fiddle crabs.

The scenic Mohegan Bluffs area is just one of the beautiful places you can visit on Block Island.

Sports

Fishing. Fishing is a favorite pastime here, and the Block Island Sound is known for striped bass, bluefish, cod, and flounder. Charted fishing boats are available, each specializing in a different type of fish. If tuna are your focus, **The Persuader** (401-783-5644) is your best bet. **G. Willie Makit,** (401-466-5151) pursues bluefish and bass. For those with no preference, **Tropical Moon** (401-763-7564) will help you catch whatever is biting. All three boats depart and return to Old Harbor. More independent anglers can captain their own rowboat. **Twin Maples,** Beach Avenue by New Harbor (401-466-5547), rents rowboats, fishing equipment, and tackle and even sells bait. If you're a landlubber, walk to the end of Coast Guard Road and cast off the beach on the Great Salt Pond.

Water Sports. Little kids can ride the waves with a boogie board rented from **Island Sport Shop,** 995 Weldon's Way; (401-466- 5001). **Block Island Parasailing,** located on the Old Harbor Dock (401-466-2474), offers canoe and kayak instruction, along with parasailing. **Oceans & Ponds,** Old Harbor, (401-466-5131), provides life jackets, paddles, and cartop equipment; **Island Outfitters,** Old Harbor, (401-466-5502) also offers diving equipment.

Horseback riding. Saddle up at **Rustic Rides,** West Side Road (401-466-5060), for a guided tour of the rocky west coast. You can also ride along the beach.

Baseball. Everyone is welcome to join in the evening youth games. Check the Block Island times for the schedule.

Historic Sites and Museums

LIGHTHOUSES

- **Southeast Point Light House,** Mohegan Bluffs off South East Light Road (401–466–5009). Once the most powerful light in New England, the lighthouse, constructed in 1875, has a beam that reaches 35 miles out to sea. The structure was moved back 400 feet from the bluffs due to erosion. The museum has exhibits on the history of lighthouses.

- **North Light Interpretive Center,** Sandy Point (401–466–3200). This lighthouse is perched on the island's northernmost point. The museum focuses on the maritime history of the island. Some of the exhibits include old lifesaving equipment used in the many wrecks in Block Island waters.

CEMETERIES

- **Block Island Historical Cemetery,** overlooking New Harbor, contains the graves of seventeenth-century settlers.

- **Indian Burial Ground,** Center Road. The graves are unusually close together because the Manisseans were buried in a sitting position.

MUSEUM

- **Block Island Historical Society,** Old Town Road (401–466–2481). This nineteenth-century inn has period furniture, pottery, and beads of the Manisses tribe, as well as mounted birds and geology displays of the region. Most city kids used to big museums won't be impressed, but try this if you're looking for a rainy-day pursuit.

Performing Arts

Oceanwest Theater, Champlin's Marina, New Harbor (401–466–2971), presents first-run movies nightly as well as rainy-day matinees from late May to mid-September.

The **Historical Society,** Old Town Road, Old Harbor (401–466–2481), is a good rainy-day activity. Two permanent exhibitions focus on the Manisseans, the Native Americans who lived here for centuries, and the mounted birds of Elizabeth Dickens, an island legend.

SPECIAL EVENTS

Festivals

Listed below are festivals and special events for **Block Island.** For more information call the Block Island Chamber of Commerce (401–466–2982 or 800–383–2474).

Great Treats for Little Kids

- **Hotel Manisses Animal Farm and Petting Zoo,** Spring Street (401–466–2063). Free admission. Open from dawn to dusk. Pet and feed the llamas, emus, black swans, Sicilian ducks, and a pygmy goat.
- **Littlefield Bee Farm,** Corn Neck Road (401–466–5364.) Open Memorial Day to Columbus Day. Learn how bees make honey and why you shouldn't be afraid of these insects, then sample the honey.
- **Island Elementary School Playground,** High Street. Crawl through the tunnels, climb on the jungle gym, and sway on the swings.
- **Block Island Kite Company,** Corn Neck Road (401–466–2033). Launch your own kite into the island breezes. Kite-flying lessons are provided.

July. July Fourth Celebration. Block Island Arts and Crafts Guild Fair. Annual Barbershop Quartet Concert.

August. Block Island Triathlon. Annual Block Island House and Garden Tour. Nature Conservancy Annual Conservation Event. Block Island Arts Festival.

September. Annual 15K Road Race.

October. National Audubon Birdwatching Weekend. Annual Harvest and Antique Car Festival.

November. Annual Block Island Christmas Shopping Stroll. Block Island Arts and Crafts Guild Fair.

WHERE TO STAY

Rental Agencies

To rent a cottage for a week or more—a cost effective and convenient way to enjoy the island—call at least six months in advance. Several companies provide rental services, including **Block Island Realty, Inc.,** Dodge Street., P.O. Box 721 (401–466–5887), and **Phelan Real Estate,** Payne Road and Water Street, P.O. Box B-2 (401–466–2816).

In addition, call these reservation services for hotel and other rentals: **Block Island Holidays Inc.,** Box 803 (401–466–3137 or 800–905–0590; www.blockisland.com/biholidays), and **Block Island Reservations,** Water Street (800–825–6254; www. blockislandhotel.com). Check out the **Block Island home page** (www.blockisland.com).

Hotels and Inns

Surf Hotel, Dodge Street (401–466–2241 or 401–466–2240), is one of the grand Victorian inns still standing on the island. Situated on the beach in the center of town, the Surf Hotel tempts with hearty breakfasts, grills for barbecuing on the porch, a playground and basketball hoop, and a parrot in the lobby. If you want to be where the action is, this is the place. But remember, it can be noisy, and most rooms have only a sink and no private bathroom. There's a six-night minimum stay in July and August.

The **Atlantic Inn,** High Street (401-466-5883 or 800-224-7422), a short walk from the Old Harbor, offers twenty-one rooms, many with good views. Amenities include a croquet court, two tennis courts, and a playhouse replica of the inn just for kids. Children under twelve stay free. Three-night stay minimum during summer weekends.

The **New Shoreham House Inn,** Water Street (401-466-2651 or 800-272-2601), in the historic downtown district, overlooks the Old Harbor. This lodging offers special family packages in July and at various times during the late spring and fall and family fun suggestions all of the time. Kids under twelve stay free, and cots and cribs are available on request. If you can visit for a week, an apartment provides more flexibility.

Built in 1890, **The 1661 Inn,** Spring Street (401-466-2421 or 401-466-2063 or 800-MANISSES), is named for the date the first non–Native American settlers arrived on the island. The inn sits on a hilltop overlooking the sea. Eight of the rooms have decks that afford views of the Old Harbor and the Atlantic Ocean. The decor, more Colonial New England than gussied-up Victorian, feels more comfortable for families. Rates include a buffet breakfast, afternoon wine, and an island tour.

> ## Block Island Club
>
> The Block Island Club, Corn Neck Road (401-466-5939), a resort club that offers weekly memberships to island visitors, is a great idea for families too energetic to just sunbathe. Besides a lifeguarded beach, the club, located on the island's Great Salt Pond, offers tennis, sailboarding, and sailing. Since the tide is gentle, the waves are manageable.

Cottages/Apartments

Although rooms in the main buildings of the following inns generally are not suitable for families, the inns do offer cottages and apartments.

Barrington Inn, Beach and Ocean Avenues (401-466-5510), offers two apartments in the old barn. These two-bedroom units welcome kids of any age, accommodate families of five, and feature kitchen facilities, barbecue grills, and private decks.

The Blue Dory Inn, Box 488 Dodge Street (401-466-5891 or 800-992-7290), overlooking Crescent Beach, has a main building, four cottages, (three of the four are suitable for families) and three suites in a separate building called the Waverly. This is only one of two properties on Block Island with direct access to a beach. Recently voted "Block Island's most romantic inn," the Blue Dory maintains that atmosphere by suggesting families stay in one of the cottages. The Tea House, the smallest cottage, comes with a kitchenette and is best for adults with just one young child. From the Tea House's porch you have a great view of the ocean. The Cottage, which has two bedrooms plus a kitchenette, accommodates up to six. The Sherman Cottage, the roomiest unit, has three bedrooms, a kitchen, and a big living room and can accommodate from six to eight people.

Wherever you stay, be sure to come by the main building for afternoon tea and cookies or wine and cheese. The Blue Dory Great Cookie, a homemade chocolate chunk treat served each afternoon, gets great reviews from guests.

With Crescent Beach only a two-minute walk away, **Gables Inn** and **Gables II,** Old Harbor (401-466-2213), is a good place for families visiting Block Island. The efficiencies can accommodate five people and offer kitchen facilities; however, in summer they must be rented by the week. The rooms do not have televisions or telephones, but the main building has a television and a phone for the use of guests. The rooms in the main building are decorated with Victorian pieces. The apartments have some period pieces combined with comfortable, contemporary furniture. The inn offers barbecue facilities, picnic tables, and beach supplies.

The Bellevue House on High Street (401-466-5268 or 401-466-2912) has two-bedroom apartments and three-bedroom cottages for rent.

The Gothic Inn, Dodge Street (401-466-2918 or 800-944-8991), overlooking the ocean, features two-bedroom efficiencies and a country cottage.

WHERE TO EAT

Seafood is Block Island's forte. Take a leisurely breakfast in the sun at **Ernies,** Old Harbor (401-466-2473), and watch the ferries pull in with new arrivals from the mainland. Later you can fill up on what some say is the best seafood on the island at **Dead Eye Dick's,** Payne's Dock, New Harbor (401-466-2654). Get goofy with the natives at sing-alongs at **Ballard's Inn,** Old Harbor (401-466-2231). This longtime island fish house has a cavernous dining room and an outdoor patio with tables. The property has a half-mile beach (often crowded); nonetheless, there is a beach. This does wonders for those can't-sit-still children who order, literally jump in the water, then dry off and eat. For après-meals, the beach has a volleyball net. Ballard's gets a good recommendation for its fried clams, fish and chips, and lobster dinners. Boaters, twentysomethings, and families all come here.

Diners at **Harborside Inn,** Water Street (401-466-5504), can eat indoors or enjoy their meals streetside or on the porch. Locals like the clam chowder. Other popular items are the scallops in garlic and herb butter and the scrod. There is a salad bar and a few nonseafood items, including hamburgers and veal dishes.

The **Mohegan Cafe and Brewery,** Water Street, opposite the ferry landing (401–466–5911 or 800–825–6524), is a lively place, and the in-season nightly music adds to the fun but noisy atmosphere. Kids and parents feel comfortable here because the restaurant is, as one islander put it, "flexible." The Mohegan Cafe will mix and match what's on hand to satisfy your child—and you. Lunch favorites include the vegetarian pita pocket and the fried clam roll. For dinner, try the linguine with clams. The seafood chowder is always a good bet.

If you're fished out, go to **Aldo's** (401–466–5871) for Italian food for the whole family and a video arcade for the kids. For pizza, **Capizzano's,** Old Harbor (401–466–2829), has all kinds from pies to calzones to plain old pizza with almost any topping you want. If you want burgers, visit **The Beachhead,** Corn Neck Road (401–466–2249). Parents, older kids, and teens appreciate dining at **Manisses** on Spring Street (401–466–2421). Heralded as one of the best restaurants on the island, Manisses features American style cuisine served in two dining rooms. The menu includes such specialties as Cajun swordfish, herb salmon, and venison. Complementing the dishes of beef, seafood, and poultry are fresh vegetables from the hotel's garden. Flaming coffee, dessert, and after-dinner drinks are served in the upstairs parlor. Try the Black Forest fruitcake crowned with fresh berries. Like the lodging, this restaurant is best suited for adults and older children.

SIDE TRIPS

On your way back from Block Island, take one of the ferries to **Newport, Rhode Island.** Tour the nineteenth-century European-style mansions cliffside along Bellevue Avenue; then stroll through Colonial Newport's brick-paved streets harborside. Music lovers should time their visit with the summertime classical, jazz, or folk festivals.

Call the Newport County Convention and Visitors Bureau, 23 America's Cup Avenue, Newport (401–849–8098 or 800–326–6030), for a free travel planner with attraction, event, and accommodation information. Web site: www.gonewport.com.

FOR MORE INFORMATION

Block Island Chamber of Commerce, Water Street, Old Harbor (401–466–2982 or 800–383–2474), has a travel planner, a helpful source of tourist information. Pick up a copy of the weekly *Block Island Times,* which has a map of the island and a list of community activities. Also, check out the island's home page, www.blockisland.com.

Emergency Numbers

Ambulance, fire, and police: 911

Block Island Medical Center, P.O. Box 919, Payne Road; (401) 466-2974

Block Island Pharmacy, P.O. Box 1179, High Street; (401) 466-5825

Block Island Police: (401) 466-3220

Coast Guard: (401) 789-0444

Poison Hotline: (401) 277-5727

Public Health Nurse, Mary Donnelly: (401) 466-2332

TORONTO

I f you shy away from city vacations because of the hassles associated with large metropolitan areas, take a trip to Toronto, Ontario, Canada's largest city and top visitor destination. This spanking-clean city on the northern shore of Lake Ontario offers families every-thing a major metropolitan area should—without the hassles. Your family will find all the things you might expect: interesting sights, kid-friendly museums, arts and entertainment, shopping, great restaurants, and a wide selection of accommodations. You'll also find some things you might not expect: a sparkling, lively waterfront; safe, clean streets; and a friendly, ethnically diverse population that adds much to Toronto's character and charm.

GETTING THERE

U.S. citizens and legal residents don't need passports or visas to enter Canada, although they are preferred. Native-born U.S. citizens should have a birth certificate or voter's registration card that shows citizenship, plus a picture I.D. Naturalized citizens need naturalization certificates or other proof of citizenship. Permanent residents who are not citizens need alien registration receipts.

Metropolitan Toronto is a major transportation center. Some thirty-five major airlines offer regular service through three terminals at **Pearson International Airport** (416-612-5100), in the northwest corner of metropolitan Toronto. Car rentals are available at the airport. Only taxis with TIA on their license plates are authorized to pick up passengers. **Toronto Island Airport** (416-868-6942) services a number of commuter airlines, including flights originating in the United States. The airport can be accessed via a brief public ferry ride that leaves from the foot of Bathurst Street.

Amtrak (800-USA-RAIL) runs trains from New York and Chicago to Toronto, where passengers can link up to the **VIA Rail Canada, Inc.** (416-868-7277), which provides rail service throughout Canada. Union Station is downtown on Front Street, directly on Toronto's subway line.

Toronto

AT A GLANCE

▶ Explore a clean, exciting, friendly, and ethnically diverse city

▶ Browse through innovative museums, including a science center and shoe museum

▶ Discover Black Creek Pioneer Village, a nineteenth-century living history community

▶ Enjoy the many parks and playspaces

▶ Tourism Toronto, (416) 203-3805 or (800) 363-1990; www.tourism-toronto.com

Greyhound, Voyageur, and regional bus lines serve Metro Toronto, arriving and departing from the bus terminal at 610 Bay Street. Fares and schedules for all bus companies may be obtained by calling (416) 393-7911.

Those coming by car can reach Toronto by one of several major routes that parallel Lake Ontario's shores: Highway 401 and Highway 2 from the west and east; Queen Elizabeth Way from the west only; and Highway 400, which connects with Highway 401, from the north.

Note: While you're at Pearson airport, check out the boutique complex at the terminal; it has only Harrod's in North America.

GETTING AROUND

Metro Toronto has consolidated its six former municipalities—the City of Toronto, the Borough of East York, and the Cities of York, North York, Scarborough, and Etobicoke—into one megacity, Metropolitan Toronto. Toronto is now the fourth-largest city in North America, after Mexico City, New York City, and Los Angeles. Transit service via Toronto Transit Commission (TTC) includes 818 miles of subway, bus, trolley and street-car, and ferry routes. Riders must have exact change or purchase TTC tickets and tokens at subway stations or from stores displaying the EXACT FARE sign. For information about routes, schedules, and fares, call (416) 393-4636, or pick up a *Ride Guide* at subway entrances.

Toronto has so many diverse neighborhoods that you may sometimes prefer your car to public transportation. The Metropolitan Toronto Convention and Visitors Association (MTCVA) has free maps that include area highways. Avoid heavy rush-hour traffic. Street parking, when you can find it, is usually limited to one hour, although you may park overnight until 7:00 A.M. Day parking is also free at outlying subway stations. The city streets are arranged in a grid pattern, running north-south and east–west.

Ferries operated by the Metro Parks Department (416–392–8193) leave from the foot of Bay Street to the three Toronto Islands on a regular schedule. Gray Coach Lines (416–594–0338) has scheduled service every twenty minutes between most major downtown hotels and the airport. Taxis cruise throughout the city.

WHAT TO SEE AND DO

Museums

Toronto's museums are inspired and innovative places where even the fussiest kid will find something to tickle his or her fancy.

One of the best is the **Ontario Science Center,** 770 Don Mills Road (416–696–3127; www.osc.on.ca). Plan on spending the better part of the day here; you'll enjoy it as much as your kids. Located in a pleasant setting about a half hour from downtown, the museum is famous throughout North America for its innovative exhibits. There are more than 800 exhibits, including **The Space Hall,** popular with older school-age children, teens, and adults. Interactive options include experiencing weightlessness by riding in a rocket chair and the **Challenger Learning Centre,** a hands-on space shuttle mission.

SPORT started as a temporary exhibit but was so well received it's now permanent. The hands-on, bodies-on exhibit includes a radar-clocked baseball pitch, climbing rock wall, bobsled video run, and the chance to judge sports performances, comparing scores with a replay of reactions from real experts.

Although especially relevant for high school students, even younger kids will be fascinated by some of the exhibits at the **Chemistry Hall,** called Matter, Energy, Change. Inside the hall an ultraviolet light makes visitors' clothes glow. Kids can leave their shadow behind, "trapped" by a strobe light on a phosphorescent vinyl wall, and witness the melting and reforming of crystals on a large screen. In the **Human Body Hall,** kids use DNA fingerprinting to catch a criminal, listen to a heart murmur, and learn about immunology.

At the center's **Shopper's Drug Mart Omnimax Theatre** watch films on an 80-foot-high domed screen.

Inquire about **OSCOTT** weekend and vacation discovery classes for ages three to thirteen.

Royal Ontario Museum (ROM), 100 Queen's Park, Bloor Street at

"Please Touch" is the policy at the Ontario Science Center, which features more than 800 hair-raising exhibits.

Avenue Road (416-586-5551), is Canada's largest museum and a real gem. Walk through a bat cave, whose 3,000 bats seem alive in the darkness; ogle mummies at the Ancient Egypt gallery; stand next to the towering skeletons of prehistoric beasts in the Dinosaur Hall; and discover a Ming tomb, complete with figures of soldiers and weapons.

The **Children's Own Museum,** which opened November 1998 and is part of ROM, presents a different kind of hands-on experience. Aimed at ages two to eight, the museum consists of one main gallery with ten different sections, each representing part of a neighborhood. To the basic shell of a house, market, construction site, back alley, and other setting, kids add furnishings, including their own handcrafted items. The concept encourages creativity and builds confidence in new ways of thinking.

Bata Shoe Museum, 327 Bloor Street West (416-979-7799), may not sound like a kid-pleaser, but it is. The only museum in the world devoted to footwear, the facility presents shoes as interpreters of culture and ritual. Kids see nut crushers, fearsome-looking foot gear with 4-inch spikes that make your grunge-loving teen covetous. The shoes were used to crush chestnuts in order to extract the tannin needed to soften leather.

Other kid-pleasers: the backwards' pointing pair worn by smugglers' in the Netherlands during World War II (the toes left a false trail, pointing in the direction opposite to the one the contrabandists actually took); as well as such celebrity footwear as John Lennon's black Beatle boots; Elton John's silver platform boots; Madonna's sequined, magenta heels;

Parks, Green Spaces, and Play Areas

A great way to experience a city with kids is to play outside, sampling the ambience and the "streetmosphere." Toronto, from May through summer when the weather is warm, offers a delightful mix of parks, green spaces, and play areas.

Ontario Place, 955 Lake Shore Boulevard West (416-314-9811; www.ontarioplace.com), occupies ninety-six acres stretching over three man-made islands in Lake Ontario. This is the place to be in summer, particularly when the sun is shining and the lake sparkles. Here you'll find strolling mimes and musicians, minigolf, and a water play area with slides, bumper boats, pedal boats, and Rush River, a raft ride. The **Children's Village** is terrific, with a LEGO creative play center, award-winning playground, rope bridges, **children's theater,** and lots more. It's fun to stroll the grounds, passing the canals, lagoons, and clusters of shops and restaurants. Evenings are lively with **Imax** movies shown in the six-story Cinesphere, as well as frequent concerts. Ontario Place is also the best spot from which to enjoy the **Benson & Hedges Symphony of Fire,** a fireworks competition held on select evenings in June and July.

Harbourfront Centre, Queen's Quay West at the foot of York Street, and including York, John, and Maple Leaf quays (416-973-3000), is a waterfront complex of shops, restaurants, galleries, and performing arts venues in what was once a rundown district of warehouses. Take time to browse the crafts shops, listen to a free summer concert at Molson Place, search for treasures at **Harbourfront Antiques Market,** 390 Queen's Quay West (416-260-2626) and play an impromptu game of Frisbee at the field near Bathurst Pier, which has one playground designated for kids seven and younger and another for older children. Ask about the **HarbourKid** programs, which vary from month to month and may include free family concerts, workshops, or a day camp for ages five to sixteen (divided into appropriate age groups). In winter York Quay, the world's largest artificial skating rink, has free ice skating.

On **Centre Island,** part of the 800-acre **Toronto Islands Park** (416-392-8186) across the harbor from downtown, is the **Centreville Amusement Park** (416-203-0405), a treat for young children. The scaled-down version of a **nineteenth-century Ontario village** has a fire station and steam engines. Little ones also like the swan-shaped paddle boats and the petting farm, whose residents include cows,

(continued)

Parks, Green Spaces, and Play Areas *(continued)*

geese, and pigs. The Avenue of the Islands, a long promenade, is great for strolling. Along with a public beach—sunning only, as the water temperature hovers in the high 50s—Centre Island has miles of bike trails that connect to the other, more residential islands. Pack a picnic and pedal your way along the scenic, tree-lined paths. It's all part of Toronto's easygoing charm.

High Park, west of downtown, south of Bloor Street and north of Queensway, is accessible by streetcar or subway. It's a good place to toss a Frisbee or take a stroll. Considered Toronto's "Central Park," the facility has a menagerie, hiking trails, sports fields, pond, and restaurant.

Kortright Centre for Conservation (416-661-6600) is south of Major MacKenzie on Pine Valley Drive in suburban Kleinburg, about a thirty-minute drive. Here kids and adults can commune with nature. Daily 1:00 P.M. programs vary according to the season, weather, and specialty of the naturalist leader. You can wade through wetlands on a stream safari, find out about wind turbines at a science workshiops, and learn about bats, owls, and things that flutter at night at a Bat Night program. Reserve in advance. The scenic hiking trails are popular with families, and there's a marsh habitat on the premises.

Ask about special seasonal events such as the fall honey festival (there's a beehouse here) and the popular maple syrup demonstrations in spring.

Toronto Zoo, in Scarborough on Highway 401 at Meadowvale Road (416-392-5900), is rated as one of the world's best. There are more than 4,000 animals, eight tropical pavilions, and Monorail and Zoomobile rides for viewing outdoor exhibits. Look for a schedule of the daily demonstrations and zookeeper talks. At the $18 million **African Savanna,** which opened in June 1998, visit with cheetahs, lions, hippos, elephants, and rhinos.

and Elvis's blue patent loafers. Before exploring the museum, ask for the family shoe bag, a hands-on activities kit designed for ages five to ten

Spend some time at the **Art Gallery of Ontario and the Grange (AGO),** 317 Dundas Street West, Grange Park (416-979-6648). With fifty galleries and thousands of works, AGO is one of North America's largest public art museums. Don't attempt to see it all, but pick your favorites. At Off the Wall!, a hands-on activity room for children eight and younger, kids can dress up like a painting and create sculptures and paintings. The Henry Moore Sculpture Center houses one of the largest collections of Moore's work; kids seem to like his flowing lines, especially the works with family themes. Other highlights are the Canadian galleries and the French Impressionist paintings.

Historical Attractions

These next two sites are fun ways for all ages to learn more about this area's fascinating past.

Fort York, Garrison Road off Fleet Street (416-392-6907). *Toronto,* a Huron word for "meeting place," was established as a French fur trading post in 1750 and colonized by the British in 1793 on this site. This is also where the Battle of York was fought in the War of 1812. The American raid of York, resulting in the burning of the parliament building, led to retribution by the British, who invaded Washington and tried to burn down the president's residence. Although the building wasn't destroyed, the scorched walls outside had to be whitewashed, resulting in what was thereafter known as the White House. All has been forgiven, of course, and today costumed soldiers and their wives give tours and are delighted to answer any questions you and the kids have. On Kidsummer Day in August, children can dress up like soldiers and take part in drills.

Black Creek Pioneer Village, 1000 Murray Ross Parkway, Downsview, northwest Toronto (416-736-1733), reconstructs a mid-nineteenth-century village in rural Ontario. Costumed interpreters are here to answer questions and demonstrate crafts of the day, such as broom making, weaving, baking, and tinsmithing. More than forty restored homes and shops plus a cafeteria and restaurant are on the premises. Be sure to ask about special weekends throughout the year, which include an apple pie baking contest (where visitors can buy what's left after the judging) and fall fair. Open mid-March to December 31.

More Attractions

At 1,815 feet and 5 inches the **CN Tower,** 301 Front Street West (416-360-8500 or 888-684-3268; www.cntower.ca), is reputedly the world's tallest free-standing structure. From the observation deck the views are spectacular. On a clear day you can see Niagara Falls. Kids especially like the glass floor that allows them to feel as if they are floating atop the city. Reopened June 1998 after a $26 million renovation, the CN Tower sports a refurbished SkyQuest Theater showing a three-minute film about human achievement, as well as new shops, restaurants, and attractions. The Maple Leaf Cinema features a twenty-two-minute film about Canada's land and people, and an arcade has two new motion simulator rides. Easy Glide Canadian Panorama takes you on a simulated airplane ride, while the Ultimate Roller Coaster tosses, twirls, and pitches just like a real thrill ride.

SkyDome is adjacent to the Tower at Front and Peter Streets, 1 Blue Jays Way (416-341-2776). The stadium has a fully retractable roof and is home to the Toronto Blue Jays baseball team, the Toronto Argonauts football team, and the Toronto Raptors basketball team. Even if there's nothing going on, sports fans will enjoy the guided tour.

Paramount **Canada's Wonderland,** Rutherford Road exit from Highway 400 (905-832-7000), a thirty-minute drive north of Toronto, is a full-service amusement park. This enormous attraction is divided into seven theme areas, including Hanna Barbera Land, Smurf Forest, and White Water Canyon. There are nine thrilling roller coasters, such as Vortex, a suspended coaster, and Top Gun, a looping coaster. Other get-you-screaming experiences are Drop Zone, which drops you 230 feet, and Xtreme Skyflyer, a shake 'em up flight ride. Younger children like Kidzville, with its smaller roller coasters, rides, and Rugrats characters. A theme water park, strolling entertainers, dolphin shows, cliff divers, restaurants, shops, free summer concerts, and more make this an all-day commitment. Arrive early.

For hockey fans, be sure to stop at the **Hockey Hall of Fame,** inside BCE Place at Front and Yonge Streets (416-360-7765; www.hhof.com). Inside the $25 million, 51,000-square-foot building, you will find museum-style exhibits, theaters that show hockey's best plays, trivia games, and a plastic ice rink that the aspiring player can glide across. Walk through a re-creation of the Montreal Canadiens' dressing room and feel the spirit that surges through Canadian hockey fans. The Hall of Fame's Bell Great Hall is expected to become the home of the precious Stanley Cup and is dedicated to Canadian hockey greats including Woody Dumart, Lanny McDonald, and Marcel Dionne. There are also a hockey simulator and memorabilia, including a collection of hockey masks and seats from famous stadiums.

Performing Arts

No matter when you visit, you're sure to find something exciting going on in the performing arts. Get the monthly events calendar *About Town* and *Where Toronto,* published by *Where* Magazines International in cooperative with Tourism Toronto. Toronto has three daily papers with listings of events, including the "What's On" section in Thursday's *Toronto Star.* The **Young People's Theater,** 165 Front Street East (416-363-5131), puts on productions geared to children.

The Toronto Symphony frequently performs young people's and special family concerts at Roy Thomson Hall (416-593-4828). The Canadian Opera Company and National Ballet of Canada performances take place at O'Keefe Center (416-393-7474). In summer the **Canadian Stage**

Company stars in the outdoor Shakespearean festival "The Dream in High Park," which older kids may enjoy, particularly because of the setting. Call (416) 367-8243 for schedules.

Toronto has a large theater industry, with plays being performed in forty-odd theaters. These include the **Pantages Theater** and the **Elgin and Winter Garden** complex, with theatrical, musical, and dance performances. If you don't mind standing in line (arrive before the noon opening), Five Star Tickets (416-596-8211) sells half-price tickets to all arts events on the day of performance from a booth in front of the Eaton Centre on Dundas and Yonge Streets.

SPECIAL EVENTS

Sporting Events

The Toronto Maple Leafs of the National Hockey League play in Maple Leaf Gardens, Carlton and Church Streets (416-977-1641). The big summer attraction is the Toronto Blue Jays, in the American League, winners of the 1992 and 1993 World Series, who play in the SkyDome. Although games sometimes sell out, you can often get tickets at the box office (416-341-1000). The Toronto Argonauts football team also plays in the SkyDome; call (416) 872-5000 for tickets. Get tickets for the Player's International Tennis Tournament, held in late July, by calling (416) 665-9777 or from TicketMaster (416-870-8000), which also can provide tickets to some (but not all) sporting, theatrical, and other events.

Fairs, Festivals, and Special Events

Call the Convention and Visitors Association for more information on the following events.

March. Children's Film Festival.

May. International Children's Festival, with acrobats, mimes, storytellers, and theater companies from around the world.

June. Benson & Hedges Symphony of Fire, fireworks competition at Ontario Place. Dragon Boat Race Festival on Toronto Islands, with traditional Chinese dragon-shaped boats and concession stands.

August. Du Maurier International Tennis Championship; Canadian National Exhibition, the world's largest annual fair. See Canadian arts, agriculture, architecture, and more at the Canadian National Exhibition.

Labor Day. Canadian National Air Show, over the harbor, can be watched from Ontario Place, Harbourfront, or Toronto Islands.

September. Toronto International Film Festival.

WHERE TO STAY

Toronto has two free reservations services: Accommodation Toronto (416-203-2500 or 800-363-1990) is operated by the Hotel Association of Metropolitan Toronto and features more than one hundred luxury, moderate, and economy properties; Econo-Lodging Services (416-494-0541) offers hotels in all price ranges as well as short-term furnished apartments. There are also a number of bed-and-breakfast reservation services listed in the *Metropolitan Toronto* publication, free from Tourism Toronto. Here are some choices for families.

Downtown

The **Delta Chelsea Inn,** 33 Gerrard Street West (416-595-1975 or 800-268-9070; www.deltahotels.com), has a family pool area, a separate adult pool, game rooms, and a Children's Creative Centre with supervised activities. The property is big, with almost 1,600 rooms.

Royal York Hotel, 100 Front Street West (416-863-6333 or 800-441-1414; www.cphotels.ca), has an elan that makes it many visitors' favorite Toronto hotel. With 1,365 rooms, the property is large. The hotel is across from Union Station and is connected to the underground shops. There's also an indoor pool.

The **Cambridge Suites Hotel,** 15 Richmond Street East (416-368-1990 or 800-463-1990; www.centennialhotels.com/cambridge), works well for families. The suites have a dining/work area and separate bedrooms, plus microwave and regrigerator.

The **Sheraton Centre Toronto Hotel,** 123 Queen Street West (416-368-2511 or 800-441-1414, www.sheratonctr.toronto.on), is another good bet for families. Conveniently located, it has access to the underground city, as well as good-size rooms, a large indoor/outdoor pool, acres of gardens, and a supervised kids' room for ages eighteen months to twelve years.

The **Westin Harbour Castle,** 1 Harbour Square (416-869-1600, 800-228-3000; www.wextin.com), is situated on Harbourfront. The property has an indoor pool and Westin Kids' Klub amenities, which include room safety kits upon request as well as a welcoming gift for kids.

Midtown

Pricey but posh, the **Four Seasons Hotel Toronto,** 21 Avenue Road (416-964-0411 or 800-268-6282; www.fourseasons.com), pampers guests with good service and large rooms. Kids can check out complimentary bicycles and video games and at turn-down, children get milk and cookies. The **Hotel Intercontinental Toronto,** 220 Bloor Street

West (416-960-5200 or 800-267-0010; www.interconti.com), also offers good service and good-size rooms, plus the property participates in Intercontinental's Kids-in-Tow program, aimed at children accompanying parents on business trips. Upon check-in kids get a backpack with some toys and parents get a guide to the city's child-friendly attractions.

Moderately priced rooms are available in summer on the campus of **Victoria University,** 140 Charles Street West (416-585-4524), near the Royal Ontario Museum. The residence hall rooms come with linens and towels, but bathrooms are down the hall.

Scarborough

The **University of Toronto,** Scarborough Campus, 1265 Military Trail; (416-287-7369) offers families lodging in eighty-one furnished town houses located in a beautiful, parklike Student Village, thirty minutes from downtown Toronto. Available from mid-May through the third week in August, units have equipped kitchens and sleep four to six in rooms with one or two twin beds (minimum stay two nights). There are no televisions, no air-conditioning, and no room phones.

WHERE TO EAT

Toronto is packed with 5,000 restaurants, many reflecting the city's diverse ethnic population, including Greek, Italian, and Chinese. If you're exploring some of the various ethnic neighborhoods on foot, watch and ask where the locals eat. (While these explorations can be fascinating for adults who enjoy local color, kids might be bored since there's not much "action" in these neighborhoods, some of them thirty to forty minutes from downtown.)

Tourism Toronto has several guides listing restaurants, including *Toronto Day and Night,* which lists both eateries and shopping by neighborhood and category. Downtown has its share of fine dining spots, including these with family appeal: **Hard Rock Cafe-SkyDome,** 1 Blue Jays Way, Suite 350 (416-341-2388), has great burgers and Canada's largest rock 'n' roll collection. Eat in style and watch your favorite team play at **Cafe on the Green,** SkyDome Hotel, 45 Peter Street South (416-341-5045), where the sports-theme dining room provides a great view of the SkyDome playing field. **The Old Spaghetti Factory,** 54 The Esplanade (416-864-9761), is economical, casual, and fun—and there's a children's menu. **Mr. Greenjeans** in the downtown Eaton Centre, an enormous shopping mall (416) 979-1212, has an entertainment theme that kids love and menus bigger than your table. (Cross the street to show the kids the World's Biggest Bookstore, on Eaton Street.) Make a "knight" of it at the **Medieval Times Dinner and Tournament,** Arts, Crafts, and Hobbies Building, Exhibition Place (416-260-1234), where you can dine and watch jousting knights astride Andalusian stallions.

Toronto has a **Planet Hollywood,** 277 Front Street West (416-596-7827), serving pastas, burgers, and salads amid movie memorabilia and multiscreen images. Hockey enthusiasts might like **Wayne Gretzky's,** 99 Blue Jays Way (416-979-PUCK), with a menu similar to Planet Hollywood's but Gretzky's hockey items on display. At **Shopsy's TV City,** 284 King Street West (416-599-5464), kids keep busy working the Sony PlayStations at each table and watching television. Folks line up early for the all-you-can-eat buffet at **Frankie Tomatto's,** 7225 Woodbine Avenue, Markham (905-940-1900). The **Kensington Kitchen,** 124 Harbord Street (416-961-3404), offers an inexpensive items such as couscous and brochettes of chicken or lamb as well as other Mediterranean-inspired dishes. The **Senator,** 249-253 Victoria Street (416-364-7517), a diner reminiscent of the 1950s, serves meat loaf, macaroni and cheese, burgers, and other comfort foods at moderate prices.

SIDE TRIPS

Niagara Falls, 90 miles from Toronto, is one of the great natural wonders of the world. En route, stop by **Royal Botanical Gardens,** Hamilton (30 minutes from downtown Toronto), and stroll the beautifully landscaped grounds. If you're headed to Montreal, stop in **Whitby,** a forty-minute drive from downtown, where **Cullen Gardens and Miniature Village** features flowers (there's a tulip festival every April), 140 miniature buildings (built to $\frac{1}{12}$ scale), puppet shows, and more. About an hour west of Toronto, near the town of Cambridge, is **African Lion Safari** (open until early October), where you can drive through game reserves in your own car or take a guided bus tour. Call (519) 623-2620.

FOR MORE INFORMATION

Tourism Toronto has multilingual information counselors and helpful publications. Call (416) 203-3805 or (800) 363-1990, or write to Tourism Toronto, Queen's Quay Terminal at Harbourfront Centre, 207 Queens Quay West, Box 126, Toronto, Ontario, Canada M51 1A7. You can stop by **Information Toronto,** 255 Front Street West, from 9:00 A.M. to 5:30 P.M. on weekdays. Or check out the Web site at www.tourism-toronto. com. On Highway 401, at Winston Churchill Boulevard exit 333 off the eastbound lanes, stop by the **Shell Info Centre,** which has year-round, twenty-four-hour interactive computer facilities and a video on the area.

For visitor's information on the Province of Ontario, visit the Ontario Ministry of Tourism and Recreation's Travel Centre in the Eaton Centre, 220 Yonge Street, or call (416) 965-4008 or (800) 268-3736.

Kid's Toronto (416-481-5696), free at many locations, is an excellent monthly source for family-oriented events. Community Information Centre of Metro Toronto (416-392-0505) offers complete information on services for the disabled, twenty-four hours a day.

Emergency Numbers

Ambulance, fire, and police: 911

Poison Information Center: (416) 598-5900

Twenty-four-hour emergency service: Hospital for Sick Children, 555 University Avenue; (416) 597-1500 and Toronto General Hospital, 200 Elizabeth Street (416) 340-4611.

Twenty-four-hour pharmacy: Shopper's Drug Mart, 700 Bay Street at Gerard (downtown); (416) 979-2424

Lake Champlain and Burlington

After the Great Lakes, Lake Champlain is the next largest inland lake in the United States. Extending southward from Canada, the 120-mile-long lake lies between New York State and Vermont, whose boundaries claim two-thirds of the lake. The bays, islands, and miles of Vermont shoreline are havens for swimming, sailing, boating, fishing, windsurfing, waterskiing—and just relaxing. (Keep an eye out for Champ, the sea monster who has allegedly been spotted several times over the years.)

Burlington, Vermont's largest city, sits on the terraced eastern slopes of Lake Champlain and is the headquarters for navigation around the lake. It's also an important business and educational center, home to the University of Vermont.

Burlington offers easy access not only to such water pursuits as boating, fishing, and cruising but also to mountain splendors. To the city's east are the Green Mountains, and across the lake rise the Adirondacks. As a result, Burlington is an excellent base for outdoor pursuits. The region offers plenty of hiking trails, plus skiing in winter and scenic road trips in fall.

GETTING THERE

Burlington International Airport (802-863-2874) is New England's third busiest. Car rentals are available at the airport.

Vermont Transit, 133 Saint Paul Street at Main (802-864-8611 or 800-642-3133—Vermont, 800-451-3292—New England). Buses go to and from other Vermont towns as well as Boston, Albany, and Montréal, with connections made with Greyhound.

Amtrak, 29 Railroad Avenue, Essex Junction (5 miles east of Burlington) (802-879-7298 or 800-USA-RAIL). Trains run to and from New

Lake Champlain and Burlington

AT A GLANCE

▶ Enjoy swimming, sailing, boating, fishing, windsurfing, waterskiing—and just relaxing—on a 120-mile lake

▶ Discover nineteenth-century folk art, artifacts, architecture at the Shelburne Museum

▶ Tour Ben & Jerry's Ice Cream factory

▶ Vacation at two full-service family resorts

▶ Dive for eighteenth- and nineteenth-century wrecks

▶ Lake Champlain Regional Chamber of Commerce, (802) 863-3489; Vermont Travel Division, (802) 828-3236; www.travel-vermont.com

York and Montréal. A bus leaves hourly for downtown Burlington.

Auto/passenger ferries link Vermont and New York at three northern crossings: Burlington to Port Kent, New York (one-hour trip): Charlotte, Vermont, to Essex, New York (eighteen minutes); and Grand Isle, Vermont, to Plattsburgh, New York (twelve minutes). All are operated by Lake Champlain Transportation Company, King Street Dock (802-864-9804).

Burlington is at the end of the scenic portion of highways I-89 and SR 116.

An interesting option in the Shelburne area is the **Shelburne Shuttle,** (800-707-3530). This restored train departs from the train station, Route 7 and Harbor Road, Shelburne. From June through Labor Day the train provides continuous service to the Shelburne Museum, the Vermont Teddy Bear Company, the Country Store, and back to the depot. Visitors are encouraged to leave their cars in any of the attractions' parking lots and take the train to visit the other sites.

Shelburne is about 9 miles south of Burlington. Vergennes is about 20 miles south of Burlington and about 11 miles south of Shelburne. South Hero, part of the Lake Champlain Islands, is about 17 miles northwest of Burlington.

GETTING AROUND

A car is a necessity. Public CCTA (Chittendon County Transit Authority) buses operate Monday through Saturday throughout the city and to outlying areas, including Shelburne, from the CCTA hub on Cherry and Church Streets.

WHAT TO SEE AND DO

Museums and Historical Sites

We're starting with the biggest and the best: **Shelburne Museum,** U.S. 7, Shelburne (802-985-3344; www.shelburnemuseum.org). The heritage of New England is celebrated here with impressive eighteenth- and nineteenth-century folk art, artifacts, and architecture. But this collection of Americana—among the best in the country—isn't presented in a boring, dry-as-dust museum manner. Instead, the history and artifacts are incorporated into a small village of thirty-seven exhibit buildings on forty-five acres, most transported from various places in Vermont: a covered bridge, 1800s homes and shops—even a lighthouse, a private, furnished **1890 railroad car** and a **vintage railroad station.**

Other favorite buildings include the **horseshoe barn** stocked with scores of carriages. The museum's founder, Electra Havermeyer Webb, desired suitable shelter for her father's extensive carriage collection. She had her craftsmen duplicate a horseshoe-shaped barn she liked in Vermont; thus came the inspiration for what eventually turned into the Shelburne Museum. The **wagons, sleighs,** and **coaches** delight children. Especially appealing for young ones is the child's cutter, circa 1887, a small red sleigh that seems perfect for Vermont winter fun. Young children, enamored of trucks, also seem to like the **early fire-fighting equipment** found in the Shaker Shed, circa 1840, from the Canterbury, New Hampshire, a Shaker community. Of particular appeal are the horse carts, ladder wagon, and pump wagon.

Kids especially like the 1830 one-room **schoolhouse;** the **1890 jail,** featuring cells, stocks, and pillory; and the **old-time general store** with barbershop, taproom, and post office.

All ages—including adults—like the **Circus Building.** Outside, take time for little ones to ride the **carousel.** Not a historic structure, this building was specifically built in the 1950s to display a 500-foot-long **miniature circus.** The tiny but detailed figures are entrancing. The circus parade features rows of marching horses, zebras, and elephants; a lion cage pulled by horses; and cowgirls and cowboys complete with lariats and boots. Opposite the glass displays are forty life-size **carousel figures,** including prancing ponies, a giraffe, a tiger, and chariots, all expertly

Shelburne Farms

Of special interest in the area is **Shelburne Farms,** 102 Harbor Road, Shelburne (802–985-8686). Designed as an "ideal" farm at the turn of the century, this property now features an inn, a barn, a carriage tour, and walking trails. Set on 1,000 acres with ample Lake Champlain frontage, the grounds are alluring. A tractor-pulled hay wagon takes you to the barn. Then meander through meadows and enjoy the splendid scenery. With little children visit the Children's Farmyard, with its goats, rabbits, and horses to pet.

Lake Champlain Camp, a weekly summer day camp for ages prekindergarten through grade 6, focuses on the environment and farm life.

Two books of special interest are available at the visitor center gift shop: Shelburne Farms Children's Farmyard and Walking Trail has a trail map and information about the farm animals. Designed for teachers but helpful for parents is Shelburne Farms Project Seasons: Hands-on Activities for Discovering the Wonders of the World. The myriad activities make learning about science and nature easy and fun for children in grades two through five.

carved by the **Gustav Dentzel Carousel Company** of Philadelphia.

Older school-age children appreciate the **Hat and Fragrance Textile Gallery,** housed in an 1800 former Shelburne distillery. The rooms display the colorful quilts and dresses, as well as the hat boxes, typical of the nineteenth century. An adjacent room exhibits the large collection of hooked rugs created by Molly Tobey of Rhode Island. Children might also enjoy the **tobacconist's figures** (otherwise known as "cigar store Indians") that inhabit the **Stagecoach Inn,** along with such other folk art objects as weather vanes crafted to look like roosters, whales, and fish. (Another reason for visiting here: Public bathrooms are around back.)

Don't miss the *Ticonderoga,* the last vertical beam sidewheel steamboat intact in the United States, which was built in Shelburne Harbor in 1906. A film on board shows the ingenious way the ship was moved to the museum. The **Toy Shop** will delight with penny banks, mechanical toys, dolls, and animals; for more dolls, as well as dollhouses, see the Variety Unit.

The **Family Activity Center** at Owl Cottage features a reading area, costume play, and art projects. From late October through late May, theme tours for children ages five and older (with adults along) are given twice on Saturdays. One theme might be searching the museum for "cats," then picking a favorite for an art activity. (Reservations are required.) In July and August the museum offers a weekly series of children's workshops. These

You and your family can learn what life was like in another era at the Shelburne Museum, which features, among other things, an authentic print shop.

fill quickly; to register in advance, call the Educational Department at (802) 985–3346, ext. 395, weekdays.

Try to time your visit to coincide with one of the special-events weekends. In late May the museum celebrates the opening of its warm-weather season with **Lilac Sunday,** nineteenth-century entertainment and leisure activities that include a Victorian picnic, croquet, carriage rides, music—and lots of fun. July Fourth is celebrated with **Old Time Farm Day,** featuring horse-drawn wagon rides, farm animals, traditional folk music, dances, games, crafts, and storytelling. Play old-time baseball and milk a cow, churn butter, make ice cream, and shell peas.

Plan on spending at least three hours, although you could easily spend much more; there's a "second day free" admission policy. The Dog Team Cafe serves sandwiches, burgers, and salads. A jitney service helps with touring the museum's forty-five acres. Baby strollers and carriers aren't permitted in some of the buildings because of the narrow hallways or fragile exhibits. A physical accessibility guide and wheelchairs are available at the McClure Visitor Center.

If you have more time in the area, the following sites offer kid-pleasing diversions.

Discovery Museum, 51 Park Street, Route 2A, Essex Junction; (802-878-8687). This small hands-on museum, located in a historic home, gears its exhibits and programs to kids up to age twelve. Attractions include a Science Center area with a 727 cockpit, fossil table, freshwater

Lake Champlain Maritime Museum

Lake Champlain Maritime Museum, on the grounds of the Basin Harbor Club resort, R.R. 3, Box 4092, Vergennes (802–475-2022; www.lcmm.org), is nautical and nice, dedicated to exploring and preserving Lake Champlain's maritime history.

From the **Coast Guard ship** on the lawn to the rowboats and a **Native American dugout canoe** on display, this museum exhibits an interesting array of watercraft. A video recounts the diversity of Lake Champlain's sunken treasures, which includes horse ferries, gunboats, and steamboats. A display explains **nautical archeology,** and visitors are welcome to watch the archeologists at work in their lab.

The museum's pride is the *Philadelphia II,* a replica of a 54-foot Revolutionary War gunboat, moored in the north harbor, down a path from the museum's buildings. The summertime gun drill performed by sailors in period dress ends with a "boom."

For local children, or guests staying in the area or at the **Basin Harbor Club,** the museum offers a Monday to Thursday **summer program** of hands-on, maritime experiences for ages three to sixteen. Kids ages three to five, launch foil boats, listen to tugboat stories, and enjoy other sea-related activities one morning each week. Various theme weeks engage ages six to eight, nine to eleven, and twelve and older. During Nautical Archeology week activities might include snorkeling, reconstructing artifacts, and drawing ship plans. For the History of 1776 week children make tricornered hats and learn about cooking and camping in the woods Colonial style. During Anchors Away week children learn navigation and seamanship skills and end the week by taking *Bruno,* a restored 1930s Coast Guard launch, for a trip on Lake Champlain. The deadline for summer class registration is June 1.

fish tank, rocks and minerals, and—everyone's favorite—bubble experiments. Call for information about weekly and monthly programs.

Ethan Allen Homestead, off Route 127 (802-865-4556). School-age children may like a visit to this restored 1787 timber farmhouse that belonged to Revolutionist Allen, leader of the famous Green Mountain Boys. Guided tours are given, and there's a multimedia show on this local hero who helped establish the state of Vermont. When you're through, enjoy a respite at the 258-acre Winooski Valley Park, with hiking trails, that surrounds the homestead.

Parks, Beaches, and Green Spaces

Burlington Waterfront, Lake Champlain. The city has done a good job of making the Lake Champlain waterfront accessible, safe, and family-friendly. For more information on Burlington's beaches and parks, contact the Parks and Recreation Department (802–864–0123).

Boat Cruises. A well-known lake sight is the **Spirit of Ethan Allen II,** Burlington Boathouse, College Street (802–862–8300), a 500-passenger triple-decker cruise ship offering a variety of cruises June through mid-October. Most children, even young ones, enjoy the ninety-minute narrated, scenic trip, especially if you remember to bring bread to feed the gulls. Other outings include sunset and dinner cruises.

At the **Burlington Community Boathouse**, College Street at the waterfront (802–865–3377), sign on for captained day sails or come aboard a fishing charter. You can also take sailing lessons and rent your own sailboat or rowboat.

Bicycling and Strolling. The **Waterfront Park and Promenade,** along Lake Champlain's waterfront from Pearl Street to Maple Street, is a great place for a family break from museums. The boardwalk sports benches, and a grassy area appeals to Frisbee throwers and children who just want to romp. For some gentle exercise, pedal or rollerblade along the bicycle path that stretches for 8.2 miles along the lake from Oakledge Park in the south to the Flynn Estate in the north (bring your own bikes; rentals are also available in town).

Just a few blocks farther north is **Battery Park,** the waterfront at Pearl Street. The site of a battle against the British in the War of 1812, this spot has a great view of the Adirondacks across the lake. In summer free jazz concerts are held at the outdoor amphitheater.

Swimming and Beaches. Even during the height of summer Lake Champlain can feel cold to those unaccustomed to brisk New England waters. Children, however, seem to splash happily. A favorite place for local swimming, and the closest to downtown, is **North Beach** (802–864–0123). To get there, take North Avenue to Institute Road. There are in-season lifeguards as well as picnic tables, rest rooms, and a food concession. The beach is free except for a nominal parking fee.

Leddy Park, north of North Beach off North Avenue, is known as Burlington's sporting park. Year-round **Leddy Arena** (802–864–0123), an indoor ice rink, entices children, and in good weather athletic youngsters take to the basketball and tennis courts. Although smaller than North Beach, there's enough of a sandy strip to keep castle-builders happy. Lifeguards patrol in season and bathrooms are available, although there are no food concessions. The park is free except for a nominal parking fee.

South of downtown Burlington is **Oakledge Park,** off Route 7 at the

Diving Lake Champlain

Explore the shipwrecks hidden under Lake Champlain's gray waters. Although many vessels sank in Lake Champlain, only five underwater wrecks have been identified and marked with yellow buoys by the Coast Guard. These comprise the **Lake Champlain Historic Underwater Preserves,** a fascinating attraction for certified scuba divers. (To learn scuba diving one must be at least twelve years old.) Three of the wrecks— the *Horse Farm,* the *Coal Barge,* and the *General Butler*—are accessible from Burlington's shores. Two others—the *Phoenix* and the *Diamond Island Stone Boat*—are located near Colchester and Vergennes. (Before diving obtain information and always follow appropriate safety precautions.)

Among the most interesting are the *Horse Farm* and the *General Butler.* Situated in Burlington Bay, the **Horse Farm** is the only known surviving example of the horse ferries, often called "teamboats." These ferries in use from the 1820s to the Civil War were powered by horses that walked on a horizontal flywheel, similar to a treadmill. These paddle wheels are the wreck's most spectacular feature. Dive down and you can view the deteriorated but still intact iron hubs and oak spokes. Be careful not to touch anything. In exploring the *Horse Farm* do not use the deck to support your weight.

Also unusual is the 1862 *General Butler,* a rare example of a sailing canal boat. This schooner-rigged commercial vessel transported cargo across the lake. With its masts removed and centerboard raised, this vessel could travel on the Champlain canal, which connected the lake to the Hudson River. On December 9, 1876, Captain William Montgomery of Isle La Motte headed out with marble blocks from the Isle La Motte quarry destined for the Burlington marble works. Caught in a powerful winter gale, the craft's steering mechanism broke. As each rough wave broke over the vessel, the force of the water lifted the *General Butler* on top of the breakwater. With the vessel in this precarious position, one by one the passengers jumped to the ice-covered stones. Montgomery was the last to make the perilous jump; moments after he landed his ship sank into the 40 feet of water where it remains to this day. Having barely escaped drowning, the passengers, drenched by the frigid waters, now faced death by exposure. Luckily, two people saw the destruction and braved the storm to row to the rescue.

To obtain information about how to explore these wrecks, contact the **Vermont Division for Historic Preservation,** 135 State Street, Montpelier (802-828-3226).

end of Flynn Ave. Drive here or follow the waterfront bicycle path south. Along with picnic tables and a swimming beach, this park has some sports facilities, including tennis courts, volleyball courts, and a baseball diamond.

Nature Center. Near Burlington there are many places for hiking and exploring. One of the nicest is the **Green Mountains Audubon Nature Center,** Sherman Hollow Road, Huntington, (802-434-3068). Trails on this 230-acre preserve wind through several typical Vermont habitats such as beaver ponds, marshes, farm fields, brooks, rivers, and woodlands. In spring get your hands busy with a Vermont tradition—help with the maple-sugaring. Call ahead for this event and for the schedule of interpretive classes.

Lake Champlain's Islands. From the mainland travel to the islands via ferry or take I-89 north of Burlington to Route 2 north, which cuts through South Hero, Grand Isle, North Hero, South Alburg, and Alburg. From South Alburg Route 129 leads to Isle La Motte. Burton Island, a family-friendly spot, is accessible via boat. Harder to reach than other Vermont spots, the Lake Champlain Islands are less developed and less crowded, offering scenic views of the lake edged by the Adirondacks to the west and the Green Mountains to the east.

A popular day trip is to the island of **North Hero,** 35 miles from Burlington. For horse lovers (and few children aren't), the islands' biggest day trip draw are the **Royal Lipizzan Stallions of Austria,** P.O. Box 213, North Hero (802-372-5683). Referred to as "the ballet dancers of the horse world," these dashing white prancers seem straight out of a fairytale. Your children may know about these "flying white stallions" from the Walt Disney movie *The Miracle of the White Stallions,* which dramatized the rescue of these horses from destruction at the end of World War II. The horses are impressive, performing high-stepping maneuvers initially taught to make them more formidable foes in battle. Children grow wide-eyed watching these beasts execute leaps and turns.

Hiking and Campgrounds. Grand Isle State Park, 36 East Shore South, U.S. 2, Grand Isle (802-372-4300 or 802-879-5674—January–May), is a 226-acre tract boasting a fitness trail, a playground, and boats for rent. For overnight stays there are thirty-four lean-tos and a cabin.

A good day stop, or overnight spot, for outdoor families is **Burton Island State Park,** Box 123, St. Albans Bay (802-524-6353 or 802-879-5674—January–May). The park, which covers 253 acres, features few crowds, good fishing, boat rentals, a naturalist center, and a swimming beach. Access to Burton Island is by boat only. The marina has one hundred slips with power hookups and fifteen moorings. Forty-two campsites are

Fun Factory Tours

The factories for two made-in-Vermont popular products are located in the Shelburne area, and each offers a factory tour. Factory tours are eye-openers, especially for young children who may never have thought beyond the store when considering where things come from.

Vermont Teddy Bear Company, 2236 Shelburne Road, Route 7 (802–985–3001 or 800–829–BEAR). The guides, who act more like vaudeville comedians than docents, enliven your factory-floor visit with bear facts and antics, almost making you believe the bears are real. At the end your children will certainly want a teddy of their own.

Arrive early. In summer waits can be as long as an hour. To pass the time the factory offers face painting, tea parties with teddy bears, checker games, bingo, and crafts for kids.

Ben & Jerry's, P.O. Box 240, Waterbury (802–244–TOUR). This ice cream factory created by two buddies started in Vermont. To please the crowds awaiting tours, various booths outside offer face painting, bubble play, and crafts. When the lines are long, skip the tour, which consists of a video about the company's beginnings and a not-too-interesting look at the factory floor; simply enjoy the outdoor activities and the ice cream.

available, of which twenty-six are lean-tos. If you don't arrive via your own boat, you can catch a passenger ferry from Kamp Kill Kare State Park.

Performing Arts

Flynn Theatre for the Performing Arts, 153 Main Street, offers excellent dance, music, and theater performances. Call (802) 88–FLYNN for ticket information. **Saint Michael's College,** Route 15, Winooski Park, puts on professional summer theater performances from late June to mid-August. Call (802) 655–0122 for schedules. A number of cultural festivals are held annually (see Special Events).

SPECIAL EVENTS

Contact the Lake Champlain Regional Chamber of Commerce for more information on the following events.

June. Discover Jazz Festival. Lake Champlain Balloon Festival, Champlain Valley Fairgrounds, Essex Junction, includes a children's petting zoo and amusement rides, entertainment, exhibits, and more.

July. Champlain Shakespeare Festival.

July–early August. Vermont Mozart Festival.

August. A Taste of Stowe and For Art's Sake, Stowe.

September. Harvest Festival, Shelburne Farms, entertainment, crafts, and hayrides.

WHERE TO STAY

Families have a wide choice of accommodations in the area, but first decide if you want to stay in town, on the lake, or at one of the full-service, year-round resorts not far from Burlington. (Actually, you might want to do all three.) *Vermont Guidebook* lists lodgings throughout the state. Here are a few with family appeal.

Burlington

Radisson Hotel Burlington, 60 Battery Street (802-658-6500 or 800-333-3333), has twenty-five rooms, many overlooking the lake and the Adirondack Mountains. Features you'll like: indoor heated swimming pool, restaurants (including a casual cafe), complimentary airport shuttle, and free covered parking. Adjacent is the Burlington Square Mall and Church Street Marketplace.

    Eliot House, 2176 Dorset Street, Shelburne (802-985-1412), a bed and breakfast in an 1865 farmhouse, has a welcoming feel as well as mountain views and a swimming pool. The three-room suite in the renovated carriage barn gives families plenty of room. In addition, the main house has two guest rooms. The sitting room has such conveniences as a refrigerator, a microwave, and a coffee maker. All rates include continental breakfast. Children ten and older are welcome.

    Inn at Shelburne Farms, Shelburne Farms, Shelburne (802-985-8498), accepts children, although the setting and fee lend themselves more to romantic retreats than family getaways. Once the mansion for the grand estate that was Shelburne Farms, this inn retains the view, grounds, and perfect setting on a hilltop overlooking Lake Champlain. The inn also retains the structure's fine woodwork, marble floors, and expansive windows. Most of the guest rooms are large. The decor is eclectic.

    The property boasts a tennis court, croquet lawn, game room, walking trails, lake fishing, and lake swimming (no pool). Older children and teens might like to stay here.

    Shelburne Travelodge, 1907 Shelburne Road; Route 7 (802-985-8037), is a typical, serviceable motel. Rooms have coffee makers and cable television, and the property has a pool.

Resorts

The **Basin Harbor Club,** Basin Road, Vergennes, 25 miles south of Burlington (802-475-2311 or 800-622-4000), offers an excellent base for your family's exploration of Shelburne. Owned and operated by the Beach family for more than a century, Basin Harbor, situated on the eastern shore of Lake Champlain, stretches for 700 acres. This full-scale resort has an eighteen-hole golf course and offers tennis, swimming, bicycling, boating, and fishing. Other family-related activities include family Olympics, hayrides, water tubing, cave exploring, and nature hikes. The **Lake Champlain Maritime Museum** (see above) is on the grounds.

The ambience of this dedicated family resort is "sophisticated country." While both the Tyler Place and Basin Harbor cater to families, Basin Harbor is both larger and more formal than the Tyler Place (see below). At Basin Harbor everyone dresses for dinner—even "young men over the age of twelve"—in the main dining room. Before dinner guests tend to linger over cocktails, sitting in Adirondack chairs (child-size chairs provided) and savoring the lake views.

At least twice a week during dinner an ensemble provides dance music (not DJ-driven rhythms), a touch that tends to amaze and occupy younger children and annoy most teenagers. It is nice, however, to see grandparents fox-trotting (or attempting to) with their grandchildren. The wine list is noteworthy, and the food is generally good. The Red Mill restaurant, a renovated barn, offers a casual alternative for dinner

Along with rooms in the main lodge, the Champlain House, and the Homestead, guests may choose individual cottages that offer several rooms. The seventy-seven cottages, several with lake views, accommodate 250 guests. Some buildings date to the 1920s, others to the 1960s, but all have been renovated. Although most cottages feature a sitting room and a bedroom, they differ in layout and locale. Before you book, consider how far you want to be from the main lodge's dining room or from the dock. Some secluded cottages with great lake views also require a long walk, sometimes, along the road, to reach the lodge and the lakefront. These are not the best choice for those with young children. The Shadyhill, a two-bedroom, two-bath cottage, has a screened porch, a wonderful asset, especially for families looking for a protective play area for young children.

During July and August, Basin Harbor offers a **children's program** for ages three to thirteen. Supervised programs operate from 9:30 A.M. to 1:30 P.M. and from 6:00 to 9:00 P.M. for Little Champs, ages three to five, and for Harbor Mates, ages six to eight. These groups can romp in their own playground. Each group also has its own air-conditioned building for gathering and for creating crafts. Daily outings include nature walks, canoe and fishing excursions, and swimming and pool games. If parents want, the children can dine at Champs table and enjoy after-dinner activities as bingo and movies. Champlain Explorers, ages nine to thirteen, have less structured activities. Generally, a morning and an afternoon activity are offered.

The summer rates include lodging, the children's program, and three meals a day. Except for swimming in the pool or the lake, there are fees for almost everything else—boating, waterskiing, fishing, bicycling, and tennis. Set a budget with your children, as these fees can add up. Spring and fall rates include a continental breakfast, and children twelve and under stay free.

The Tyler Place on Lake Champlain, P.O. Box 500, Highgate Springs (802-868-3301), understands families, making a vacation as much fun for parents as for children. Vacations at this low-key, all-inclusive resort are booked by the week, and many families come back year after year. The Tyler Place, stretching for a mile along the shores of Lake Champlain, covers 165 acres and offers lots of activities, including organized programs, divided into six groups, for infants to sixteen-year-olds.

Care for infants and toddlers is extra. The programs are geared to Junior Midgets, ages two and a half to three; Senior Midgets, ages four to five; Juniors, ages six to seven; and Preteens, ages eight to ten. These programs continue from breakfast through lunch, resuming for dinner and after-dinner activities and ending at 8:30 P.M. Young children enjoy storytelling, nature walks, and wading in pools. Senior Midgets and Juniors try hayrides, soccer, parachute games, softball, picnics, and scavenger hunts. Preteens keep busy with windsurfing instruction, canoeing, kayaking, pontoon boat rides, and DJ parties. Programs for Junior Teens, ages eleven to thirteen, and Senior Teens, ages fourteen to sixteen, also start at breakfast, run through lunch, and continue through dinner. Junior Teens' programs end at 9:30 P.M. and Senior Teens' end by 10:30 P.M. Junior and Senior Teens have a complete sports and outing program similar to that for Preteens, plus instruction in archery and waterskiing and evening pizza parties and get-togethers.

The children's programs don't operate in the afternoons so that families can spend time together and children can enjoy less structured fun. The informal evening gatherings are appropriate for adults and children (although kids often are busy in their own groups) and include singalongs, costume parties, bonfires, and dances.

The resort takes advantage of its lake location by offering canoeing, sailing, kayaking, and windsurfing instruction. Tennis courts are on the grounds, and golf is nearby. The accommodations, although plain, are adequate. Except for those lodgings in the resort's Inn, all have kitchenettes. In May, June, and September, rates are 15 to 30 percent lower than during high season. All rates include lodging, meals, sports, children's and teens' programs, and evening activities.

All-Season Resorts

Two popular family resorts near Lake Champlain are Bolton Valley and Smuggler's Notch.

Bolton Valley Resort, Bolton, 19 miles from Burlington (802-434-2131 or 800-451-3220—hotel reservation, 800-451-5025—condos), offers hotel rooms (some with kitchens) or modern, trailside condominiums (all with kitchens) in a splendid mountain setting. The resort's nature center has daily summer activities, rotated during the week, that might include nature photography, a moose watch, or mountain biking classes, plus guided nature walks. Camp Bear Paw occupies the days of ages six to twelve, and there's a nursery for ages three months to six years. In winter the nursery is open, and there are preski and childcare programs for ages four and five, plus full-day skiing sessions for ages five to fifteen (divided by ages).

Smuggler's Notch, Route 108, 30 miles northeast of Burlington International Airport (802-644-8851 or 800-451-8752—United States, 800-356-8679—Canada), consistently ranks among the top family ski resorts in North America. Much has to do with what it does for kids and parents. Alice's Wonderland childcare for ages six weeks and older, with indoor and outdoor play, is open in summer and winter seasons.

In winter the resort has ski camps for ages three to six and seven to twelve and a teen program that includes sports and evening dance parties. Ski Week packages feature family game nights and sledding parties, while the five-day FamilyFest includes camp and one free Parent's Night Out—selected supervised evenings for ages three to twelve.

Summer brings day camps for ages three to seventeen. Older kids are challenged by ropes courses, nature programs, and painting and photography classes When the kids aren't in camp, they head to the three water slides or two pools (there are toddler wading pools, too). Mountainside lodgings, from motel units to five-bedroom condos, are in the walkabout village, where you'll also find a miniature golf course, horseback riding stables and hayrides, restaurants, a convenience store, a deli, and indoor and outdoor tennis.

WHERE TO EAT

If you feel like a formal dinner, but one that welcomes children, reserve a table in the main dining room at **Basin Harbor Club,** Vergennes, (802-475-2311 or 800-622-4000). Dinner is a five-course meal. Lunch at the

Ranger Room is a bounteous buffet of hot and cold pasta, seafood, and salads, plus burgers and sandwiches. Children especially like the ice cream sundaes. **The Red Mill,** a renovated barn, offers casual dining of burgers and seafood.

Reservations are required at the **Inn at Shelburne Farms,** Shelburne Farms, Shelburne (802-985-8498). This elegant sixty-room Queen Anne–style manor house built in 1899 functions as an inn but is also open to the public for breakfast and dinner. Furnished with family pieces, some fine, some merely representative of the period, the house has an elegant feel. The proportions are grand, the setting overlooking Lake Champlain are dramatic, and the details, from the elaborate molding to the tiled fireplaces and corded oak paneling, are impressive.

Interestingly, well-behaved children are welcome as overnight guests (see above) and at meals. For grade-school children enthralled by mansions, a breakfast here would be a special treat. (Dinner seems too formal and too expensive, geared more to romance than children.) After breakfast, you are entitled to walk in the gardens and enjoy the Lake Champlain views.

Vermont Pasta restaurants (at 5 Green Street, 1 miles south of the junction of Routes 22A and 7, Vergennes, 802-877-3413; and 156 Church Street, Burlington, 802-658-2575) are known for their fresh homemade pastas and sauces. The restaurants provide a comfortable atmosphere and lots of menu "pastabilities." Although younger children will most likely want their pasta plain or with tomato sauce, the restaurant appeals to grown-ups and teens too. Specialties include pasta with shrimp and scallops, and tortellini with smoked chicken.

Carbur's, 115 St. Paul Street (802-862-4106), is known as much for its amusing sixteen-page menu and funky decor as for its "granwiches," super-sized sandwiches. The high-ceilinged dining room, with its lacquered tables, is accented with Victorian antiques (signs, sideboards, tools, barrels, etc.). This restaurant also serves ribs and seafood, but the sandwiches and salads are a better deal. Children like the oversized cakes and ice cream sundaes. For parents: Carbur's bills itself as having Vermont's largest beer list.

The trendy **Daily Planet,** 15 Center Street (802-862-9647), has bright oilcloth tablecloths at lunch and a more formal linen setting for dinner. Lunch may be the best bet for families, with a selection of burgers, nachos, and fajitas. Dinner can be more adventuresome for those children willing to sample such entrees as grilled swordfish and Thai chicken.

Perry's Fish House, 1080 Shelburne Road, South Burlington (802-862-1300), is popular with locals. While the decor of fish nets, ships' wheels, and buoys is typically nautical, the food is atypical—good and fresh. For nonseafood fans, Perry's serves prime rib, pasta, and chicken. Children can be reasonably noisy here, and no one will take offense.

SIDE TRIPS

A popular winter ski resort, the Stowe area is more peaceful in the summer, when it offers a wealth of recreational possibilities. At the **Stowe Mountain Resort,** take a gondola ride on Mount Mansfield, the highest peak in Vermont, and enjoy spectacular vistas. There's also an alpine slide ride (adults can accompany younger kids). On Sunday evenings concerts are held at the Trapp Family Concert Meadow (yes, the *Sound of Music* family offspring operate a lodge in town). Biking, swimming, hiking, golfing, tennis, and loads of special events are all at your fingertips. Call (802) 253-3000 or (800) 24-STOWE for information and central reservations.

FOR MORE INFORMATION

Summer and winter editions of the *Vermont Traveler's Guidebook,* including the Burlington area and other literature, can be obtained from **Vermont Travel Division,** 134 State Street, Montpelier 05602 (802-828-3236). Contact **Lake Champlain Regional Chamber of Commerce** for their *Vermont Area Guide* to the region: P.O. Box 453, 209 Battery Street, Burlington 05402 (802-863-3489). Or stop by the **Information Center,** Church Street Marketplace, corner of Church and Bank, mid-May through mid-October. Call (802-828-3239) for fall foliage reports. Check out Vermont online, www.travel-Vermont.com.

The **Vermont Chamber of Commerce** publishes a *Winter Travel Guide;* call (802) 223-3443. For cross-country ski information, call the Vermont Association of Snow Travelers (VAST) at (802) 229-0005; www. virtualvermont.com/chamber/vast). For general information, call (800) VERMONT. For the state's automated fax service, call (800) 833-9756.

Emergency Numbers

Ambulance, fire, and police: 911

Poison Control: (802) 658-3456

Twenty-four-hour care for minor or major emergencies: Medical Center Hospital of Vermont, 111 Colchester Avenue; (802) 656-2345

Twenty-four-hour pharmacy: Price Chopper, 555 Shelburne Road (U.S. 7, 2 miles south of downtown); (802) 864-8505

WOODSTOCK AND QUECHEE

Woodstock, in the foothills of the Green Mountains, was settled in the 1760s. Restored eighteenth- and nineteenth-century homes grace the streets of this picture-book pretty Vermont town, complete with a village green and a covered bridge. Woodstock is also among Vermont's most cosmopolitan towns, offering fine restaurants and lodging (the noted Woodstock Inn & Resort is here), along with up-market shops, boutiques, and art galleries.

But Woodstock isn't just a town for well-heeled couples wanting city amenities in a country setting. Despite its upscale feel, or maybe because of it, families feel comfortable here.

There's lots to see and do, and the scenic Ottauquechee River valley offers prime hiking and cross-country skiing trails.

The speed limit through town, along Central Street, Route 4, is 25 mph. The frequent tourist traffic may not ever allow you to go above 25 mph, but if you do, beware: The police do give speeding tickets.

Quechee, 8 miles east of Woodstock on U.S. Route 4, a once bustling mill town, has now stretched to include a large condominium and vacation home development. Highlights are the Quechee Gorge and Simon Pearce Glass.

GETTING THERE

Woodstock is 13 miles west of White River Junction. By car take I–89 or I–91 to U.S. Route 4 west.

GETTING AROUND

A car is essential if you want to explore more than just the town.

Woodstock and Quechee

AT A GLANCE

▶ Learn how to train oxen, milk cows, and quilt at Billings Farm and Museum

▶ Cross-country and downhill ski

▶ Stroll Quechee Gorge's paths for wonderful fall foliage views

▶ Relax at the country-elegant Woodstock Inn & Resort

▶ Woodstock Area Chamber of Commerce, (802) 457-3555

▶ Quechee Chamber of Commerce, (802) 295-7900

WHAT TO SEE AND DO

Museums and Nature Centers

Woodstock has some particularly appealing attractions for families. Two must-sees are the Billings Farm and Museum and the Vermont Institute of Natural Science and Raptor Center.

The **Billings Farm & Museum,** P.O. Box 489 (off Route 12), Woodstock (802-457-2355), is a beautiful place—Victorian-era barns, prized Jersey cows grazing in lush green pastures, and acres and acres of rolling terrain dotted by groves of trees. The dairy farm, first established in 1871 by Frederick Billings (who went on to become a railroad magnate) as a state-of-the-art enterprise, now serves as "a living museum of Vermont's rural heritage." It's a treat just to walk here.

The facility labels itself "one of this country's premier agricultural museums." Several buildings house exhibits of nineteenth-century farm necessities. The barn features a collection of horse-drawn conveyances, including hay wagons, hansom carriages, and a parade wagon. These are intriguing to look at, but the descriptions of the items are standard placards that fail to engage kids. The farm manager's house, with its restored 1890s decor, gives kids a sense of rural home life from the proper parlor, fit for meeting with the minister, to the office, complete with rolltop desk and farm ledgers. The second floor of the entry building has a permanent display of old farm tools, threshing equipment, butter churns, and other once invaluable items.

More enjoyable, however, than the static displays are the living history demonstrations about centuries-old farming skills. Kids learn how to milk cows, how to train oxen (slowly and with much repetition), why blacksmiths were so important, and what makes a quilt. Because this facility is still a working farm and one that uses modern techniques, your kids will see a high-tech calf nursery and modern tractors. Pointing this out to children helps eliminate confusion about new and old techniques.

The gift shop has a very good selection of books about farming and farm animals, especially books geared to young kids. Another place not to miss: the snack bar in the dairy barn (around back). Here you can buy raspberry sherbet, lemonade, trail mix, and, of course, Vermont cheddar cheese (no sandwiches). Families are invited to relax at the farm's picnic area (bring your own meals) and simply enjoy the scenery.

Check the Billings Farm & Museum's schedule for special activities and festivals. A favorite is the October Harvest Celebration that includes a barn dance, a husking bee, and the arrival of the giant pumpkin pulled by the farm's friendly oxen. Ages two to adult.

The Billings Farm & Museum is part of the Marsh Billings National Historic Park, which also features a mansion, available for tours seasonally, and Mount Tom.

The **Vermont Institute of Natural Science and Raptor Center** (VINS), R.R. 2, Box 532, Woodstock (802–457–2779), is an educational and rehabilitative center devoted to raptors, or birds of prey. A horseshoe-shaped path takes you by twenty-four species of birds, all of which have wounds that make them unreleasable. Kids get to view such majestic creatures as bald eagles, peregrine falcons, barred owls, snowy owls, red-tailed hawks, and ravens.

Because the flight cages are big, shaded, and designed with rafters and tree branches, it can be difficult to find these often well-camouflaged feathered wonders. Bring binoculars to make viewing easier. VINS also has nature trails and some live animals and insects, including snakes and bees.

VINS generally hosts an annual Family Weekend at the Woodstock Inn & Resort, featuring workshops and special programs. VINS four-day summer discovery day camp is geared to kids entering grades 1, 2, and 3. In fall the two-hour nature program Itsy Bitsy Spiders is usually held for preschoolers. Winter events include stargazing and snow-tracking workshops, a Holiday Naturefest in November with crafts and storytelling, a Winter Celebration Family Day in February complete with hikes and igloo building, and a Sugar on Snow Festival in March featuring maple sugaring the old-fashioned way over an open fire.

If your kids like historical homes, then visit the **Dana House Museum,** home to the Woodstock Historical Society, Elm Street, around the corner from the Village Green, (802-457-1822). This 1807 residence, once the home of the prominent Dana family, now features period furnishings. Kids are most interested in the silver coins, antique toys, tools, skis, and sled.

Play Spaces

Unless you're looking for it, you probably won't notice the **George Perkins Marsh Man and Nature Park,** Route 4, Central Street (just off the bridge between 43 and 47 Central Street). Beside a small stone bridge and literally just steps down from the often busy main drag, this park is a great mini-oasis. It's surprising how relaxing it can be to get just a little bit away from the crowds on Central Street. Buy some homemade ice cream or muffins and pies from the **Mountain Creamery** (see Where to Eat) first, then come here for a sweet moment's respite.

The **Woodstock Recreation Center,** 54 River Street (802-457-1502), is a good place to know about if your summer lodging doesn't come with a pool but your kids just need to get wet to work off some energy. The Rec Center's two outdoor pools are chock full of local children. Yours are quite likely to make some new friends here. The Friday family swim nights are popular, too. Check the calendar for special events. A favorite fund-raiser is the early-October chili cook-off on the village green. Local restaurants and individuals compete to be the best of the beans. Fees per activity.

Shopping

Your preteens and teens will appreciate a browse at **Who is Sylvia?,** 26 Central Street, Woodstock (802-457-1502), a vintage clothing store. Many a "too-cool" party dress, from innocent white cottons to slinky and sequined formals, has been found among the racks of 1880s to 1950s gowns. Parents can tip their hats to Momma by trying on those pillboxes and simple veiled numbers she (and Jackie Kennedy) wore. The shop also features a small selection of jewelry, lace, and linens.

Central Avenue, the burg's main street, features several blocks of boutiques and art galleries. **Stephen Huneck Gallery,** 49 Central Street, P.O. Box 59, Woodstock (802-457-3290 or 800-449-2580), features whimsical pet- and animal-centered art that pleases children. His furniture incorporates dogs (lots of Dalmatians), cats, and rainbow trout. Bring Fido along, too, as dogs are welcome and some of the artwork is thoughtfully mounted low on the wall for easy viewing by the family pooch. Kids like posing with the carving of a man walking five wooden dogs that is outside the shop.

F. H. Gillingham and Sons, the Vermont General Store, 16 Elm Street, Woodstock (802-457-2100 or 800-344-6668), has been in business

Outdoor Activities

- **Hike Mount Tom and Mount Peg.** The trail heads are near town, and trail maps are available from the Woodstock Inn & Resort and from the information booth on the village green.
- **Ski cross-country.** A top-ranked facility, the **Woodstock Ski Touring Center,** headquarters at the Woodstock Country Club, Route 106 (802–457–2114) offers 75 kilometers of trails, 60 kilometers of which are groomed. Trails wind through the golf course and along paths on Mount Tom.
- **Ski downhill.** Managed by the Woodstock Inn & Resort, **Suicide Six Ski Area** (802–457–6674), which opened in 1937, was one of the first downhill areas in the nation. Nonintimidating, with just a 650-foot vertical drop, the majority of the nineteen trails cater mostly to beginners and intermediates. Snowboarders have a half-pipe to play in. There are no special kids-only classes, but here, as at other ski areas, families can book their own private family lesson that includes children as young as four.

The **Woodstock Inn's Family Ski Week packages,** generally available at selected times each season, save families money. These packages typically include complimentary lift tickets and rental equipment, plus one group lesson per person, free breakfast and dinner for children, and a complimentary horse-drawn sleigh ride. (For more information, see Where to Stay).

- **Ride horses.** The **Kendron Valley Stables,** Route 106 about 4.5 miles south of Woodstock (802–457–1480), offers a range of riding options, including beginner scenic rides and instruction in a riding ring.
- **Explore Quechee Gorge,** Route 4 (between Woodstock and White River Junction), Hartford. The gorge, cut by the Ottauquechee River, offers some dramatic scenery as well as a relatively flat path that's fine for young kids. In fall the birch, maple, and beech trees form a quilt of colors. From the bridge on Route 4 look down to the cascading waters of the river 165 feet below, or take the stairs (adjacent to the gift shop and parking area) to the path along the river. It's an easy stroll to a waterfall and an old mill.
- **Paddle a canoe. Wilderness Trails,** Quechee (802–886–2215), rents canoes and leads river float trips on Silver Lake in Silver Lake State Park, Barnard, Vermont.
- **Swim and boat. Silver Lake State Park,** Barnard, 11 miles north of Woodstock, (802–234–9451 or 802–886–2434), has thirty-four acres of trails and boating facilities.

since 1886. This shop combines the everything-you-need hardware and housewares of a typical country store with an up-market selection of Vermont products, gourmet groceries (jams, jellies, cheese, wine, etc.), and kitchen gadgets. Of particular interest to families is Gillingham's toy department. In keeping with the store's spirit, all the toys are handcrafted, many made of wood. Popular items are the wooden blocks, puzzles, and airplanes.

A 32,000 square foot "restored" woolen mill now houses **Simon Pearce Glass** at the mill, Quechee (802-295-1470). The shop sells clear glass items, pottery, and furniture handcrafted by artisans. There's also a pleasant restaurant overlooking the river and mill falls (see page 323) and downstairs, a glassblowing furnace where visitors can watch craftsmen employing traditional techniques. Kids like seeing the long blow pipes and watching how the molten glass becomes a vase, goblet, or bowl. Check the shop's seconds area for good buys on slightly irregular items.

SPECIAL EVENTS

February. Winter Carnival with concerts, sleigh rides, square dances.

June. Quechee Hot Air Balloon Festival; Woodstock Inn and Resort Teddy Bear Weekend.

July. Crafts Fair and Fourth of July Fireworks.

October. Harvest and Crafts Fair.

December. Christmas Wassail Weekend features a parade of carriages and concerts.

WHERE TO STAY

Campgrounds
Silver Lake State Park, Barnard, 11 miles north of Woodstock (802-234-9451 or 802-886-2434), is open from January to May and offers forty-seven camping sites, including seven lean-tos.

Another good spot is **Quechee Gorge State Park,** Route 4, Hartford, between Woodstock and White River Junction. Administrative office: 190 Dewey Mills Road, White River Junction, (802-295-2990 or 802-886-2434—January–May). Open early May to mid-October. The park has fifty-four sites, including lean-tos.

Inns, Motels and Condominiums
The Woodstock/Quechee area has a number of inns and motels, as well as one well-noted inn, the Woodstock Inn & Resort. Because of the size of their rooms, antique furnishings, and fine and expensive dining, many of

the inns and bed and breakfasts do not really welcome children even if, by law, they allow them.

If you want easy-to-handle, moderately priced accommodations, consider staying at nearby motels. Two clean, serviceable, and well-located motels are the **Shire Hotel,** 46 Pleasant Street, Woodstock (802-457-2211), whose rooms have televisions and refrigerators, and the **Quality Inn at Quechee Gorge,** Route 4, 1 mile east of the bridge at Quechee Gorge, Quechee, (802-295-7600), which has rooms plus several suites with kitchenettes. Conveniently located across from an entrance to Quechee Gorge State Park, the Quality Inn features an outdoor heated pool.

The imposing **Parker House Inn,** 16 Main Street, Quechee (802-295-6077) was built in 1857 for wool tycoon Joseph Parker. Today it's owned and operated by Walt and Barbara Forester and is next door to the Simon Pearce Glass (see above). This conveniently located property offers pleasant Victorian-accented rooms. The main floor has two dining rooms open to the public in the evening. As a result, though, the first floor doesn't have that home-away-from-home feel many people want in an inn.

"We accept kids of any age," says Walt Forester, "but we don't seek them out." Nevertheless, upstairs a sitting area with a television and a few board games enables kids to feel at home. Several of the rooms are large enough for families. A treat for young grade-schoolers is a stay in Emily's room. The dressing room is big enough for a crib, but the highlight is the antique desk that unfolds to become a single bed.

WHERE TO EAT

The village of Woodstock features many restaurants. We've listed some good, moderately priced family picks.

Bentley's, 3 Elm Street, Woodstock (802-457-3232) is the pleasant result of mixing a pub, a parlor, and a party place. Casually tasteful, Bentley's is lively, often noisy, but still cozy, especially if you're seated on one of the raised platforms. These booths and some others employ Victorian settees instead of banquettes. The fringed table lamps and Oriental rugs, along with the sofas, suggest a gussied up 1890s parlor. But come 10:00 P.M. the Victorian feel fades as the recessed ceiling is lowered to become a dance floor, turning Bentley's into a nightspot popular with couples.

Gourmet has called Bentley's the "best luncheon spot in Woodstock." Locals rave about the Five Star Chili, loaded with ground turkey, and the French tart, a flaky pastry crust filled with fresh vegetables and cheddar cheese. The Maple Mustard Chicken, with pecans, mustard, and maple syrup, and the seared Vermont lamb steak, with horseradish crème fraîche and sweet balsamic sauce, are generally good and representative of the dinner entrees. Children's menu available.

Woodstock Inn & Resort

The premier **Woodstock Inn & Resort,** 14 The Green, opposite the village green, Woodstock (802–457–1100 or 800–448–7900), is.a treat for travelers. The magazine *Condé Nast Traveler* ranked this four-diamond, four-star property as among the top fifty resorts in the United States. More of a fine hotel because of scale and services than an inn, the Woodstock Inn & Resort exudes a country elegance. The lobby has a huge fieldstone fireplace, wooden mantle, and sitting area of handcrafted wooden benches. The guest rooms, some of which feature fireplaces, are decorated in hunt colors—lots of green and burgundy. The beds sport quilts, and Vermont handicrafts, such as boxes and carved ducks, add regional touches to the rooms. Guests have free use of the indoor pool, sauna, steam room, whirlpool, and exercise room. For an additional charge, guests may use the indoor and outdoor tennis courts as well as racquetball courts at the **Sports Center.**

The inn has spaces that work well for families and for adults only. Kids are as welcome to use the **putting green** (near the outdoor pool) as are adults. Putters are free and available from the front desk. Your budding duffers will be happy to know that kids are allowed on the golf course, "as long as they can keep up,"

notes the manager. The **library** has comfortable chairs and tables suitable for playing board games; some are provided, as are kids' books (but it would be nice to have a better selection of both). The second-floor **game room,** open 8:30 A.M. to 11:00 P.M., has chess and checkers, books, and a billiard table.

Afternoon tea, served in an airy garden room, comes with coffee and hot chocolate, as well as cookies or pastries. This is a great way to wind down after a day of touring and it's perfectly okay to take some goodies back to your room with you so you can snack and relax before dinner. **Richardson's Tavern,** the only indoor smoking space in the inn, is a strictly adult lounge. The oak paneling, Oriental rugs, hunt prints, and paintings create a clubby New England atmosphere.

In June the hotel hosts a **Teddy Bear Weekend.** Kids bring their own bears for a parade, lawn party, and tea. Most of the year there are no drop-off-your-kids programs, but during holidays and some summer weekends, selected activities appropriate to families may be offered. Check at the front desk. In addition, during Christmas/New Year's **Camp Friendship,** a program of children's dinner and games, typically convenes every

(continued)

Woodstock Inn & Resort *(continued)*

other night from 5:00 to 11:00 P.M. for ages three and older.

The resort has a **golf course,** plenty of **hiking trails** in summer, and **cross-country** and **downhill trails** in winter, plus an indoor pool, sauna, and tennis and racquetball courts at the nearby **Health and Fitness Center.** The center has a family activities field, Timothy Knox Meadows, named for Woodstock's first settler, who arrived in 1765. The open space is great for romping, impromptu games of kickball, and just plain strolling. A shuttle van departs regularly from the main inn to the center.

The Eagle Cafe, Woodstock Inn & Resort, 14 The Green, opposite the village green, Woodstock (802-457-1100 or 800-448-7900), a sunny space near the main dining room, features more moderately priced fare than the inn's formal restaurant, although both restaurants feature the same children's menu of hot dogs, chicken fingers, and other kid favorites. Two things are noteworthy: You can order from this reduced-priced, kid-pleasing menu for your children ages fourteen and younger instead of the usual age twelve cutoff; and you can order from the dining room menu, a nice touch if you want fine food but your kids want a casual atmosphere. The main courses at the Eagle (same menu for lunch and dinner) cover a range of offerings, from turkey club sandwiches to burgers, designer pizza, and swordfish.

The **Mountain Creamery,** 33 Central Street, Route 4, Woodstock (802-457-1715), is a find. This cafe serves good food at moderate prices, has a bakery, offers homemade ice cream, and has take-out. The atmosphere is casual and the decor simple but welcoming. The pine booths have cranberry or hunter green oilcloths, and the wooden tables are set with hand-painted tiles. The menu features salads and deli sandwiches, as well as the popular Vermont gobbler, a mix of turkey, cranberry sauce, and sprouts. Leave room for dessert. This place is famous for its tasty slices of homemade pies, especially the Mile High Apple Pie, which has no less than 3 pounds of apples. Top sellers in the homemade ice cream department are maple walnut and vanilla, and kids never complain about the make-your-own sundae option.

Chumley's Bakery and Lunch Cafe, 9 Main Street, Quechee (802-295-3380), housed in a little yellow clapboard house across the street from the Simon Pearce Mill, is a good place for families to know about. At the counter you can order tuna, turkey, and chicken club sandwiches, plus cookies, a Danish, and apples. Eat at the tables in the adjoining room or take the food to go. These are the quickest, least expensive lunch meals in Quechee.

Simon Pearce Restaurant, at the Mill, Quechee (802-295-1470), could be right out of a feature in *Martha Stewart Country Living.* The large glass windows overlook the mill falls and the covered bridge. The exposed brick walls, old oak floors, and pine beams create a pleasing blend of textures. Reservations recommended.

For families, lunch is the best bet, as it's more casual and affordable than dinner, especially since a children's menu is not offered at either sitting. For lunch, kids generally like the shepherd's pie and the soups when they're not too fancy. Adults like the shepherd's pie, too, as well as the vegetable sandwich with portobello mushrooms. Dinner entrees often include roast duck and sesame tuna.

SIDE TRIPS

Farther north in the Lake Champlain/Burlington, Vermont, area is the noted **Shelburne Museum,** 5555 Shelburne Road, Shelburne (802-985-3344), a collection of buildings, crafts, artifacts, and architecture representative of eighteenth- and nineteenth-century New England. Kids especially like the circus miniatures, the 1890s jail, the lighthouse, and the *Ticonderoga,* a sidewheel steamboat. (See the Lake Champlain and Burlington, Vermont Chapter.)

Vermont also offers lots of great skiing. A particularly family-friendly ski area is **Okemo Mountain** (802-228-4041). The resort offers day care for ages six weeks to eight years plus good kids' skiing classes for ages four to twelve and a mini-rider program for ages five to twelve.

FOR MORE INFORMATION

In summer and fall (late June through mid-October) there's a **town information booth** on the village green (802-457-1042). This facility provides maps, attraction information, and assistance with lodging. Contact the **Woodstock Area Chamber of Commerce,** 18 Central Street, P.O. Box 486, Woodstock, 05091 (802-457-3555). The **Quechee Chamber of Commerce,** Quechee Gorge (802-295-7900), operates an information booth at Quechee Gorge from mid-May to mid-October.

Woodstock Emergency Numbers

Emergency: 911

Woodstock Village Police Department (non-emergency): (802) 457-1420

Vermont Poison Center: (802) 658-3456

Local Pharmacy: Shire Apothecary, 13 Elm Street; (802) 457–2707.
Pharmacy hours: Monday to Saturday 8:00 A.M. to 6:00 P.M., Sunday
8:00 A.M. to 1:00 P.M.

Local Ambulance: (802) 457–2323

Ottauquechee Health Center (on-call physicians and emergency room):
(802) 457–3030

Quechee Emergency Numbers

Emergency: 911

Hartford Police Department (non-emergency): (802) 295–9425

Vermont Poison Center: (802) 658–3456

Local Pharmacy: Corner Drug, 213 Maple Street, White River Junction;
(802) 295–2501. Pharmacy hours: Monday to Friday 8:30 A.M. to 7:00
P.M., Saturday 9:00 A.M. to 5:00 P.M., Sunday 10:00 A.M. to 1:00 P.M.
(About 7 miles from Quechee.)

Dartmoth Hitchcock Medical Center (on-call physicians and emergency
room): 1 Medical Center Drive, Lebanon, New Hampshire; (603)
650–5000. (About 10 miles from Quechee.)

INDEX

O

P